PE
1127
.S6
W48
1993

SIDE BY SIDE
A Multicultural Reader

Harvey S. Wiener *Adelphi University*

Charles Bazerman *Georgia Institute of Technology*

Houghton Mifflin Company   Boston   Toronto
Dallas   Geneva, Illinois   Palo Alto   Princeton, New Jersey

CREDIT

Leonard Abramson, "Uncaring Women's Health Care." *The New York Times,* May 14, 1990. Copyright © 1990 by The New York Times Company. Reprinted by permission.

From I KNOW WHY THE CAGED BIRD SINGS by Maya Angelou. Copyright © 1969 by Maya Angelou. Reprinted by permission of Random House, Inc.

James Baldwin, "If Black English Isn't a Language, Then Tell Me, What Is?" *The New York Times,* July 29, 1979. Copyright © 1979 by The New York Times Company. Reprinted by permission.

Charles F. Berlitz, "The Etymology of the International Insult," from *Penthouse Magazine.* Copyright © 1970 by Penthouse International Ltd., and reprinted with permission of the copyright owner and the author.

From Fabiola Cabeza de Baca, "The Women of New Mexico," WE FED THEM CACTUS. Copyright © 1979 by The University of New Mexico Press. Reprinted by permission.

Albert Camarillo, "Zoot Suit Riots," from CHICANOS IN CALIFORNIA: A History of Mexican Americans in California. Copyright © 1984 by Boyd & Fraser Publishing Company, San Francisco, CA 94118. Reprinted by permission.

Stephen L. Carter, "I Am an Affirmative Action Baby," OP-ED, *The New York Times,* August 5, 1991. Copyright © 1991 by The New York Times Company. Reprinted by permission.

Janice Castro, et al, "Spanglish Spoken Here," *Time,* July 11, 1988. Copyright 1988 Time Warner Inc. Reprinted by permission.

Credits continued on p. 462.

Sponsoring Editor: *Mary Jo Southern*
Managing Development Editor: *Melody Davies*
Production/Design Coordinator: *Renée LeVerrier*
Electronic Publishing Specialist: *Victoria Levin*
Manufacturing Coordinator: *Sharon Pearson*
Marketing Manager: *George Kane*

Printed in the U.S.A.

ISBN: 0-395-63684-1

Library of Congress Catalog Card Number: 92-72404

23456789-AH-96 95 94 93

Contents

UNIT TWO

Selves: True Colors   75

UNIT THREE

Language: Our Words, Our Voices   149

U N I T   F O U R

Jobs: Dollars and Dreams   227

UNIT SIX

Side by Side: the Sum of the Parts   381

Rhetorical Contents *

*Most selections are listed under more than one rhetorical strategy.

EXAMPLE AND ILLUSTRATION

NARRATION

PROCESS ANALYSIS

Preface

Side by Side is a multicultural reader for writers devoted to a curriculum of inclusion; its aim is to capture the varieties of American experience, drawn from diverse ethnic, social, and cultural groups, and to present a range of readings that help define our country and enrich its written legacy. Our collection of readings reflects the unprecedented mix of students now filling college classrooms across the country. Content-rich selections and extensive apparatus lead students to analyze what they read, apply their own experiences and knowledge of the topic of the selection, and then justify and develop their responses in writing.

THEMATIC ORGANIZATION

We have divided the sixty fiction and non-fiction readings into six sections, each organized around a theme that links the readings:

> *Childhood: Born in the USA* presents the common experience of growing up from the perspectives of children with different cultural backgrounds.
> *Selves: True Colors* focuses on individuals searching for their identities through their culture and heritage.
> *Language: Our Words, Our Voices* explores languge and its effect on our culture and behavior.
> *Jobs: Dollars and Dreams* shows how Americans of all backgrounds can struggle in their pursuit of the "American Dream."
> *Prejudices: Tears in the Rainbow Fabric* looks at the damaging effects of racism and discrimination.
> *Side by Side: The Sum of the Parts* celebrates the individuality and diversity of the people of our nation.

Taken together, these themes, we believe, represent the dreams and aspirations, the joys and disappointments, the aches and longings of the men, women, and children who people our nation.

APPARATUS ████████████████████████████

To guide study and to focus conversation, we offer a rich set of apparatus. A brief overview focuses on the issues that emerge from the selections in each unit.

- *Prereading Journal* questions ask students to explore their background knowledge and opinions of the ideas presented in the unit.
- An *explanatory headnote* provides context for the selection that follows.
- *Key vocabulary* gives definitions for difficult words in the reading.
- *Details and Their Meanings* asks students to explore their comprehension of the details and ideas of the readings.
- *Reading and Critical Thinking* leads students to examine inferential meanings and judge the writer's ideas.
- *The Writer's Strategies* require students to analyze the rhetorical techniques that advance the writer's meaning in the selection.
- *Thinking Together* encourages students to draw on collaborative learning techniques to discuss and apply an essential issue related to the reading selection.
- A *vocabulary* exercise helps students integrate unfamiliar words and phrases into the students' linguistic resources.
- *Writing Workshop* offers varied opportunities for students' writing. First, "Critical Thinking in Writing" provides challenging tasks to stimulate short essays on the ideas expressed in the readings. Next, "Connecting Ideas" guides students to link issues raised in one selection with related issues from other readings throughout the text. This activity encourages multiple perspectives on major topics in the text.
- At the end of each unit, *Side by Side* prompts students to reflect in writing about the units' themes. Students can return to their prereading journal entries and consider how the chapter essays provided new insights or confirmed old ones.

ACKNOWLEDGEMENTS ███████████████████

Many people helped us with this book by providing valuable comments in early stages of the manuscript. We would like to thank the following reviewers:

Gretchen Cupp, Yuba Community College, CA; Connie Eggers, Western Washington University; Grace Y. Kountz, SUNY—Old Westbury; Linda Weeks, Dyersburg Community College, TN; Ann Steiner, Central State University, OH.

INTRODUCTION

Writing and Reading

Each of us has a mental picture of the complex world we live in. Everyday experiences contribute to our world view and to our understanding of the peoples and cultures that occupy our planet, our country, our city, our neighborhood. Certainly all the reading we do, both formal and informal, plays a major role in shaping how we think; reading brings detail, focus, and specificity to our mental picture. Indeed, the selections in *Side by Side* will sharpen and expand your concept of the world community. But only by sharing information with others—by speaking and by writing—can you be sure that your conclusions about issues are sound and that your mental picture takes into account the thoughts and experiences of other people.

THE WRITING-READING CONNECTION

The writing-reading connection helps us to develop an informed vision of the world. Reading places before our eyes a range of thoughts and ideas that we otherwise might never encounter. Writing helps us share our understanding so that others see how we think and can react to our ideas. Writing helps us sharpen our thoughts on a subject because clear writing demands thinking about an idea in a rigorous way.

In this book, we examine readings not only to explore their multicultural content and their perspectives on the American experience but also to analyze how writers write, what effects they achieve, and how they achieve those effects. This plan enables us to evaluate how the experience of reading affects our thoughts about a subject and can shape our written responses to what we have read.

All through your education you have explored different kinds of readings. In your earliest schooldays, you read for facts or for entertainment. As you advanced through the grades, your teachers assigned material that required you to interact with the ideas and information. Some selections pleased and entertained more than others, but probably the common thread that connected the readings was that each one helped to focus your picture of the world. Readings of value add to your information base, expand your point of view about a topic, help you to analyze or evaluate your situations, introduce fresh perspectives on issues, and challenge you to develop and justify your own beliefs.

Reading for meaning is different from reading for pleasure or even reading for facts. To know that you understand a selection, you need to apply the material in some way, to incorporate it into your thinking and use it to help you understand the world. The most constructive way to use the material is to write about it.

CRITICAL THINKING THROUGH WRITING ——

Writing helps you think critically about what you read. The first step in critical thinking is comparing or applying your own experience or prior thoughts about a subject to the selection you have just read. Your own experience is a valuable tool because it is the resource that you have most readily at hand. Even though many of the selections in this book deal with topics far removed from your everyday experience, your thoughts and emotions are good guides to whether a writer is presenting ideas sincerely and accurately.

The activities in *Side by Side* ask you to write regularly about the issues emerging from the selections. Generally, we make specific assignments that highlight a focused and dynamic issue from the selection, one that may require a particular rhetorical strategy for appropriate essay development.

In the writing assignments, we have provided a variety of tasks. The most basic kind of writing that we encourage is summary writing. In a summary, you need to reproduce the information of a selection in your own words in order to state what a reading means. You identify the main idea, the essential support that the writer provides, and the conclusion (if any) that the writer draws. In a summary, you don't have to worry about whether you agree with the writer or whether the selection seems logical or true. Those critical judgments come later.

In other places, we ask you to react informally to what you have read—that is, to provide an initial emotional or intellectual response to one or more key issues that emerge from the selection. We suggest that you write a journal entry or a letter to stimulate a flow of ideas independent of any formal essay requirements. But we do not neglect the formal essay: many of the assignments you will do here require some command of essay conventions—for example, introduction, thesis, body, rhetorical strategies, transitions, convincing details, and conclusions. We encourage library research when a topic takes you into areas about which you have limited knowledge or information from your own experience. Many of the questions we ask about the selections reflect these concerns, so you should be primed to apply to your own writing what we have highlighted about essay form and technique for each piece in *Side by Side.*

Another approach we take to stimulate writing about your reading is to ask you in "Connecting Ideas" to compare and contrast various selections that you have read. In some instances, you can create a *synthesis* of two or more pieces by combining the information into a picture of the subject that is larger and more coherent than the picture you had after reading only one of the selections. However, you may find that writers offer opposing views about the same topic or that they present a problem similarly yet disagree about the course of action to follow. In those situations, you will need to weigh carefully the support a writer uses to back up an argument. You can start by asking what is the writer's *warrant* for making a particular assertion. A warrant is the authority, justification, or grounds that support a particular claim. Direct experience is usually a good warrant for some issues, but not always. Ask yourself how much experience the writer has with the topic, whether he or she has any ideological or personal stake in advancing a certain claim, whether he or she is presenting information fairly or slanting it. Once you have evaluated the writer's support, you can render a reasoned judgment of your own about the topic.

PRE-WRITING ━━━━━━━━━━━━━━━━━━━━━━━━━━

As you try to frame a written response to your reading, look carefully at the questions we have provided. Wherever you can, use them or questions your instructor gives you to help you start thinking about a topic that interests you. Narrow the topic, if necessary, to suit your own concerns. Talk with your friends, roommates, and teachers about the issues that prod your thoughts.

There are a number of informal techniques that can help you get started in formulating a written reaction to a selection.

Freewriting

An easy, enjoyable kind of writing to stimulate thought is called *freewriting*. When you freewrite, you write nonstop on a topic for a set amount of time (fifteen minutes, for example) without worrying about where your thoughts are going or how your writing will look. Nobody will ever judge what you freewrite, so you need not slow down to make sure that your grammar and spelling are correct. Your ideas don't even have to follow any logical order. Freewriting is exactly like talking to yourself about something.

The point of talking to yourself on paper is to help you identify feelings, clarify responses, and develop ideas that you will be able to use later in a formal assignment. Committing ideas to paper in this way can be useful even months later to remind you of your reaction to a particular topic or selection.

Journal Writing

Since writing, like any other activity, usually gets easier the more you do it, a good place to gather your responses is in a *writing journal* that you update regularly. All the units in *Side by Side* begin with some suggestions for journal assignments, and the more writing you do in your journal, the deeper and richer your writing will become. Journal writing is closer to freewriting than to the formal essay-writing process. In some of the journal entries that we recommend, you will freewrite your ideas and feelings about a subject; in others, you will set down your thoughts and observations. Because journals are portable, you can add to an entry whenever an idea occurs to you. Because journals are also private, you can write what you wish and pay little attention to grammar and spelling. Concentrate only on getting your unedited thoughts down on paper.

Brainstorming

Another technique for getting started is *brainstorming*. It is usually a group activity in which a few people or even a whole class verbalizes ideas without worrying about how good those ideas are. Maybe you'll have a terrible idea that will make the next person think of something that will help you improve your own idea, which in turn can stimulate another person to say something really profound. Brainstorming is an excellent strategy to follow in the various group activities we encourage throughout *Side by Side*. Once you get started with this process of free-associating, the ideas are likely to grow better and better.

Asking Reporters' Questions

A useful start-up technique that many investigative reporters use is asking *who, what, when, where, why* and *how* questions. These questions help clarify and focus a topic, generate specific details, and even highlight aspects of a thought that may need special attention. Reporters' questions enable you to limit and focus a topic. The five *w* and one *h* questions can be used again at any time in the writing process when you get stuck on a point.

Making a List

To stimulate ideas in responses to an essay question, you can simply make a list of everything that comes to mind about a subject. Do not worry about the connections between ideas that you generate or whether the ideas flow logically from one to the other. Later you can connect related thoughts and eliminate anything that seems inappropriate. Your initial goal is to fill a page with random thoughts that, when expanded, can yield fruitful essay responses.

Making Rough Outlines

As a topic stimulates their thinking, some writers jot information down in a *rough outline*. Major areas of thought appear in headings; possible supporting thoughts, in subheadings. Rough outlines allow you to develop ideas and loosely organize them at the same time. Don't fuss about using roman and arabic numerals or capital and lowercase letters to list your ideas in a rough outline. Simply indicate broad areas suggested by the topic, and place under them any supporting or related ideas.

Whether you are working from a freewriting paragraph, a list, or a rough outline, once you finish you will have a tangible document in your hands, something concrete that marks the beginning of the writing process. You are now approaching the point at which you can begin your formal writing.

LIMITING AND DEVELOPING YOUR TOPIC ──

Limiting Your Topic

Before you begin producing a draft, start limiting your topic by eliminating and grouping information from your prewriting exercise. Doing so will make writing a formal essay easier and more precise. Grouping related ideas together in an informal outline creates a basis for paragraphs. If you find one idea that doesn't go anywhere or fit in with your other ideas, you might want to leave it out of your essay. If you produced a rough outline during pre-writing flesh it out. If you used some other pre-writing strategy, grouping or outlining will help you to limit your topic and organize your initial responses.

Besides grouping, there are several helpful guidelines for limiting a topic. You need to ask yourself, "Who will read this paper— who is my *audience*?" In just the same way that you speak to your grandparents differently from the way you speak to your classmates, knowing who will read your essay will help you decide how elaborate your explanations should be, how formally you need to approach a topic, and how much detail and support you should provide. How much do your readers already know about a topic? With what terms and concepts will they already be familiar? Which ones will you need to explain?

Another important question that will help you limit your topic is "What is the *purpose* of this paper?"—that is, what response are you looking for from your reader? If you are telling a funny story, then the response you want is laughter. If you are giving instructions for loading a disk into a computer, then you want your reader to be able to perform that task successfully. If you are writing about the benefits of recycling, then you want your reader to agree that recycling is a good idea. With your audience and purpose in mind, you can make appropriate word choices and construct sentences designed to achieve your goals.

Generating a Thesis

Once you finish your outline and other efforts to limit your topic, the next essential step is to generate a *thesis*. Every piece of writing you do should have at its heart a main point, an assertion, a belief, a discovery. The thesis is a one-sentence statement of what you want to communicate to your reader. It informs the reader about the topic, and it indicates your attitude toward, or opinion about, the topic. A good thesis tells the reader exactly what you want to assert in the essay and what the reader will understand if he or she reads what you have written. Often you can construct an effective thesis from the language in the assignment that you have been given, so read the writing task statement carefully. Suppose that the assignment is this:

> Do you personally identify more with your roots or with some newer version of evolving American culture? Write an essay describing the culture that you feel part of or want to be part of.

You can construct a thesis like this, which draws on the words from the task:

> As the American daughter of Korean immigrant parents, I always identified with a newer born-in-America version of our evolving culture until my shocking adventures on a trip to Seoul, home of my mother's parents.

In other cases, as with a broadly stated assignment, you'll have to construct the thesis exclusively from your own language resources. For example, if your announced topic is simply *affirmative action*, you might propose one of these sentences as your thesis:

> Affirmative action policies have allowed many minority women to move upward on the career ladder in high-level academic jobs. The attacks on affirmative action policies by some government leaders have had devastating effects on how white America views job opportunities for black men and women.

In the early stages of your writing, you should view your thesis as tentative: it will change as you continue thinking about the ideas and details of your essay. Experienced writers often tinker with their thesis statements right up to the final draft. But in all the examples given above, notice how the writer states a limited topic and makes an assertion about it.

SELECTING RHETORICAL STRATEGIES ───────

After you have written a tentative thesis and have weighed your audience and purpose, consider the various rhetorical strategies available to you as you develop your essay. Most college writing is expository—designed to inform and explain something about a topic. So you will find it helpful to consider some of the subgroups under the writing category "exposition" as ways of developing an idea clearly and thoughtfully. The following list identifies and defines these subgroups and shows how a writer might develop an essay response to a typical topic by using various rhetorical techniques.

Topic: Affirmative Action

Technique	Example
Description: Provide a picture.	Describe a scene at McDonald's in which members of a multiethnic work force, created through affirmative action, work together harmoniously.
Narration: Tell a story.	Tell a story about how a relative was accepted for a job-training program because of affirmative action guidelines.
Illustration: Explain by giving examples.	Illustrate three cases of how affirmative action policies helped people turn their lives around.
Comparison and Contrast: Explain by showing similarities and differences.	Indicate what an office was like before and after the employer established affirmative action guidelines.
Process Analysis: Explain by showing how to do or make something.	Identify the steps to be taken to make affirmative action policies work on your campus.

Technique	Example
Causal Analysis: Explain the cause and effects of some issue or event.	Analyze the reasons why affirmative action policies were developed, or analyze the consequences of those policies on the job.
Classification: Explain an idea by setting up categories.	Classify the kinds of responses that communities can make to affirmative action policies.
Definition: Explain by giving an expanded meaning.	Define affirmative action in the twenty-first century.
Argumentation: Take sides on a controversial point.	Argue for (or against) continuing affirmative action policies in government employment.

The writing assignments in *Side by Side* sometimes specify the rhetorical task—"Write a narrative essay to show how you moved beyond some restrictions of your childhood to discover a bigger world," for example. Other assignments are more open-ended, and you should choose a method or combination of methods of development on your own. Your thesis, audience, and purpose all will affect your selection of the most appropriate developmental mode.

DRAFTING ━━━━━━━━━━━━━━━━━━━━━━━━━━━━━━━

When the preliminary tasks are out of the way, you can concentrate on crafting your essay. Your first attempt is called the *first draft.* Sometimes—when you are doing an in-class test, for instance—the first draft is all you have time to write. Don't worry. If you have followed the steps described above, you will be able to do a good, though somewhat rough, job of presenting your ideas even when you have time only for one draft. Despite the press of time in an in-class essay exam, do not sacrifice prewriting, even if you can give only a few minutes to it.

In most college writing courses, however, the first draft is just a rough draft. You will have time to go over your work several times, making each draft better and a little more polished. Try to make the rough draft a relaxed effort. Don't censor yourself or inhibit the flow of ideas. The main purpose of a rough draft is to get consecutive sentences on paper about a topic that you've thought about carefully.

After you get through your essay once, let it sit for a while. Do something else. You will produce a better revision if you get a fresh perspective. Taking a break between drafts helps clear your mind and makes you more objective.

This is often a good stage at which to let someone else take a look at your work. Another reader is often useful for clarifying for you the kind of revision that is needed. But whether there is another reader or you are the only person reading your rough draft, the same issues should guide you toward a revised draft.

Two essential issues are unity and coherence, and any revision must address them carefully. *Unity* refers to the idea that all sentences in an essay must relate to the thesis as well as to each other. *Coherence* refers to the idea that all written thoughts must connect to each other logically, clearly, and smoothly. Unity and coherence are the writer's and reader's guarantee that the piece makes sense.

In your revision efforts, pay attention to how you have ordered the details in your paper. Especially in a narrative or process essay, you may want to organize information chronologically, that is according to a clear time sequence. In a descriptive paper, you may wish to present details spatially—top to bottom, front to back, or side to side, for example. Or you might wish to consider arranging details in order of importance, where you build to an essential point by presenting the less important information before you tell the reader the most important details.

As you revise, you need to ask questions like these: "Does the writing make sense?" "Did I leave anything out?" "Could the essay be clearer if I changed the order of ideas?" "Do I need more examples or more specific details?" "Are there some things I should leave out?" "Can the beginning or ending be stronger?" "Have I presented my ideas in a grammatically fluent way without too many spelling, punctuation, or other kinds of errors?"

If you handwrite or type your paper, you might use a different colored pencil or pen at this stage to cross out or draw lines indicating where to move words and sentences. Insert new pages with changes. Write notes to yourself in the margins; put arrows or stars where you want to add material. Don't worry about the mess. The key aim of revision is to produce a guide for the next draft. As long as you produce a useful document, you are revising correctly. If you use a computer, your revisions will be much easier to accomplish; move words around and insert phrases using the various options of your word-processing program.

Start with a fresh sheet of paper for the second draft. Work slowly to make sure you integrate all the changes from the first draft. Make sure you proofread for both content and grammar. Make sure you copy everything exactly as you want it to be, without missing anything or copying something incorrectly.

When you are finished with the second draft, put it aside for a while before you come back to it. When you reread it, be strict with yourself. Can you rewrite any sentences to make them clearer? Are your most important statements in the most important places in your paragraphs? Could your language be more precise, livelier, more direct? Are there mistakes in grammar, spelling, sentence structure, or punctuation? If you are satisfied with your responses to each question, you may decide it is time to hand the essay in. If you are not satisfied, writing another draft is a good idea.

You'll have lots of opportunity to read and write from the selections in *Side by Side*. Enjoy—and learn.

UNIT 1

Childhood: Growing Up in the USA

INTRODUCTION

America is a country of many contrasts—between the future and the past, tradition and change, poverty and wealth, glaciers and rain forests, high-tech cities and simple country towns, and children and adults. Sometimes it isn't easy to cope with the sharp divisions and contradictions of American life. All Americans are constantly pulled in many directions, between the need to fit in and the need to be themselves, between the desire to preserve the past and the desire to embrace the future, between their ethnic identities and the dominant American culture.

Children only gradually discover that growing up in America can be a difficult challenge. In this unit, you will read about children past and present, from many parts of the country, who are of different classes and ethnic groups. You will discover what they learned about America and how they struggled to make difficult decisions. In "An American Dream," by Rosemary Santini, you will read about the struggle between heritage and change. In "The Struggle to Be an All-American Girl," by Elizabeth Wong, the struggle is between American and ethnic cultures.

Parents and other relatives are often important teachers, easing the road to maturity—or making it more complex. In "Moon on a Silver Spoon," Eudora Welty tells how she learned a most important lesson from her mother. Sometimes parents can help children make their way in the world, as we see in "Momma," by Dick Gregory and "Two Worlds," by Jim Yoshida. At other times, grown-ups can be the source of conflict, as Langston Hughes recalls in "Salvation," a moving portrayal of a religious experience in his youth. There are even times when a child must reject his or her parents' world completely, as Sam Moses points out dramatically in "A New Dawn," an account of a teenager's daring escape from Cuba.

What binds these essays from many cultural perspectives is the intensely realized efforts of the writers to understand the ways of childhood in an increasingly complicated world.

PREREADING JOURNAL

Before you go to the selections in Unit One, write about one of the following topics in your journal.

1. Compare your experiences of growing up with what you know or imagine were your parents' experiences. What do you think was especially easy or hard about growing up then? How do the challenges and opportunities faced by your parents differ from the challenges and opportunities facing you? How was America a different place for them than it is for you?

2. What was the most important lesson you learned in growing up? How did you learn it? Who taught it to you? Write about the events surrounding this experience.

3. Write about a time in your childhood when you were in conflict about being a member of your family and part of the world at large. The reason for the conflict might be something you wanted to do despite your parents' opposition. Or there might have been a conflict between the identity you wanted for yourself and the identity your parents wanted for you. Or the conflict could have been between your family and outsiders, such as your friends.

Two Worlds

Jim Yoshida,
with Bill Hosokawa

Jim Yoshida is a writer who grew up in the Seattle area. In this selection, he describes the parental challenges he faced to become a high school football player.

KEY WORDS

rationalize (par. 2) to think of self-satisfying but inaccurate reasons for one's behavior.
apprehension (par. 7) fear, misgiving.
averted (par. 20) deflected, blocked.
transgression (par. 21) misdeed, sin.
exhilaration (par. 30) joyous enthusiasm.
ardent (par. 34) eager, dedicated.

1   WHEN I WAS FIFTEEN years old and a freshman in a Seattle high school, I stood 5 feet 7 inches tall and weighed 168 pounds. Many of my friends signed up to try out for the freshman football team. I couldn't because I had to go to Japanese school.

2   Still, I figured it wouldn't hurt to watch football practice for a little while. I sat on the sidelines, glancing at my watch frequently to make sure I would leave in time to get to Japanese school. On the third day of practice, the freshmen engaged in a scrimmage, and I couldn't tear myself away. I had played some sandlot football, and I figured I could do just as well as the freshmen in uniform. Before I knew it, it was too late to get to Japanese school on time. It didn't take me long to rationalize that being absent was only a little worse than being tardy. I decided that I might just as well watch football practice for the remainder of the day. Before long, nothing seemed to be more important than playing football with the freshman team. I approached the coach and told him I wanted to try out.

3   Coach Heaman looked at my stocky frame. "What's your name?" he asked.

4   "Jim Yoshida," I replied.

5   He reached into a pocket and pulled out a form. "You have to get your parents' permission," he said. "Take this home and get it signed. Come down to the locker room after school tomorrow and check out a uniform."

6   My heart sank. Here I was being invited to try out for the team, and parental permission—an impossible obstacle—blocked the way.

7   Full of apprehension, I went home at the normal time. Apparently Mom was unaware of my absence from Japanese school, and if my sister Betty had noticed, she hadn't said anything. I knew that Mom could sense when I had something on my mind. Besides, I wanted to talk to her before Dad came home, so I came straight to the point.

8   "Mom," I ventured, "I want to try out for the football team at school."

9   After hesitating a moment she replied, "What if you were injured playing football? Besides, what would you do about Japanese school? I think you had better forget about football."

10   I knew it was useless to try to change her mind and even more useless to talk to Dad.

11   Next day during a study period, I gave myself permission to play football. My hands were clammy when I gave the slip to Coach Heaman. I was sure he could hear the pounding of my heart and see the look of guilt that I knew was written on my face. He failed to notice, however, and routinely filed the permission form and issued me an ancient, hand-me-down uniform and a pair of ill-fitting shoes.

12   I made the team as a running guard. This meant I pulled out of the line and ran interference for the ballcarrier. If I did what I was supposed to do and threw a good block, the ballcarrier had a chance of making a good gain.

13   At the end of the freshman season, I was one of several freshman players invited to suit up with the varsity. In the season finale, the varsity coach let me play half the game.

14   Meanwhile, for some reason I have never understood, my absence from Japanese school went unnoticed until Betty brought home her Japanese-school report card right after the football season ended. Mom and Dad grinned as they examined her record. I knew what was coming next; Dad turned to me and asked to see my report card.

15   "Sir," I said, "I don't have one."

16   His eyebrows shot up. "Why not? Did you lose it?"

17   "No, sir, I haven't been attending Japanese school."

18   He fixed me with a stare that bored right through me. We were at the dinner table, and all of us had hot boiled rice to eat with cooked meat and vegetables. Steam rose from the bowl in front of my father, and I could see his temper rising too.

19   "Explain yourself," Dad ordered.

20   So I told him the whole story, including the way I had signed the form, and his frown grew darker and darker. Mom averted a very explosive situation by suggesting that the dinner table was not the place for a scolding. She suggested we finish our dinner and then talk about the problem.

21   Sometime during the meal, Dad must have seen the humor of my transgression. Perhaps he remembered pranks he had pulled as a boy. I was relieved to see his anger had given way to simply a serious mood when finally the dishes were cleared away.

22   First he lectured me about how wrong it was to deceive one's parents, and I had to agree with him. Eventually he got around to football. "I can understand why you would want to play the game," he said. "You should, however, take an interest in a Japanese sport like judo."

23   Judo is like wrestling, a sport in which a smaller and weaker person learns to use an opponent's strength to defeat the opponent. I didn't have much enthusiasm for judo.

24   Dad was saying, "Judo will give you the discipline you need. You must learn to grow tougher physically, mentally, and morally."

25   Then I saw a way that I might be able to play football next season. I apologized for what I had done. I *was* truly sorry. I agreed to go back to Japanese school and try my best to make up for what I had missed. I said I would go to judo class—if I could play football again next year.

26   The smile that had started to take shape on Dad's face vanished. Then he said, "All right, play football if it's that important to you, but remember there are things that are important to me too. So go to Japanese school and try to learn a little about the language; and go to judo classes and learn a little about discipline." We shook hands.

27   Several nights later, when I came home from Japanese school, Dad introduced me to a man who was about ten years older than I. His name was Kenny Kuniyuki; he was an instructor at a judo school. Dad told me Kenny would be my judo teacher. I liked Kenny immediately. We had dinner together, and then he drove me to the judo school.

28   For the next three weeks, every Monday, Wednesday, and Friday, I went to the school and learned to fall. Falling without hurting yourself is an art in itself. Gradually I learned to roll to absorb the impact as I hit the mat and to break the momentum with my arms and legs and shoulders before I crashed to the floor. Then Kenny began on the holds and throws. From seven to nine-thirty I would practice throwing and being thrown with the other students. After everyone else had left, Kenny had me stay and practice with him.

29   I must admit that I thought about quitting, especially on mornings after a particularly strenuous workout. I knew, though, that if I dropped judo, I could forget about playing football.

30   Approximately six months after I began judo lessons, everything began to fall into place. I was tough physically; I had learned, finally, to take the hardest falls without hurting myself; and I was able to coordinate my skill with my strength. I found a new exhilaration and excitement in judo. Judo was as much fun as football!

31   Soon I was good enough to skip over all the intermediate steps—yellow, green, brown, and purple—and get a black belt. It usually takes a student three or four years of hard work to win black-belt rating. I had done it in a fraction of that time. Mom and Dad beamed approval.

32   Dad raised no objection when I turned out for football in the fall of my sophomore year. I had kept my end of the bargain, and he kept his. I made the team as a running guard and was lucky enough to be an all-city selection even though we didn't win a single game. I still continued practicing my judo after the daily football workouts.

33   When I returned to school for my junior year, I had 190 muscular pounds on my 5-foot-9½-inch frame. The judo training had given me a better sense of balance, which helped me as a football player. I had no trouble making the team, and at the end of the season, I was again named all-city.

34   By the time my senior year rolled around, both my parents had become ardent football fans, and they came to watch me play. My new coach shifted me to fullback. I guess the move was a success because even though we still didn't win a game, we scored a touchdown—the first in three years. I was the one who carried the ball over the line! As I picked myself up after scoring, I saw Dad standing just outside the end zone with a big grin on his face. I think the sight of that grin made me the happiest of all!

EXERCISES

Details and Their Meanings

1. At the beginning of this piece, how old is Jim Yoshida, and how tall and heavy is he?
2. What prior commitment keeps Jim from trying out for football?
3. How does Jim's mother feel about his playing football?
4. Who is Betty? What role does she play in getting Jim in trouble?
5. What deal does Jim work out with his father?
6. How long does it take Jim to become good at judo? What at first is the hardest thing to learn about judo? How does judo help Jim to become a better football player?
7. How good is Jim's high school football team? What position does Jim first play on the team? What position does he eventually get to play?

Reading and Critical Thinking

1. Why is playing football so important to Jim? What information helps you to answer this question?
2. Why do you suppose Jim and Betty's parents want them to attend Japanese school?
3. Why does Jim decide to disobey his parents' wishes? What gives him the courage to do so?
4. Why does Jim's father not punish him for lying? What kind of person does Jim's father seem to be? Why does Jim's father feel that judo is more appropriate for Jim than football?
5. Why do you think Jim is able to skip all the intermediate belts in judo?
6. Why do Jim's parents become football fans?

The Writer's Strategies

1. What is Jim Yoshida's main purpose in writing this selection? Where is his purpose stated?
2. What is the meaning of the title? What are the two worlds?
3. Narrative is the major rhetorical strategy used in this selection. Why did Yoshida choose the narrative form? How does the writer make use of description to support his main rhetorical strategy?
4. Why does the writer use dialogue?

5. Why does Yoshida use chronological order? Outline the sequence of events briefly.
6. How old is Yoshida in the concluding paragraph? Why does the writer end the selection there and not carry it forward to the present?

Thinking Together

Parental permission slips are an important part of every student's life, even college students. How much authority do you think parents should have over their children's activities? As a class, brainstorm to develop a list of high school and college situations that require signed approvals. Then, working in small groups, decide which situations really merit parental approval and which ones should be left for the student to decide. When all groups have finished, come back together and compare lists. Where was the most disagreement? Why?

Vocabulary

The following sports terms are used in the selection. You can figure out the meaning of some from context clues—that is, by reading the piece carefully. But you may have to look up the meaning of others. Write a definition for each term in your own words.

1. scrimmage (par. 2)
2. running guard (par. 12)
3. ballcarrier (par. 12)
4. varsity (par. 13)
5. black belt (par. 31)
6. fullback (par. 34)
7. end zone (par. 34)

WRITER'S WORKSHOP ———————

Critical Thinking in Writing

1. Write an essay about a time you deceived one of your relatives—your parents, sister or brother, or spouse. What made you take such action? How did this experience work out? How did you feel afterward?

2. Both judo and football helped make Jim Yoshida physically stronger and more disciplined. How important are discipline and physical fitness to you? Did discipline and physical fitness in your youth influence your adulthood? How? Write an essay about the activities you pursue to keep you strong and teach you the value of discipline.

3. Imagine that you are forced to choose between an activity you really enjoy and one that your parents believe is necessary for your welfare. How will you and your parents resolve this conflict? Write an essay in which you describe the process that you and your parents will undertake and the kind of negotiation that might take place.

Connecting Ideas

Read Elizabeth Wong's "The Struggle to Be an All-American Girl" (page 32). How is Wong's experience with her ethnic tradition different from Jim Yoshida's? What obstacles does Wong face that Yoshida does not face or is able to overcome? Yoshida and Wong draw different conclusions about American culture. Why do they do so?

A New Dawn

Sam Moses

Journalist Sam Moses has written for a number of periodicals, among them Sports Illustrated. *In this piece, he introduces us to Lester Moreno Perez, a young Cuban American with a remarkable story.*

KEY WORDS

annals (par. 1)   recorded histories.
counterrevolutionary (par. 3)   moving against radical changes in government—in this case, opposing Fidel Castro.
infrared (par. 12)   a kind of radiation below visible light, given off by objects that radiate heat.
wishbone (par. 16)   a y-shaped bone.
odyssey (par. 17)   an epic journey.
blitz (par. 19)   an all-out, sudden attack.

1   IN THE ANNALS OF great escapes, the flight by 17-year-old Lester Moreno Perez from Cuba to the U.S. surely must rank as one of the most imaginative. At 8:30 on the night of Thursday, March 1, Lester crept along the beach in Varadero, a resort town on the north coast of Cuba, and launched his sailboard into the shark-haunted waters of the Straits of Florida. Guided first by the stars and then by the hazy glow from concentrations of electric lights in towns beyond the horizon, Lester sailed with 20-knot winds, heading for the Florida Keys, 90 miles away.

2   Two hours past daybreak on Friday, Lester was sighted by the Korean crew of the *Tina D*, a Bahamian-registered freighter. The boom on his craft was broken, and he was just barely making headway, 30 miles south of Key West. The astonished crew pulled Lester aboard, fed him spicy chicken and white rice, and then radioed the U.S. Coast Guard, which sent the patrol boat *Fitkinak* to take him into custody. After five days in the Krome Detention Center in

12

Miami while paperwork was being processed, he was issued a visa by U.S. immigration officials and released into the welcoming arms of his relatives.

3   Except for his rich imagination and broad streak of courage, Lester could be any 17-year-old who decides to leave home. He was raised in the shoreside town of Varadero, the second-oldest of five children in his family. "As soon as I started thinking a little bit— when I was seven or eight years old—I wanted to come to America," he says. Independent thinking ran in the family; his grandfather, Urbino, had been imprisoned for attending a counterrevolutionary meeting early in Fidel Castro's regime and spent nearly five years in jail. Furthermore, Lester's sister Leslie, who had been on the national swim team and had traveled to several foreign countries, had told intriguing tales of life outside Cuba. Lester also did not like the idea of serving three years in the Cuban army and then facing the possibility of having his career chosen for him by the Communist Party. There was also trouble at home; he and his stepfather, Roberto, were at odds, mostly over politics. So Lester decided he wanted to go to America, not Angola.

4   When he was 10 years old, Lester taught himself to windsurf by hanging around the European and Canadian tourists who rented boards on the beach at Varadero. "If you made friends with them, they would sometimes let you use their equipment," he says. As he grew older and got better at the sport, he found he liked the isolation and freedom of the sea. "Sometimes I would sail for eight hours without stopping, and go very far out," he says. His windsurfing to freedom seemed destined.

5   Recently, Lester sat in a big easy-chair in the Hialeah, Fla., apartment of Ana and Isidro Perez, the great-aunt and great-uncle who took him in. Lester is so skinny—5'6", 130 pounds—that it seems there is room for two or three more of him in the chair. On his head he wears Walkman earphones, which he politely removes when a visitor enters the room. He has been in America only a few weeks, but he has already been interviewed several times and has been chauffeured all over Miami in a limo on a radio station-sponsored shopping spree. The tops of his feet are still covered with scabs, the result of the hours he spent in the sailboard's footstraps; but his hands show no blisters, only hard, white calluses.

6   As he waits for a translator to arrive, Lester rocks back and forth in the chair like a hyperactive child. He clicks the television on with the remote control, passes a Spanish-language station and stops at a morning show on which a man is explaining, in English, how to prevent snoring by placing a Ping-Pong ball between your shoulder

blades, a move that forces one to sleep facedown. When a visitor demonstrates this to Lester through gestures and snores, the young man rolls his dark eyes, smiles and says in perfect English, "People are all crazy here."

7   A few minutes later, the translator, who owns a windsurfing shop in Miami, arrives, and Lester begins to tell his story through him.

8   "I had only been thinking of making the trip on a sailboard for about a month," he says. "Before that, I'd been thinking of leaving the country by marrying a Canadian girl—every couple of months a few would come that were pretty nice-looking. But I decided to sail because I was training hard and was confident I would be able to make the trip easily. I had windsurfed in bad weather, and even surfed during Hurricane Gilbert, so I was already out in really rough conditions and wasn't worried about it.

9   "Right before I left, I was watching the wind patterns. A cold front had passed by and it was pretty strong, so I waited until it subsided a little. Usually after a cold front passes, the wind shifts to the east, and it's just a straight reach to the U.S., so I waited for that. Then I told two of my friends, who said they would help me. I wasn't hungry, but I ate a lot—three or four fried eggs, some rice and half a liter of milk—so I would be strong for the journey." His friends also persuaded him to take along some water, a can of condensed milk and a knife.

10   At 7:00 on the evening of March 1, Lester, who had said nothing to his family, slipped out of his house and went down to the Varadero beach, where he worked at a windsurfing rental booth by day, while attending high school at night. Earlier that day, he had carefully rigged the best mast and strongest boom he could find with a big 5.0-square-meter sail. Then he had lashed the sail rig in the sand with the rental boards. Under cover of darkness, he unlocked the shed where the privately owned boards were kept and removed his sleek and durable Alpha model. It had been a gift to him from a man who sympathized with his plight—a generous East German whom Lester called Rambo for the camouflage hat he always wore. Lester fastened the sail rig to the board and carried it to the water. He waded into the ocean until he was knee-deep, glanced over his shoulder to make sure he hadn't been seen, and stepped onto the board. His ride on the wind to freedom had begun.

11   "I wasn't nervous," he says. "I had to be very clear minded once I decided to go; otherwise they would catch me and I would be in a lot of trouble. It would have meant three or four years in prison if I had been caught. No lie about what I was doing was possible."

12   About one and a half blocks away from the beach was a tower usually manned by guards with infrared binoculars. Lester, who was sailing without lights, also had to keep an eye out for freighters and pleasure boats that would be cruising in the busy Straits of Florida.

13   "At first I wasn't able to get my feet in the footstraps," he says, "because there wasn't enough wind for my sail. But as I got farther out and was able to get fully powered up, I began feeling more confident. The swells were very steep, maybe four or five meters, and I was going so fast I had no choice but to jump them."

14   As he recalls the moment, Lester rises from his chair, plants his bare feet on the tile floor and extends his thin arms, grasping an imaginary boom. He begins in English, "Wind coming, coming, coming . . . out, out, out . . . is very strong." He's hanging in his invisible harness now, arms stretched wide, eyes lit up, flying over the waves. "Whoosh!" he cries. "Is good!"

15   For 10 hours he rode the wind, never once fearing failure, or drowning. He thought of his family and how worried they would be when they discovered he was missing. But he wasn't alone out there. "Ever since I left, I could see the sharks coming out and in, coming up on the board. I was hoping and thinking they were dolphins, but when the sun came up, I could see there was no way they were dolphins."

16   Around daybreak, the aluminum boom broke, separating the connection to the mast like pieces of a wishbone. He tried fixing the boom with his knife but couldn't, so he sailed on, clutching the pieces of the broken wishbone. This made control of the board extremely difficult, and he couldn't rest in the harness he had rigged. "My arms and hands were getting really tired, but by then I could already see the big kites of the fishermen, so I wasn't really worried. When I saw the freighter, I tried to point [into the wind] as much as I could and sail toward it."

17   A similar crossing was made in January 1984, by Arnaud de Rosnay, a Frenchman who boardsailed from Key West to Cuba as a personal challenge and a publicity stunt. De Rosnay, one of the best boardsailors in the world, had sailed in daylight with a chase boat. His trip included two stops for repairs and two stops to rest, and he completed the crossing in about seven hours. (In November of the same year, de Rosnay vanished while trying to cross the Straits of Formosa.) But only a month before Lester's odyssey, another young Cuban had perished attempting to reach the Keys in a raft.

18   Not surprisingly, Hollywood has come knocking on Lester's door. "The story is a natural," says Paul Madden, the president of

Madden Movies. "It's *Rocky* and *The Old Man and the Sea* in one. If this picture is done right, by the end of it the audience will be standing up in the theater and cheering." Madden might not be one of those doing the cheering; he was outbid for the rights to Lester's story by Ron Howard's Imagine Films.

19   Lester has handled the movie offers—assumed to have reached six figures—and the media blitz with uncommon courtesy and self-assurance. A new acquaintance has even invited him to spend the summer at Hood River, Ore., where he will be able to jump the formidable swells of the Columbia River. This sounds good to Lester. But right now, one of his teenage friends has invited him to go sailing off Miami Beach. That sounds like the most fun of all.

_____

EXERCISES

Details and Their Meanings

1. Who is Lester Moreno Perez? How old is he? Where did he grow up? How did he learn to windsurf? Who helped him?
2. What members of Lester's family influenced his decision to leave Cuba?
3. What convinced Lester that the time had come to leave Cuba?
4. What means of escape from Cuba presented themselves? Which method did Lester choose? Why did he reject the others?
5. What would have happened to Lester if he had been caught?
6. How did Lester know the weather would be good for a crossing? How did he know he was heading in the right direction?
7. What difficulties did Lester face crossing to Florida? Who eventually rescued him?

Reading and Critical Thinking

1. What can we infer about life in Cuba from Lester's actions?
2. Why did Lester choose to risk his life when other means of escape presented themselves? What choice do you think other people would make in the same situation?

3. Why do armed guards occupy watch towers on the coast of Cuba? What are they guarding against? What does their presence tell you about Cuba?
4. Why didn't Lester tell his parents what he was doing? What might have happened if he had confided in them? Do you think he made the right decision? Why or why not?
5. What makes Lester Moreno Perez's story appealing to movie producers? Which actor would you cast as Lester? Why?
6. What evidence does the writer give about how well Lester is adjusting to life in America? How would you react to life in a new culture without your immediate family to support you?

The Writer's Strategies

1. What is the meaning of the title, "A New Dawn"?
2. How does Sam Moses use narration? How does he use description?
3. What is the writer's attitude toward his subject? Why did he write about Lester Perez? Why doesn't he discuss negative aspects of life in Cuba?
4. In which paragraphs does the writer cite secondhand information? How reliable is it?
5. Why does the writer tell about Arnaud de Rosnay in paragraph 17? What is his purpose in doing so?

Thinking Together

Imagine that you are living in a politically repressive country like Cuba. Do you have a responsibility to stay and work for change, or should you run away and make a better life for yourself elsewhere? Brainstorm with your classmates to develop a list of reasons for each option, and then discuss which reasons you think are the strongest.

Vocabulary

The following nautical terms are used in the selection. Write a definition for each term.

1. Straits (par. 1)
2. knot (par. 1)
3. freighter (par. 2)

4. windsurf (par. 4)
5. boom (par. 10)
6. swells (par. 13)
7. mast (par. 16)

WRITER'S WORKSHOP ━━━━━━━━━━

Critical Thinking in Writing

1. Assume that you are Lester Perez. Write a journal entry describing your thoughts and feelings during key periods of your escape.
2. Write an essay explaining the decision you made in *Thinking Together* about whether it is better to flee oppression or to stay and fight against it.
3. Assume that you are in Lester Perez's situation. Write a letter to your parents to explain why you are leaving the country of your birth.

Connecting Ideas

Read Armando Rendón's "Kiss of Death" (p. 91) and Gary Soto's "Looking for Work" (p. 231). How would Lester Perez respond to these authors, who are critical about life in America? What could Perez remind them about?

Salvation

Langston Hughes

Langston Hughes is best remembered as a poet, but he was also an accomplished essayist, journalist, and playwright, as well as one of the major figures in the growth of African-American culture during the Harlem Renaissance of the 1920s. In this piece from his autobiography The Big Sea *(1940), Hughes offers an irreverent account of how his conversion "saved" him.*

KEY WORDS

dire (par. 3)   frightening, dreadful.
gnarled (par. 4)   bent and twisted, like knots in a tree.
rounder (par. 6)   usually someone who walks on rounds like a policeman but here probably a drifter.
deacons (par. 6)   members of a congregation who assist the minister.
serenely (par. 7)   very peacefully.
knickerbockered (par. 11)   wearing loose, knee-length pants, called *knickers* for short.

1   I WAS SAVED FROM sin when I was going on thirteen. But not really saved. It happened like this. There was a big revival at my Auntie Reed's church. Every night for weeks there had been much preaching, singing, praying, and shouting, and some very hardened sinners had been brought to Christ, and the membership of the church had grown by leaps and bounds. Then just before the revival ended, they held a special meeting for children, "to bring the young lambs to the fold." My aunt spoke of it for days ahead. That night I was escorted to the front row and placed on the mourners' bench with all the other young sinners, who had not yet been brought to Jesus.

2   My aunt told me that when you were saved you saw a light, and something happened to you inside! And Jesus came into your life! And God was with you from then on! She said you could see and

hear and feel Jesus in your soul. I believed her. I had heard a great many old people say the same thing and it seemed to me they ought to know. So I sat there calmly in the hot, crowded church, waiting for Jesus to come to me.

3   The preacher preached a wonderful rhythmical sermon, all moans and shouts and lonely cries and dire pictures of hell, and then he sang a song about the ninety and nine safe in the fold, but one little lamb was left out in the cold. Then he said: "Won't you come? Won't you come to Jesus? Young lambs, won't you come?" And he held out his arms to all us young sinners there on the mourners' bench. And the little girls cried. And some of them jumped up and went to Jesus right away. But most of us just sat there.

4   A great many old people came and knelt around us and prayed, old women with jet-black faces and braided hair, old men with work-gnarled hands. And the church sang a song about the lower lights are burning, some poor sinners to be saved. And the whole building rocked with prayer and song.

5   Still I kept waiting to *see* Jesus.

6   Finally all the young people had gone to the altar and were saved, but one boy and me. He was a rounder's son named Westley. Westley and I were surrounded by sisters and deacons praying. It was very hot in the church, and getting late now. Finally Westley said to me in a whisper: "God damn! I'm tired o' sitting here. Let's get up and be saved." So he got up and was saved.

7   Then I was left all alone on the mourners' bench. My aunt came and knelt at my knees and cried, while prayers and songs swirled all around me in the little church. The whole congregation prayed for me alone, in a mighty wail of moans and voices. And I kept waiting serenely for Jesus, waiting, waiting—but he didn't come. I wanted to see him, but nothing happened to me. Nothing! I wanted something to happen to me, but nothing happened.

8   I heard the songs and the minister saying: "Why don't you come? My dear child, why don't you come to Jesus? Jesus is waiting for you. He wants you. Why don't you come? Sister Reed, what is this child's name?"

9   "Langston," my aunt sobbed.

10   "Langston, why don't you come? Why don't you come and be saved? Oh, Lamb of God! Why don't you come?"

11   Now it was really getting late. I began to be ashamed of myself, holding everything up so long. I began to wonder what God thought about Westley, who certainly hadn't seen Jesus either, but who was now sitting proudly on the platform, swinging his knickerbockered legs and grinning down at me, surrounded by deacons and old

women on their knees praying. God had not struck Westley dead for taking his name in vain or for lying in the temple. So I decided that maybe to save further trouble, I'd better lie, too, and say that Jesus had come, and get up and be saved.

12   So I got up.

13   Suddenly the whole room broke into a sea of shouting, as they saw me rise. Waves of rejoicing swept the place. Women leaped in the air. My aunt threw her arms around me. The minister took me by the hand and led me to the platform.

14   When things quieted down, in a hushed silence, punctuated by a few ecstatic "Amens," all the new young lambs were blessed in the name of God. Then joyous singing filled the room.

15   That night, for the last time in my life but one—for I was a big boy twelve years old—I cried. I cried, in bed alone, and couldn't stop. I buried my head under the quilts, but my aunt heard me. She woke up and told my uncle I was crying because the Holy Ghost had come into my life, and because I had seen Jesus. But I was really crying because I couldn't bear to tell her that I had lied, that I had deceived everybody in the church, that I hadn't seen Jesus, and that now I didn't believe there was a Jesus any more, since he didn't come to help me.

EXERCISES

Details and Their Meanings

1. Where and when do the events take place?
2. Who is responsible for bringing young Hughes to church?
3. What has Hughes been told to expect will happen in church?
4. Where do the children sit while they are waiting to be saved? What is the significance of the name of the area?
5. Who is Westley? Why is he important?
6. What emotion motivates Hughes to get up? How does the congregation react when he gets up?
7. What does Hughes do when he is alone in his room?

Reading and Critical Thinking

1. What point is Langston Hughes making about his experience at the revival?

2. Why is the title of this piece ironic—that is, suggesting the opposite of what it appears to be saying?
3. How does the writer describe the people at the revival?
4. Why does Hughes expect that Westley will be punished?
5. Why does Hughes cry at the end of the story? What does Aunt Reed think is the reason for his tears?
6. In the last paragraph, the writer says he cried for the last time in his life but one. What other event do you think might have made him cry?
7. What do you think would have happened to Hughes if he had not come forward to declare his faith?

The Writer's Strategies

1. How old is the narrator? From what perspective is this narrative written?
2. Which paragraphs serve as the introduction?
3. What ordering strategy does the writer use?
4. Paragraphs 5 and 12 are each one sentence long. Why does the writer use such short paragraphs?
5. Which paragraph serves as an epilogue? (An epilogue is additional material describing events that take place after the ending of a narrative.)

Thinking Together

The narrator in "Salvation" finally gives in to the pressures from his surroundings, despite a struggle with his conscience. What other circumstances cause young people to go against what they know and believe is right? How do peer pressures influence a person's behavior? Working in groups, make a list of the elements that influence young people to challenge what they believe is right. Share your list with other groups in the class. At your instructor's suggestion, after your discussion write a short essay sharing your thoughts on this issue.

Vocabulary

The following terms from the selection are associated with religion. Write a short definition of each.

1. revival (par. 1)
2. preacher (par. 3)

3. sermon (par. 3)
4. altar (par. 6)
5. deacons (par. 6)
6. congregation (par. 7)

WRITER'S WORKSHOP

Critical Thinking in Writing

1. Religion is a very personal experience for most people. Write about your own faith or the faith of someone close to you. What is it based on? Did you ever attend a revival meeting? If you did, was your experience different from Langston Hughes's? Write a brief description of the revival and your reaction to it.

2. Should children be expected to embrace the religion of their parents and guardians, or should they be allowed to make up their own minds about faith? What conflicting issues are raised by this question? What ideas can you think of to support each position? Write a brief paper to explore these issues.

3. Write a narrative about a pivotal experience that you believe helped you grow up.

Connecting Ideas

Read James Baldwin's piece on black English on page 199. In paragraph 7, Baldwin says that it was the genius of the black church to create a unique black speech and culture. What kind of culture do you see at work in "Salvation"? How is Hughes participating in something larger than a personal religious experience? What would Baldwin say that Hughes isn't getting about the church experience?

An American Dream

Rosemarie Santini

Rosemarie Santini has published articles in many publications and her books include The Secret Fire, Abracadabra, A Swell Style of Murder, *and* The Disenchanted Diva. *This account, which first appeared in the magazine section of a Sunday newspaper, tells how life has changed over the years for a family of three generations of Italian Americans who live together in the Queens section of New York City. Santini suggests that reaching for the American Dream has resulted in a gradual forgetting of the rich traditions of the past.*

KEY WORDS

tenements (par. 1)   inexpensive, crowded apartment houses occupied by working-class people.
affluent (par. 19)   well-to-do.
reiterates (par. 22)   repeats.
melodramatic (par. 24)   extremely emotional and overacted.
tumultuous (par. 27)   full of turmoil.
oblivious (par. 29)   not aware.

1   "WHERE ARE THE CHILDREN?" Ida Rinaldi asks as she breaks one egg after another into a large mound of flour, first breaking each egg into a glass and inspecting it for any discoloration. It is a process learned in the old days, in the tenements on Thompson St., when the eggs were often bad and destroyed whatever they were put into. "My mother taught me how to do this," she says.

2   Resting on the tablecloth that covers her kitchen table is a large, wooden board on which she begins to knead the mixture. On the counter nearby, other necessities for her Italian cuisine are in evidence: tomatoes, canned, of course, in Italia, tomato paste from the same country—very expensive—beef meats, and stale bread mixed in milk, all ready to be rolled into large meatballs. She enjoys her chores, part of a process which will take hours. She is preparing fet-

tucine as her Neapolitan mother taught her. "Let's see, eight people, eight eggs," she counts with peasant logic.

3   It is hot in the kitchen this August day, and she puts her hand to her forehead, smearing her tanned complexion with white flour. "Where are the children?" she asks again, although there is no one to answer.

4   At 67, Mrs. Rinaldi does not fit the popular picture of an Italian Mama. She is chic, petite, and slender. She wears the tight pants of the '70s, a shell blouse and tiny gypsy earrings. On the left finger of her right hand are a diamond engagement ring and a wedding band in an antique setting. They are not the original ones. In 1931 when she married, she was given no engagement ring and her wedding band was of plain silver.

5   Other things were different then, too. Now her house is a three-story brick-attached house in a lovely section in Queens. A backyard, a porch, a lawn are her proud possessions. Her apartment on the second floor could be featured in *The Sunday News* interior decorating pages. It is modern and sleek, and the only signs of her Italian heritage are tiny Botticelli angels in antique gold, which liven up the living room.

6   In 1931, her wedding home was an unheated, three-room tenement apartment in the Italian section of Greenwich Village. There, while working as a dressmaker, she raised her family, keeping the small apartment spotless, cooking on an old stove, cooling her groceries in an ice box; a living-room couch was her children's bed. Enduring these hardships, Ida Rinaldi and her husband worked and saved for the fulfillment of their American Dream, a house of their own. Finally, when their daughter Kathleen married and had a family, the Rinaldi-DeGiovanni clan moved from the tenements to the suburban splendor of Queens.

7   Here the brick houses all stand in a row, attached but separated by fence lines announcing ownership in this working-class neighborhood. Most owners, like the Rinaldi family, spent their entire life savings on the down payments. Only the electrical wires, hanging like kite lines over the pretty streets, mar the vista of this lovely neighborhood, an effect which the homeowners add to by stringing up clothesline in the backyards, probably a hangover from tenement days. Although most houses have washer-dryers, old habits die hard, and the Italians prefer their clothes bleached and dried in the sun, a custom inherited from ancestors who washed clothes in the village brooks of Italy.

8   Other neighbors have planted tomatoes in their gardens, but not this family. In the Rinaldi house there is a *House Beautiful* quality of

floors polished almost too clean, of furniture oiled, of dustlessness, and in the duplex below, where the DeGiovannis live, the same cleanliness dominates all.

9   The other dominating interest in this household is "What's for dinner?" Today, it is the egg fettucine specialty, hand-rolled, to be served with a thick meat sauce. Mrs. Rinaldi explains that she is spending so much time on this delicacy as a treat for the children, her two grandsons, teenagers Paul and John, who were, of course, a major reason for the Rinaldi-DeGiovanni move from Greenwich Village. But where are the children?

10   Kathleen DeGiovanni brings her mother the news. Her two sons have baseball games to play. After that, they are going to the DeGiovanni beach club for a swim and a party.

11   Mrs. Rinaldi's eyes look sad. "What about the egg noodles?" she asks.

12   "Can we keep them?" her tall, brunette daughter suggests.

13   Sighing, the older woman cuts the dough carefully in strips, then carries the long, thin pasta into the extra bedroom. "Well, no one's using the extra bedroom. We can lay them out here," she says, laying the pasta carefully on the bed.

14   Afterwards, she pours a cup of espresso. "It's all changed," she says. "When we first came here, our life was more centered in this house. It was the '60s, and we were so glad to get out of the tenements. This seemed like a good place for our grandchildren to play and grow up. Now, everyone is going this way and that. I guess that's life."

15   She spoons three sugars into her tiny demitasse cup. "I hope it doesn't get damp. Noodles are impossible to keep separate when it gets damp." As she sits, her hands move with infinite patience and care, a habit from another era when hands were important for darning, sewing, crocheting, knitting, making pasta.

16   Does she miss the old style of living in the Italian section of Greenwich Village? "I loved it, but now everyone has either died or moved away. When I walk down the streets, I don't know anyone." But weekly, she does walk down the streets, riding the bus and subway into the city to have her hair done, buying ricotta and mozzarella in the old cheese store across the street from the church, the same store where she shopped as a young bride whenever she could afford it. Once in a while, she runs into an old neighbor or friend who tells her how terrible living in the Village is nowadays.

17   Sometimes she wonders whether her life has really improved, although they have more room and more conveniences. Later, her

daughter Kathleen comments on this: "I grew up sleeping on a living-room couch. Here, my sons have a bedroom to themselves. We moved into a brand-new area where everyone was mostly Italian and mostly friendly. When the kids were small, I could leave them on the front lawn and not worry about them."

18   But the kids were no longer small, and Kathleen and her husband spend most of their time working in the city, going to church and school meetings, chauffeuring the boys to baseball games, grabbing a moment or two at the beach club, where a swim, a game of tennis give them much pleasure, not returning home until it is time to sleep.

19   The boys do not even mow the lawn nowadays, even though their weekly allowance from their grandfather should influence them to do so. Their major interests are sports, dancing, music, visiting more affluent neighborhoods, attending rock concerts, meeting new girls. John and Paul, 15 and 17, are tall, solid, muscular young men who say they want to live farther out on Long Island, near the sea, in a house complete with a boat moored at a dock, an office nearby in town, and lots and lots of privacy.

20   Dark-haired, studious Felix DeGiovanni agrees with his sons. "My parents were immigrants, born in Europe. They didn't have any choice on how to live when they arrived here. I had to compromise, too, and live in Queens, instead of farther out, because I work in the city."

21   Although Mr. DeGiovanni likes suburban living, he feels that his boys have been too much sheltered. "I learned all about life very young, on the city streets. I was working in the neighborhood pasta store after school when I was 13. My kids will be put through college without having to work. They have everything they need. They don't know how to take care of themselves, and I'm not sure that's good for them."

22   Mr. DeGiovanni earned his M.A. in engineering by going to night school and working as a draftsman during the day. Because his children do not have to struggle, he feels they are not as mature as he was at their age. Also, he reiterates a familiar parental theme, questioning whether his sons have any respect for authority.

23   Grandfather Rinaldi agrees that life is very, very different from the time he came over on a boat from Italy. "Then we worked hard and respected our parents and our family." White-haired, retired from the U.S. Post Office, Mr. Rinaldi sits on the porch in his rocking chair, pensively smoking his pipe as he watches the comings and goings in the neighborhood, talking about how different his life would have been if his parents were not immigrants.

24   If he had stayed in Italy, he might wander down to the town's square where he would find the other older men sitting and pondering the past and would argue with them, raising his voice in melodramatic splendor. If he had remained in Greenwich Village, he might walk over to the private men's club where Italian men play bocce and pinochle and talk about politics. But in Queens there are only a few senior-citizen centers for this kind of social interchange, and Mr. Rinaldi says the people there are too old.

25   Still, he is happy that he has at last attained his idea of a successful life: a house he owns out of what he considers the city, a safe place far removed from tenement living. Yet, there is a bittersweet element to his satisfaction, as if now he has everything, what does he really have?

26   "When we lived in Italy, I felt superior," he explains. "My parents were respected. We lost all that when we came to America. For years, I couldn't speak the language properly. Other kids from the neighborhoods called me names. I had to fight a lot, and I didn't understand the ways of living here. It took me a long time to get accustomed to America. That's why I worked so hard to better myself. To get what I had dreamed of all these years."

27   What is this dream anyhow, and has it worked for these former city dwellers in their effort for a better life? There is a lack of primitiveness here on these residential streets, so far from the tumultuous streets of their youth in the city . . . a sterility, almost a disease of cleanliness, where a speck of trash spills over onto their private thoughts and peaceful existence. Yet the neighborhood concepts which most of these former tenement dwellers grew up with are still in evidence. There are eyes in every second-story window, observing any stranger on the streets in minute detail, and visitors are associated with this house and that. There are pleasantries on the street, greeting of neighbors and friends.

28   Then, suddenly, the streets are empty. It is 5:30, dinner time in an Italian working-class neighborhood. The men have walked or driven home from their jobs. The children have stopped playing. In the Rinaldi-DeGiovanni home, the beautiful homemade noodles lie on the bed in the guest bedroom, uncooked, waiting for the meat sauce and imported, expensive cheese.

29   In the kitchen of the top floor apartment, the Rinaldi grandparents are eating vegetables in garlic oil with fresh Italian bread, waiting for the third generation of the family to be available from their busy life. This third generation is swimming in the beach-club pool, clowning with friends, listening to rock music, drinking soda pop, eating frankfurters, oblivious to the lifetime of dedication and hard-

ship represented by the plates of rare and delicious fettucine in marvelous sauce that await them.

_____

EXERCISES

Details and Their Meanings

1. Where does the piece take place? Where is the Rinaldi-
   DeGiovanni house? In what room does the action occur? In what
   ways is the setting significant?
2. Where did Ida Rinaldi learn to inspect eggs? Where else in the
   essay is that place mentioned? How many times is it mentioned?
   In what ways does that place contrast with Ida's current location?
3. What details indicate the way Ida cooks? What details indicate
   the way she dresses? How does the way she cooks contrast with
   the way she dresses? What does the contrast indicate?
4. Who is present at the beginning of the selection? Who is present
   later? Who never appears? What is significant about the order in
   which the family members appear? Where are the grandsons
   when the piece begins? Where are they later in the afternoon?
   Where are they when the piece ends? How often are they asked
   about? What is the significance of where they are and where
   they are not?
5. Where did Mr. DeGiovanni grow up? What did his childhood
   teach him that he is afraid his boys aren't learning? How do the
   boys spend their time, and what are their ambitions?
6. What sacrifices did Grandfather Rinaldi make and for what purpose? What were the results of his sacrifice? Did he get something of the sort he had hoped for? Does he miss anything he
   may have left behind in his struggle?

Reading and Critical Thinking

1. What values are important for the grandfather? for the father?
   for the children? How have these values changed from one generation to the next? Do you agree that the grandsons are not
   learning important values? Why or why not?

2. In what ways is the boys' life better than the childhoods of their parents and grandparents? In what way might the boys' child-hood be less satisfactory than their parents' and grandparents'?
3. How does the old life in the Greenwich Village neighborhood compare with current life in Queens? Which do you feel is pref-erable?
4. How much are the grandsons aware of the Italian traditions? Ought they be more aware? Is their lack of knowledge a natural part of becoming an American?

The Writer's Strategies

1. Look at the opening sentence. How does the question help set up the thesis of the selection?
2. How many places and ways of life are contrasted in this piece? List all the contrasts you can find, and identify the main point established by each.
3. How does the topic of conversation switch when each new per-son enters the room? How do these multiple perspectives enrich the main point?
4. How many mentions of food and cooking can you find? In what ways does food establish the ethnic culture of the selection? What does the concern about food tell you about the family's way of life? What is the significance of the dinner's having to be postponed until the children return?

Thinking Together

In discussion groups of three or four students, share the story of how your parents and grandparents lived and how your lives may be dif-ferent from theirs. Compare where they lived, the houses they lived in, the food they ate, and the amusements they had with those you experience.

Vocabulary

The following italicized words refer to details of Italian culture men-tioned in the essay. From the context in which the words appear and from your knowledge of Italian culture, identify the meaning of each term.

1. other necessities for her Italian *cuisine* (par. 2)
2. tomatoes, canned, of course, *in Italia* (par. 2)
3. She is preparing *fettucine* (par. 2)

 4. as her *Neapolitan* mother taught her (par. 2)
 5. tiny *Botticelli* angels in antique gold (par. 5)
 6. pours a cup of *espresso* (par. 14)
 7. into her tiny *demitasse* cup (par. 15)
 8. buying *ricotta* and *mozzarella* in the old cheese store (par. 16)
 9. working in the neighborhood *pasta* store after school (par. 21)
 10. where Italian men play *bocce* and *pinochle* (par. 24)

WRITER'S WORKSHOP

Critical Thinking in Writing

1. Do you think modern American youth have it "too easy"? What does having it "too easy" mean, and what are the consequences of it? State your position about the current generation in three or four paragraphs.
2. What values did your parents hope you would develop? Did you in fact develop those values? Do your values come from what your parents told you or from the challenges you have faced? Write several paragraphs describing your parents' efforts to transmit values to you and the results of those efforts.
3. Do you believe that becoming affluent and leading a comfortable life necessarily means losing contact with one's ethnic identity? Write an essay of about a page stating your position and giving reasons for your beliefs.

Connecting Ideas

Compare the view in this selection with the process of Americanization described in Elizabeth Wong's "The Struggle to Be an All-American Girl" (page 32). Do you think the boys in "An American Dream" and the girl in "The Struggle" would have the same or different attitudes toward their ethnic heritage? In what ways might the Rinaldis' and DeGiovannis' feeling about the boys be similar to the regrets Elizabeth Wong feels as an adult? Write an essay of three or four paragraphs exploring these connections.

The Struggle to Be an All-American Girl

Elizabeth Wong

The writer looks back on her childhood and on the way the culture she was born into interfered with her attempts to be an American. Notice how Elizabeth Wong's attitudes about the culture of her birth may have changed since she was a child.

KEY WORDS

stoically (par. 1)   in a manner unaffected by joy, grief, pleasure, or pain.
kowtow (par. 6)   to show respect by bowing deeply.
phonetic (par. 6)   speech sounds represented by symbols, each of which stands for a separate and distinct sound.
pidgin (par. 10)   speech that is a mixture of two or more languages.
Cinco de Mayo (par. 13)   the Fifth of May, Mexican Independence Day.

1   IT'S STILL THERE, THE Chinese school on Yale Street where my brother and I used to go. Despite the new coat of paint and the high wire fence, the school I knew 10 years ago remains remarkably, stoically the same.

2   Every day at 5 P.M., instead of playing with our fourth- and fifth-grade friends or sneaking out to the empty lot to hunt ghosts and animal bones, my brother and I had to go to Chinese school. No amount of kicking, screaming, or pleading could dissuade my mother, who was solidly determined to have us learn the language of our heritage.

3   Forcibly, she walked us the seven long, hilly blocks from our home to school, depositing our defiant tearful faces before the stern principal. My only memory of him is that he swayed on his heels like a palm tree, and he always clasped his impatient twitching hands

behind his back. I recognized him as a repressed maniacal child killer, and knew that if we ever saw his hands we'd be in big trouble.

4   We all sat in little chairs in an empty auditorium. The room smelled like Chinese medicine, an imported faraway mustiness. Like ancient mothballs or dirty closets. I hated that smell. I favored crisp new scents. Like the soft French perfume that my American teacher wore in public school.

5   There was a stage far to the right, flanked by an American flag and the flag of the Nationalist Republic of China, which was also red, white and blue but not as pretty.

6   Although the emphasis at the school was mainly language—speaking, reading, writing—the lessons always began with an exercise in politeness. With the entrance of the teacher, the best student would tap a bell and everyone would get up, kowtow, and chant, "Sing san ho," the phonetic for "How are you, teacher?"

7   Being ten years old, I had better things to learn than ideographs copied painstakingly in lines that ran right to left from the tip of a *moc but,* a real ink pen that had to be held in an awkward way if blotches were to be avoided. After all, I could do the multiplication tables, name the satellites of Mars, and write reports on *Little Women* and *Black Beauty.* Nancy Drew, my favorite book heroine, never spoke Chinese.

8   The language was a source of embarrassment. More times than not, I had tried to disassociate myself from the nagging loud voice that followed me wherever I wandered in the nearby American supermarket outside Chinatown. The voice belonged to my grandmother, a fragile woman in her seventies who could outshout the best of the street vendors. Her humor was raunchy, her Chinese rhythmless, patternless. It was quick, it was loud, it was unbeautiful. It was not like the quiet, lilting romance of French or the gentle refinement of the American South. Chinese sounded pedestrian. Public.

9   In Chinatown, the comings and goings of hundreds of Chinese on their daily tasks sounded chaotic and frenzied. I did not want to be thought of as mad, as talking gibberish. When I spoke English, people nodded at me, smiled sweetly, said encouraging words. Even the people in my culture would cluck and say that I'd do well in life. "My, doesn't she move her lips fast," they would say, meaning that I'd be able to keep up with the world outside Chinatown.

10   My brother was even more fanatical than I about speaking English. He was especially hard on my mother, criticizing her, often cruelly, for her pidgin speech—smatterings of Chinese scattered like chop suey in her conversation. "It's not 'What it is,' Mom," he'd say

in exasperation. "It's 'What *is* it, what *is* it, what *is* it'!" Sometimes Mom might leave out an occasional "the" or "a," or perhaps a verb of being. He would stop her in midsentence: "Say it again, Mom. Say it right." When he tripped over his own tongue, he'd blame it on her: "See, Mom, it's all your fault. You set a bad example."

11   What infuriated my mother most was when my brother cornered her on her consonants, especially "r." My father had played a cruel joke on Mom by assigning her an American name that her tongue wouldn't allow her to say. No matter how hard she tried, "Ruth" always ended up "Luth" or "Roof."

12   After two years of writing with a *moc but* and reciting words with multiples of meanings, I finally was granted a cultural divorce. I was permitted to stop Chinese school.

13   I thought of myself as multicultural. I preferred tacos to egg rolls; I enjoyed Cinco de Mayo more than Chinese New Year.

14   At last, I was one of you; I wasn't one of them.

15   Sadly, I still am.

EXERCISES

Details and Their Meanings

1. When it was time to go to Chinese school, how did Elizabeth Wong and her brother behave? What attitude toward the school did their behavior reveal? How did the children's behavior contrast with the attitude of their mother? How did the children's behavior contrast with the appearance of the school and the principal?

2. How did the auditorium smell? How did the American teacher smell? Which smell did young Elizabeth prefer? Which flag did she prefer, the flag of the Nationalist Republic of China or the flag of the United States? Which language, Chinese or English, did she prefer? What attitude do you think these preferences expressed?

3. What politeness exercises did the students have to do each day? What can you infer about Wong's attitude toward these exercises?

4. What kind of work did Wong do in Chinese school? in American school? In which school was she more advanced? In which was the work more interesting to her? What were the rewards and penalties for her accomplishments in each school?
5. When did Wong see people speak Chinese? Who were the people? What was her impression of spoken Chinese?
6. How did Chinese people react to Wong's skill in English? How did other people react to it?
7. What mistakes did Wong's mother make in English? How did Wong's brother respond to his mother's errors? What attitude about language did the children's feelings toward their mother's and grandmother's use of language show?
8. When and how did Wong's experience with Chinese school end? What attitude did she seem to have toward Chinese school when she stopped attending? What foods and holidays did she prefer at that time? Did those foods and holidays represent the dominant American culture or something else?

Reading and Critical Thinking

1. What seems to be Elizabeth Wong's general attitude toward her cultural background and the training she received in it? Why do you think she feels that way? Is that feeling warranted? How do you think that attitude may have influenced her behavior?
2. Overall, how do you characterize the experience the writer and her brother had in Chinese school? Do you believe their experience is typical of the experiences of many children who receive some kind of cultural training? Why or why not? Do you believe such training has value? In what ways?
3. How did the writer and her brother generally feel about the traditional Chinese language and culture of their family? Is it typical for children to feel embarrassed by or even hostile toward the traditional culture and language of their family? Is the problem worse for children of immigrants or for other groups. Is the embarrassment inevitable? Is there anything parents can do to avoid the problem? Are there any positive aspects to this cultural discomfort?
4. What is the significance of Elizabeth Wong's interest in French perfume and language and Mexican food and holidays? What does she mean about being an "All-American girl"? What does America represent to her? Do you agree with her view of what

it means to be all-American? Do you think all Americans share her view?

5. What do the closing paragraphs of the essay indicate about the way Elizabeth Wong now views her experiences at Chinese school? Has her attitude changed? Do you think the change in attitude reflects a deep change in the goals she will pursue in her life or just reflects some passing feelings? What could she now do to act on those feelings? Would those actions be likely to lead her to adopt a totally Chinese way of life?

The Writer's Strategies

1. What are the opening three words of the essay? In the opening paragraph, what impression is the writer trying to give of the Chinese school? Why? How does the opening set up the issues discussed in the rest of the essay? What is the significance of the school's solidity and endurance for the young children and for Wong as an adult?

2. What is Wong's thesis? In paragraphs 2 through 5, what story does Wong tell? What points does she make by this story? Why does she use a narrative to make these points? Why does she use a generalized narrative about "every day" instead of a specific narrative about "one day"?

3. In what paragraphs can you find comparisons? What are the items being compared? What is the point of the comparisons? How do the various comparisons support the overall conflict of this essay? What is that conflict?

4. What associations does the writer make with various smells? What kinds of evaluative words does she associate with the use of different languages? How do these associations help develop the themes of this essay?

5. In the last four paragraphs, several rapid changes in attitude are expressed. What are the attitudes? What time in the writer's life does each of the attitudes express? How does the inclusion of these changing statements of attitude change the meaning or interpretation of the essay?

6. The last two sentences, which are the last two paragraphs, are very short and repeat words and sentence patterns. Describe these repeated patterns, and discuss how they achieve a special effect.

Thinking Together

As a class, brainstorm about the various ways in which you are formally and informally taught about the cultures of your birth—including parochial or ethnic schooling, community cultural celebrations, and family experiences and discussions. Then, in small groups, compare your experiences of this kind, and describe your feelings about them.

Do you feel that these experiences were totally positive? Do you ever feel that they were unpleasant or something you did not want to do? Have you ever felt that aspects of your birth culture were standing in the way of your being part of the dominant American culture or any other group? Do you feel differently about these issues now from the way you felt as a child?

Vocabulary

The following words from the selection contain one or more small words or roots. The meaning of each small word or root is related to the meaning of the larger word in which it is embedded. Identify the small word or root; then define the larger word and explain its relation to the smaller units.

1. forcibly (par. 3)
2. repressed (par. 3)
3. maniacal (par. 3)
4. mustiness (par. 4)
5. painstakingly (par. 7)
6. ideograph (par. 7)
7. lilting (par. 8)
8. pedestrian (par. 8)
9. chaotic (par. 9)
10. fanatical (par. 10)

WRITER'S WORKSHOP ────────────────

Critical Thinking in Writing

1. Does growing up in America make children feel proud and happy or uncomfortable and embarrassed about their family,

ethnic, or cultural background? How does this feeling affect how children learn and develop? Write an essay exploring your ideas about the effect of ethnic identity on children growing up in America.

2. Write an essay describing your curiosity about cultures other than your own as you were growing up. Did you ever feel that other cultures were more interesting than or preferable to your own? What cultures were you curious about? Did you ever try to act in accordance with that other culture? Was your curiosity or behavior encouraged or discouraged? Did it create any tension within your family?

3. Write a narrative about how you learned or were introduced to some cultural practice or belief that was part of your family's background. Reveal directly or indirectly how you felt about that experience then and how you feel about it now.

Connecting Ideas

Look ahead to the essay "Minority Student" by Richard Rodriguez. What similar issues do Rodriguez and Wong raise? How are their perspectives different? How do their separate cultures influence those perspectives, do you think? Write a one-page essay comparing and contrasting the two selections.

Momma

Dick Gregory

Dick Gregory is one of the most influential recorders of the modern black experience. In this passage from Nigger *(1964), his autobiography, you see (and feel) the influence of the writer's mother on his family.*

KEY WORDS

fatback (par. 1)   a strip of fat from the upper part of a side of pork.

---

1   LIKE A LOT OF NEGRO kids, we never would have made it without our Momma. When there was no fatback to go with the beans, no socks to go with the shoes, no hope to go with tomorrow, she'd smile and say: "We ain't poor, we're just broke." Poor is a state of mind you never grow out of, but being broke is just a temporary condition. She always had a big smile, even when her legs and feet swelled from high blood pressure and she collapsed across the table with sugar diabetes. You have to smile twenty-four hours a day, Momma would say. If you walk through life showing the aggravation you've gone through, people will feel sorry for you, and they'll never respect you. She taught us that man has two ways out in life—laughing or crying. There's more hope in laughing. A man can fall down the stairs and lie there in such pain and horror that his own wife will collapse and faint at the sight. But if he can just hold back his pain for a minute she might be able to collect herself and call the doctor. It might mean the difference between his living to laugh again or dying there on the spot.

2   So you laugh, so you smile. Once a month the big gray relief truck would pull up in front of our house and Momma would flash that big smile and stretch out her hands. "Who else you know in this neighborhood gets this kind of service?" And we could all feel proud when the neighbors, folks who weren't on relief, folks who had Daddies in their houses, would come by the back porch for some

39

of those hundred pounds of potatoes, for some sugar and flour and salty fish. We'd stand out there on the back porch and hand out the food like we were in charge of helping poor people, and then we'd take the food they brought us in return.

3   And Momma came home one hot summer day and found we'd been evicted, thrown out into the streetcar zone with all our orange-crate chairs and secondhand lamps. She flashed that big smile and dried our tears and bought some penny Kool-Aid. We stood out there and sold drinks to thirsty people coming off the streetcar, and we thought nobody knew we were kicked out—figured they thought we *wanted* to be there. And Momma went off to talk the landlord into letting us back in on credit.

4   But I wonder about my Momma sometimes, and all the other Negro mothers who got up at 6 A.M. to go to the white man's house with sacks over their shoes because it was so wet and cold. I wonder how they made it. They worked very hard for the man, they made his breakfast and they scrubbed his floors and they diapered his babies. They didn't have too much time for us.

5   I wonder about my Momma, who walked out of a white woman's clean house at midnight and came back to her own where the lights had been out for three months, and the pipes were frozen and the wind came in through the cracks. She'd have to make deals with the rats: leave some food out for them so they wouldn't gnaw on the doors or bite the babies. The roaches, they were just like part of the family.

6   I wonder how she felt telling those white kids she took care of to brush their teeth after they ate, to wash their hands after they peed. She could never tell her own kids because there wasn't soap or water back home.

7   I wonder how Momma felt when we came home from school with a list of vitamins and pills and cod liver oils the school nurse said we had to have. Momma would cry all night, and then go out and spend most of the rent money for pills. A week later, the white man would come for his eighteen dollars rent and Momma would plead with him to wait until tomorrow. She had lost her pocketbook. The relief check was coming. The white folks had some money for her. Tomorrow. I'd be hiding in the coal closet because there was only supposed to be two kids in the flat, and I would hear the rent man curse my Momma and call her a liar. And when he finally went away, Momma put the sacks on her shoes and went off to the rich white folks' house to dress the rich white kids so their mother could take them to a special baby doctor.

8   Momma had to take us to Homer G. Phillips, the free hospital for Negroes. We'd stand on line and wait for hours, smiling and Uncle Tomming every time a doctor or a nurse passed by. We'd feel good when one of them smiled back and didn't look at us as though we were dirty and had no right coming down there. All the doctors and nurses at Homer G. Phillips were Negro, too.

9   I remember one time when a doctor in white walked up and said: "What's wrong with him?" as if he didn't believe that anything was.

10   Momma looked at me and looked at him and shook her head. "I sure don't know, Doctor, but he cried all night long. Held his stomach."

11   "Bring him in and get his damned clothes off."

12   I was so mad at the way he was talking to my Momma that I bit down hard on the thermometer. It broke in my mouth. The doctor slapped me across the face.

13   "Both of you go and stand in the back of the line and wait your turn."

14   My Momma had to say: "I'm sorry, Doctor," and go to the back of the line. She had five other kids at home and she never knew when she'd have to bring another down to the City Hospital.

15   And those rich white folks Momma was so proud of. She'd sit around with the other women and they'd talk about how good their white folks were. They'd lie about how rich they were, what nice parties they gave, what good clothes they wore. And how they were going to be remembered in their white folks' wills. The next morning the white lady would say, "We're going on vacation for two months, Lucille, we won't be needing you until we get back." Damn. Two-month vacation without pay.

16   I wonder how my Momma stayed so good and beautiful in her soul when she worked seven days a week on swollen legs and feet, how she kept teaching us to smile and laugh when the house was dark and cold and she never knew when one of her hungry kids was going to ask about Daddy.

17   I wonder how she kept from teaching us hate when the social worker came around. She was a nasty bitch with a pinched face who said: "We have reason to suspect you are working, Miss Gregory, and you can be sure I'm going to check on you. We don't stand for welfare cheaters."

18   Momma, a welfare cheater. A criminal who couldn't stand to see her kids go hungry, or grow up in slums and end up mugging people in dark corners. I guess the system didn't want her to get off relief,

the way it kept sending social workers around to be sure Momma wasn't trying to make things better.

19   I remember how that social worker would poke around the house, wrinkling her nose at the coal dust on the chilly linoleum floor, shaking her head at the bugs crawling over the dirty dishes in the sink. My Momma would have to stand there and make like she was too lazy to keep her own house clean. She could never let on that she spent all day cleaning another woman's house for two dollars and carfare. She would have to follow that nasty bitch around those drafty three rooms, keeping her fingers crossed that the telephone hidden in the closet wouldn't ring. Welfare cases weren't supposed to have telephones.

20   But Momma figured that some day the Gregory kids were going to get off North Taylor Street and into a world where they would have to compete with kids who grew up with telephones in their houses. She didn't want us to be at a disadvantage. She couldn't explain that to the social worker. And she couldn't explain that while she was out spoon-feeding somebody else's kids, she was worrying about her own kids, that she could rest her mind by picking up the telephone and calling us—to find out if we had bread for our baloney or baloney for our bread, to see if any of us had gotten run over by the streetcar while we played in the gutter, to make sure the house hadn't burnt down from the papers and magazines we stuffed in the stove when the coal ran out.

21   But sometimes when she called there would be no answer. Home was a place to be only when all other places were closed.

EXERCISES

Details and Their Meanings

1. What details in the opening paragraph indicate the poverty of Dick Gregory's family? What is the attitude that Gregory's mother suggests the children have toward their poverty? What incidents show that attitude? What effect do you think Momma's attitude had on the writer?
2. What kind of work did Momma do? What were the hardships of that work? What effect did that work have on how she could

take care of her own family? How did the conditions in the house where she worked compare with the conditions in her own home?

3. What did Momma think about the family she worked for? How did they treat her? What does her attitude toward that family reveal about her character?

4. What medical difficulties did Momma's own children have? What hardships and indignities did she face in order to take care of her children's medical needs?

5. Why was the Gregory house not kept clean? What did the social worker think about the Gregory house? Why did Momma have to hide the telephone? Why did she need a telephone?

Reading and Critical Thinking

1. What is the effect of Momma's positive attitude toward the difficulties of life? What is the effect of Momma's attitude on the attitude of the writer? Do you think her attitude was appropriate? What do you think might have been the source of her attitude? Do you think she would have the same attitude toward her situation now as she had about fifty years ago? Would any of her behaviors be different now? Which ones? Why do you think they would be different?

2. What is the writer's attitude toward his mother's sacrifices? Do you think her sacrifices made him an obedient and grateful child? Why?

3. How does Momma support the family? What attitude do her employers show toward her? What attitudes does she show toward them? Do her work and loyalty to her employers create any conflicts or potential conflicts in her emotions or thoughts? What do you think of her responses to her employers' treatment of her?

4. Which of the indignities described here come from racism and which come from poverty? Can the two causes be separated in these cases? What connections are there between racism and poverty in this piece?

5. Does the selection in any way appear dated, representing an earlier time in history? If you think it is dated, what details make you think so? In what ways might the writer be describing something happening today?

6. What kind of portrayal does this piece give of the welfare system? In what ways does the welfare system help the family? In

what ways does the system hurt the family? Does the welfare system still operate in these ways, or has it changed?

The Writer's Strategies

1. What is the main idea, stated in the opening sentence? Why does Dick Gregory begin with such a direct statement of the thesis? What is the relation of this thesis to the details reported in the rest of the essay?
2. In the second sentence, how is the family's poverty described and how does Momma characterize their poverty? What is unusual about how these details are presented? What is the effect of presenting the ideas in this way? Are any sentences phrased in similar ways later in the essay? How does the attitude reflected in this phrasing go with the ideas of this essay?
3. In which paragraphs are there contrasts between the house and family where the mother works and her own house and family? What is the effect of presenting these contrasts?
4. Identify all the times the writer begins a paragraph with "I wonder." What kind of material is presented in each of these paragraphs? What does the writer wonder about in each of these paragraphs? What is the overall effect of this repeated phrase?
5. Look at the last paragraph. What do the two short sentences imply? Why did the writer end this way? Why didn't he stop at the end of the previous paragraph or go on to state fully what is implied in those sentences?

Thinking Together

This selection presents a picture of parental sacrifice to raise children well. Within small groups, discuss what you feel parents' obligations are to their children and whether parents today live up to those obligations. Then discuss how you think you would live up to those obligations and whether you desire to do so. Also raise questions about special problems that your own children may face.

Vocabulary

Write definitions for the verbs below taken from the selection. Check the paragraphs indicated for the appropriate context.

1. collapse (par. 1)
2. aggravate (par. 1)

3. evict (par. 3)
4. plead (par. 7)
5. flash (par. 2)

WRITER'S WORKSHOP ━━━━━━━━

Critical Thinking in Writing

1. In an essay, compare the welfare system of fifty years ago with that of today. Consider what improvements (if any) have been made and whether either the current system or the earlier one provided any help or hindrance to the aspirations of the families on welfare. Develop your own thoughts about how the welfare system might be improved.
2. From your personal experience, write an essay about how attitude can affect the outcome of an unfortunate or a difficult situation.
3. Write a narrative of about a page describing a time when your parents made sacrifices to protect you or provide you with something that would help or give you pleasure.

Connecting Ideas

Read Susan Tifft's "Fighting the Failure Syndrome" (page 46), and write a short essay comparing the disadvantages of the young black males described there to the difficulties of the Gregory children. Also compare Momma's solution to the difficulties to the solutions proposed by Tifft.

Fighting the Failure Syndrome

Susan Tifft,
with Bruce Henderson and Julie Johnson

Susan Tifft, Bruce Henderson, and Julie Johnson are reporters and staff writers for Time *magazine. In this piece, they explain a controversial plan to change the way schools in the United States educate young African-American males.*

KEY WORDS

pathologies (par. 1) diseases, harmful characteristics.
tutelage (par. 2) an informal teaching relationship.
emulate (par. 5) to imitate.
detractors (par. 10) people opposed to an idea.

1 THE SIGNS OF CRISIS are everywhere. Nearly 1 in 4 black men, ages 20 to 29, is in jail, on probation or on parole. Black men are less likely to attend college than black females or whites of either gender, and when they do go, they often drop out. Homicide, including fatalities resulting from clashes with police, is the leading cause of death among black males, ages 15 through 34. Says Secretary of Health and Human Services Louis Sullivan: "When you look at a long list of social pathologies, you find black men No. 1."

2 To reverse this downward spiral, a vocal minority of black educators are pushing a radical idea: putting elementary-school-age black boys in separate classrooms, without girls or whites, under the tutelage of black male teachers. Critics of the proposal say segregating classrooms by race and gender flies in the face of more than 25 years of civil rights gains. But supporters argue that such concerns are less important than the urgent need to rescue African-American males from a future of despair and self-destruction. "The boys need

more attention," says Spencer Holland, a Washington educational psychologist and champion of the black-male classroom concept. "The girls are not killing each other."

3   Advocates of this approach believe low expectations and low self-esteem are largely responsible for the poor academic performance of African-American boys. A recent study of the New Orleans public schools, for example, showed that black males accounted for 80% of the expulsions, 65% of the suspensions and 58% of the non-promotions, even though they made up just 43% of the students. "Black boys are viewed by their teachers as hyperactive and aggressive," says Jewelle Taylor Gibbs, a clinical psychologist at the University of California, Berkeley. "Very early on, they get labeled."

4   The absence of positive male role models may also cripple black boys' development. Nationally, 55.3% of black families with children under 18 are maintained by the mother, many of them living in inner cities. Moreover, most elementary-school teachers are female, leading black boys to view academic success as "feminine."

5   Bill Cosby, Jesse Jackson and other black celebrities are too remote to offer realistic models of responsible manhood. The adult males whom many black boys try to emulate come from their own neighborhoods, and in tough urban areas, these "models" are all too often involved in drugs and crime. One lesson boys learn from such men is that doing well in school is for sissies or, worse yet, for blacks who are trying to "act white."

6   Three years ago, in an attempt to overcome these problems, a school in Florida's Dade County opened two classrooms for black boys with no fathers at home, one in kindergarten and one in first grade. The results were encouraging. Daily attendance rates increased 6%, test scores jumped 6% to 9%, and there was a noticeable decrease in hostility. But after only a year, the U.S. Education Department brought an abrupt halt to the experiment because it violated civil rights laws.

7   Since then, the closest thing to a black-males-only class is an effort in Washington, run by a group called Concerned Black Men. Launched two years ago at Stanton Elementary School, in the city's drug-infested southeast section, the program brings some three dozen black male lawyers, architects and other professionals into second-grade classrooms each week as teachers and mentors.

8   Although the classes include both genders, the main goal is to lift the sights and spirits of black boys, most of whom live only with their mothers or grandmothers. "The whole concept is to get the kids to look at themselves," says Albert Pearsall III, a computer security-

programs manager at the U.S. Department of Justice who teaches black history, along with a traditional second-grade curriculum. "If I can work effectively in a professional career, why can't these kids?"

9   Some critics of the all-black, all-male classroom idea are concerned that separating students by sex and race could intensify black boys' feelings of anger and inferiority. Others argue that the notion's underlying assumptions do not hold up. If poor, female-headed families are bad for black boys, they say, then they must be equally disastrous for black girls and whites of both sexes.

10   Detractors also contend that there is no clear link between self-esteem and academic performance and that a variety of people—not just black men—can effectively teach African-American boys. "It's helpful to have role models from one's own group," says child psychiatrist James Comer, director of the Child Study Center at Yale. "But there's probably no need to have role models exclusively from that group."

11   Supporters counter that black males are more frequently tracked into special-education classes than black girls or their white peers and would be no worse off segregated for normal instruction. "Black boys are already in classes by themselves," points out Jawanza Kunjufu, author of *Countering the Conspiracy to Destroy Black Boys.*

12   Such passionate debate makes it unlikely that primary-grade classrooms for black boys will become the norm anytime soon. Still, unless something else is done to make single-parent black homes more supportive of these children, or to help reduce their soaring dropout and suspension rates, the idea could attract more disciples —ironically hastening the day when "separate but equal" may actually help black youths rather than hurt them.

EXERCISES

Details and Their Meanings

1. According to the writers, what proportion of black men ages 20 to 29 are in prison, on parole, or on probation? What is your reaction to these data?
2. What is the leading cause of death among black men ages 15 through 34? What do these data tell you about the nature of existence for American blacks?

3. What percentage of black households with children under 18 is maintained by women? Why are women bearing this responsibility without the help of men?
4. What was the result of the Dade County experiment with all-black-male classrooms?
5. What is the purpose of comparing Bill Cosby and Jesse Jackson with "neighborhood" role models?
6. Why was the Dade County experiment halted by the U.S. Department of Education?
7. Explain the partnership that Concerned Black Men has entered into with second-grade classrooms.

Reading and Critical Thinking

1. What do statistics suggest about young black men in school?
2. Why is the idea of separate classes for black males considered radical? Do you find it radical? Why or why not? Where else do you find single-group education?
3. What do the writers suggest is one problem for a black male being raised by his mother alone? What other problems can you think of? Is being raised by a single mother necessarily a problem for a young male? Why or why not?
4. According to supporters, what are some of the problems that can be addressed by keeping male and female students apart? In which situations could you support separating boys from girls? In which situations would you not support separation?
5. What can you conclude about concerns that all-black, all-male classrooms will intensify feelings of anger and inferiority? Are these feelings correct? Are they racist?
6. From the title of Jawanza Kunjufu's book, what can you infer about his belief regarding black American boys? Do you agree with his position? Why or why not?
7. What do the writers of this piece believe about the possible value of all-black, all-male classrooms? Do you agree with them? Why or why not?
8. What is James Comer's view of segregated classrooms? How would people you know respond to his view?
9. Why do you think the selection does not dwell on the educational problems of black females? What are some of those problems?

The Writer's Strategies

1. Which sentence in paragraph 2 is the thesis of this essay? Restate the thesis in your own words. How does the title of the selection relate to the thesis?
2. How does paragraph 1 serve as an introduction to the essay? What data in the introduction attract and hold your attention? Where else in the essay do you find data thoughtfully and dramatically presented?
3. Many argumentative strategies are used? Where, for example, do the writers present the opposition's point of view, only to refute it? Do you find the technique effective? Why or why not?
4. Writers sometimes appeal to authority by citing comments made by credible people—researchers or individuals in important positions who know the issue. Where in this selection do you find such appeals, including quotations from reliable sources? Do these appeals convince you of the writers' position? Why or why not?
5. The writers provide examples or illustrations as a rhetorical technique. In paragraphs 6 and 7, for example, how do the writers use examples to support their point?
6. Where in the essay do you find instances of comparison and contrast? Why do the writers use this strategy?
7. Comment on the last paragraph, the conclusion of the essay. Is it effective? Why or why not? What elements of summary do you find? The last paragraph does more than summarize the key issues. What other features distinguish this paragraph? With what ideas does the conclusion leave the reader?

Thinking Together

Brainstorm on the issue of how to improve education for minority students, and make a list of *five* steps that you believe would help. Then form groups of three to five students, and decide on the *three* steps that the group feels are most important. Share the three items identified by your group with the other groups in class. Finally, as a class, write a letter to your local newspaper or to *Time* magazine to indicate the recommendations your class would make to improve education for minority students.

Vocabulary

The following list includes words that indicate someone who is in favor of something, a *supporter*, and someone who is opposed to something, a *detractor*. Each word presents a different shade of meaning. Identify each item as a *supporter* (*S*) or a *detractor* (*D*). Then define each word.

1. advocate
2. critic
3. champion
4. mentor
5. proponent
6. opponent
7. adversary
8. sponsor
9. enemy
10. benefactor
11. nemesis
12. skeptic
13. cynic
14. antagonist

WRITER'S WORKSHOP

Critical Thinking in Writing

1. Would you like to be a member of a segregated classroom in which everyone is the same race or gender as you? Write your opinions for or against such a classroom.
2. Assume that you are writing a report for the U.S. Department of Education on the all-black, all-male classroom. Summarize the results of the various pilot programs, and make a recommendation about whether more programs should be implemented.
3. Some critics argue that to improve education for minority students, more minority teachers must teach them and more minority administrators must manage their schools. Do some research in the library, or conduct a survey of students and faculty at your school. Develop a position on the issue. Then write an argument in which you support your point with data or testimony gathered in your research.

Connecting Ideas

Read Felicia R. Lee's "Model Minority" (page 112); then write an essay to explore some of the factors that troubled Asian-American youngsters have in common with African Americans. How do the problems of these groups differ? Can the experience of one group be used to predict what will work with another group? Why or why not?

The Jacket

Gary Soto

Gary Soto describes his feelings about growing up by telling a story about an article of clothing that seems to sum up his social failures. This selection may make you think about the old saying "The clothes make the man."

KEY WORDS

guacamole (par. 2)   a yellow-green spread made from mashed avocados.

————————

1   MY CLOTHES HAVE FAILED me. I remember the green coat that I wore in fifth and sixth grades when you either danced like a champ or pressed yourself against a greasy wall, bitter as a penny toward the happy couples.

2   When I needed a new jacket and my mother asked what kind I wanted, I described something like bikers wear: black leather and silver studs with enough belts to hold down a small town. We were in the kitchen, steam on the windows from her cooking. She listened so long while stirring dinner that I thought she understood for sure the kind I wanted. The next day when I got home from school, I discovered draped on my bedpost a jacket the color of day-old guacamole. I threw my books on the bed and approached the jacket slowly, as if it were a stranger whose hand I had to shake. I touched the vinyl sleeve, the collar, and peeked at the mustard-colored lining.

3   From the kitchen mother yelled that my jacket was in the closet. I closed the door to her voice and pulled at the rack of clothes in the closet, hoping the jacket on the bedpost wasn't for me but my mean brother. No luck. I gave up. From my bed, I stared at the jacket. I wanted to cry because it was so ugly and so big that I knew I'd have to wear it a long time. I was a small kid, thin as a young tree, and it would be years before I'd have a new one. I stared at the jacket, like an enemy, thinking bad things before I took off my old jacket whose sleeves climbed halfway to my elbow.

4   I put the big jacket on. I zipped it up and down several times, and rolled the cuffs up so they didn't cover my hands. I put my hands in the pockets and flapped the jacket like a bird's wings. I stood in front of the mirror, full face, then profile, and then looked over my shoulder as if someone had called me. I sat on the bed, stood against the bed, and combed my hair to see what I would look like doing something natural. I looked ugly. I threw it on my brother's bed and looked at it for a long time before I slipped it on and went out to the backyard, smiling a "thank you" to my mom as I passed her in the kitchen. With my hands in my pockets I kicked a ball against the fence, and then climbed it to sit looking into the alley. I hurled orange peels at the mouth of an open garbage can and when the peels were gone I watched the white puffs of my breath thin to nothing.

5   I jumped down, hands in my pockets, and in the backyard on my knees I teased my dog, Brownie, by swooping my arms while making bird calls. He jumped at me and missed. He jumped again and again, until a tooth sunk deep, ripping an L-shaped tear on my left sleeve. I pushed Brownie away to study the tear as I would a cut on my arm. There was no blood, only a few loose pieces of fuzz. Damn dog, I thought, and pushed him away hard when he tried to bite again. I got up from my knees and went to my bedroom to sit with my jacket on my lap, with the lights out.

6   That was the first afternoon with my new jacket. The next day I wore it to sixth grade and got a D on a math quiz. During the morning recess Frankie T., the playground terrorist, pushed me to the ground and told me to stay there until recess was over. My best friend, Steve Negrete, ate an apple while looking at me, and the girls turned away to whisper on the monkey bars. The teachers were no help: they looked my way and talked about how foolish I looked in my new jacket. I saw their heads bob with laughter, their hands half-covering their mouths.

7   Even though it was cold, I took off the jacket during lunch and played kickball in a thin shirt, my arms feeling like braille from goose bumps. But when I returned to class I slipped the jacket on and shivered until I was warm. I sat on my hands, heating them up, while my teeth chattered like a cup of crooked dice. Finally warm, I slid out of the jacket but a few minutes later put it back on when the fire bell rang. We paraded out into the yard where we, the sixth graders, walked past all the other grades to stand against the back fence. Everybody saw me. Although they didn't say out loud, "Man, that's ugly," I heard the buzz-buzz of gossip and even laughter that I knew was meant for me.

8   And so I went, in my guacamole jacket. So embarrassed, so hurt, I couldn't even do my homework. I received Cs on quizzes, and forgot the state capitals and the rivers of South America, our friendly neighbor. Even the girls who had been friendly blew away like loose flowers to follow the boys in neat jackets.

9   I wore that thing for three years until the sleeves grew short and my forearms stuck out like the necks of turtles. All during that time no love came to me—no little dark girl in a Sunday dress she wore on Monday. At lunchtime I stayed with the ugly boys who leaned against the chainlink fence and looked around with propellers of grass spinning in our mouths. We saw girls walk by alone, saw couples, hand in hand, their heads like bookends pressing air together. We saw them and spun our propellers so fast our faces were blurs.

10   I blame that jacket for those bad years. I blame my mother for her bad taste and her cheap ways. It was a sad time for the heart. With a friend I spent my sixth-grade year in a tree in the alley waiting for something good to happen to me in that jacket, which had become the ugly brother who tagged along wherever I went. And it was about that time that I began to grow. My chest puffed up with muscle and, strangely, a few more ribs. Even my hands, those fleshy hammers, showed bravely through the cuffs, the fingers already hardening for the coming fights. But that L-shaped rip on the left sleeve got bigger; bits of stuffing coughed out from its wound after a hard day of play. I finally Scotch-taped it closed, but in rain or cold weather the tape peeled off like a scab and more stuffing fell out until that sleeve shriveled into a palsied arm. That winter the elbows began to crack and whole chunks of green began to fall off. I showed the cracks to my mother, who always seemed to be at the stove with steamed-up glasses, and she said that there were children in Mexico who would love that jacket. I told her that this was America and yelled that Debbie, my sister, didn't have a jacket like mine. I ran outside, ready to cry, and climbed the tree by the alley to think bad thoughts and watch my breath puff white and disappear.

11   But whole pieces still casually flew off my jacket when I played hard, read quietly, or took vicious spelling tests at school. When it became so spotted that my brother began to call me "camouflage," I flung it over the fence into the alley. Later, however, I swiped the jacket off the ground and went inside to drape it across my lap and mope.

12   I was called to dinner: steam silvered my mother's glasses as she said grace; my brother and sister with their heads bowed made ugly faces at their glasses of powdered milk. I gagged too, but eagerly ate

big rips of buttered tortilla that held scooped up beans. Finished, I went outside with my jacket across my arm. It was a cold sky. The faces of clouds were piled up, hurting. I climbed the fence, jumping down with a grunt. I started up the alley and soon slipped into my jacket, that green ugly brother who breathed over my shoulder that day and ever since.

EXERCISES

Details and Their Meanings

1. What did Gary Soto want his new jacket to look like? Why do you think he wanted that kind of jacket? How would such a jacket make him appear among his schoolmates? How did he communicate his desired style to his mother? Do you think she understood what he wanted?

2. What was the jacket like that Soto's mother got him? What was his reaction to it? What size was it? Why was the size important? Why do you think his mother got him this kind of jacket? In what ways did he accept his mother's choice? In what ways did he not accept it?

3. What happened the first time Soto wore the jacket? Why do you think he did not repair the jacket immediately? What attempts did he make to repair it? What happened to the rip over time? What did that rip seem to signify?

4. How did Soto's classmates and friends react to his jacket? Was their reaction temporary or long lasting?

5. What happened to Soto's grades? to his social standing? to his friendships with girls? Why did he believe these events were caused by the jacket?

6. In what ways did Soto try to hide the jacket, not wear it, or otherwise try not to make it conspicuous? Why couldn't he get rid of it altogether? Why did his brother start to call him "camouflage"? How did his effort to avoid appearing in public because of the jacket reflect on his social presence and confidence during those years?

7. How did the jacket come to look over time? How did that appearance seem to reflect Soto's attitude toward his life?

Reading and Critical Thinking

1. To what extent do you think Gary Soto exaggerates the effect of the jacket? Do these exaggerations reflect the thinking of the young boy or the adult writer?
2. What was the psychological impact of the jacket and people's reaction to it on the young boy? Do you believe clothes can have such a psychological impact?
3. In what ways does Soto blame his misfortunes on his mother for purchasing the jacket? What does his attitude toward his mother's purchase of the jacket reveal about his relationship with her?
4. Were Soto's teenage years happy or unhappy? What do you think were the causes of those feelings? To what extent were those feelings caused by either the jacket or the mother?
5. What does this piece tell you about growing up? Does it in any way reflect on the particular experience of Hispanic youths, or are youths in all groups likely to go through something similar?

The Writer's Strategies

1. What is the opening sentence? How does that sentence relate to the narrative that follows? Is that sentence an accurate portrayal of the causes of the boy's difficulties? If it is not, why do you think the writer insists on blaming the jacket?
2. Why does the writer state in the opening paragraph that "in fifth and sixth grades . . . you either danced like a champ or pressed yourself against a greasy wall"? How does this choice set up the problem of the selection?
3. The writer presents a number of similes (comparisons using *like* or *as*), such as "bitter as a penny" and "arms feeling like braille." Find other similes. For both of the similes presented here and for others that you find, explain the meaning that is conveyed and tell how the simile supports the ideas and mood of the selection.
4. In how many places is it mentioned that the mother's glasses were steamed up as she cooked? What is happening between the mother and Soto at each of those times? What is the writer trying to show by this repeated imagery of the mother's glasses fogged by cooking?
5. In what order are the events told? What is the general progress of the writer's life over that period? What is the condition of the jacket over that period? How do these three elements fit together in a single pattern?

6. What parts of the piece seem exaggerated? Why does the writer exaggerate? What impression is the writer trying to give? Does the exaggeration strengthen or weaken the selection?

7. The writer ends by comparing the jacket to a "green ugly brother." Where does he make that comparison earlier? What does the writer mean by it? Why does he end the piece with that comparison? Why does he say that the "green ugly brother . . . breathed over my shoulder that day and ever since"?

Thinking Together

In small groups, compare the kinds of clothes you had as you grew up, particularly as you entered your teen years. Discuss which clothes you hated and why and which clothes you liked. Discuss which clothes your parents picked for you and when you were allowed to choose your own clothes. Which clothes made you feel part of a group. Which made you stand out in a positive way, and which made you appear to be an outsider? Then each group should write a description of the most excellent and most awful outfits for both male and female teenagers. Be prepared to consider in a general class discussion why each outfit would result in social acceptance or rejection.

Vocabulary

The following words appear in the selection. Define each one in terms that fit its context.

1. braille (par. 7)
2. scab (par. 10)
3. vicious (par. 11)
4. camouflage (par. 11)
5. tortilla (par. 12)

WRITER'S WORKSHOP ────────────

Critical Thinking in Writing

1. Clothes and external appearances are very important to children entering their teen years. What does this preoccupation say about children at that age and about the nature of their relationships? Write an essay about the importance of appearance to preteens and teenagers.

2. To what extent does Gary Soto blame other people or external events for his own misfortunes? Is he correct to do so? Have you ever done this? Write a short essay exploring how you focus your discontents by blaming someone or something outside yourself.

3. Have you ever had a conflict with your parents over the clothes you wear? How did the conflict turn out? What were the consequences? Write a biographical narrative recalling the incident and its implications.

Connecting Ideas

Read "Cultural Barriers and the Press to Americanize," by Margaret A. Gibson (page 65). Compare the barriers to belonging faced by the Punjabi youths described in that piece to the barriers faced by Gary Soto. How do the Punjabi students and Soto contend with those barriers? What are the results of the different conditions and strategies? Write a page or two of an informal journal entry thinking through these comparisons.

Moon on a Silver Spoon

Eudora Welty

Eudora Welty is one of America's foremost writers. Her work includes fiction, poetry, and criticism, much of it concerned with the South. In this selection from One Writer's Beginnings *(1984), her autobiography, she discusses her family's love of reading.*

KEY WORDS

initiating (par. 10)   introducing.

keystone (par. 10)   the stone in an arch that holds everything together.

acute (par. 13)   sharp.

opulence (par. 15)   showy richness.

reposing (par. 15)   reclining, lying down.

insatiability (par. 16)   the condition of not being able to be satisfied.

cadence (par. 18)   beat or rhythm; in this case, the rhythm of words in a text.

---

1   ON A VISIT TO my grandmother's in West Virginia, I stood inside the house where my mother had been born and where she grew up.

2   "Here's where I first began to read my Dickens," Mother said, pointing. "Under that very bed. Hiding my candle. To keep them from knowing I was up all night."

3   "But where did it all *come* from?" I asked her at last. "All that Dickens?"

4   "Why, Papa gave me that set of Dickens for agreeing to let them cut off my hair," she said. "In those days, they thought very long, thick hair like mine would sap a child's strength. I said *No!* I wanted my hair left the very way it was. They offered me gold earrings first. I said *No!* I'd rather keep my hair. Then Papa said, 'What about

books? I'll have them send a whole set of Charles Dickens to you, right up the river from Baltimore, in a barrel.' I agreed."

5   My mother had brought that set of Dickens to our house in Jackson, Miss.; those books had been through fire and water before I was born, she told me, and there they were, lined up—as I later realized, waiting for *me.*

6   I learned from the age of two or three that any room in our house, at any time of day, was there to read in, or to be read to. My mother read to me. She'd read to me in the big bedroom in the mornings, when we were in her rocker together, which ticked in rhythm as we rocked, as though we had a cricket accompanying the story. She'd read to me in the dining room on winter afternoons in front of the coal fire, with our cuckoo clock ending the story with "Cuckoo," and at night when I'd get in my own bed. I must have given her no peace.

7   It had been startling and disappointing to me to find out that storybooks had been written by *people,* that books were not natural wonders, coming up of themselves like grass. Yet regardless of where they came from, I cannot remember a time when I was not in love with them—with the books themselves, cover and binding and the paper they were printed on, with their smell and their weight and with their possession in my arms, captured and carried off to myself.

8   Neither of my parents had come from homes that could afford to buy many books, but though it must have been something of a strain on his salary, my father was all the while carefully selecting and ordering away for what he and Mother thought we children should grow up with.

9   Besides the bookcase in the living room, which was always called the library, there were the encyclopedia tables and dictionary stand under windows in our dining room. There was a full set of Mark Twain and a short set of Ring Lardner in our bookcase, and those were the volumes that in time united us as parents and children.

10   I live in gratitude to my parents for initiating me—and as early as I begged for it, without keeping me waiting—into knowledge of the word, into reading and spelling, by way of the alphabet. They taught it to me at home in time for me to begin to read before starting school. I believe the alphabet is no longer considered an essential piece of equipment for traveling through life. In my day it was the keystone to knowledge. You learned the alphabet as you learned

"Now I lay me" and the Lord's Prayer and your father's and mother's name and address and telephone number, all in case you were lost.

11   My love for the alphabet, which endures, grew out of reciting it, but before that, out of seeing the letters on the page. In my own storybooks, before I could read them for myself, I fell in love with various winding, enchanted-looking initials at the heads of fairy tales. In "Once upon a time," an "O" had a rabbit running it as a treadmill, his feet upon flowers. When the day came, years later, for me to see the Book of Kells, Gospels from the ninth century, all the wizardry of letter, initial and word swept over me, a thousand times over, and the illumination, the gold, seemed a part of the word's beauty and holiness that had been there from the start.

12   In my sensory education I include my physical awareness of the word. Of a certain word, that is; the connection it has with what it stands for. Around age six, perhaps, I was standing by myself in our front yard waiting for supper, just at that hour in a late summer day when the sun is already below the horizon and the risen full moon in the visible sky stops being chalky and begins to take on light. There comes the moment, and I saw it then, when the moon goes from flat to round. For the first time it met my eyes as a globe. The word "moon" came into my mouth as though fed to me out of a silver spoon. Held in my mouth the moon became a word. It had the roundness of a Concord grape that Grandpa took off his vine and gave me to suck out of its skin and swallow whole, in Ohio.

13   Long before I wrote stories, I listened for stories. Listening *for* them is something more acute than listening *to* them. I suppose it's an early form of participation in what goes on. Listening children know stories are *there*. When their elders sit and begin, children are just waiting and hoping for one to come out, like a mouse from its hole.

14   When I was six or seven, I was taken out of school and put to bed for several months for an ailment the doctor described as "fast-beating heart." I never dreamed I could learn away from the schoolroom, and that bits of enlightenment far-reaching in my life went on as ever in their own good time.

15   An opulence of storybooks covered my bed. As I read away, I was Rapunzel, or the Goose Girl, or the princess in one of the *Thousand and One Nights* who mounted the roof of her palace every night and of her own radiance faithfully lighted the whole city just by reposing there.

16   My mother was very sharing of this feeling of insatiability. Now, I think of her as reading so much of the time while doing something else. In my mind's eye *The Origin of Species* is lying on the shelf in the pantry under a light dusting of flour—my mother was a bread maker; she'd pick it up, sit by the kitchen window and find her place, with one eye on the oven.

17   I'm grateful, too, that from my mother's example, I found the base for worship—that I found a love of sitting and reading the Bible for myself and looking up things in it.

18   How many of us, the Southern writers-to-be of my generation, were blessed in one way or another, if not blessed alike, in not having gone deprived of the King James Version of the Bible. Its cadence entered into our ears and our memories for good. The evidence, or the ghost of it, lingers in all our books.

19   "In the beginning was the Word."

EXERCISES

Details and Their Meanings

1. Where did Eudora Welty's mother grow up? Where did Welty grow up?
2. Why did Welty's mother receive a complete set of Dickens? Why did the mother carry her books from one place to another?
3. What is the first word the narrator associates with an object in the world?
4. Which authors did the family read?
5. What book was most important in shaping Welty's ear as a writer?
6. How did Welty learn the alphabet?

Reading and Critical Thinking

1. Why did Welty's mother read Dickens under the covers at night? What does this tell you about her?
2. What can you infer from the fact that the collection of Dickens survived "fire and flood"? What books would you protect from damage?

3. Why did the father feel that buying books was a priority? How much of a priority is buying books for families today? Explain your answer.
4. Why does Welty associate words with religion?
5. Why does Welty decide to become a writer? What critical facility does she possess that her mother did not?
6. Where does Welty criticize modern culture? What is her criticism? Is this criticism justified? Why or why not?

The Writer's Strategies

1. How many different age periods does Welty refer to? Where is this account told from an adult's perspective? Where is it told from a child's perspective?
2. How do narration and description serve in developing the essay?
3. Where does the writer use sensory details? What are some of the most vivid?
4. What is the significance of the title? ·
5. What is the conclusion of this selection? What new idea is introduced in the conclusion?

Thinking Together

Evidently, Welty's parents believed that providing their daughter with a love of reading was important to her future. If you have children, what important skills or enthusiasms will you try to encourage in them? Develop a list in small groups; then compare your answers as a class.

Vocabulary

The following items mentioned in the selection are likely to be familiar to you. Write a brief description of each. If necessary, consult a dictionary or an encyclopedia.

1. Charles Dickens (par. 4)
2. Mark Twain (par. 9)
3. Ring Lardner (par. 9)
4. Book of Kells (par. 11)
5. Rapunzel (par. 15)
6. Goose Girl (par. 15)
7. *A Thousand and One Nights* (par. 15)
8. *The Origin of Species* (par. 16)
9. King James Bible (par. 18)

WRITER'S WORKSHOP ━━━━━━━━━━━━

Critical Thinking in Writing

1. Which books were important to you as you grew up? Describe some of the books that you loved the most as a child.

2. In many households, television and videocassettes have replaced books as the primary source of entertainment for children. Is there anything wrong with that? Can television and videocassettes convey the wonder and mystery that Welty got from books?

3. What should be the role of parents in influencing their children's activities such as reading? Should parents leave children to develop their own interests and tastes or should parents take a strong hand in guiding their children—to books and away from television, for example? Write an essay discussing your views on the matter.

Connecting Ideas

Read "See Spot Run," by Ellen Tashie Frisina (page 165). How does the experience of reading presented in that selection differ from Welty's account? What principal differences between the Welty and Frisina households can you discover? What is the reason for their different attitudes toward books?

Cultural Barriers and the Press to Americanize

Margaret A. Gibson

This selection is from a sociological study of Punjabi students in an American high school. In this part of the study, Margaret A. Gibson discusses the students' conflict between keeping their cultural values and behaviors and adopting American ways.

KEY WORDS

Punjabi (par. 1)   a person from the Punjab region of northwest India.

applicable (par. 1)   useful, related.

defer (par. 1)   to give way.

reluctant (par. 1)   unwilling.

initiate (par. 1)   to start, begin.

refrained (par. 14)   avoided.

incompetent (par. 14)   not skilled.

accordance (par. 15)   agreement.

legitimacy (par. 17)   lawfulness and authoritativeness.

1   ALL PUNJABI STUDENTS WERE faced with conflicting sets of expectations regarding appropriate behavior, one set applicable to their Punjabi world and the other to the world of school. At home, for example, Punjabi young people learned to defer to their elders and to remain respectfully quiet in their presence. When Punjabis first entered American schools, whether as small children or teenagers, they were reluctant to speak in class except to respond with factual information to a teacher's direct question. Punjabi students were especially uncomfortable with the American technique of "brainstorming," one elementary teacher observed, and fell silent

65

when expected to express their own ideas. High school teachers made similar observations. "'I don't know,' is their answer almost before the question is asked," one English teacher responded, when asked if Punjabi students participated in class discussions. It was rare, said another, for Punjabi girls "to be outgoing enough to initiate conversation in class." Part of the difficulty stemmed from the coeducational nature of American high schools.

2   In village Punjab teenage boys and girls traditionally avoid conversation with one another and even eye contact. In Indian schools, girls are not faced with the necessity of mixing with boys or speaking up in their presence. Classroom interaction is structured differently and, in most cases, secondary schooling is segregated by sex. At Valleyside High the Punjabi girls, including those born in America, participated only with great reluctance in coeducational activities, especially those that appeared competitive, such as physical education classes. They did not wish to draw attention to themselves in the presence of the opposite sex.

3   Just talking to boys could pose difficulty, particularly for the newer arrivals: "A family that has just come over gets really upset if they see their [teenage] daughter talking to some guy," one student explained. Even for the American-educated students informal conversation between the sexes did not always come easily: "When I came here [to the high school] from eighth grade and saw girls talking to guys I thought, 'Oh my God, what are you doing?' I had never thought of myself doing that. And if a guy came I'd go the other way." Most Punjabi girls did talk to boys at school, we discovered, but not in front of their parents. One student explained in an interview:

4   **Interviewer:** Does it bother your parents if you just speak to fellow students who are guys?

5   **Girl:** A lot of guys . . . come by [my house] and say "Hi, how are you?" I tell them not to stop [by] . . . because my mom and dad would get mad. They say, "Okay, we understand." I talk to guys here at school, and if my parents were to find out they would probably kick me out of school.

6   **Interviewer:** Just for chatting with them?

7   **Girl:** They are afraid . . . the guy might start liking me.

8   **Interviewer:** How do they feel about your making friends with American girls?

9   **Girl:** They don't say anything about that, just as long as I stay away from boys and going out on dates.

10   **Interviewer:** So you can mix with all kinds of girls?

11   **Girl:** Yes. . . . I enjoy talking to everybody. I even like to talk to boys. I've always been shy, but I enjoy talking to them. . . . If you don't talk to people they might say, "She thinks she's too good." I don't consider myself too good to talk to anybody. I think everybody is equal.

12   **Interviewer:** It must be awfully hard on the girls when they know their parents would really get upset.

13   **Girl:** Just about every girl here [at the high school] talks to every-body. If their parents were to be with them, they would have to face the other way. It's like in India. You hardly can look at anybody at all.

14   Punjabi students had learned to behave one way at home, an-other at school, but even in school the separation between the sexes remained. In sharp contrast to Valleysider social patterns, Punjabi boys and girls were never seen walking or sitting together. In group meetings, such as a get-together of the Asian Club, girls and boys sat separately. Most girls also refrained from speaking up in these sorts of gatherings, not, they said, because they felt incompetent to do so, but because it was their way of showing respect for the opposite sex.

15   Coeducational schooling posed the most obvious difficulties for Punjabis, but the constant attention given to preparing young peo-ple to go off on their own and to make decisions in accordance with individual rather than family wishes provided equal cause for ten-sion. The entire high school curriculum carried an implicit emphasis on teaching students that they had both the responsibility and the right to make decisions independent of their elders' views. So strong was the individualist orientation that it had become formalized in a social studies course titled "On Your Own." This course or one simi-lar to it was required for graduation.

16   In this class students learned how to rent an apartment, get mar-ried, plan the family budget, and even arrange a funeral—all on their own. Punjabi students were distinctly uncomfortable with this class, which from start to finish presumed white, middle-class val-ues. Lessons dealing with marriage and family life, always taught from a Western point of view, were embarrassing to Punjabi adoles-cents, as were units dealing with contraception, abortion, and di-vorce, particularly in the coeducational setting of the American classroom. Outside of class Punjabi girls were teased by Punjabi boys for having to pair off with members of the opposite sex for some of their assignments, in accordance with the teacher's instruc-tions. In spite of their discomfort with this and many other class as-signments, however, the girls reported that "whatever the teacher says, we have to do."

17   Even some Valleysider parents expressed concern about the heavy emphasis by school personnel on independent decision making for young people. The high school, they felt, was undercutting parental authority, teaching students, for example, not to believe something just because "your parents believe it." Some objected to the message that at age eighteen the child, then legally an adult, could "do as he pleases, at school, at home, or any place else, and the parents don't have anything to say about it." Those Valleysiders who wished the schools would do more to support parental authority were also those who reinforced the legitimacy of school authority. In this respect, some Valleysider parents sounded very much like their Punjabi counterparts.

18   Most Punjabi students in time learned to juggle the different demands and expectations of home and school. There were occasions, however, when Punjabi girls resisted complying with class requirements, even at the risk of losing credit. Physical education raised the most difficult problems. Two years of physical education were mandatory for high school graduation. Students received full credit if they attended class regularly, changed into gym clothes (short shorts and shirt), and made a reasonable effort to do what was asked of them. Although requirements seemed straightforward to Valleysider teachers, for many of the Punjabi girls in the senior sample they were simply beyond the pale. "Our children cannot change for sports," said one Punjabi parent; "this is against our culture." Almost no Punjabi parents wanted their daughters to expose their legs in the presence of boys or men. Some girls wore street clothes to class until they realized they would fail. Then they changed to sweat pants, no matter the temperature. . . .

19   Quite a few Punjabi parents were opposed to all sports for adolescent girls, especially if they were expected to run around in the presence of boys and men. In village Punjab only little girls played outside. An older girl, one man pointed out, would be seen "walking with her head low." Right or wrong, he concluded, Punjabi parents wanted the same from their daughters in Valleyside. . . .

20   In spite of all the pressures and counterpressures, Punjabi students made every effort to meet the demands of the formal curriculum, only rarely refusing to comply with a teacher's demands or school regulations, and then only in matters perceived to affect family and community honor. This was true even though Punjabi students often found the values of the classroom incompatible with those advocated by their parents. The easy give and take between the sexes and between students and teachers, the emphasis on indi-

vidual decision making and on asserting one's own ideas, and the underlying assumption that majority-group norms should prevail were examples of home-school discontinuities with which all Punjabi students had to contend and with which, in fact, they were successfully contending, by working out a multicultural modus vivendi.

21   Punjabis did not view compliance with school rules or doing what one must to succeed academically as symbols of majority-group conformity, and they rewarded those who excelled in school. Diligence in matters academic and the acceptance of school authority were not equated, in the Punjabi view, with "acting white" or "like the Americans." Furthermore, although Punjabi teenagers condemned peers who acted "like whites," they enjoyed American burgers, wore designer jeans, and, if they could possibly manage it, zoomed down a highway standing on the seat in an open Trans-Am.

EXERCISES

Details and Their Meanings

1. What practices in American high school classes were the Punjabi students uncomfortable with? How did these classroom practices conflict with Punjabi culture?
2. In Punjabi culture what is the traditional pattern of communication between boys and girls? How is this pattern reinforced by the attitudes of parents and of fellow Punjabi students? In what ways do American schools require different communication patterns? What kinds of tensions are created for Punjabi girls?
3. What were students expected to accomplish in the "On Your Own" course? What parts of this course were embarrassing or tension filled for the Punjabi students? How did the Punjabi students cope with this course?
4. What was the attitude of the Punjabi parents to the independence the high school was trying to foster in their children? How did this independence conflict with the parents' cultural values? Did any other parents share the views of the Punjabi parents? Is there a fundamental conflict of values between schools and most parents?

5. What particular problems were created for Punjabi girls by physical education classes?
6. What aspects of American life did the Punjabi students seem to enjoy? What do these pleasures suggest about the attitude of the students toward American values and ways?

Reading and Critical Thinking

1. In what ways did the Valleyside school attempt to develop individualist values? How might individualist values undermine respect for tradition, traditional values, and the authority of parents and other elders? Do you think Valleyside is typical of other American schools in this regard? Should schools be less concerned with developing individual confidence and independence?
2. In what ways were the Punjabi students not totally honest with their parents about what went on in school? Why? Were they right to keep some things from their parents?
3. What kinds of restrictions did the Punjabi parents wish to put on their daughters? Were they right to do this? What kinds of pressures did the parental restrictions put on the girls? Were the restrictions and pressures on the girls greater than those on the boys? What does this difference suggest about the roles of males and females in Punjabi culture?
4. Which culture do you think the Punjabi children preferred—American or Punjabi? Would you predict that ten years from now these students would identify more with American or with Punjabi values? Why?

The Writer's Strategies

1. In what sentence is the thesis identified? How do all the separate topics discussed in the selection relate to that main point?
2. This selection is written in a formal, academic style. Identify examples of generalizations, conceptual vocabulary, lengthy sentences, and the analytical organization of ideas.
3. In what way is the last paragraph built on a contradiction in attitudes that reflects the basic conflict of the entire selection?

Thinking Together

Discuss in small groups what aspects of school life, if any, you had to hide from your parents because they would not understand, would disapprove, or would otherwise create tensions, difficulties, or embarrassment for you. Were any cultural patterns involved, or were the tensions just typical of parent-child relations. At the end of the discussion, the group should make up a list of the three most common areas of tension between students' lives and parents' values. The groups should then compare the lists as part of a general class discussion.

Vocabulary

Paragraphs 20 and 21 contain some of the most difficult vocabulary in the selection because they summarize the students' situation in sociological terms. Using the context of the paragraphs, your understanding of the ideas in the selection, and a dictionary when needed, define each of the following words.

1. pressures (par. 20)
2. counterpressures (par. 20)
3. curriculum (par. 20)
4. regulations (par. 20)
5. perceived (par. 20)
6. incompatible (par. 20)
7. underlying (par. 20)
8. assumption (par. 20)
9. discontinuities (par. 20)
10. multicultural (par. 20)
11. modus vivendi (par. 20)
12. compliance (par. 21)
13. conformity (par. 21)
14. diligence (par. 21)

WRITER'S WORKSHOP ⎯⎯⎯⎯⎯⎯⎯⎯⎯

Critical Thinking in Writing

1. Restate the ideas of the last two paragraphs of the selection. Make sure you show full understanding of all the details by expressing them in your own words.
2. As you grew up, did you have to reconcile new values that you learned in school or among friends with traditional values that you learned from your family and your family's culture? Write an essay of several paragraphs exploring any value-related conflicts in your life and describing how you handled them.

3. In an essay of several paragraphs, describe a group of students in your high school, presenting their problems and conflicts as though you were a sociologist observing them from outside the school.

Connecting Ideas

Think of all the selections in this unit on childhood. Did students or children in any of the other selections face dilemmas similar to those faced by the Punjabi students? How did the tensions compare to the ones described here, and how did the other students' solutions compare to the solutions of the Punjabi students? Write a one-page essay discussing these comparisons.

S I D E B Y S I D E

1. Which of the selections in this unit was closest to your own experience of childhood? With which character or situation did you identify most closely? Explain what you identified with in the piece. In what ways is your own experience different from what you read?
2. Write a definition paper in which you discuss the phrase "Born in the USA." What does this phrase mean to you? How do the selections in this unit help you to understand its meaning?
3. Imagine that you are going to write a letter to a child from another country about what to expect from growing up in the United States. From your own experiences and what you have read in this unit, tell the child what to be aware of, what to look out for, and what challenges and opportunities to be prepared to face.

UNIT 2

Selves: True Colors

INTRODUCTION ━━━━━━━━━━━━━━━━━━━━━━

What gives us our identity? Do we fashion it out ourselves from education, experience, and choice? Or is it a gift from our families, our cultures, and our ethnic heritage? How much of us belongs to the past, to the geographical locations of our ancestors, to the beliefs they held, and perhaps even to the beliefs about them developed and passed down by others over the centuries? How much of what we have become is the product of our own choices, and how much is the result of prejudices for or against members of our group?

One of the lasting myths about America is the idea that the United States is a melting pot, a vast cauldron into which people from all over the world flow and out of which streams a single culture, a single standard, a single unified and coherent way of life. Despite the popularity of this myth and its impact on our consciousness, the lives of people living side by side in the United States often challenge the melting-pot vision. The single melting pot sometimes vanishes, and several different pots are visible on the stove.

In this unit you will read about Americans who have grappled with the idea of the melting pot. Leslie Marmon Silko explores the relation between Native American culture and Christian belief. Although Martin Luther King, Jr. and others wrote in hope that a unified society would fulfill America's promise of liberty and justice for all, the context for many of their pleas is an American society that lacks racial harmony and that must adjust to meet the needs and talents of a multifaceted community. Armando Rendón and Fabiola Cabeza de Baca remind us of the need to hold on to our separate identities and to take pride in our ancestors and their cultures. Stephen Carter asks us to reconsider our assumptions about the present as we work toward a new harmony. Richard Rodriguez points toward a future that promises a new synthesis of cultures.

Throughout these selections, interesting writers explore the issues of self, identity, and American culture.

PREREADING   JOURNAL

1. Write about what you consider to be the typical American household. What do you think of when you hear the phrase "typical American family"? How does this family live? What kind of house do they have? What is an average day like for this family? In what ways is your family a typical American one? In what ways is it not typical?

2. Write about something that reflects your ethnic heritage: a holiday celebration, a wedding ceremony, funeral rites, the foods you eat, the clothes you wear, traditional customs that you practice. Who taught you about these things? How do they help you understand your heritage?

3. Psychologists, philosophers, and religious leaders, among others, have tried to define the self. What do you think the self is? What elements contribute to your self? How do racial, cultural, and religious backgrounds influence the self? What role does physical appearance play in how we define the self?

The Fight

Maya Angelou

Maya Angelou is an important voice in modern American literature. In this excerpt from one of her best-known books, I Know Why the Caged Bird Sings *(1968), Angelou describes a late 1930s fight between heavyweight champ Joe Louis (the "Brown Bomber") and former champ Primo Carnera, showing that Louis's fights were critical events in African American culture and sports.*

KEY WORDS

apprehensive (par. 2)   filled with doubt or worry.
cracker (par. 3)   slang word for an ignorant white person.
maimed (par. 16)   crippled.
hewers (par. 17)   cutters.
ambrosia (par. 27)   in Greek mythology, the drink of the gods.

1   THE LAST INCH OF space was filled, yet people continued to wedge themselves along the walls of the Store. Uncle Willie had turned the radio up to its last notch so that youngsters on the porch wouldn't miss a word. Women sat on kitchen chairs, dining-room chairs, stools and upturned wooden boxes. Small children and babies perched on every lap available and men leaned on the shelves or on each other.

2   The apprehensive mood was shot through with shafts of gaiety, as a black sky is streaked with lightning.

3   "I ain't worried 'bout this fight. Joe's gonna whip that cracker like it's open season."

4   "He gone whip him till that white boy call him Momma."

5   At last the talking was finished and the string-along songs about razor blades were over and the fight began.

6   "A quick jab to the head." In the Store the crowd grunted. "A left to the head and a right and another left." One of the listeners cackled like a hen and was quieted.

7   "They're in a clench, Louis is trying to fight his way out."

8   Some bitter comedian on the porch said, "That white man don't mind hugging that niggah now, I betcha."

9   "The referee is moving in to break them up, but Louis finally pushed the contender away and it's an uppercut to the chin. The contender is hanging on, now he's backing away. Louis catches him with a short left to the jaw."

10   A tide of murmuring assent poured out the doors and into the yard.

11   "Another left and another left. Louis is saving that mighty right . . ." The mutter in the Store had grown into a baby roar and it was pierced by the clang of a bell and the announcer's "That's the bell for round three, ladies and gentlemen."

12   As I pushed my way into the Store I wondered if the announcer gave any thought to the fact that he was addressing as "ladies and gentlemen" all the Negroes around the world who sat sweating and praying, glued to their "master's voice."

13   There were only a few calls for R. C. Colas, Dr. Peppers, and Hire's root beer. The real festivities would begin after the fight. Then even the old Christian ladies who taught their children and tried themselves to practice turning the other cheek would buy soft drinks, and if the Brown Bomber's victory was a particularly bloody one they would order peanut patties and Baby Ruths also.

14   Bailey and I lay the coins on top of the cash register. Uncle Willie didn't allow us to ring up sales during a fight. It was too noisy and might shake up the atmosphere. When the gong rang for the next round we pushed through the near-sacred quiet to the herd of children outside.

15   "He's got Louis against the ropes and now it's a left to the body and a right to the ribs. Another right to the body, it looks like it was low . . . Yes, ladies and gentlemen, the referee is signaling but the contender keeps raining the blows on Louis. It's another to the body, and it looks like Louis is going down."

16   My race groaned. It was our people falling. It was another lynching, yet another Black man hanging on a tree. One more woman ambushed and raped. A Black boy whipped and maimed. It was hounds on the trail of a man running through slimy swamps. It was a white woman slapping her maid for being forgetful.

17   The men in the Store stood away from the walls and at attention. Women greedily clutched the babes on their laps while on the porch the shufflings and smiles, flirtings and pinching of a few minutes before were gone. This might be the end of the world. If Joe lost we were back in slavery and beyond help. It would all be true, the accusations that we were lower types of human beings. Only a little higher than the apes. True that we were stupid and ugly and lazy and dirty and, unlucky and worst of all, that God Himself hated us and ordained us to be hewers of wood and drawers of water, forever and ever, world without end.

18   We didn't breathe. We didn't hope. We waited.

19   "He's off the ropes, ladies and gentlemen. He's moving towards the center of the ring." There was no time to be relieved. The worst might still happen.

20   "And now it looks like Joe is mad. He's caught Carnera with a left hook to the head and a right to the head. It's a left jab to the body and another left to the head. There's a left cross and a right to the head. The contender's right eye is bleeding and he can't seem to keep his block up. Louis is penetrating every block. The referee is moving in, but Louis sends a left to the body and it's the uppercut to the chin and the contender is dropping. He's on the canvas, ladies and gentlemen."

21   Babies slid to the floor as women stood up and men leaned toward the radio.

22   "Here's the referee. He's counting. One, two, three, four, five, six, seven . . . Is the contender trying to get up again?"

23   All the men in the store shouted, "NO."

24   "—eight, nine, ten." There were a few sounds from the audience, but they seemed to be holding themselves in against tremendous pressure.

25   "The fight is all over, ladies and gentlemen. Let's get the microphone over to the referee . . . Here he is. He's got the Brown Bomber's hand, he's holding it up . . . Here he is . . ."

26   Then the voice, husky and familiar, came to wash over us—"The winnah, and still heavyweight champeen of the world . . . Joe Louis."

27   Champion of the world. A Black boy. Some Black mother's son. He was the srongest man in the world. People drank Coca-Colas like ambrosia and ate candy bars like Christmas. Some of the men went behind the Store and poured white lightning in their soft-drink bottles, and a few of the bigger boys followed them. Those who were

not chased away came back blowing their breath in front of themselves like proud smokers.

28   It would take an hour or more before the people would leave the Store and head for home. Those who lived too far had made arrangements to stay in town. It wouldn't do for a Black man and his family to be caught on a lonely country road on a night when Joe Louis had proved that we were the strongest people in the world.

EXERCISES

Details and Their Meanings

1. What is the setting of this piece? What details help you to decide?
2. What brand-name products are mentioned? What do you think is the writer's purpose in making so many specific references?
3. Who is Uncle Willie? Why is he an important figure in the community?
4. How do the people in the store separate themselves by age and sex? Why do you think they separate like this?
5. Why have all the people come to hear the fight? Why do they consider it an important event?
6. Where is the fight taking place? What is the outcome? How do the people feel after the fight is over?
7. What does the outcome of the fight suggest to the people in town about themselves? Why is the outcome important to their self-esteem?

Reading and Critical Thinking

1. What can you infer about the townspeople described in the selection? What kind of people are they?
2. Why do the people place so much significance on this fight? What is Maya Angelou assuming that you understand about the 1930s? Is her assumption justified in your case?
3. What can you infer about the age and sex of the narrator? Why are these elements important to your understanding of this

piece? Where does Angelou allow an adult's perspective to take over her narrative?

4. In paragraph 16, what does Angelou suggest would be the consequences of Louis's losing the fight? What is she implying?
5. When Louis wins, what does the narrator conclude about her race?
6. How much of the selection is a description of the fight?

The Writer's Strategies

1. State in your own words what you believe is the thesis.
2. Why does the writer focus on a group of ordinary townspeople when she is writing an appreciation of Joe Louis? Why does Louis remain so distant from the people in this narrative?
3. What main strategy is the writer using? Where does description play an important role?
4. The writer uses dialogue, but what is her reason for not having anyone talk to anyone else? How does this strategy heighten the effect of the piece?
5. To what primary sense does Angelou appeal—sound, smell, sight, taste, or touch? Why is this appropriate? Find the most unforgettable images of that sense.
6. Which paragraphs present the conclusion of this piece? How does the conclusion introduce a new element?

Thinking Together

Today, cable television and satellites enable people all around the world to experience major sports events in a much more direct way than was possible in the late 1930s when the Louis-Carnera fight took place. Can your class think of a recent sporting event that had a global or national impact? Why do sports events—football, baseball, soccer games or major boxing matches—ignite such deep passions worldwide?

Vocabulary

Angelou uses a number of poetical expressions. Use your own words to explain the meaning of these expressions—that is, to explain the literal meaning lying underneath the figurative language.

1. as a black sky is streaked with lightning (par. 2)
2. cackled like a hen (par. 6)
3. a tide of murmuring assent (par. 10)
4. near-sacred quiet (par. 14)
5. raining the blows (par. 15)
6. drank Coca-Colas like ambrosia (par. 27)
7. ate candy bars like Christmas (par. 27)

WRITER'S WORKSHOP

Critical Thinking in Writing

1. Sports figures continue to be models for young people. Do you admire, look up to, or wish to emulate any athletes? If you do, discuss who and why. If you do not, discuss why not. Write an essay to present your points.
2. Joe Louis in his day was an important model for black Americans. What current figure do you think serves as a model for his or her people? Choose a particular racial, ethnic, or religious group; identify an appropriate model for that group; and defend your choice in a well-detailed essay.
3. In the 1930s and 1940s, Joe Louis's fights united the black community. Indeed, Louis's defeat of Max Schmeling, a German boxer who was a favorite of Hitler, was an important symbolic event for all Americans opposed to Nazism. What contemporary event would everybody in the United States or everyone from a particular group be likely to watch? Present your thoughts on this subject in an essay.

Connecting Ideas

Read "Salvation," by Langston Hughes (page 19). What similar elements of rural black culture can you find in Hughes's and Angelou's selections? The events in Angelou's piece take place twenty years later than the events in Hughes's. What signs can you find in Angelou's piece of changes that have occurred in Southern life and attitudes in that twenty-year period?

I Am an Affirmative Action Baby

Stephen Carter

Stephen Carter is a professor at Yale Law School. In this selection from his book Reflections of an Affirmative Action Baby *(1991), Carter urges people of color to put aside their differences on affirmative action and work together.*

KEY WORDS

pejoratively (par. 1) in a negative or belittling way.
moorings (par. 5) the anchoring that holds a ship in place.
corollary (par. 7) a consequence of a proposition or a proposition that is incidentally proved by another proposition.
portend (par. 9) to indicate, forecast.
nullification (par. 9) voiding, doing away with.
neoconservatism (par. 11) modern political doctrine that advocates dismantling government programs that interfere with or take the place of individual initiative.
abject (par. 12) pitiful, miserable.

1   I CALL US—black professionals of my generation—the affirmative action babies. I know that this term is sometimes used pejoratively, but it is my intention to invert that meaning, to embrace the term, not reject it.

2   Had I not enjoyed the benefits of a racial preference in professional school admission, I would not have accomplished what I have in my career. I was afforded the opportunity for advanced professional training at one of the finest law schools in the country, Yale, and I like to think that I have made the most of this privilege. So, yes, I *am* an affirmative action baby, and I do not apologize for that.

3   By the term "affirmative action baby," I mean to imply only a temporal identification: that is the name, and an accurate one, of the civil rights age in which we live. My generation was in or about to

start high school when a nation torn by violent racial strife and shattered by the murder of Martin Luther King Jr. decided to try preferential admission and hiring policies as a form, it was hoped, of corrective justice. We entered college around the dawn of the era of affirmative action in admission.

4   My law school classmates and I agonized as preferential policies went through their first major crisis, a partial rejection by the Supreme Court in the Bakke case. And now, as I look around the classrooms at the Yale Law School, where I have taught for almost a decade, I realize that the bright and diverse students of color I see before me have a shot, and a good one, at being the last members of the affirmative action generation—or, what is better still, the first members of the post-affirmative action generation, the professionals who will say to a doubting world, "Here are my accomplishments; take me or don't take me on my merits."

5   In recent years, however, affirmative action has slipped its moorings and started to drift. The drift has been slow, so slow that it has scarcely been noticed, but it has carried the programs a long and dangerous distance from the relatively placid waters of the provision of opportunities for developing talent. Nowadays, affirmative action is being transformed into a tool for representing the "points of view" of excluded groups.

6   The argument one now hears is that people of color have a distinctive voice, a vision of the world, that is not being represented in the places where vital decisions are made: the boardroom, the bureaucracy, the campus. In the new rhetoric of affirmative action, it seems, the reason to seek out and hire or admit people of color is that one can have faith that their opinions, their perspective, will be different from the opinions and perspectives of people who are white—who evidently have a distinctive set of views of their own.

7   The unfortunate logical corollary is that if the perspective a particular person of color can offer is *not* distinctive, if it is more like the "white" perspective than the "black" one, then that person is not speaking in an authentically black voice—an accusation that has become all too common.

8   As a black intellectual, I see my role as one of trying, if possible, to foster reconciliation, to promote the educational conversation from which all of us who care about the future of black people will benefit. There is no reason for us to be at each other's throats when there is so much on both sides of the argument from which all can learn. Our task, I think, should be to find the common ground, to be at once realistic about the world and sensitive to each other.

9   Let us, then, be frank: there is good reason, given today's politics, to think that we are looking toward the end of most racial preferences. For those of us who have been positioned to take advantage of what it offers, the affirmative action era has been a decidedly mixed blessing. The prospect of its end should be a challenge and a chance; it does not portend disaster. We must never turn affirmative action into a crutch, and therefore we must reject the common claim that an end to preferences would be a disastrous situation, amounting to a virtual nullification of the 1954 desegregation ruling.

10   We should be concentrating on constructive dialogue about how to solve the problems of the real and continuing victims of the nation's legacy of racist oppression: the millions of struggling black Americans for whom affirmative action and entry to the professions are stunningly irrelevant.

11   Mine is not, I hope, a position that will be thought inauthentically black. It is not, I think, evidence of that most fatal of diseases (for a black intellectual), neoconservatism; my views on many other matters are sufficiently to the left that I do not imagine the conservative movement would want me. (Neither, I think, would the left—but that is fine with me, for it is best for intellectuals to be politically unpredictable.)

12   Surely the abject and sometimes desperate circumstances that confront so many of us who have not been fortunate enough to gain access to college and professional school are reason enough for us to stop sniping at one another. If not, we can be sure of two things: first, as professionals and intellectuals, we who are black and middle class will likely endure; second, as they struggle through the violent prisons that many inner cities have become, millions of other black people may not.

13   So perhaps, for a golden moment, we can pause in our quarreling and talk *to* one another, instead of continuing an endless, self-defeating argument over who is the authentic keeper of the flame.

———

EXERCISES

Details and Their Meanings

1. How has Stephen Carter benefited from affirmative action?
2. What subject does the writer teach? How many years has he been teaching?

3. During what time period did the writer grow up?
4. In the writer's opinion, how has affirmative action changed over the years?
5. What does the writer mean by the phrase "distinctive voice"?
6. How does the writer see his role as a black intellectual?
7. What does Carter expect for his students? How does he describe them?
8. How does Carter characterize *neoconservatism*?

Reading and Critical Thinking

1. Which groups do you think are involved in the conflict Carter describes? Are you part of either group?
2. Carter considers affirmative action "a decidedly mixed blessing," although he does not develop this point. Where in the essay can you find reasons to support his point? Do you agree with the "mixed blessing" idea? Why or why not?
3. Does Carter fault American society for the problems faced by black people? Why or why not? Which paragraph helps you to answer this question?
4. Which segments of the black community have criticized Carter? Which paragraphs help you to identify them? Do you agree or disagree with the criticism? Why?
5. In which paragraphs does Carter praise affirmative action? What does he say about it? Where does he criticize affirmative action? How would you evaluate this major social program in America?
6. What evidence does Carter give to support his conclusion that "we are looking toward the end of most racial preferences"? Do you agree with him? Why or why not?

The Writer's Strategies

1. What is Carter's purpose in titling this essay "I Am an Affirmative Action Baby"? Why does he use *baby* and not *man, person,* or some other word?
2. Which paragraphs make up the introduction?
3. What are the writer's main points? Where does he state them?
4. Where does Carter begin his conclusion? What warning does he give there?
5. What transitional words does the writer use to connect ideas?

6. Where does Carter first define affirmative action? Where does he describe it the second time? How does the definition change?
7. Who is the intended audience for this piece? What assumption is the writer making about his readers' knowledge of current politics? Is his assumption accurate in your case?

Thinking Together

Carter refers to the Bakke case, assuming that his readers will be familiar with the details of it. Look up the Bakke case in an encyclopedia or in some other reference work. What was the issue? What did the Supreme Court decide? Do you agree with its decision? Discuss your findings and responses in groups.

Vocabulary

Look in a dictionary of political terms or a book about politics to define the following terms.

1. left
2. right
3. conservative
4. liberal
5. neoconservative

WRITER'S WORKSHOP ━━━━━━━━━━━━━━━

Critical Thinking in Writing

1. What are your views on affirmative action? Do you believe it is necessary to continue preferential treatment of groups who have been historically ignored? Write an essay to explain your thoughts.
2. During his Supreme Court nomination hearing in 1991, Judge Clarence Thomas, another Yale graduate, articulated the black neoconservative position that blacks did not benefit from affirmative action in any important way and that the goal of government should be to create a single standard for all Americans. How do you think Stephen Carter would respond to Thomas's

argument? What merits can you find in each position? With whom do you agree? Write your response in an argumentative essay.

3. Carter asserts that the task for those who care about the future of black people "should be to find the common ground, to be at once realistic about the world and sensitive to each other." How might this statement serve as a kind of pact or creed for those who care about the future of humanity? Write an essay called "Finding the Common Ground" in which you argue how being realistic about the world and sensitive to each other will benefit the varied racial and ethnic groups of our country. Draw on your own experience and (or) your readings to provide a well-detailed argument.

Connecting Ideas

Read Martin Luther King's "I Have a Dream" speech (page 139). In what ways have King's hopes for the future been realized by people like Stephen Carter? What concerns expressed by King does Carter share?

Kiss of Death

Armando Rendón

Armando Rendón is a journalist, a scriptwriter, and an executive in a Chicago counseling firm. In this selection from his Chicano Manifesto *(1971), Rendón describes growing up in Texas and California and the challenges to his ethnic identity.*

KEY WORDS

factionalized (par. 9)   split into small, contending groups.
gilt (par. 11)   cheap gold-colored covering meant to look like real gold.
acculturized (par. 13)   became comfortable with a culture.
mystique (par. 15)   a charmed air, charisma.

1   I NEARLY FELL VICTIM to the Anglo. My childhood was spent in the West Side barrio of San Antonio. I lived in my grandmother's house on Ruiz Street just below Zarzamora Creek. I did well in the elementary grades and learned English quickly.

2   Spanish was off-limits in school anyway, and teachers and relatives taught me early that my mother tongue would be of no help in making good grades and becoming a success. Yet Spanish was the language I used in playing and arguing with friends. Spanish was the language I spoke with my *abuelita*, my dear grandmother, as I ate *atole* on those cold mornings when I used to wake at dawn to her clattering dishes in the tiny kitchen; or when I would cringe in mock horror at old folk tales she would tell me late at night.

3   But the lesson took effect anyway. When, at the age of ten, I went with my mother to California, to the San Francisco Bay Area where she found work during the war years, I had my first real opportunity to strip myself completely of my heritage. In California the schools I attended were all Anglo except for this little mexicanito. At least, I never knew anyone who admitted he was Mexican and I certainly

never thought to ask. When my name was accented incorrectly, Réndon instead of Rendón, that was all right; finally I must have gotten tired of correcting people or just didn't bother.

4   I remember a summertime visit home a few years after living on the West Coast. At an evening gathering of almost the whole family —uncles, aunts, nephews, nieces, my *abuelita*—we sat outdoors through the dusk until the dark had fully settled. Then the lights were turned on; someone brought out a Mexican card game, the Lotería El Diablito, similar to bingo. But instead of rows of numbers on a pasteboard, there were figures of persons, animals, and objects on cards corresponding to figures set in rows on a pasteboard. We used frijoles (pinto beans) to mark each figure on our card as the leader went through the deck one by one. The word for tree was called: *Arbol!* It completed a row; I had won. Then to check my card I had to name each figure again. When I said the word for tree, it didn't come at all as I wanted it to; AR-BOWL with the accent on the last syllable and sounding like an Anglo tourist. There was some all-around kidding of me and good-natured laughter over the incident, and it passed.

5   But if I had not been speaking much Spanish up until then, I spoke even less afterward. Even when my mother, who speaks both Spanish and English fluently, spoke to me in Spanish, I would respond in English. By the time I graduated from high school and prepared to enter college, the break was nearly complete. Seldom during college did I admit to being a Mexican-American. Only when Latin American students pressed me about my surname did I admit my Spanish descent, or when it proved an asset in meeting coeds from Latin American countries.

6   My ancestry had become a shadow, fainter and fainter about me. I felt no particular allegiance to it, drew no inspiration from it, and elected generally to let it fade away. I clicked with the Anglo mind-set in college, mastered it, you might say. I even became editor of the campus biweekly newspaper as a junior, and editor of the literary magazine as a senior—not bad, now that I look back, for a tortillas-and-beans Chicano upbringing to beat the Anglo at his own game.

7   The point of my "success," of course, was that I had been assimilated; I had bought the white man's world. After getting my diploma I was set to launch out into a career in newspaper reporting and writing. There was no thought in my mind of serving my people, telling their story, or making anything right for anybody but myself. Instead I had dreams of Pulitzer Prizes, syndicated columns,

foreign correspondent assignments, front-page stories—that was for me. Then something happened.

8   A Catholic weekly newspaper in Sacramento offered me a position as a reporter and feature writer. I had a job on a Bay Area daily as a copyboy at the time, with the opportunity to become a reporter. But I'd just been married, and there were a number of other reasons to consider: there'd be a variety of assignments, Sacramento was the state capital, it was a good town in which to raise a family, and the other job lacked promise for upward mobility. I decided to take the offer.

9   My wife and I moved to Sacramento in the fall of 1961, and in a few weeks the radicalization of this Chicano began. It wasn't a book I read or a great leader awakening me, for we had no Chávezes or Tijerinas or Gonzálezes at the time; and it was no revelation from above. It was my own people who rescued me. There is a large Chicano population in Sacramento, today one of the most activist in northern California, but at the time factionalized and still dependent on the social and church organizations for identity. But together we found each other.

10   My job soon brought me into contact with many Chicanos as well as with the recently immigrated Mexicans, located in the barrios that Sacramento had allocated to the "Mexicans." I found my people striving to survive in an alien environment among foreign people. One of the stories I covered concerned a phenomenon called Cursillos de Cristiandad (Little Courses in Christianity), intense, three-day group-sensitivity sessions whose chief objective is the re-Christianization of Catholics. To cover the story properly I talked my editor into letting me make a Cursillo.

11   Not only was much revealed to me about the phony gilt lining of religion which I had grown up believing was the Church, but there was an added and highly significant side effect—cultural shock! I rediscovered my own people, or perhaps they redeemed me. Within the social dimension of the Cursillo, for the first time in many years I became reimmersed in a tough, *macho ambiente* (an entirely Mexican male environment). Only Spanish was spoken. The effect was shattering. It was as if my tongue, after being struck dumb as a child, had been loosened.

12   Because we were located in cramped quarters, with limited facilities, and the cooks, lecturers, priests, and participants were men only, the old sense of *machismo* and *camarada* was revived and given new perspective. I was cast in a spiritual setting which was a perfect background for reviving my Chicano soul. Reborn but imperfectly, I

still had a lot to learn about myself and my people. But my understanding deepened and renewed itself as the years went by. I visited bracero camps with teams of Chicanos; sometimes with priests taking the sacraments; sometimes only Chicanos, offering advice or assistance with badly needed food and clothing, distributed through a bingo-game technique; and on occasion, music for group singing provided by a phonograph or a guitar. Then there were barrio organization work; migrant worker programs; a rural self-help community development project; and confrontation with antipoverty agencies, with the churches, with government officials, and with cautious Chicanos, too.

13   In a little San Francisco magazine called *Way*, I wrote in a March 1966 article discussing "The Other Mexican-American":

> The Mexican-American must answer at the same time: Who am I? and Who are we? This is to pose then, not merely a dilemma of self-identity; but of self-in-group-identity. . . . Perhaps the answer to developing a total Mexican-American concept must be left in the hands of the artist, the painter, the writer, and the poet, who can abstract the essence of what it is to be Mexican in America. . . . When that understanding comes . . . the Mexican-American will not only have acculturized himself, but he will have acculturized America to him.

14   If anyone knew what he was talking about when he spoke of the dilemma of who he was and where he belonged, it was this Chicano. I very nearly dropped out, as so many other Mexican-Americans have, under the dragging pressure to be someone else, what most of society wants you to be before it hands out its chrome-plated trophies.

15   And that mystique—I didn't quite have it at the time, or the right word for it. But no one did until just the last few years when so many of us stopped trying to be someone else and decided that what we want to be and to be called is Chicano.

16   I owe my life to my Chicano people. They rescued me from the Anglo kiss of death, the monolingual, monocultural, and colorless Gringo society. I no longer face a dilemma of identity or direction. That identity and direction have been charted for me by the Chicano —but to think I came that close to being sucked into the vacuum of the dominant society.

EXERCISES

Details and Their Meanings

1. In what city did Armando Rendón first live? What language did he use in school? When did he use another language?
2. How did the writer's view of his heritage change as he moved from childhood to adolescence?
3. What is Lotería El Diablito?
4. In what college situations did Rendón find it an advantage to be of Spanish descent?
5. When did the writer rediscover his heritage? What organization helped him? What other experiences helped Rendón to strengthen his ties to the Chicano community?
6. What activities did Rendón embrace to help other Chicanos?

Reading and Critical Thinking

1. What was Rendón's mother's attitude toward Mexican culture? How do you know? Was her attitude appropriate? Why or why not?
2. From information in paragraph 3, you can tell that this selection begins during which decade?
3. How does Rendón describe Anglo culture? What doesn't he like about it? Do you think he is accurate in his criticism? Why or why not?
4. What was the purpose of the Cursillos de Cristiandad? Who was the target audience of these courses?
5. What are some elements of typical Mexican-American culture, according to Rendón? What does it mean to him to be Chicano?
6. What does Rendón mean when he says, "I owe my life to my Chicano people" (paragraph 16)? What does he imply would have happened had he not rediscovered his heritage?

The Writer's Strategies

1. Where does the writer state his thesis? What is it?
2. Why does Rendón use Spanish words? What effect does the use of Spanish produce?
3. What phrases does the writer use to show the disparaging way people looked on Spanish culture?

4. According to the writer, what is the difference between a Chicano and a Mexican? Why is the distinction important in the selection?
5. What order does Rendón use to organize this piece?
6. Where does Rendón include a passage from another article that he wrote? What is his purpose in doing so?
7. Who is the intended audience for this piece, Anglos or Chicanos? How can you tell?

Thinking Together

Does Rendón present a balanced view of Anglo and Chicano cultures? What leads you to your conclusion? How does Rendón define Anglo culture? Break into groups and see if you can reach consensus on these questions. Report your findings to the rest of the class.

Vocabulary

Write definitions of the following Spanish words. Some are defined in the text, but you may need to look up others in a Spanish-English dictionary.

1. barrio (par. 1)
2. abuelita (par. 2)
3. atole (par. 2)
4. Lotería El Diablito (par. 4)
5. frijoles (par. 4)
6. arbol (par. 4)
7. Cursillo (par. 10)
8. macho ambiente (par. 11)
9. camarada (par. 12)
10. bracero (par. 12)

WRITER'S WORKSHOP ———————————

Critical Thinking in Writing

1. Is Rendón correct to say that Anglo culture is "monolingual, monocultural, and colorless"? Write an essay describing your experience of American culture. What do you find are its

strengths and weaknesses? How do your impressions conform to or challenge Rendón's?

2. Rendón has apparently rejected biculturalism in favor of an exclusively Chicano perspective. Do you think this is a valid choice? Should people try to stay exclusively within their ethnic identities? What is gained or lost as a result of locking oneself within one culture? Present your views in an essay.

3. Write an essay in which you define *ethnic identity* or *cultural identity*.

Connecting Ideas

Read Roberto Suro's "Mexicans Come Looking to Work but Find Dead Ends" (page 250). What in that account strikes you as reinforcing Rendón's observations about Mexican-American culture and the problems facing Chicanos in the United States?

Family Ghosts

Maxine Hong Kingston

Maxine Hong Kingston was born in California. She is the author of several works, including the award-winning memoir The Woman Warrior *(1976), from which this excerpt is taken. In this selection, Hong Kingston relates several ghost stories that she learned as a child.*

KEY WORDS

magistrate (par. 7)   a government official who administers justice.
incur (par. 9)   to provoke.
morsels (par. 10)   bite-size pieces of food.
anonymous (par. 11)   nameless, unknown.

1   WHEN THE THERMOMETER IN our laundry reached one hundred and eleven degrees on summer afternoons, either my mother or my father would say that it was time to tell another ghost story so that we could get some good chills up our backs. My parents, my brothers, sisters, great-uncle, and "Third Aunt," who wasn't really our aunt but a fellow villager, someone else's third aunt, kept the presses crashing and hissing and shouted out the stories. Those were our successful days, when so much laundry came in, my mother did not have to pick tomatoes. For breaks we changed from pressing to sorting.

2   "One twilight," my mother began, and already the chills travelled my back and crossed my shoulders; the hair rose at the nape and the back of the legs, "I was walking home after doctoring a sick family. To get home I had to cross a footbridge. In China the bridges are nothing like the ones in Brooklyn and San Francisco. This one was made from rope, laced and knotted as if by magpies. Actually it had been built by men who had returned after harvesting sea swallow nests in Malaya. They had had to swing over the faces of the Ma-

98

layan cliffs in baskets they had woven themselves. Though this bridge pitched and swayed in the updraft, no one had ever fallen into the river, which looked like a bright scratch at the bottom of the canyon, as if the Queen of Heaven had swept her great silver hairpin across the earth as well as the sky."

3   One twilight, just as my mother stepped on the bridge, two smoky columns spiraled up taller than she. Their swaying tops hovered over her head like white cobras, one at either handrail. From stillness came a wind rushing between the smoke spindles. A high sound entered her temple bones. Through the twin whirlwinds she could see the sun and the river, the river twisting in circles, the trees upside down. The bridge moved like a ship, sickening. The earth dipped. She collapsed to the wooden slats, a ladder up the sky, her fingers so weak she could not grip the rungs. The wind dragged her hair behind her, then whipped it forward across her face. Suddenly the smoke spindles disappeared. The world righted itself, and she crossed to the other side. She looked back, but there was nothing there. She used the bridge often, but she did not encounter those ghosts again.

4   "They were Sit Dom Kuei," said Great-Uncle. "Sit Dom Kuei."

5   "Yes, of course," said my mother. "Sit Dom Kuei."

6   I keep looking in dictionaries under those syllables. "Kuei" means "ghost," but I don't find any other words that make sense. I only hear my great-uncle's river-pirate voice, the voice of a big man who had killed someone in New York or Cuba, make the sounds—"Sit Dom Kuei." How do they translate?

7   When the Communists issued their papers on techniques for combating ghosts, I looked for "Sit Dom Kuei." I have not found them described anywhere, although now I see that my mother won in ghost battle because she can eat anything—quick, pluck out the carp's eyes, one for Mother and one for Father. All heroes are bold toward food. In the research against ghost fear published by the Chinese Academy of Science is the story of a magistrate's servant, Kao Chung, a capable eater who in 1683 ate five cooked chickens and drank ten bottles of wine that belonged to the sea monster with branching teeth. The monster had arranged its food around a fire on the beach and started to feed when Kao Chung attacked. The swan-feather sword he wrested from this monster can be seen in the Wentung County Armory in Shantung today.

8   Another big eater was Chou Yi-han of Changchow, who fried a ghost. It was a meaty stick when he cut it up and cooked it. But before that it had been a woman out at night.

9   Chen Luan-feng, during the Yuan Ho era of the T'ang dynasty (A.D. 806–820), ate yellow croaker and pork together, which the thunder god had forbidden. But Chen wanted to incur thunderbolts during drought. The first time he ate, the thunder god jumped out of the sky, its legs like old trees. Chen chopped off the left one. The thunder god fell to the earth, and the villagers could see that it was a blue pig or bear with horns and fleshy wings. Chen leapt on it, prepared to chop its neck and bite its throat, but the villagers stopped him. After that, Chen lived apart as a rainmaker, neither relatives nor the monks willing to bring lightning upon themselves. He lived in a cave, and for years whenever there was drought the villagers asked him to eat yellow croaker and pork together, and he did.

10   The most fantastic eater of them all was Wei Pang, a scholar-hunter of the Ta Li era of the T'ang dynasty (A.D. 766–779). He shot and cooked rabbits and birds, but he could also eat scorpions, snakes, cockroaches, worms, slugs, beetles, and crickets. Once he spent the night in a house that had been abandoned because its inhabitants feared contamination from the dead man next door. A shining, twinkling sphere came flying through the darkness at Wei. He felled it with three true arrows—the first making the thing crackle and flame; the second dimming it; and the third putting out its lights, sputter. When his servant came running in with a lamp, Wei saw his arrows sticking in a ball of flesh entirely covered with eyes, some rolled back to show the dulling whites. He and the servant pulled out the arrows and cut up the ball into little pieces. The servant cooked the morsels in sesame oil, and the wonderful aroma made Wei laugh. They ate half, saving half to show the household, which would return now.

11   Big eaters win. When other passers-by stepped around the bundle wrapped in white silk, the anonymous scholar of Hanchow took it home. Inside were three silver ingots and a froglike evil, which sat on the ingots. The scholar laughed at it and chased it off. That night two frogs the size of year-old babies appeared in his room. He clubbed them to death, cooked them, and ate them with white wine. The next night a dozen frogs, together the size of a pair of year-old babies, jumped from the ceiling. He ate all twelve for dinner. The third night thirty small frogs were sitting on his mat and staring at him with their frog eyes. He ate them too. Every night for a month smaller but more numerous frogs came so that he always had the same amount to eat. Soon his floor was like the healthy banks of a pond in spring when the tadpoles, having just turned, sprang in the wet grass. "Get a hedgehog to help eat," cried his fam-

ily. "I'm as good as a hedgehog," the scholar said, laughing. And at the end of the month the frogs stopped coming, leaving the scholar with the white silk and silver ingots.

EXERCISES

Details and Their Meanings

1. Where does the narrator work? How are ghost stories helpful to her work?
2. What does the mother normally do for a living? What other jobs does she perform?
3. Where does the mother's encounter with ghosts take place? How many other times has she seen ghosts?
4. What is the secret to combating ghosts? What is Maxine Hong Kingston's source for this information?
5. Who is Kao Chung? When did he live? Why is he important in the piece?
6. What character does the writer describe as the "most fantastic eater of them all"? Do you believe this portrait? Why or why not?

Reading and Critical Thinking

1. Do the stories related in the selection take place in America or China? Do the writer and her family live in America or China? What clues help you to answer each question? What is the connection that emerges in this piece between China and America?
2. What does the phrase "Sit Dom Kuei" mean? How does the writer make figuring out the meaning of this phrase important to her narrative?
3. What are the physical characteristics of ghosts in Chinese stories? What different kinds of figures are considered ghosts in this selection? How do they compare with what you think of as ghosts?
4. Why is it necessary for the characters in several of the stories to eat the fantastic creatures they encounter? What do you suppose would happen if they didn't eat them?

5. What is the narrator's attitude toward ghosts? Does she believe in them? How can you tell?

6. Why do most of the ghost stories related here take place in the distant past? Why does the writer include just one recent example?

7. From the accounts of blue pigs and bears with "horns and fleshy wings," what can you say about the kind of place China is? What is the attitude of people there to fantastic creatures? How is their reaction likely to be different from that of Americans'?

The Writer's Strategies

1. What is the thesis of this selection? Where does the writer state it?

2. Who is the narrator? How many narrators are there? Where does the shift take place?

3. How many different age perspectives does the writer provide? What purpose does the shift in perspective serve?

4. Where does the writer make use of sensory details? Provide examples of the most vivid and original sensory images.

5. Is the primary audience for this selection Chinese or American? How can you tell?

Thinking Together

Conduct a survey in your classroom to find out how many students or their parents, spouses, or extended families believe in ghosts. Tally the results. Then find out how many of your classmates have a firsthand ghost story to tell. How many know someone who has had a ghostly encounter? Share some of these stories with the class. How do the students who do not believe in ghosts respond to them?

Vocabulary

Maxine Hong Kingston creates memorable word pictures. Write your understanding of the following images.

1. branching teeth (par. 7)
2. froglike evil (par. 11)
3. swan-feather sword (par. 7)
4. smoke spindles (par. 3)
5. river-pirate voice (par. 6)
6. rope, laced and knotted as if by magpies (par. 2)

WRITER'S WORKSHOP ━━━━━━━━━

Critical Thinking in Writing

1. What was your favorite story as a child? In a narrative essay, re-tell this story in your own words, using as much detail as you can.

2. Most educated people in America do not believe in the existence of ghosts, supernatural phenomena, or magic. From the modern scientific perspective, they all come under the heading "super-stitions." Nevertheless, belief in them persists. How can you explain the persistence of such beliefs? Write an essay in which you explain why you feel superstitions continue to play a role in modern society.

3. Ghost and horror stories often reflect cultural values. Relate a ghost or horror story that you know and analyze what information about cultural values and beliefs the story presents.

Connecting Ideas

Read "The Man to Send Rain Clouds," by Leslie Marmon Silko (page 104). How does the Chinese folk tradition presented by Maxine Hong Kingston in "Family Ghosts" differ from the Native American tradition described in Silko's piece? What generalizations can you make about the similarities and differences between these two cultures?

The Man to Send Rain Clouds

Leslie Marmon Silko

In this selection, Leslie Marmon Silko shows how Christian culture is absorbed into the beliefs and practices of the Native American people. Notice how the people give their own interpretation to the foreign Christian beliefs.

KEY WORDS

arroyo (par. 1)   dry creek bed.
pueblo (par. 3)   village.
Angelus (par. 12)   call to Catholic prayers.

1   THEY FOUND HIM UNDER a big cottonwood tree. His Levi jacket and pants were faded light blue so that he had been easy to find. The big cottonwood tree stood apart from a small grove of winterbare cottonwoods which grew in the wide, sandy arroyo. He had been dead for a day or more, and the sheep had wandered and scattered up and down the arroyo. Leon and his brother-in-law, Ken, gathered the sheep and left them in the pen at the sheep camp before they returned to the cottonwood tree. Leon waited under the tree while Ken drove the truck through the deep sand to the edge of the arroyo. He squinted up at the sun and unzipped his jacket—it sure was hot for this time of year. But high and northwest the blue mountains were still in snow. Ken came sliding down the low, crumbling bank about fifty yards down, and he was bringing the red blanket.

2   Before they wrapped the old man, Leon took a piece of string out of his pocket and tied a small gray feather in the old man's long white hair. Ken gave him the paint. Across the brown wrinkled forehead he drew a streak of white and along the high cheekbones he drew a strip of blue paint. He paused and watched Ken throw pinches of corn meal and pollen into the wind that fluttered the

small gray feather. Then Leon painted with yellow under the old man's broad nose, and finally, when he had painted green across the chin, he smiled.

3   "Send us rain clouds, Grandfather." They laid the bundle in the back of the pickup and covered it with a heavy tarp before they started back to the pueblo.

4   They turned off the highway onto the sandy pueblo road. Not long after they passed the store and post office they saw Father Paul's car coming toward them. When he recognized their faces he slowed his car and waved for them to stop. The young priest rolled down the car window.

5   "Did you find old Teofilo?" he asked loudly.

6   Leon stopped the truck. "Good morning, Father. We were just out to the sheep camp. Everything is O.K. now."

7   "Thank God for that. Teofilo is a very old man. You really shouldn't allow him to stay at the sheep camp alone."

8   "No, he won't do that any more now."

9   "Well, I'm glad you understand. I hope I'll be seeing you at Mass this week—we missed you last Sunday. See if you can get old Teofilo to come with you." The priest smiled and waved at them as they drove away.

10   Louise and Teresa were waiting. The table was set for lunch, and the coffee was boiling on the black iron stove. Leon looked at Louise and then at Teresa.

11   "We found him under a cottonwood tree in the big arroyo near sheep camp. I guess he sat down to rest in the shade and never got up again." Leon walked toward the old man's bed. The red plaid shawl had been shaken and spread carefully over the bed, and a new brown flannel shirt and pair of stiff new Levi's were arranged neatly beside the pillow. Louise held the screen door open while Leon and Ken carried in the red blanket. He looked small and shriveled, and after they dressed him in the new shirt and pants he seemed more shrunken.

12   It was noontime now because the church bells rang the Angelus. They ate the beans with hot bread, and nobody said anything until after Teresa poured the coffee.

13   Ken stood up and put on his jacket. "I'll see about the gravediggers. Only the top layer of soil is frozen. I think it can be ready before dark."

14   Leon nodded his head and finished his coffee. After Ken had been gone for a while, the neighbors and clanspeople came quietly to embrace Teofilo's family and to leave food on the table because

the gravediggers would come to eat when they were finished.

15   The sky in the west was full of pale yellow light. Louise stood out-side with her hands in the pockets of Leon's green army jacket that was too big for her. The funeral was over, and the old men had taken their candles and medicine bags and were gone. She waited until the body was laid into the pickup before she said anything to Leon. She touched his arm, and he noticed that her hands were still dusty from the corn meal that she had sprinkled around the old man. When she spoke, Leon could not hear her.

16   "What did you say? I didn't hear you."

17   "I said that I had been thinking about something."

18   "About what?"

19   "About the priest sprinkling holy water for Grandpa. So he won't be thirsty."

20   Leon stared at the new moccasins that Teofilo had made for the ceremonial dances in the summer. They were nearly hidden by the red blanket. It was getting colder, and the wind pushed gray dust down the narrow pueblo road. The sun was approaching the long mesa where it disappeared during the winter. Louise stood there shivering and watching his face. Then he zipped up his jacket and opened the truck door. "I'll see if he's there."

21   Ken stopped the pickup at the church, and Leon got out; and then Ken drove down the hill to the graveyard where people were wait-ing. Leon knocked at the old carved door with its symbols of the Lamb. While he waited he looked up at the twin bells from the king of Spain with the last sunlight pouring around them in their tower.

22   The priest opened the door and smiled when he saw who it was. "Come in! What brings you here this evening?"

23   The priest walked toward the kitchen, and Leon stood with his cap in his hand, playing with the earflaps and examining the living room—the brown sofa, the green armchair, and the brass lamp that hung down from the ceiling by links of chain. The priest dragged a chair out of the kitchen and offered it to Leon.

24   "No thank you, Father. I only came to ask you if you would bring your holy water to the graveyard."

25   The priest turned away from Leon and looked out the window at the patio full of shadows and the dining-room windows of the nuns' cloister across the patio. The curtains were heavy, and the light from within faintly penetrated; it was impossible to see the nuns inside eating supper. "Why didn't you tell me he was dead? I could have brought the Last Rites anyway."

26   Leon smiled. "It wasn't necessary, Father."

27   The priest stared down at his scuffed brown loafers and the worn hem of his cassock. "For a Christian burial it was necessary."

28   His voice was distant, and Leon thought that his blue eyes looked tired.

29   "It's O.K. Father, we just want him to have plenty of water."

30   The priest sank down into the green chair and picked up a glossy missionary magazine. He turned the colored pages full of lepers and pagans without looking at them.

31   "You know I can't do that, Leon. There should have been the Last Rites and a funeral Mass at the very least."

32   Leon put on his green cap and pulled the flaps down over his ears. "It's getting late, Father. I've got to go."

33   When Leon opened the door Father Paul stood up and said, "Wait." He left the room and came back wearing a long brown overcoat. He followed Leon out the door and across the dim churchyard to the adobe steps in front of the church. They both stooped to fit through the low adobe entrance. And when they started down the hill to the graveyard only half of the sun was visible above the mesa.

34   The priest approached the grave slowly, wondering how they had managed to dig into the frozen ground; and then he remembered that this was New Mexico, and saw the pile of cold loose sand beside the hole. The people stood close to each other with little clouds of steam puffing from their faces. The priest looked at them and saw a pile of jackets, gloves, and scarves in the yellow, dry tumbleweeds that grew in the graveyard. He looked at the red blanket, not sure that Teofilo was so small, wondering if it wasn't some perverse Indian trick—something they did in March to ensure a good harvest—wondering if maybe old Teofilo was actually at sheep camp corralling the sheep for the night. But there he was, facing into a cold dry wind and squinting at the last sunlight, ready to bury a red wool blanket while the faces of his parishioners were in shadow with the last warmth of the sun on their backs.

35   His fingers were stiff, and it took him a long time to twist the lid off the holy water. Drops of water fell on the red blanket and soaked into dark icy spots. He sprinkled the grave and the water disappeared almost before it touched the dim, cold sand; it reminded him of something—he tried to remember what it was, because he thought if he could remember he might understand this. He sprinkled more water; he shook the container until it was empty, and the water fell through the light from sundown like August rain that fell while the sun was still shining, almost evaporating before it touched the wilted squash flowers.

36   The wind pulled at the priest's brown Franciscan robe and swirled away the corn meal and pollen that had been sprinkled on the blanket. They lowered the bundle into the ground, and they didn't bother to untie the stiff pieces of new rope that were tied around the ends of the blanket. The sun was gone, and over on the highway the eastbound lane was full of headlights. The priest walked away slowly. Leon watched him climb the hill, and when he had disappeared within the tall, thick walls, Leon turned to look up at the high blue mountains in the deep snow that reflected a faint red light from the west. He felt good because it was finished, and he was happy about the sprinkling of the holy water; now the old man could send them big thunderclouds for sure.

EXERCISES

Details and Their Meanings

1. How are Ken and Leon dressed, and what are they doing at the beginning of this selection? What can you infer about who they are?

2. What do Ken and Leon do to the body of the old man? What do you think is the meaning of the various actions they take? What can you infer about the culture of all three?

3. What beliefs does Father Paul have? Is he from the same people and region as Leon, Ken, and Teofilo? What indications are there that he represents a foreign culture? Why don't Leon and Ken tell him the truth? What are the consequences of the truth being withheld? What does Father Paul say when he finds out the truth?

4. What role does Louise play in the ceremony? What does she request?

5. How does Father Paul react to the request at first? What pictures are in the magazine that he picks up? What is the significance of the pictures and of his reactions to them? What does he think about the mixture of Catholic and local traditions? What does he finally do? Why do you think he changes his mind?

6. What is important about the sprinkling of holy water for the priest? For Leon? Do they interpret the ceremonies in the same way?

Reading and Critical Thinking

1. How did Ken, Leon, and Louise react to the body? With what desire do they associate care of the body? What does that reflect about their culture?
2. What is Ken, Leon, and Louise's relation to the Catholic priest and the church?
3. Are Ken, Leon, and Louise concerned with proper Christian burial? Why do they ask for the priest's cooperation? How do they incorporate Christian ceremony into their own? Is the final ceremony more Native American or Christian? How do they think about the priest?
4. What do you think the priest thinks about the ceremony he participates in? Why does he cooperate? Do you think he is totally satisfied with what has happened, with what effect his participation will have?
5. What does the piece suggest about the relative strengths of Christian and traditional beliefs among this group of Native Americans?

The Writer's Strategies

1. What is the main idea? Is it ever stated as a thesis? How do you come to find out the main idea?
2. In what way is not speaking directly part of the piece? What facts does the reader figure out only gradually? What does the priest figure out only gradually?
3. What order does the writer use to present events? What are the basic events of the selection? How does the external series of events represent a cultural and psychological process that reveals how the characters think and feel?
4. At the end of the piece, what has happened to Father Paul? Whose thoughts end the selection? What culture do those thoughts represent, and how do they reinterpret the meaning of the Christian ceremony? What is the significance of the ending?

Thinking Together

In groups of three or four, discuss religious or cultural customs you have observed that seemed to mix the traditions of two or more groups. Also discuss whether you know of any customs that you now think of as belonging to a single group but that historically came from a combining of cultures. After you have discussed some examples, decide which example shows the deepest mixing of cultures. Then as a group write a description and explanation of this case of cultural mixing.

Vocabulary

Some of the words in the following list bring to mind the life, surroundings, and customs of Native Americans. Others bring to mind the Catholic church. Indicate whether each reflects Native American (NA) or the Catholic (C) way of life; then define each word, using context clues from the selection.

1. cottonwood (par. 1)
2. arroyo (par. 1)
3. pickup (par. 3)
4. pueblo (par. 3)
5. Levi's (par. 11)
6. Angelus (par. 12)
7. holy water (par. 19)
8. moccasins (par. 20)
9. mesa (par. 20)
10. cloister (par. 25)
11. Last Rites (par. 25)
12. missionary (par. 30)
13. pagans (par. 30)
14. adobe (par. 33)
15. tumbleweeds (par. 34)

WRITER'S WORKSHOP ——————————

Critical Thinking in Writing

1. How do religions change when they come in contact with new cultures? Write an essay about any case you know of when the religions or cultures of two different peoples met and mixed.
2. This piece describes people's resistance to Christian culture even while they are incorporating its rituals. How might this behavior be indicative of Native American reaction to Anglo culture? Write an essay describing the cultural attitudes expressed in this selection.
3. Write a few paragraphs describing a dramatic incident, such as reaction to a death, that reveals people's beliefs and attitudes.

Connecting Ideas

How does the response to white culture described by Leslie Marmon Silko differ from Armando Rendón's response, described in "Kiss of Death" (page 91)? Write one paragraph comparing the writers' responses and another paragraph discussing which response (if either) you feel is more appropriate or preferable.

Model Minority

Felicia R. Lee

Felicia R. Lee examines the commonly held view of Asian schoolchildren as super students who effortlessly excel in all their classes, especially math and science. She shows how even positive stereotyping sometimes puts pressure on people to live up to false expectations.

KEY WORDS

émigrés (par. 4)   people who have left their homeland permanently.

docile (par. 4)   peaceful and tame.

harassment (par. 9)   continual annoyance.

advocacy (par. 10)   arguing in favor of something.

stoicism (par. 11)   a philosophy in which the ideal is to rise above both pleasure and pain and to accept all situations in the same calm way.

schizophrenic (par. 31)   suffering from a mental illness.

---

1   ZHE ZENG, AN 18-YEAR-OLD junior at Seward Park High School in lower Manhattan, translates the term "model minority" to mean that Asian-Americans are terrific in math and science. Mr. Zeng is terrific in math and science, but he insists that his life is no model for anyone.

2   "My parents give a lot of pressure on me," said Mr. Zeng, who recently came to New York from Canton with his parents and older brother. He has found it hard to learn English and make friends at the large, fast-paced school. And since he is the only family member who speaks English, he is responsible for paying bills and handling the family's interactions with the English-speaking world.

3   "They work hard for me," he said, "so I have to work hard for them."

4   As New York's Asian population swells, and with many of the new immigrants coming from poorer, less-educated families, more

and more Asian students are stumbling under the burden of earlier émigrés' success—the myth of the model minority, the docile whiz kid with one foot already in the Ivy League. Even as they face the cultural dislocations shared by all immigrants, they must struggle with the inflated expectations of teachers and parents and resentment from some non-Asian classmates.

5   Some students, like Mr. Zeng, do seem to fit the academic stereotype. Many others are simply average students with average problems. But, in the view of educators and a recent Board of Education report, all are more or less victims of myth.

6   "We have a significant population of Chinese kids who are not doing well," said Archer W. Dong, principal of Dr. Sun Yat Sen Junior High School near Chinatown, which is 83 percent Chinese. "But I still deal with educators who tell me how great the Asian kids are. It puts an extra burden on the kid who just wants to be a normal kid."

7   **The Dropout Rate Rises**   Perhaps the starkest evidence of the pressures these students face is the dropout rate among Asian-American students, which has risen to 15.2 percent, from 12.6 percent, in just one year, though it remains well below the 30 percent rate for the entire school system. In all, there are about 68,000 Asians in the city's schools, a little more than 7 percent of the student population.

8   Behind these figures, the Board of Education panel said, lies a contrary mechanism of assumed success and frequent failure. While teachers expect talent in math and science, they often overlook quiet Asian-American students who are in trouble academically.

9   The report also said that Asian students frequently face hostility from non-Asians who resent their perceived success. And though New York's Asian population is overwhelmingly Chinese, this resentment is fed by a feeling in society that the Japanese are usurping America's position as a world economic power. Some educators said that because they are often smaller and quieter, Asian students seem to be easy targets for harassment.

10   Teresa Ying Hsu, executive director of an advocacy group called Asian-American Communications and a member of the board panel, described what she called a typical exchange at a New York City school. One student might say, "You think you're so smart," she said, then "someone would hit a kid from behind and they would turn around and everyone would laugh."

11   Since Asian cultures dictate stoicism, she explained, students in many cases do not openly fight back against harassment or com-

plain about academic pressures. But though they tend to keep their pain hidden, she said, it often is expressed in ailments like headaches or stomach troubles.

12   **"Acutely Sensitive"**   "We have a group of youngsters who are immigrants who are acutely sensitive to things other students take in stride, like a door slamming in their face," said John Rodgers, principal of Norman Thomas High School in Manhattan.

13   Norman Thomas, whose student body is about 3 percent Asian, had two recent incidents in which Chinese students were attacked by non-Asian students. The attackers were suspended.

14   But tensions escalated after a group of 30 Chinese parents demanded that the principal, John Rodgers, increase security, and rumors spread that "gangs of blacks" were attacking Chinese. Both incidents, however, were one-on-one conflicts and neither attacker was black. In some cases, Mr. Rodgers said, Chinese students say they are attacked by blacks but that they cannot identify their attackers because all blacks look alike to them.

15   In response to the parents' concerns, Mr. Rodgers said, he increased security and brought in a speaker on cross-cultural conflict.

16   Traditionally, Asian parents have not been that outspoken, educators say. While they often place enormous pressures on their children to do well, most Asian parents tend not to get involved with the schools.

17   Lisa Chang, a 17-year-old senior at Seward Park—which is 48 percent Asian—recalled being one of six Asians at a predominantly black intermediate school.

18   "Inside the school was no big deal," she said. "I was in special classes and everyone was smart. Then I remember one day being outside in the snow and this big black boy pushed me. He called me Chink.

19   "Then, at home, my parents didn't want me to dress a certain way, to listen to heavy metal music," Ms. Chang said. When she told her dermatologist that she liked rock and roll, the doctor accused her of "acting like a Caucasian."

20   Ms. Chang and other students say there are two routes some Asian students take: they form cliques with other Asians or they play down their culture and even their intelligence in hopes of fitting in.

21   **Wedged Between Two Cultures**   Most Asian students are acutely aware of being wedged between two cultures. They say their parents want them to compete successfully with Americans but not become

too American—they frown on dating and hard-rock music. There is also peer pressure not to completely assimilate. A traitor is a "banana"—yellow on the outside, white on the inside.

22   There is anger, too, over the perception that they are nerdy bookworms and easy targets for bullies.

23   "A lot of kids are average; they are not what the myth says," said Doris Liang, 17, a junior at Seward Park. "In math, I'm only an average student and I have to work really hard."

24   Ms. Liang said she sometimes envies the school's Hispanic students.

25   **"Not Make Any Mistakes"**   "The Hispanic kids, in a way they are more open," she said. "They're not afraid to bring their dates home. If you're Chinese and you bring your date home they ask a lot of questions. My parents only went to junior high school in China, so when we got here they wanted us to do well in school."

26   Nicole Tran, a 15-year-old senior who spent the early part of her life in Oregon, said she believes her generation will be far more assertive.

27   "We are the minority minority," said Ms. Tran. "We are moving too fast for them," she said of the dominant white culture.

28   Dr. Jerry Chin-Li Huang, a Seward Park guidance counselor, said he believes that Asians in New York are in part experiencing the cultural transformations common to all immigrants.

29   He notes that more of the new Asian immigrants—whose numbers in New York have swelled 35 to 50 percent in the past five years to about 400,000—are coming from smaller towns and poorer, less educated families.

30   It was the early waves of educated, middle-class Asian immigrants whose children became the model minority, Dr. Huang said. Many of the students he sees have problems.

31   For one thing, Dr. Huang said many Asian parents are reluctant to admit that their children need help, even in severe cases. He said he had a schizophrenic Chinese student who began constantly wearing a coat, even on the hottest summer days. The parents were of little help.

32   "I have other children who run away from home because of the pressures," said Dr. Huang. "I had two sisters who had to go to school, then work in the factories, sewing. Their parents could not speak English so they were helping them with the bills. The girls said they barely had time to sleep."

33   Dr. Huang said many non-Asian teachers come to him for his insights because they have few Asian co-workers. Asians are 1.4 per-

cent of all school counselors; 0.8 percent of all principals, and 1.4 percent of all teachers in New York City.

34   Among its recommendations, the task force called for more Asian counselors and teachers.

35   People like Ms. Hsu, of Asian-American Communications, are optimistic that the situation for Asian students will improve as students and educators talk openly about it.

36   "I gave a workshop and I talked about the quotas, the Chinese exclusion act," said Ms. Hsu. "Two black girls came up to me. One said: 'You know, I always thought the Chinese kids were snooty. Now after hearing what you went through I feel you're my brothers and sisters.' "

EXERCISES

Details and Their Meanings

1. What are the experiences of Zhe Zeng, Lisa Chang, Doris Liang, and Teresa Hsu? What do their experiences have in common?
2. What are the dropout rates for Asian-American students in New York high schools? How have they changed? How do they compare with the rates for other students?
3. What has been happening to the immigration rate of Asians in the past few years? What does this change imply for New York schools? How do recent Asian immigrants differ from earlier immigrants? Why are the differences significant?
4. What stereotypes and standards do Asian students feel they have to live up to? What is the source of these pressures? To whom are the stereotypes positive and to whom negative? Why?
5. In what ways do the students interviewed by the writer find themselves in tension or conflict over the pressures created by the stereotypes?
6. What are the percentages of Asian-American counselors, principals, and teachers in the New York schools? How do those statistics compare to the percentage of Asian-American students? What consequences and implications does the comparison suggest?
7. What incidents have occurred in schools between Asian-American students and other students? What is the meaning of those incidents?

8. How do professionals and experts view the pressures on Asian students? Do they agree about how the future will be for Asian-American students in the New York schools?

Reading and Critical Thinking

1. In what way are parents' and teachers' expectations about Asian-American students similar to the stereotypes? What effect do these expectations have on the students? Overall, are these expectations simply good or bad? Is their effect different on different people?
2. In what ways are the expectations of and pressures on Asian students similar to or different from the expectations of and pressures on children of different ethnicities?
3. How do people of one ethnic group react to the expectations of and pressures on other groups? How do the expectations of and pressures from students of different ethnic groups create new pressures and tensions?
4. What difficulties or pressures do expectations of any kind create? Would you prefer to grow up with or without any of these kinds of expectations? How might expectations be made more individually appropriate rather than applied simply to a whole group?
5. How do different cultural characteristics influence how the Asian students react to ethnic stereotyping? To what extent do you think saying that people of a particular background share personality characteristics or social attitudes is itself a form of inappropriate stereotyping?
6. What is the special meaning of the word *banana* described in the selection? Are there other terms with similar meanings used by members of other ethnic groups? What purposes do the terms serve? What harm do they do? What kind of behavior and thinking do the terms encourage or discourage?

The Writer's Strategies

1. In what paragraph does Felicia R. Lee present her overall idea or thesis? How do the first three paragraphs lead up to that thesis? Why does the article start in this way?
2. How do paragraphs 5 and 6 add new ideas that make the main point more complex? How are these new ideas supported and

developed in the following paragraphs? What examples does the writer use to develop these ideas and how do the examples show the complexity of the issues?

3. Where does Lee use statistics? How do they support or develop her ideas? Does the writer indicate sources of the statistics? Why or why not?

4. Who are the various people interviewed for this piece, and what do their different statements contribute? Which interviewees are the Asian-American students who are Lee's subject? Which interviewees contribute background information? Which interviewees express opinions on the situations described by Lee?

5. What points does the writer make in the last few paragraphs through the comments of Dr. Huang and Ms. Hsu? How do these quotations provide a conclusion to the piece? What tone do they give the conclusion?

Thinking Together

In groups of three or four, discuss whether people expect too much or too little of you because of your membership in a particular group. How do you respond to any inappropriate expectations? Describe one specific incident in which inappropriate expectations were applied to you. Then compare the different incidents in an attempt to understand the different kinds of expectations and different kinds of responses. Next discuss more generally what role people's expectations have had in influencing your development in positive or negative ways.

Vocabulary

The following phrases appear in the selection. Define the italicized word in each one.

1. handling the family's *interactions* (par. 2)
2. face cultural *dislocations* (par. 4)
3. *inflated* expectations of teachers (par. 4)
4. resent their *perceived* success (par. 9)
5. Asian cultures *dictate* stoicism (par. 11)
6. tensions *escalated* (par. 14)
7. peer pressure not to completely *assimilate* (par. 21)
8. experiencing the cultural *transformations* (par. 28)

WRITER'S WORKSHOP

Critical Thinking in Writing

1. Write a personal essay describing how you are different from the various perceptions people have of you.
2. When have you been the victim of unrealistic expectations and perceptions? Write a narrative piece about an occasion in which people expected too much of you.
3. Can stereotypes be positive? Are positive stereotypes ever harmful? What is the effect of being stereotyped? Write an essay describing and evaluating several positive and negative stereotypes associated with young people.

Connecting Ideas

Write a one-page essay discussing how "Model Minority" relates to Elizabeth Wong's "The Struggle to Be an All-American Girl" (page 32) and Margaret A. Gibson's "Cultural Barriers and the Press to Americanize" (page 65). How are the pressures, conflicts, and difficulties of students described by Wong and Gibson the same as or different from those described by Felicia R. Lee?

My Husband's Nine Wives

Elizabeth Joseph

Elizabeth Joseph is a lawyer who lives in Utah. In this essay, she defends her decision to enter into a surprising marriage.

KEY WORDS

paradox (par. 4)   a riddle, a seeming contradiction.
at first blush (par. 4)   at the beginning.
commiserate (par. 10)   to talk sympathetically with another person.
spontaneity (par. 13)   unplanned action.

1   I MARRIED A MARRIED MAN.

2   In fact, he had six wives when I married him 17 years ago. Today, he has nine.

3   In March, the Utah Supreme Court struck down a trial court's ruling that a polygamist couple could not adopt a child because of their marital style. Last month, the national board of the American Civil Liberties Union, in response to a request from its Utah chapter, adopted a new policy calling for the legalization of polygamy.

4   Polygamy, or plural marriage, as practiced by my family is a paradox. At first blush, it sounds like the ideal situation for the man and an oppressive one for the women. For me, the opposite is true. While polygamists believe that the Old Testament mandates the practice of plural marriage, compelling social reasons make the life style attractive to the modern career woman.

5   Pick up any women's magazine and you will find article after article about the problems of successfully juggling career, motherhood and marriage. It is a complex act that many women struggle to manage daily; their frustrations fill up the pages of those magazines and consume the hours of afternoon talk shows.

6   In a monogamous context, the only solutions are compromises. The kids need to learn to fix their own breakfast, your husband needs to get used to occasional microwave dinners, you need to divert more of your income to insure that your pre-schooler is in a good day care environment.

7   I am sure that in the challenge of working through these compromises, satisfaction and success can be realized. But why must women only embrace a marital arrangement that requires so many trade-offs?

8   When I leave for the 60-mile commute to court at 7 A.M., my 2-year-old daughter, London, is happily asleep in the bed of my husband's wife, Diane. London adores Diane. When London awakes, about the time I'm arriving at the courthouse, she is surrounded by family members who are as familiar to her as the toys in her nursery.

9   My husband Alex, who writes at night, gets up much later. While most of his wives are already at work, pursuing their careers, he can almost always find one who's willing to chat over coffee.

10   I share a home with Delinda, another wife, who works in town government. Most nights, we agree we'll just have a simple dinner with our three kids. We'd rather relax and commiserate over the pressures of our work day than chew up our energy cooking and doing a ton of dishes.

11   Mondays, however, are different. That's the night Alex eats with us. The kids, excited that their father is coming to dinner, are on their best behavior. We often invite another wife or one of his children. It's a special event because it only happens once a week.

12   Tuesday night, it's back to simplicity for us. But for Alex and the household he's dining with that night, it's their special time.

13   The same system with some variation governs our private time with him. While spontaneity is by no means ruled out, we basically use an appointment system. If I want to spend Friday evening at his house, I make an appointment. If he's already "booked," I either request another night or if my schedule is inflexible, I talk to the other wife and we work out an arrangement. One thing we've all learned is that there's always another night.

14   Most evenings, with the demands of career and the literal chasing after the needs of a toddler, all I want to do is collapse into bed and sleep. But there is also the longing for intimacy and comfort that only he can provide, and when those feelings surface, I ask to be with him.

15   Plural marriage is not for everyone. But it is the life style for me. It offers men the chance to escape from the traditional, confining

roles that often isolate them from the surrounding world. More important, it enables women, who live in a society full of obstacles, to fully meet their career, mothering and marriage obligations. Polygamy provides a whole solution. I believe American women would have invented it if it didn't already exist.

———

EXERCISES

Details and Their Meanings

1. Who is Alex Joseph? What is his occupation? How many wives does he have? How long has Elizabeth Joseph been married to him? Which number wife is she?
2. How many children does the writer mention? Which ones belong to her?
3. Where is there a movement to support polygamy? What recent court rulings support polygamy? What advantages of polygamy does Elizabeth Joseph mention? Why do you think she considers legal issues?
4. How far does Elizabeth Joseph commute every day? Who takes care of her daughter? Why does she provide these details?
5. What special problems does Elizabeth Joseph have as a result of her marriage? How does she manage them?
6. What does the Old Testament say about polygamy? Why does the writer cite the Bible?

Reading and Critical Thinking

1. What about polygamy seems like a paradox for women? Do you think a woman would be most likely to accept or reject polygamy? How would men today most likely feel about it?
2. Can women have multiple husbands in Elizabeth Joseph's culture? Why or why not? Do you think this situation is appropriate? Why or why not?
3. According to paragraph 3, what complaints do most women have about marriage? How valid are these complaints?
4. Why does the writer mention only two other wives? Why do you think she chose not to name them all?

5. How many of Alex Joseph's wives live in the same house? Why does Alex eat with Elizabeth only one night a week? With whom does he eat on the other nights? What problem do you see with this arrangement?
6. Is Elizabeth Joseph advocating polygamy for all Americans? Why or why not?
7. What is the occasion for writing this essay? What event probably occurred around the time it was written?

The Writer's Strategies

1. Where does the writer state her thesis? What is it? How does the first sentence of the essay catch the reader's attention as it relates to the thesis?
2. Why does the writer take eight paragraphs to explain her family's schedule? Why is that an important issue?
3. What primary strategy for developing this essay is Joseph using? What role do narration, illustration, and comparison-contrast play?
4. Who is the audience for this selection? What information does Joseph assume her audience has? Is her assumption accurate in your case?
5. What is the conclusion of this essay? What position is the writer advocating in the conclusion?
6. What words does the writer use to signal transitions?

Thinking Together

Imagine that you are a participant in a polygamous marriage. What are the advantages and disadvantages of this way of life? In small groups, brainstorm to develop responses to that question. Compare your findings with those of the rest of the class. Do more men or more women in your class favor polygamy?

Vocabulary

The following italicized words are either defined in the text, or their meanings emerge through context. Write definitions in your own words.

1. *Polygamy,* or plural marriage, . . . is a paradox. (par. 4)
2. In a monogamous context, the only solutions are *compromises.* (par. 6)

3. the Old Testament *mandates* the practice of plural marriage (par. 4)
4. why must women only embrace a *marital* arrangement that requires so many trade-offs? (par. 7)
5. if my schedule is *inflexible,* I talk to the other wife and we work out an arrangement. (par. 13)
6. to fully meet their career, motherhood and marriage *obligations* (par. 15)

WRITER'S WORKSHOP

Critical Thinking in Writing

1. Write an essay in which you argue in favor of or against polygamy.
2. Does a group of individuals have the right to make up rules governing social behavior, even if those rules challenge society's accepted principles? On what grounds can you say yes or no? What danger is there in imposing majority standards on everybody? Write your responses in a well-argued essay.
3. Write a narrative from the point of view of a child in a polygamous marriage. Tell about how you would relate to your mother, to your father's other wives, to your father, and to your brothers and sisters.

Connecting Ideas

Read Jim Yoshida's "Two Worlds" (page 5) and Elizabeth Wong's "The Struggle to Be an All American Girl" (page 32). How do the family units and structures represented in these selections compare with Elizabeth Joseph's family structure? How do you think polygamous relations would affect Yoshida's and Wong's families?

Minority Student

Richard Rodriguez

Richard Rodriguez is a writer and teacher in San Francisco, where he was born. In this selection from Hunger of Memory: The Education of Richard Rodriguez *(1982), his autobiography, he wrestles with the conflict between his ethnic and mainstream identities.*

KEY WORDS

juxtaposition (par. 3)   placing side by side or close together.
implicated (par. 4)   connected with, mixed up in.
rhetorically (par. 9)   for effect only.
los pobres (par. 13)   Spanish phrase meaning "the poor wretches."
fawning (par. 17)   acting in a submissive, cringing way.

1   MINORITY STUDENT—THAT WAS the label I bore in college at Stanford, then in graduate school at Columbia and Berkeley: a nonwhite reader of Spenser and Milton and Austen.

2   In the late 1960s nonwhite Americans clamored for access to higher education, and I became a principal beneficiary of the academy's response, its programs of affirmative action. My presence was noted each fall by the campus press office in its proud tally of Hispanic-American students enrolled; my progress was followed by HEW statisticians. One of the lucky ones. Rewarded. Advanced for belonging to a racial group "underrepresented" in American institutional life. When I sought admission to graduate schools, when I applied for fellowships and summer study grants, when I needed a teaching assistantship, my Spanish surname or the dark mark in the space indicating my race—"check one"—nearly always got me whatever I asked for. When the time came for me to look for a college teaching job (the end of my years as a scholarship boy), potential employers came looking for me—a minority student.

3   Fittingly, it falls to me, as someone who so awkwardly carried the label, to question it now, its juxtaposition of terms—minority, student. For me there is no way to say it with grace. I say it rather with irony sharpened by self-pity. I say it with anger. It is a term that should never have been foisted on me. One I was wrong to accept.

4   In college one day a professor of English returned my term paper with this comment penciled just under the grade: "Maybe the reason you feel Dickens's sense of alienation so acutely is because you are a minority student." *Minority student.* It was the first time I had seen the expression; I remember sensing that it somehow referred to my race. Never before had a teacher suggested that my academic performance was linked to my racial identity. After class I reread the remark several times. Around me other students were talking and leaving. The professor remained in front of the room, collecting his papers and books. I was about to go up and question his note. But I didn't. I let the comment pass; thus became implicated in the strange reform movement that followed.

5   The year was 1967. And what I did not realize was that my life would be radically changed by deceptively distant events. In 1967, their campaign against southern segregation laws successful at last, black civil rights leaders were turning their attention to the North, a North they no longer saw in contrast to the South. What they realized was that although no official restrictions denied blacks access to northern institutions of advancement and power, for most blacks this freedom was only theoretical. (The obstacle was "institutional racism.") Activists made their case against institutions of higher education. Schools like Wisconsin and Princeton long had been open to blacks. But the tiny number of nonwhite students and faculty members at such schools suggested that there was more than the issue of access to consider. Most blacks simply couldn't afford tuition for higher education. And, because the primary and secondary schooling blacks received was usually poor, few qualified for admission. Many were so culturally alienated that they never thought to apply; they couldn't imagine themselves going to college.

6   I think—as I thought in 1967—that the black civil rights leaders were correct: Higher education was not, nor is it yet, accessible to many black Americans. I think now, however, that the activists tragically limited the impact of their movement with the reforms they proposed. Seeing the problem solely in racial terms (as a case of *de facto* segregation), they pressured universities and colleges to admit more black students and hire more black faculty members. There were demands for financial aid programs. And tutoring help. And more aggressive student recruitment. But this was all. The aim was

to integrate higher education in the North. So no one seemed troubled by the fact that those who were in the best position to bene-fit from such reforms were those blacks least victimized by racism or any other social oppression—those culturally, if not always econom-ically, of the middle class.

7   The lead established, other civil rights groups followed. Soon Hispanic-American activists began to complain that there were too few Hispanics in colleges. They concluded that this was the result of racism. They offered racial solutions. They demanded that Hispanic-American professors be hired. And that students with Spanish surnames be admitted in greater numbers to colleges. Shortly after, I was "recognized" on campus: a Hispanic-American, a "Latino," a Mexican-American, a "Chicano." No longer would people ask me, as I had been asked before, if I were a foreign student. (From India? Peru?) All of a sudden everyone seemed to know—as the professor of English had known—that I was a minority student.

8   I became a highly rewarded minority student. For campus offi-cials came first to students like me with their numerous offers of aid. And why not? Administrators met their angriest critics' demands by promoting any plausible Hispanic on hand. They were able, more-over, to use the presence of conventionally qualified nonwhite students like me to prove that they were meeting the goals of their critics.

9   In 1968, the assassination of Dr. Martin Luther King, Jr., prompted many academic officials to commit themselves publicly to the goal of integrating their institutions. One day I watched the na-tionally televised funeral; a week later I received invitations to teach at community colleges. There were opportunities to travel to foreign countries with contingents of "minority group scholars." And I went to the financial aid office on campus and was handed special forms for minority student applicants. I was a minority student, wasn't I? the lady behind the counter asked me rhetorically. Yes, I said. Care-lessly said. I completed the application. Was later awarded.

10   In a way, it was true. I was a minority. The word, as popularly used, did describe me. In the sixties, *minority* became a synonym for socially disadvantaged Americans—but it was primarily a numeri-cal designation. The word referred to entire races and nationalities of Americans, those numerically underrepresented in institutional life. (Thus, without contradiction, one could speak of "minority groups.") And who were they exactly? Blacks—all blacks—most ob-viously were minorities. And Hispanic-Americans. And American Indians. And some others. (It was left to federal statisticians, using elaborate surveys and charts, to determine which others precisely.)

11   I was a minority.

12   I believed it. For the first several years, I accepted the label. I certainly supported the racial civil rights movement; supported the goal of broadening access to higher education. But there was a problem: One day I listened approvingly to a government official defend affirmative action; the next day *I* realized the benefits of the program. I was the minority student the political activists shouted about at noon-time rallies. Against their rhetoric, I stood out in relief, unrelieved. *Knowing:* I was not really more socially disadvantaged than the white graduate students in my classes. *Knowing:* I was not disadvantaged like many of the new nonwhite students who were entering college, lacking good early schooling.

13   Nineteen sixty-nine. 1970. 1971. Slowly, slowly, the term *minority* became a source of unease. It would remind me of those boyhood years when I had felt myself alienated from public (majority) society—*los gringos. Minority. Minorities. Minority groups.* The terms sounded in public to remind me in private of the truth: I was not—in a *cultural* sense—a minority, an alien from public life. (Not like *los pobres* I had encountered during my recent laboring summer.) The truth was summarized in the sense of irony I'd feel at hearing myself called a minority student: The reason I was no longer a minority was because I had become a student.

14   *Minority student!*

15   In conversations with faculty members I began to worry the issue, only to be told that my unease was unfounded. A dean said he was certain that after I graduated I would be able to work among "my people." A senior faculty member expressed in confidence that, though I was unrepresentative of lower-class Hispanics, I would serve as a role model for others of my race. Another faculty member was sure that I would be a valued counselor to incoming minority students. (He assumed that, because of my race, I retained a special capacity for communicating with nonwhite students.) I also heard academic officials say that minority students would someday form a leadership class in America. (From our probable positions of power, we would be able to lobby for reforms to benefit others of our race.)

16   In 1973 I wrote and had published two essays in which I said that I had been educated away from the culture of my mother and father. In 1974 I published an essay admitting unease over becoming the beneficiary of affirmative action. There was another article against affirmative action in 1977. One more soon after. At times, I proposed contrary ideas; consistent always was the admission that I was no longer like socially disadvantaged Hispanic-Americans. But

this admission, made in national magazines, only brought me a greater degree of success. A published minority student, I won a kind of celebrity. In my mail were admiring letters from right-wing politicians. There were also invitations to address conferences of college administrators or government officials.

17   My essays served as my "authority" to speak at the Marriott Something or the Sheraton Somewhere. To stand at a ballroom podium and hear my surprised echo sound from a microphone. I spoke. I started getting angry letters from activists. One wrote to say that I was becoming the *gringos'* fawning pet. What "they" want all Hispanics to be. I remembered the remark when I was introduced to an all-white audience and heard their applause so loud. I remembered the remark when I stood in a university auditorium and saw an audience of brown and black faces watching me. I publicly wondered whether a person like me should really be termed a minority. But some members of the audience thought I was denying racial pride, trying somehow to deny my racial identity. They rose to protest. One Mexican-American said I was a minority whether I wanted to be or not. And he said that the reason I was a beneficiary of affirmative action was simple: I was a Chicano. (Wasn't I?) It was only an issue of race.

EXERCISES

Details and Their Meanings

1. What minority group does Richard Rodriguez belong to? Where in the essay does this information appear?
2. When did the writer go to college? What historical events coincided with his college years?
3. When did the writer realize that he was a minority student? When did other students realize that he is Hispanic?
4. Why did it suddenly become an advantage for Rodriguez to identify himself as a minority student? When did he begin to question his status as a minority student? What compelled him to speak out on the question of minorities?
5. How did Hispanic activists react to Rodriguez's public statements?

6. What factors other than race or ethnic group does Rodriguez feel are important in deciding who should receive affirmative action?

Reading and Critical Thinking

1. What economic class does the writer belong to? How can you tell? How do you think class influences the writer's point of view?
2. In what sense did the term *socially disadvantaged* not apply to Richard Rodriguez? Why didn't university officials care whether it applied to him or not? Do you think they should have cared? Why or why not?
3. How did the writer become an authority on affirmative action? How does this designation underscore the paradox of his situation?
4. Why do you think Rodriguez received support from right-wing groups? Why are left-wing groups unlikely to embrace his position?
5. How do you explain Rodriguez's decision to question his status as a member of a minority group?
6. In what paragraphs does Rodriguez mention black students? How does he see himself differently from them? Do you agree with his point of view? Why or why not?

The Writer's Strategies

1. Where does the writer state his thesis? What is it?
2. How does Rodriguez order the information in this selection?
3. Where does he use comparison and contrast to help make his point?
4. Give an example of irony in this essay—where the writer says one thing but means the opposite.
5. Does Rodriguez advance this essay more by facts or by opinions? Provide evidence to support your answer.
6. How does Rodriguez define *minority student*? Why is the definition of this phrase crucial to understanding this selection?
7. How would you characterize the tone of this essay—that is, what is the writer's attitude toward his subject?
8. What is the conclusion of this essay? Why is the conclusion so tentative?

Thinking Together

Imagine that your class has been appointed as a government commission with the responsibility of overhauling affirmative action guidelines for college admission and financial aid. In small groups, develop definitions of *minority, socially disadvantaged, underrepresented* and *economically deprived*. How will you ensure that the funds and assistance you set aside reach the right people?

Vocabulary

The following words and phrases have become part of the American discourse on affirmative action and equal opportunity. Write a definition of each.

1. nonwhite (par. 1)
2. Hispanic-American (par. 2)
3. institutional racism (par. 5)
4. culturally alienated (par. 5)
5. *de facto* segregation (par. 6)
6. Latino (par. 7)
7. Chicano (par. 8)

WRITER'S WORKSHOP ━━━━━━━━━━━━━━━

Critical Thinking in Writing

1. In paragraph 3 Rodriguez points out his discomfort with the label *minority student,* even though it brought him many advantages. Write an essay to explain how you feel about a label used to describe you or your group. What advantages are there for you in using the label? What are the disadvantages?
2. According to Richard T. Schaefer's "Minority, Racial, and Ethnic Groups" (page 179), the designation "minority" is imposed on people by others. If that is so, does Rodriguez's discomfort with his status matter? Does the fact that he feels he has benefited unfairly from affirmative action mean that affirmative action is not working? Should educated, middle-class minority people like Richard Rodriguez receive the same benefits of affirmative action as socially disadvantaged minority people? Why or why not? Address these concerns in a brief essay.
3. Write your own essay definition of the term *minority student.*

Connecting Ideas

Read Stephen Carter's "I Am an Affirmative Action Baby" (page 89). In what ways do Carter's concerns parallel Rodriguez's? How do the two writers' conclusions differ? Why have they arrived at different views of affirmative action? Which writer has your support in this debate? Why?

The Women of New Mexico

Fabiola Cabeza de Baca

In this selection from her history of New Mexico, Fabiola Cabeza de Baca celebrates the role of women, including her ancestors, in the development of the state. Notice how in her praise for the women she also praises the tradition, class, and culture that she is part of.

KEY WORDS

Llano (par. 1)   rolling plains in southeastern New Mexico.
Ceja (par. 1)   a region in southeastern New Mexico.
La Liendre (par. 5)   highlands in northern New Mexico.

1   THE WOMEN ON THE Llano and Ceja played a great part in the history of the land. It was a difficult life for a woman, but she had made her choice when in the marriage ceremony she had promised to obey and to follow her husband. It may not have been her choice since parents may have decided for her. It was the Spanish custom to make matches for the children. Whether through choice or tradition, the women had to be a hardy lot in order to survive the long trips by wagon or carriage and the separation from their families, if their families were not among those who were settling on the Llano.

2   The women had to be versed in the curative powers of plants and in midwifery, for there were no doctors within a radius of two hundred miles or more.

3   The knowledge of plant medicine is an inheritance from the Moors, and brought to New Mexico by the first Spanish colonizers. From childhood we are taught the names of herbs, weeds, and plants that have curative potency; even today, when we have doctors at our immediate call, we still have great faith in plant medicine. Certainly this knowledge of home remedies was a source of comfort to the

133

women who went out to the Llano, yet their faith in God helped more than anything in their survival.

4   Every village had its curandera or médica, and the ranchers rode many miles to bring the medicine woman or the midwife from a distant village or neighboring ranch.

5   Quite often the wife of the patrón was well versed in plant medicine. I know that my grandmother, doña Estéfana Delgado de Baca, although not given the name of médica, because it was not considered proper in her social class, was called every day by some family in the village, or by their empleados, to treat a child or some other person in the family. In the fall of the year she went out to the hills and valleys to gather her supply of healing herbs. When she went to live in La Liendre, there were terrible outbreaks of smallpox and she had difficulty convincing the villagers that vaccination was a solution. Not until she had a godchild in every family was she able to control the dreaded disease. In Spanish tradition a godmother takes the responsibility of a real mother, and in that way grandmother conquered many superstitions which the people had. At least she had the power to decide what should be done for her godchildren.

6   From El Paso, Texas, she secured vaccines from her cousin Dr. Samaniego. She vaccinated her children, grandchildren, and godchildren against the disease. She vaccinated me when I was three years old, and the vaccination has passed many doctors' inspections.

7   As did my grandmother, so all the wives of the patrones held a very important place in the villages and ranches on the Llano. The patrón ruled the rancho, but his wife looked after the spiritual and physical welfare of the empleados and their families. She was the first one called when there was death, illness, misfortune, or good tidings in a family. She was a great social force in the community— more so than her husband. She held the purse strings, and thus she was able to do as she pleased in her charitable enterprises and to help those who might seek her assistance.

8   There may have been class distinction in the larger towns, but the families on the Llano had none; the empleados and their families were as much a part of the family of the patrón as his own children. It was a very democratic way of life.

9   The women in these isolated areas had to be resourceful in every way. They were their own doctors, dressmakers, tailors, and advisers.

10   The settlements were far apart and New Mexico was a poor territory trying to adapt itself to a new rule. The Llano people had no

opportunity for public schools before statehood, but there were men and women who held classes for the children of the patrones in private homes. They taught reading in Spanish and sometimes in English. Those who had means sent their children to school in Las Vegas, Santa Fe, or Eastern states. If no teachers were available, the mothers taught their own children to read, and many of the wealthy ranchers had private teachers for their children until they were old enough to go away to boarding schools.

11   Doña Luisa Gallegos de Baca, who herself had been educated in a convent in the Middle West, served as teacher to many of the children on the Llano territory.

12   Without the guidance and comfort of the wives and mothers, life on the Llano would have been unbearable, and a great debt is owed to the brave pioneer women who ventured into the cruel life of the plains, far from contact with the outside world. Most of them have gone to their eternal rest, and God must have saved a very special place for them to recompense them for their contribution to colonization and religion in an almost savage country.

EXERCISES

Details and Their Meanings

1. What difficulties made the life of the women difficult? How did the hardships affect their character?
2. What did the women have to know about plant medicine and midwifery? Why? How did they acquire this knowledge?
3. What did the writer's grandmother, doña Estéfana Delgado de Baca, know and do? In what ways was the grandmother typical of other women of the region?
4. What were the responsibilities of the patrón's wife? Why was it important for her to live up to these responsibilities?
5. According to the writer, what was the relation between the patrón's family and the family of the empleados?
6. What arrangements were made for schooling the children? Whose children received education? From whom did they receive it? What was the role of women in education?

7. How does the writer evaluate the role and character of the women?
8. Does this selection describe all the women of New Mexico or only the women in a specific part? What is the significance of the answer to that question?

Reading and Critical Thinking

1. What choices did the women have? How did they cope with what was given to them? What responsibilities were thrust on them? What sort of character did they need to develop?
2. Why was the grandmother not given the title *médica*? What does that reason suggest about the writer's family? How do you think the attitude of the piece reflects her family's history and class?
3. How was the role of wife of a patrón different from the role of wife of an empleado? What does the difference suggest about the relative power, influence, and responsibilities of the two groups of women? What was the role of the patrón? How do you think the patrón related to the empleados? How did the patrón's wife's role balance and support her husband's?
4. How do the opportunities for education compare for all children on any rancho? What does the pattern of educational opportunity suggest about class distinctions on the rancho?
5. Overall, do you agree with the writer's statement that there were no class differences on the ranchos of the Llano? Why do you think the writer made that statement?
6. What do you believe was the importance of having community leaders like the women described? In what other communities have you observed similar roles taken on by women? Give some examples. How are these women's leadership roles different from male leadership roles in such traditional communities?
7. How much choice did women such as those described in this selection have over what they would do with their lives? Does lack of choice make their lives less admirable or more admirable?
8. In paragraph 3, why does the writer mention "we"? How many people mentioned in the selection are likely to be related to her? Are there any other indications that she identifies with the women she describes? How might her sense of identification be related to the overall evaluation she gives to the women? How

might the sense of belonging to a proud family relate to class divisions within her community?

The Writer's Strategies

1. What two different ideas does the writer express in the first two sentences? How do these sentences balance each other to present a fuller picture of the women's lives? How do they provide a framework for thinking about the rest of the selection? Would you say that they represent the thesis? Why or why not?
2. Identify all the positive evaluative terms the writer uses to describe the women. How else does she show that she admires them?
3. What purpose is served by the details about medicine and education? How do the examples of two de Baca women strengthen the presentation?
4. In what way do the tone and style of the writing reflect the attitude of the writer and her attachment to the culture she describes?
5. How does the ending of the selection reinforce the attitude of the writer toward her subject?

Thinking Together

In small groups, discuss any situations you are familiar with that have produced strong women capable of taking on major responsibilities for the welfare of a community. At the end of your discussion, list the circumstances that encourage women to fulfill such roles.

Vocabulary

Several Spanish words are used to describe places and roles that were part of the old way of life. These terms can be understood from the context in which they are used. Find the context in which the following words appear, and define each term in English.

1. curandera (par. 4)
2. médica (par. 4)
3. patrón (par. 5)
4. empleados (par. 5)
5. rancho (par. 7)

WRITER'S WORKSHOP ───────────

Critical Thinking in Writing

1. Write a paragraph or two speculating on what the lives of the empleados' wives were like.
2. Describe in several paragraphs the responsibilities and difficulties of a strong woman you know, and explain how she manages them.
3. Does personal character actually get stronger when a person has important responsibilities or faces great difficulties? Write an essay analyzing this idea, using experiences from your life or the lives of people you know.

Connecting Ideas

Write several paragraphs comparing the role and responsibilities of the patrón's wife described here with the role and responsibilities of the women described in Elizabeth Joseph's "My Husband's Nine Wives" (page 120). Which do you think is more admirable? more progressive?

I Have a Dream

Martin Luther King, Jr.

Dr. Martin Luther King was a Baptist minister, founder and president of the Southern Christian Leadership Conference, the national symbol of the civil rights movement and the author of many articles and books. He is the only American born in this century whose birthday is now a national holiday. This selection, his keynote address to the 1963 March on Washington, is considered one of the greatest examples of oratory in modern American history.

KEY WORDS

fivescore (par. 2)   five twenties or one hundred
manacles (par. 2)   restraints such as handcuffs
languishing (par. 3)   wasting away
hallowed (par. 6)   sacred, holy
inextricably (par. 11)   connected so as not to be separated out
tribulation (par. 15)   hardship
redemptive (par. 15)   fulfilling, saving
wallow (par. 16)   lie in mud, remain stuck
exalted (par. 22)   raised up
jangling (par. 24)   irritatingly noisy, discordant
prodigious (par. 26)   mighty, superior

---

1   I AM HAPPY TO join with you today in what will go down in history as the greatest demonstration for freedom in the history of our nation.

2   Fivescore years ago, a great American, in whose symbolic shadow we stand today, signed the Emancipation Proclamation. This momentous decree came as a great beacon light of hope to millions of Negro slaves who had been seared in the flames of withering injustice. It came as a joyous daybreak to end the long night of their captivity.

3   But one hundred years later, the Negro still is not free; one hundred years later, the life of the Negro is still sadly crippled by the manacles of segregation and the chains of discrimination; one hundred years later, the Negro lives on a lonely island of poverty in the midst of a vast ocean of material prosperity; one hundred years later, the Negro is still languishing in the corners of American society and finds himself in exile in his own land.

4   So we've come here today to dramatize a shameful condition. In a sense we've come to our nation's capital to cash a check. When the architects of our republic wrote the magnificent words of the Constitution and the Declaration of Independence, they were signing a promissory note to which every American was to fall heir. This note was the promise that all men, yes, black men as well as white men, would be guaranteed the unalienable rights of life, liberty, and the pursuit of happiness.

5   It is obvious today that America has defaulted on this promissory note in so far as her citizens of color are concerned. Instead of honoring this sacred obligation, America has given the Negro people a bad check; a check which has come back marked "insufficient funds." We refuse to believe that there are insufficient funds in the great vaults of opportunity of this nation. And so we've come to cash this check, a check that will give us upon demand the riches of freedom and the security of justice.

6   We have also come to this hallowed spot to remind America of the fierce urgency of now. This is no time to engage in the luxury of cooling off or to take the tranquilizing drug of gradualism. Now is the time to make real the promises of democracy; now is the time to rise from the dark and desolate valley of segregation to the sunlit path of racial justice; now is the time to lift our nation from the quicksands of racial injustice to the solid rock of brotherhood; now is the time to make justice a reality for all God's children. It would be fatal for the nation to overlook the urgency of the moment. This sweltering summer of the Negro's legitimate discontent will not pass until there is an invigorating autumn of freedom and equality.

7   Nineteen sixty-three is not an end, but a beginning. And those who hope that the Negro needed to blow off steam and will now be content, will have a rude awakening if the nation returns to business as usual.

8   There will be neither rest nor tranquility in America until the Negro is granted his citizenship rights. The whirlwinds of revolt will continue to shake the foundations of our nation until the bright day of justice emerges.

9   But there is something that I must say to my people, who stand on the warm threshold which leads into the palace of justice. In the process of gaining our rightful place, we must not be guilty of wrongful deeds.

10   Let us not seek to satisfy our thirst for freedom by drinking from the cup of bitterness and hatred. We must forever conduct our struggle on the high plain of dignity and discipline. We must not allow our creative protest to degenerate into physical violence. Again and again we must rise to the majestic heights of meeting physical force with soul force.

11   The marvelous new militancy which has engulfed the Negro community must not lead us to a distrust of all white people, for many of our white brothers, as evidenced by their presence here today, have come to realize that their destiny is tied up with our destiny and they have come to realize that their freedom is inextricably bound to our freedom. This offense we share mounted to storm the battlements of injustice must be carried forth by a biracial army. We cannot walk alone.

12   And as we walk, we must make the pledge that we shall always march ahead. We cannot turn back. There are those who are asking the devotees of civil rights, "When will you be satisfied?" We can never be satisfied as long as the Negro is the victim of the unspeakable horrors of police brutality.

13   We can never be satisfied as long as our bodies, heavy with fatigue of travel, cannot gain lodging in the motels of the highways and the hotels of the cities. We cannot be satisfied as long as the Negro's basic mobility is from a smaller ghetto to a larger one.

14   We can never be satisfied as long as our children are stripped of their selfhood and robbed of their dignity by signs stating "for whites only." We cannot be satisfied as long as a Negro in Mississippi cannot vote and a Negro in New York believes he has nothing for which to vote. No, we are not satisfied, and we will not be satisfied until justice rolls down like waters and righteousness like a mighty stream.

15   I am not unmindful that some of you have come here out of excessive trials and tribulation. Some of you have come fresh from narrow jail cells. Some of you have come from areas where your quest for freedom left you battered by the storms of persecution and staggered by the winds of police brutality. You have been the veterans of creative suffering. Continue to work with the faith that unearned suffering is redemptive.

16   Go back to Mississippi; go back to Alabama; go back to South Carolina; go back to Georgia; go back to Louisiana; go back to the

slums and ghettos of the northern cities, knowing that somehow this situation can, and will be changed. Let us not wallow in the valley of despair.

17   So I say to you, my friends, that even though we must face the difficulties of today and tomorrow, I still have a dream. It is a dream deeply rooted in the American dream that one day this nation will rise up and live out the true meaning of its creed—we hold these truths to be self-evident, that all men are created equal.

18   I have a dream that one day on the red hills of Georgia, sons of former slaves and sons of former slave-owners will be able to sit down together at the table of brotherhood.

19   I have a dream that one day, even the state of Mississippi, a state sweltering with the heat of injustice, sweltering with the heat of oppression, will be transformed into an oasis of freedom and justice.

20   I have a dream my four little children will one day live in a nation where they will not be judged by the color of their skin but by content of their character. I have a dream today!

21   I have a dream that one day, down in Alabama, with its vicious racists, with its governor having his lips dripping with the words of interposition and nullification, that one day, right there in Alabama, little black boys and black girls will be able to join hands with little white boys and white girls as sisters and brothers. I have a dream today!

22   I have a dream that one day every valley shall be exalted, every hill and mountain shall be made low, the rough places shall be made plain, and the crooked places shall be made straight and the glory of the Lord will be revealed and all flesh shall see it together.

23   This is our hope. This is the faith that I go back to the South with.

24   With this faith we will be able to hear out of the mountain of despair a stone of hope. With this faith we will be able to transform the jangling discords of our nation into a beautiful symphony of brotherhood.

25   With this faith we will be able to work together, to pray together, to struggle together, to go to jail together, to stand up for freedom together, knowing that we will be free one day. This will be the day when all of God's children will be able to sing with new meaning—"my country 'tis of thee; sweet land of liberty; of thee I sing; land where my fathers died, land of the pilgrim's pride; from every mountain side, let freedom ring"—and if America is to be a great nation, this must become true.

26   So let freedom ring from the prodigious hilltops of New Hampshire.

27   Let freedom ring from the mighty mountains of New York.

28   Let freedom ring from the heightening Alleghenies of Pennsylvania.

29   Let freedom ring from the snow-capped Rockies of Colorado.

30   Let freedom ring from the curvaceous slopes of California.

31   But not only that.

32   Let freedom ring from Stone Mountain of Georgia.

33   Let freedom ring from Lookout Mountain of Tennessee.

34   Let freedom ring from every hill and molehill of Mississippi, from every mountainside, let freedom ring.

35   And when we allow freedom to ring, when we let it ring from every village and hamlet, from every state and city, we will be able to speed up that day when all of God's children—black men and white men, Jews and Gentiles, Catholics and Protestants—will be able to join hands and to sing in the words of the old Negro spiritual, "Free at last, free at last; thank God Almighty, we are free at last."

EXERCISES

Details and Their Meanings

1. What event that took place in 1863 is King referring to in the opening of this piece?
2. What conditions in 1963 has King come to address?
3. What dangers does King address in paragraph 6?
4. What does King say will result if his warning is not heeded?
5. What danger does King identify within the black community?
6. What specific grievances does King enumerate in paragraphs 13 through 15?
7. In what places, according to King, is life particularly difficult for black people? Which paragraph introduces the list?
8. What are some specific hopes that King has for the future?

Reading and Critical Thinking

1. What definition of the American dream does King give? Where do you find this definition?

2. What specific proposals for legislation and social changes does King make? Has any of these proposals become law as far as you know?

3. What information does King assume his listeners have about the conditions of American life in 1963? How does this assumption change the context of his speech for an audience of the 1990s?

4. What triumphs does King mention? What is his purpose in naming them?

5. How is King using this speech as a platform to set the future agenda for the civil rights movement? Where in the essay does he present elements of this platform?

6. Recent events in Los Angeles and other American cities suggest that the problems King identified are still simmering powerfully under the surface of American society. How do you think King would address racial tensions in America today? How would he have reacted to the beating of Rodney King, a black man, by white police officers and then the acquittal of those officers by an essentially white jury? What role might King have played as cities burned in May 1992?

The Writer's Strategies

1. What is King's thesis?
2. Why did King use the title "I Have a Dream"? What senses of the word *dream* inform this piece?
3. Who is King's immediate audience? Who else is he addressing?
4. Why does King make so many allusions—that is, references to other works or events? Name some of the sources King draws on.
5. How does King make use of repetition? What is his purpose in doing so? Why does he include so many place names in the final paragraphs? What is his purpose in doing so?
6. Which paragraphs mark the introduction? Comment on its effectiveness.
7. Where does the conclusion begin? Why are the concluding paragraphs so short?

Thinking Together

See if your library has a videotape or a recording of Martin Luther King, Jr., delivering this speech. Listen to it in class. Then in groups discuss how the experience of hearing it differs from reading it.

What are the major differences in the two experiences? What do King's voice, body language, and gestures add to his words?

Vocabulary

Identify the following, using reference books if necessary; then write a description of each item.

1. Emancipation Proclamation (par. 2)
2. interposition (par. 21)
3. nullification (par. 21)
4. "my country 'tis of thee" (par. 25)
5. Thomas Edison

WRITER'S WORKSHOP ————————————

Critical Thinking in Writing

1. In an essay, compare the dream that Martin Luther King, Jr., articulated thirty years ago with the reality of the modern America you know. Which parts of King's dream have come true? Which parts remain to be fulfilled?
2. Most American historians consider this work among the most brilliant speeches made by an American. What makes it so good? Write a critique of "I Have a Dream," enumerating its strengths and, if you can find any, its weaknesses.
3. What is your dream for America? Write an essay called "I Have a Dream" in which you share your goals, ambitions, and hopes for our country.

Connecting Ideas

Read Susan Tifft's "Fighting the Failure Syndrome" (page 46), Marcus Mabry's "Confronting Campus Racism" (page 350), or both. In light of King's piece, how do Tifft's and Mabry's proposals for improving schools strike you? What do you suppose King would argue about American education?

S I D E B Y S I D E

1. Drawing on the selections in this unit, write an essay in which you argue whether America should be a monocultural or a pluralistic society. What are the advantages and disadvantages of each position? What do Americans stand to gain or lose?

2. Revisit the issue of the *self*, which you considered in your prereading journal. Drawing on your journal entry, the essays in this chapter, and your conversations about them, write a paper in which you define the self and the special role that ethnic identity plays in that definition.

3. If the United States is to remain divided by race, ethnic culture, and class, what can be done to ensure that American society will be just? How can every individual be guaranteed equal opportunities for education and success, equal protection under the law, and equal access to the benefits of citizenship? Write a well-detailed proposal for maintaining a fair America, including provisions for enforcing this protection.

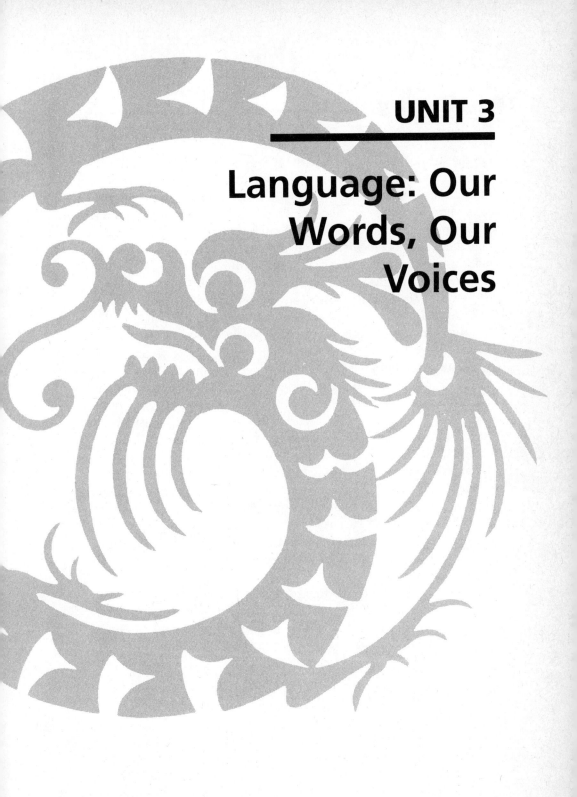

UNIT 3

Language: Our Words, Our Voices

INTRODUCTION

On the surface, the English language seems to be a powerful unifying force in American culture. Although only a small proportion of immigrants spoke English when they first came to this country, today English is the language in which Russian Americans in New York can speak to Chicanos in San Francisco. English is the predominant language of television, music and motion pictures, and the malls and shopping centers across the nation.

American English, however, is not the same language that the British brought to this country in the seventeenth century. James Baldwin points out in "If Black English Isn't a Language . . . What Is?" that Africans brought to America as slaves adapted British English to their own needs, creating what he argues is a separate language, one that enriches the way all Americans talk. In "*Macho* and *Machismo* as Loan Words" and "Spanglish," Constance Sullivan and Janice Castro, respectively, detail the rich influence of Spanish on American English in many parts of the country and consider the blend of Spanish and English called Spanglish.

This unit also explores several questions of language itself. In "Women's Language" Robin Lakoff describes how English exercises control over the way women speak and relate to their world. Ellen Tashie Frisina, in "'See Spot Run'" and Paule Marshall in "From the Poets in the Kitchen," discuss how the lives of women are enriched by learning to read and write. In "Minority, Racial, and Ethnic Groups," Richard T. Schaefer investigates how racial concepts and stereotypes develop.

Language is both the tie that binds us to a range of people across the nation and around the world and a key to our individual cultures and personalities. The essays in this section examine these often contradictory elements.

PREREADING JOURNAL

1. Make a list of words or phrases used in your home that come from your heritage. They can be words from another language, slang expressions, or even regional words, like *submarine, hoagie,* or *hero,* which all mean the same thing—a large sandwich made on a long roll that is split lengthwise.

2. Words are the building blocks of thoughts. Do you feel that the more words you know, the more things you can think about? Do the words you use to describe the world around you and to think about yourself help to shape how you see the world and how you feel about yourself? Write a journal entry in which you consider these questions.

3. "Sticks and stones may break my bones, but names can never hurt me." Is this old schoolyard saying true? Can the names that people call you do any harm to the way you feel about yourself or shape the kind of person you become? Write a journal entry about names you have been given—nicknames, diminutives (shortened forms, such as Mike for Michael or Sam for Samantha), pet names, and hurtful names that people directed at you because of your physical appearance, habits or personality traits, religion, or race. How did these various types of names make you feel?

From the Poets in the Kitchen

Paule Marshall

Paule Marshall remembers listening to her mother and her mother's friends talk in the kitchen when she was a child. She reveals why their talk was so important to her development as a writer.

KEY WORDS

Flatbush (par. 9)   a section of Brooklyn, New York.
incarnate (par. 15)   given a bodily form.

───────

1   SOME YEARS AGO, WHEN I was teaching a graduate seminar in fiction at Columbia University, a well-known male novelist visited my class to speak on his development as a writer. In discussing his formative years, he didn't realize it but he seriously endangered his life by remarking that women writers are luckier than those of his sex because they usually spend so much time as children around their mothers and their mothers' friends in the kitchen.

2   What did he say that for? The women students immediately forgot about being in awe of him and began readying their attack for the question and answer period later on. Even I bristled. There again was that awful image of women locked away from the world in the kitchen with only each other to talk to, and their daughters locked in with them.

3   But my guest wasn't really being sexist or trying to be provocative or even spoiling for a fight. What he meant—when he got around to explaining himself more fully—was that, given the way children are (or were) raised in our society, with little girls kept closer to home and their mothers, the woman writer stands a better chance of being exposed, while growing up, to the kind of talk that goes on among women, more often than not in the kitchen; and that this experience gives her an edge over her male counterpart by instilling in her an appreciation for ordinary speech.

153

4   It was clear that my guest lecturer attached great importance to this, which is understandable. Common speech and the plain, workaday words that make it up are, after all, the stock in trade of some of the best fiction writers. They are the principal means by which characters in a novel or story reveal themselves and give voice sometimes to profound feelings and complex ideas about themselves and the world. Perhaps the proper measure of a writer's talent is skill in rendering everyday speech—when it is appropriate to the story—as well as the ability to tap, to exploit, the beauty, poetry and wisdom it often contains.

5   "If you say what's on your mind in the language that comes to you from your parents and your street and friends you'll probably say something beautiful." Grace Paley tells this, she says, to her students at the beginning of every writing course.

6   It's all a matter of exposure and a training of the ear for the would-be writer in those early years of apprenticeship. And, according to my guest lecturer, this training, the best of it, often takes place in as unglamorous a setting as the kitchen.

7   He didn't know it, but he was essentially describing my experience as a little girl. I grew up among poets. Now they didn't look like poets—whatever that breed is supposed to look like. Nothing about them suggested that poetry was their calling. They were just a group of ordinary housewives and mothers, my mother included, who dressed in a way (shapeless house-dresses, dowdy felt hats and long, dark, solemn coats) that made it impossible for me to imagine they had ever been young.

8   Nor did they do what poets were supposed to do—spend their days in an attic room writing verses. They never put pen to paper except to write occasionally to their relatives in Barbados. "I take my pen in hand hoping these few lines will find you in health as they leave me fair for the time being," was the way their letters invariably began. Rather, their day was spent "scrubbing floor," as they described the work they did.

9   Several mornings a week these unknown bards would put an apron and a pair of old house shoes in a shopping bag and take the train or streetcar from our section of Brooklyn out to Flatbush. There, those who didn't have steady jobs would wait on certain designated corners for the white housewives in the neighborhood to come along and bargain with them over pay for a day's work cleaning their houses. This was the ritual even in the winter.

10   Later, armed with the few dollars they had earned, which in their vocabulary became "a few raw-mouth pennies," they made their way back to our neighborhood, where they would sometimes

stop off to have a cup of tea or cocoa together before going home to cook dinner for their husbands and children.

11   The basement kitchen of the brownstone house where my family lived was the usual gathering place. Once inside the warm safety of its walls the women threw off the drab coats and hats, seated themselves at the large center table, drank their cups of tea or cocoa, and talked. While my sister and I sat at a smaller table over in a corner doing our homework, they talked—endlessly, passionately, poetically, and with impressive range. No subject was beyond them. True, they would indulge in the usual gossip: whose husband was running with whom, whose daughter looked slightly "in the way" (pregnant) under her bridal gown as she walked down the aisle. That sort of thing. But they also tackled the great issues of the time. They were always, for example, discussing the state of the economy. It was the mid and late 30's then, and the aftershock of the Depression, with its soup lines and suicides on Wall Street, was still being felt.

12   Some people, they declared, didn't know how to deal with adversity. They didn't know that you had to "tie up your belly" (hold in the pain, that is) when things got rough and go on with life. They took their image from the bellyband that is tied around the stomach of a newborn baby to keep the navel pressed in.

13   They talked politics. Roosevelt was their hero. He had come along and rescued the country with relief and jobs, and in gratitude they christened their sons Franklin and Delano and hoped they would live up to the names.

14   If F.D.R. was their hero, Marcus Garvey was their God. The name of the fiery, Jamaican-born black nationalist of the 20's was constantly invoked around the table. For he had been their leader when they first came to the United States from the West Indies shortly after World War I. They had contributed to his organization, the United Negro Improvement Association (UNIA), out of their meager salaries, bought shares in his ill-fated Black Star Shipping Line, and at the height of the movement they had marched as members of his "nurses' brigade" in their white uniforms up Seventh Avenue in Harlem during the great Garvey Day parades. Garvey: He lived on through the power of their memories.

15   And their talk was of war and rumors of wars. They raged against World War II when it broke out in Europe, blaming it on the politicians. "It's these politicians. They're the ones always starting up all this lot of war. But what they care? It's the poor people got to suffer and mothers with their sons." If it was *their* sons, they swore they would keep them out of the Army by giving them soap to eat

each day to make their hearts sound defective. Hitler? He was for them "the devil incarnate."

16   Then there was home. They reminisced often and at length about home. The old country. Barbados—or Bimshire, as they affectionately called it. The little Caribbean island in the sun they loved but had to leave. "Poor—poor but sweet" was the way they remembered it.

17   And naturally they discussed their adopted home. America came in for both good and bad marks. They lashed out at it for the racism they encountered. They took to task some of the people they worked for, especially those who gave them only a hard-boiled egg and a few spoonfuls of cottage cheese for lunch. "As if anybody can scrub floor on an egg and some cheese that don't have no taste to it!"

18   Yet although they caught H in "this man country," as they called America, it was nonetheless a place where "you could at least see your way to make a dollar." That much they acknowledged. They might even one day accumulate enough dollars, with both them and their husbands working, to buy the brownstone houses which, like my family, they were only leasing at that period. This was their consuming ambition: to "buy house" and to see the children through.

—————

EXERCISES

Details and Their Meanings

1. What did the visiting male novelist say? Why did he say it? How did the women in the seminar react? Why? What was Paule Marshall's reaction? Why? What do the various reactions to the writer's statement indicate about attitudes toward women's experiences?
2. Why are novelists interested in everyday speech? Why is listening to everyday speech good training for would-be writers? How does this view of everyday speech influence how you think of Paule Marshall's mother and her mother's friends?
3. Did the mother and her friends dress or act like poets? How did they dress and act? What did they do for work? When did they talk? What did they talk about? Describe the atmosphere in the

place where they talked. How might that atmosphere have influenced the way they talked?

4. What special ways did the mother and her friends have of talking? What special phrases does Marshall quote? What do the quotations reveal about how the women used language? What about their attitudes? What do you find surprising about the attitudes they revealed?

5. What did the women think about race relations, politics, and opportunities?

6. Where were Paule Marshall and her sister when this talk was going on? How much did they hear? Did they participate? What interest do you think they had?

Reading and Critical Thinking

1. Why did Marshall comment that the visiting novelist "seriously endangered his life" by his comment? Why did the graduate students think his point was sexist? Do you agree? Why or why not? Do you think the experiences and ideas presented in this essay reinforce gender stereotypes or shed new light on women's experiences?

2. Does the selection show that girls have better training in language than boys? What does it show about women's and girls' language experience? Do you think the language experience of women and girls in the culture portrayed here is similar to the experience of women and girls in other cultures? Do women generally have an edge over men in appreciating everyday speech? Do men have experiences of certain kinds of everyday speech that are unfamiliar to women?

3. Did the jobs of the writer's mother and the other women indicate social power? What skills did their jobs require? How did the conversations in the kitchen reveal another side of these women?

4. What underlying attitudes of the women are revealed by their talk? What do these attitudes indicate about the women's motivations, awareness, and intelligence?

5. Did the women feel they had any control over the events they discussed? What could they influence? How did the limits of their control affect how they lived their lives?

6. Why do you think the women discussed the matters they did? How did the talk help them and enrich their lives?

7. Do you think Paule Marshall felt closer to the well-known novelist or to the women in her mother's kitchen? Whom do you think she believes taught her more about being a writer? Which do you think is more important for learning to become a writer, childhood language experiences or expert advice received in adulthood?

The Writer's Strategies

1. What is the thesis of this selection?
2. Where does the essay open? Why doesn't it open with a description of the women in the kitchen? What kinds of ideas are expressed in the seminar? How do these ideas give a different point of view on the kitchen talk? What problems would Paule Marshall have had in expressing these ideas if the essay had started out in the kitchen?
3. Why does Marshall describe the ordinary looks and hard work of the women before she discusses their talk?
4. How does Marshall demonstrate the women's skillful use of language?
5. What attitude is expressed toward the women? How does the tone of the piece support this attitude?
6. For whom do you think Marshall wrote this piece? What do you think was her purpose?
7. What is the order in which the women's topics of discussion are presented? What reason can you find for the order? What is the last topic presented? How does that topic provide an appropriate closing issue?

Thinking Together

As a class, brainstorm about the different places in which men and women gather to trade stories and talk and the different kinds of talk that goes on in these different groupings. Then in small groups of three or four exchange stories of how you as a child listened to or took part in one of those groups and learned about how language is used in them. Reflect on the language, skills, attitudes, and relations you learned from those groups. Each group should report its conclusions to the entire class in a general discussion.

Vocabulary

Define each of the italicized words, using hints from the context in which the word appears.

1. a graduate *seminar* in fiction at Columbia University (par. 1)
2. trying to be *provocative* or even *spoiling for* a fight (par. 3)
3. those early years of *apprenticeship* (par. 6)
4. these unknown *bards* would put an apron and a pair of old house shoes in a shopping bag (par. 9)
5. *indulge* in the usual gossip (par. 11)
6. They took their image from the *bellyband* that is tied around the stomach of a newborn baby to keep the navel pressed in. (par. 12)
7. They *reminisced* often and at length about home. (par. 16)
8. This was their *consuming* ambition (par. 18)

WRITER'S WORKSHOP ━━━━━━━━━━━━

Critical Thinking in Writing

1. Write two or three paragraphs describing an individual or group of individuals you know who are natural storytellers or otherwise naturally eloquent speakers.
2. In a one-page essay, compare and contrast males' and females' different experiences with language as they grow up, the nature of the differences, and the consequences of the differences for adult males and females.
3. Write a few paragraphs discussing the ways in which writing is or is not like speaking and the ways in which skill in speaking may or may not help you learn to write.

Connecting Ideas

Compare the view of the language of women presented here with the view presented in Robin Lakoff's "Women's Language" (page 190). In a few paragraphs, examine the language styles and attitudes learned by women and the relation of these language details to the overall development of women's personality and character. Discuss as well which selection presents a more positive view of women's language. If you find significant differences between the selections, you may wish to consider whether they both can be true. If so, how? If not, why not?

Spanglish

Janice Castro, with Dan Cook and Cristina Garcia

Janice Castro and her co-authors are staff writers for Time *maga-zine. In this piece, they describe the growing influence of Spanish on American English.*

KEY WORDS

linguistic (par. 2)   having to do with the study of language.
syntax (par. 3)   the arrangement of words into meaningful sentences.
implicit (par. 5)   understood though not openly expressed.
hybrids (par. 6)   mixed products of two distinct things.
gaffes (par. 10)   embarrassing mistakes.
mangled (par. 10)   butchered or deformed.

1   IN MANHATTAN A FIRST-GRADER greets her visiting grandparents, hap-pily exclaiming, "Come here, *siéntate!*" Her bemused grandfather, who does not speak Spanish, nevertheless knows she is asking him to sit down. A Miami personnel officer understands what a job applicant means when he says, "*Quiero un* part time." Nor do drivers miss a beat reading a billboard alongside a Los Angeles street advertising CERVEZA—SIX-PACK!

2   This free-form blend of Spanish and English, known as Span-glish, is common linguistic currency wherever concentrations of Hispanic Americans are found in the U.S. In Los Angeles, where 55% of the city's 3 million inhabitants speak Spanish, Spanglish is as much a part of daily life as sunglasses. Unlike the broken-English ef-forts of earlier immigrants from Europe, Asia and other regions, Spanglish has become a widely accepted conversational mode used casually—even playfully—by Spanish-speaking immigrants and native-born Americans alike.

3   Consisting of one part Hispanicized English, one part Ameri-canized Spanish and more than a little fractured syntax, Spanglish is

a bit like a Robin Williams comedy routine: a crackling line of cross-cultural patter straight from the melting pot. Often it enters Anglo homes and families through the children, who pick it up at school or at play with their young Hispanic contemporaries. In other cases, it comes from watching TV; many an Anglo child watching *Sesame Street* has learned *uno dos tres* almost as quickly as one two three.

4   Spanglish takes a variety of forms, from the Southern California Anglos who bid farewell with the utterly silly *"hasta la* bye-bye" to the Cuban-American drivers in Miami who *parquean* their *carros.* Some Spanglish sentences are mostly Spanish, with a quick detour for an English word or two. A Latino friend may cut short a conversation by glancing at his watch and excusing himself with the explanation that he must *"ir al* supermarket."

5   Many of the English words transplanted in this way are simply handier than their Spanish counterparts. No matter how distasteful the subject, for example, it is still easier to say "income tax" than *impuesto sobre la renta.* At the same time, many Spanish-speaking immigrants have adopted such terms as VCR, microwave and dishwasher for what they view as largely American phenomena. Still other English words convey a cultural context that is not implicit in the Spanish. A friend who invites you to *lonche* most likely has in mind the brisk American custom of "doing lunch" rather than the languorous afternoon break traditionally implied by *almuerzo.*

6   Mainstream Americans exposed to similar hybrids of German, Chinese or Hindi might be mystified. But even Anglos who speak little or no Spanish are somewhat familiar with Spanglish. Living among them, for one thing, are 19 million Hispanics. In addition, more American high school and university students sign up for Spanish than for any other foreign language.

7   Only in the past ten years, though, has Spanglish begun to turn into a national slang. Its popularity has grown with the explosive increases in U.S. immigration from Latin American countries. English has increasingly collided with Spanish in retail stores, offices and classrooms, in pop music and on street corners. Anglos whose ancestors picked up such Spanish words as *rancho, bronco, tornado* and *incommunicado,* for instance, now freely use such Spanish words as *gracias, bueno, amigo* and *por favor.*

8   Among Latinos, Spanglish conversations often flow easily from Spanish into several sentences of English and back.

9   Spanglish is a sort of code for Latinos: the speakers know Spanish, but their hybrid language reflects the American culture in which they live. Many lean to shorter, clipped phrases in place of the longer, more graceful expressions their parents used. Says Leonel de

la Cuesta, an assistant professor of modern languages at Florida International University in Miami: "In the U.S., time is money, and that is showing up in Spanglish as an economy of language." Conversational examples: *taipiar* (type) and *winshi-wiper* (windshield wiper) replace *escribir a máquina* and *limpiaparabrisas*.

10   Major advertisers, eager to tap the estimated $134 billion in spending power wielded by Spanish-speaking Americans, have ventured into Spanglish to promote their products. In some cases, attempts to sprinkle Spanish through commercials have produced embarrassing gaffes. A Braniff airlines ad that sought to tell Spanish-speaking audiences they could settle back *en* (in) luxuriant *cuero* (leather) seats, for example, inadvertently said they could fly without clothes (*encuero*). A fractured translation of the Miller Lite slogan told readers the beer was "Filling, and less delicious." Similar blunders are often made by Anglos trying to impress Spanish-speaking pals. But if Latinos are amused by mangled Spanglish, they also recognize these goofs as a sort of friendly acceptance. As they might put it, *no problema*.

━━━━━━━━━

EXERCISES

Details and Their Meanings

1. How many Hispanics are living in the United States? What American cities are centers of Hispanic culture?
2. What kinds of words do Spanish-speaking Americans borrow from English? How does Spanglish function as a kind of code? What other languages have contributed hybrids?
3. What kinds of words do English-speaking Americans borrow from Spanish?
4. Why do advertisers use Spanish to sell products? How does this strategy sometimes backfire?
5. How does Spanglish enter English-speaking households?

Reading and Critical Thinking

1. Why do you think the phenomenon of Spanglish is only about ten years old? What is a fair prediction to make about the future use of Spanglish? Do you use Spanglish? When? Where?
2. Why is the use of Spanglish mostly an urban phenomenon?

3. Is the sentence "In the U.S., time is money" an example of a fact or an opinion? How can you tell?
4. Why do you think English adopted Spanish words such as *bronco* and *tornado*?
5. What do the writers imply is the reason Spanish-speakers adopt English words and phrases? What is the reason English-speakers will adopt Spanish words and phrases? Do such adoptions weaken or enrich the language in your opinion?
6. Why might speakers of other hybrid forms of English be mystified by Spanglish?

The Writer's Strategies

1. Where do the writers state their thesis? What is it?
2. What is the writers' purpose in writing this piece? Who is their audience?
3. In which paragraphs do the writers support their points with examples? Where do the writers make use of definition?
4. What ordering technique is used?
5. Where do the writers state the conclusion? What is it?

Thinking Together

The English language began as a hybrid of Germanic, Celtic, and French languages; Spanish began as a form of Latin. In groups of three to five, discuss whether you believe American English will someday become a hybrid form as it absorbs more and more Spanish or will remain essentially unchanged as Spanish-speaking Americans assimilate into the mainstream culture. What factors, such as the media and education, will promote or stand in the way of developing a new hybrid.

Vocabulary

The following Spanish expressions are defined in the text. Look each item up in the essay, and write a definition of it.

1. uno dos tres (par. 3)
2. impuesto sobre la renta (par. 5)
3. almuerzo (par. 5)
4. escribir a máquina (par. 9)
5. limpiaparabrisas (par. 9)
6. en cuero (par. 10)
7. encuero (par. 10)

WRITER'S WORKSHOP ━━━━━━━━━

Critical Thinking in Writing

1. Despite vast influences on English by other languages, most Americans do not know another language well enough to speak or write it. Why is this so? Why, unlike European and Canadian children, for example, don't American schoolchildren learn well a language other than their own?

2. Look up the words *chocolate, algebra, zero, potato, television, dessert, camel, diesel, tycoon, macho, hurricane,* and *banjo* in an etymological dictionary. Where do these words come from? Write a short essay about what you think English would be like if it were not influenced by other languages.

3. Consider the influences (other than language) that Spanish culture has had on American culture—and vice versa. Write an essay providing examples of these influences and explaining whether you think they are positive or negative.

Connecting Ideas

Read James Baldwin's "If Black English Isn't a Language . . . What Is?" (page 199). Apply to Spanglish Baldwin's discussion of the reasons new dialects emerge and eventually become languages. In what sense is the use of Spanglish protective?

"See Spot Run"

Ellen Tashie Frisina

In this selection, Ellen Tashie Frisina recalls with affection how she as a fourteen-year-old helped her seventy-year-old grandmother learn to read.

KEY WORDS

differentiated (par. 1)   separated, distinguished.
stealthily (par. 2)   secretly.
authoritatively (par. 4)   commandingly, in an expert way.
baklava (par. 13)   a dessert consisting of pastry, honey, and nuts.

1   WHEN I WAS 14 years old, and very impressed with my teenage status (looking forward to all the rewards it would bring), I set for myself a very special goal—a goal that so differentiated me from my friends that I don't believe I told a single one. As a teenager, I was expected to have deep, dark secrets, but I was not supposed to keep them from my friends.

2   My secret was a project that I undertook every day after school for several months. It began when I stealthily made my way into the local elementary school—horror of horrors should I be seen; I was now in junior high. I identified myself as a *graduate* of the elementary school, and being taken under wing by a favorite fifth grade teacher, I was given a small bundle from a locked store-room—a bundle that I quickly dropped into a bag, lest anyone see me walking home with something from the "little kids" school.

3   I brought the bundle home—proudly now, for within the confines of my home, I was proud of my project. I walked into the living room, and one by one, emptied the bag of basic reading books. They were thin books with colorful covers and large print. The words were monosyllabic and repetitive. I sat down to the secret task at hand.

4   "All right," I said authoritatively to my 70-year-old grandmother, "today we begin our first reading lesson."

165

5   For weeks afterward, my grandmother and I sat patiently side by side—roles reversed as she, with a bit of difficulty, sounded out every word, then read them again, piece by piece, until she understood the short sentences. When she slowly repeated the full sentence, we both would smile and clap our hands—I felt so proud, so grown up.

6   My grandmother was born in Kalamata, Greece, in a rocky little farming village where nothing much grew. She never had the time to go to school. As the oldest child, she was expected to take care of her brother and sister, as well as the house and meals, while her mother tended to the gardens, and her father scratched out what little he could from the soil.

7   So, for my grandmother, schooling was out. But she had big plans for herself. She had heard about America. About how rich you could be. How people on the streets would offer you a dollar just to smell the flower you were carrying. About how everyone lived in nice houses—not stone huts on the sides of mountains—and had nice clothes and time for school.

8   So my grandmother made a decision at 14—just a child, I realize now—to take a long and sickening 30-day sea voyage alone to the United States. After lying about her age to the passport officials, who would shake their heads vehemently at anyone under 16 leaving her family, and after giving her favorite gold earrings to her cousin, saying "In America, I will have all the gold I want," my young grandmother put herself on a ship. She landed in New York in 1916.

9   No need to repeat the story of how it went for years. The streets were not made of gold. People weren't interested in smelling flowers held by strangers. My grandmother was a foreigner. Alone. A young girl who worked hard doing piecework to earn enough money for meals. No leisure time, no new gold earrings—and no school.

10   She learned only enough English to help her in her daily business as she traveled about Brooklyn. Socially, the "foreigners" stayed in neighborhoods where they didn't feel like foreigners. English came slowly.

11   My grandmother had never learned to read. She could make out a menu, but not a newspaper. She could read a street sign, but not a shop directory. She could read only what she needed to read as, through the years, she married, had five daughters, and helped my grandfather with his restaurant.

12   So when I was 14—the same age that my grandmother was when she left her family, her country, and everything she knew—I took it upon myself to teach my grandmother something, something I already knew how to do. Something with which I could give back to her some of the things she had taught me.

13   And it was slight repayment for all she taught me. How to cover the fig tree in tar paper so it could survive the winter. How to cultivate rose bushes and magnolia trees that thrived on her little piece of property. How to make baklava, and other Greek delights, working from her memory. ("Now we add some milk." "How much?" "Until we have enough.") Best of all, she had taught me my ethnic heritage.

14   First, we phonetically sounded out the alphabet. Then, we talked about vowels—English is such a difficult language to learn. I hadn't even begun to explain the different sounds "gh" could make. We were still at the basics.

15   Every afternoon, we would sit in the living room, my grandmother with an afghan covering her knees, giving up her crocheting for her reading lesson. I, with the patience that can come only from love, slowly coached her from the basic reader to the second-grade reader, giving up my telephone gossiping.

16   Years later, my grandmother still hadn't learned quite enough to sit comfortably with a newspaper or magazine, but it felt awfully good to see her try. How we used to laugh at her pronunciation mistakes. She laughed more heartily than I. I never knew whether I should laugh. Here was this old woman slowly and carefully sounding out each word, moving her lips, not saying anything aloud until she was absolutely sure, and then, loudly, proudly, happily saying, "Look at Spot. See Spot run."

17   When my grandmother died and we faced the sad task of emptying her home, I was going through her night-table drawer and came upon the basic readers. I turned the pages slowly, remembering. I put them in a paper bag, and the next day returned them to the "little kids" school. Maybe someday, some teenager will request them again, for the same task. It will make for a lifetime of memories.

EXERCISES

Details and Their Meanings

1. How old is the narrator? How old was her grandmother when she came to the United States? Why is that information significant?

2. Where did the writer's grandmother come from? What kind of place was it? What did the grandmother believe about America? Where did she settle in the United States?
3. Where did the writer get the books to teach her grandmother? Whom did she say they were for?
4. What reading level did the grandmother achieve? How long did this accomplishment take? How successful was the narrator at teaching her grandmother?
5. What jobs did the grandmother have? Which one lasted longest?
6. What kinds of things did the narrator learn from her grandmother?

Reading and Critical Thinking

1. Why do you think the granddaughter and not one of the old woman's children tried to teach the old woman?
2. Why did the grandmother need to lie in order to be allowed into America? Was the lie justified, do you think? Why or why not? If she were coming here in the 1990's instead of 1916 would she still have had to lie? Explain your opinion.
3. What does the grandmother's decision to come to America reveal about her character?
4. What factors discouraged the grandmother from learning to read well? Why was the grandmother able to read a menu but not a newspaper?
5. What is a safe generalization to make about the grandmother's desire to learn to read?
6. What do you think was the granddaughter's motivation for teaching her grandmother to read? Are grandchildren today likely to assume the responsibility of teaching their grandparents? Why or why not?

The Writer's Strategies

1. What is the significance of the title of this piece?
2. What is the effect of the first-person narration ("I," "me," "my")?
3. How does dialogue advance the narrative?
4. Why does the writer use narrative as the major organizing principle of the essay? Where do you find a narrative within the narrative? What is the effect of the writer's telling of her grandmother's life in Greece and travel to America?

5. What is the writer's main purpose? Where does the purpose become clear? What is the writer's thesis?

Thinking Together

Brainstorm to develop a list of the steps you would take if you were going to teach someone to read. What materials would you use? What homework or exercises would you assign?

Vocabulary

The following words from the selection are adverbs—that is, words that modify verbs, adjectives, or other adverbs to tell how something was done. Write a definition of each word.

1. stealthily (par. 2)
2. authoritatively (par. 4)
3. patiently (par. 5)
4. vehemently (par. 8)
5. phonetically (par. 14)
6. heartily (par. 16)

WRITER'S WORKSHOP ━━━━━━━━━━

Critical Thinking in Writing

1. Obviously, coming to America alone was very hard for the grandmother. What was the hardest thing you ever decided to do? What made it difficult? How did the situation turn out? Write a narrative in which you indicate how you faced your most difficult challenge.
2. Have you ever taught someone how to do something? What was it? What was the experience of teaching like for you? What did you find agreeable about it? What was hard or frustrating? How good a job did you do? Address some of these questions in a short essay.
3. Learning to read was a profound challenge for the old woman in this selection. What other challenges face old people in America today? Write an essay in which you describe and analyze some of these challenges.

Connecting Ideas

Read Roberto Suro's "Mexicans Come to Work but Find Dead Ends" (page 250). What details in that selection seem similar to the experience of the grandmother in "'See Spot Run'"? What generalizations about the immigrant experience can you base on this comparison?

Classrooms of Babel

Connie Leslie, with Daniel Glick and Jeanne Gordon

Connie Leslie and her co-authors describe how public education is meeting the challenge of increasing numbers of foreign-born and foreign-language-speaking children in almost all schools in the United States. Notice the different approaches that different communities take to the challenge.

KEY WORDS

Urdu (par. 1)   a major language of India and Pakistan.
Tagalog (par. 6)   a major language of the Philippines.

1   FOR PICTURE DAY AT New York's PS 217, a neighborhood elementary school in Brooklyn, the notice to parents was translated into five languages. That was a nice gesture, but insufficient: more than 40 percent of the children are immigrants whose families speak any one of 26 languages, ranging from Armenian to Urdu.

2   At the Leroy D. Feinberg Elementary School in Miami, a science teacher starts a lesson by holding up an ice cube and asking "Is it hot?" The point here is vocabulary. Only after the students who come from homes where English is not spoken learn the very basics will they move on to the question of just what an ice cube might be.

3   The first grade at Magnolia Elementary School in Lanham, Md., is a study in cooperation. A Korean boy who has been in the United States for almost a year quizzes two mainland Chinese girls who arrived 10 days ago. Nearby, a Colombian named Julio is learning to read with the help of an American-born boy.

4   In small towns and big cities, children with names like Oswaldo, Suong, Boris or Ngam are swelling the rolls in U.S. public schools, sitting side by side with Dick and Jane. Immigration in the 1980s brought an estimated 9 million foreign-born people to the United States, slightly more than the great wave of 8.8 million immigrants that came between 1901 and 1910. As a consequence, at least

2 million children or 5 percent of the total kindergarten-through-12th-grade population have limited proficiency in English, according to a conservative estimate from the U.S. Department of Education. In seven states including Colorado, New Mexico, New York and Texas, 25 percent or more of the students are not native-English speakers. And all but a handful of states have at least 1,000 foreign-born youngsters. As a result, says Eugene Garcia, of the University of California, Santa Cruz, "there is no education topic of greater importance today."

5   How to teach in a Tower of Babel? Since a 1974 Supreme Court decision, immigrant children have had the right to special help in public schools. But how much? And what kind? Many districts have responded by expanding the bilingual-education programs they've been using for the past two decades. In these classes, students are taught subjects like social studies, science and math in their native language on the theory that children must develop a firm foundation in their mother tongue before they can learn academic subjects in a new language. Proponents say that even with bilingual education it takes between four and seven years for a non-native to reach national norms on standardized tests of most subject material.

6   In most schools, it's not economically feasible to hire bilingual teachers unless there are 20 or more students who speak the same language in the same grade. Even then, there aren't many math, chemistry or biology teachers who can handle Vietnamese or Tagalog. In addition, critics like author and former Newton, Mass., teacher Rosalie Pedalino Porter argue that the typical bilingual programs for Spanish speakers used over the last two decades haven't worked. The clearest indication of the failure, she charges, is the high dropout rate for Hispanic children—35.8 percent compared with 14.9 percent for blacks and 12.7 percent for whites.

7   Bilingual classes aren't an option in a classroom where a dozen languages are spoken. In schools such as Elsik High in Houston and New York's PS 217, all immigrant children are mixed in ESL (English as a second language) classes on their grade level. ESL teachers give all instruction in English; their special training helps them work with kids who start out not knowing a single word. Some students remain in ESL classes for three or four years. Others move into regular classes but return to an ESL room for remedial periods.

8   Still other schools such as Houston's Hearne Elementary School use the "total immersion" method. With 104 of Hearne's 970 students speaking one of 23 languages, principal Judith Miller has encouraged all of her teachers to take ESL training so that immigrant youngsters can remain in classes with their native-English-speaking

peers. "The limited-English children are able to interact with their peers better and learn social skills. They also seem much happier," says Miller. Opponents see total immersion as a euphemism for "the good old days" when non-English-speaking students sank or swam in mainstream America without special treatment.

9   **Nurturing Atmosphere**   Some schools have found that immigrant parents can be a great resource, either as volunteers or hired aides. When members of New York's PS 217 Parents Association noticed that non-English-speaking families rarely made any connection with the school, they won a $10,000 grant and hired five mothers of immigrant students as outreach workers. One day each week, these women, who speak Urdu, Chinese, Russian, Haitian-Creole or Spanish, do everything from acting as interpreters at parent-teacher conferences to helping families find city services.

10   California is experimenting with "newcomer" schools that act as a one-year stopover for foreign-born children before they move on to a neighborhood school. These centers mix children of all ages in a given classroom and offer comprehensive services such as immunizations and other health care. Bellagio Road Newcomer School for grades four through eight is one of two such schools in Los Angeles. While most classrooms are Spanish bilingual, other students are taught in English. Teaching assistants who speak a variety of languages help out with translating. Principal Juliette Thompson says the aim is to provide a nurturing atmosphere for a year while the children, many of whom carry psychological scars from living in war-torn countries like El Salvador, learn some fundamentals of English. The newcomer schools seem to be working well, but they don't reach many kids. "Unfortunately," says Laurie Olsen, a project director for an advocacy group, California Tomorrow, "the real norm is far less optimistic than what you see happening in the newcomer schools."

11   A method borrowed from Canada recognizes that the problem is not one-sided. Called "two-way immersion," the program requires students to learn subject matter in both languages. Classes in the voluntary enrichment program encourage mixed groups of native speakers and English speakers to acquire new vocabulary. Public schools like PS 84 in Manhattan also use two-way immersion to attract upper-middle-class parents. Lawyer Holly Hartstone and her husband, a doctor, enrolled their 9-year-old son Adam in PS 84, where nine of the school's 25 classes are involved in voluntary Spanish two-way immersion. When Adam grows up, his parents expect that he'll live in a global community and need more than one lan-

guage. These programs are catching on around the country. Two-way immersion in Japanese, which began three years ago in a Eugene, Ore., elementary school has spread to Portland, Anchorage and Detroit. And the French program at Sunset Elementary School in Coral Gables, Fla., recently received a grant from the French government.

12   **Young Yankees**   Being a stranger in a strange land is never easy. "All the English-speaking kids should learn a foreign language. Then they'd know how hard it is for us sometimes," says 17-year-old Sufyan Kabba, a Maryland high-school junior, who left Sierra Leone last year. But here they are, part of the nation's future, young Yankees who in the end must rely on the special strength of children: adaptability.

EXERCISES

Details and Their Meanings

1. Into how many languages was the notice from PS 217 translated? Why wasn't that enough? In the first three paragraphs, what languages are mentioned or alluded to? In paragraph 4, what children's names are mentioned? What continents or parts of the world are represented by these languages and names? What do these languages and places suggest about the backgrounds of students in American classrooms who do not speak English?
2. How many immigrants came to the United States during the 1980s? What statistics indicate their impact on education? In how many states are more than one-fourth of the students not native speakers of English? Are you surprised by any of the states listed? Why or why not?
3. What obligation do the public schools have to immigrant children?
4. Describe the bilingual approach to education. How does it work? How rapidly does it work for most children? How widely is it used? What are the obstacles to providing bilingual education for all students?

5. How does ESL instruction differ from bilingual education? How does the total immersion method differ from both? What are the arguments for and against total immersion?
6. How have schools and programs used immigrant parents to help? How does the use of parents suggest that the problems faced by the schools involve more than simply teaching English vocabulary and grammar?
7. What are newcomer schools? What services do they provide? What is the idea behind them? Are they succeeding? Are they widespread?
8. What is two-way immersion? What is the concept behind it? In what kinds of neighborhoods has it been used? Is it spreading to other districts?

Reading and Critical Thinking

1. How do bilingualism, ESL, and immersion differ in concept and practice? Which do you think is the best general approach? Why?
2. To what extent does each of the various programs described seem to respond to special sets of conditions or to the general problem of students whose first language is not English? Which program seems to provide the most help? Which seems most appropriate for the conditions it is addressing?
3. Why is immersion compared to "the good old days"? Do you think those days were really good? What is wrong or right with letting students sink or swim? Do you think immersion really is the same as "the good old days"? How is the idea expressed in paragraph 12, relying on children's adaptability, the same as or different from the strategy of letting them sink or swim?
4. Do you think two-way immersion is a good idea? Has it been succeeding? What goals has it served for which children? For those who are not English-speakers, does it offer the same advantages and disadvantages as total immersion or does it work differently? Would you like to have been a participant in such a program? How does two-way immersion compare to newcomer schools in terms of goals, the children served, and the neighborhoods served? Why do you think two-way immersion is spreading and newcomer schools are not?
5. Do you think special services should be provided to immigrant children? What services (if any) would you support?

6. The United States has always been considered a land of opportunity for immigrants. In recent years, what has changed to cast a shadow on this view of America? Do you agree that a record number of immigrant children poses one of the greatest problems for American education? Why or why not?

7. Why do you think Sufyan Kabba says in paragraph 12 that English-speaking children should have to learn a foreign language? Do you agree? Why or why not?

8. Where does the final statement of the essay place responsibility for children's success in American schools? Do you agree with the point made there? Does the last sentence undermine all that has gone before? Does it free the educational system of responsibility? Or is it an accurate statement, in your view? Where do you believe the responsibility for learning should lie? How should that responsibility be divided among the system, the children, and the parents?

The Writer's Strategies

1. With what incident does the selection open? In what ways is that incident striking or memorable? How does the incident serve to introduce the issues raised in the piece? What would you say is the writers' thesis?

2. What is the main idea of the first four paragraphs? Where is it stated most directly? How does the opening sentence of paragraph 5 change the focus of the essay? How many questions are asked in paragraph 5?

3. To what extent and in what way are the questions posed in paragraph 5 answered in the rest of the selection? Are the writers concerned more with presenting the problem or with providing definite answers? What phrases or statements indicate their attitude toward providing definite answers?

4. Where do the writers provide lists of foreign names and foreign languages? How do these lists illustrate the ideas of the essay? How are they related to its title?

5. Where, other than in the title, is Babel mentioned? What is the Tower of Babel? Why have the writers used this image? Is it fair or appropriate to use the Tower of Babel as a major image for this piece?

6. How many school programs are described? Why do the writers show so many?

7. Why does the closing paragraph turn from discussing programs to considering the attitudes of individual students? Should the

writers have used this strategy earlier and more completely, or should they not have used it at all? How does the ending shift the point of the entire piece?

Thinking Together

In small groups, share your memories of classmates who did not speak English well. How did they succeed at their schoolwork? What kinds of difficulties did they seem to have? Try to put yourself in the shoes of these children. If you yourself are not a native speaker of English, describe your own memories and feelings. After group discussion, each group member should write a paragraph that describes an immigrant child's struggles and ends by saying what the school did or could have done to ease the movement of the child into the educational mainstream.

Vocabulary

Define each of the italicized words, using hints from the context in which the word appears.

1. a nice gesture, but *insufficient* (par. 1)
2. limited *proficiency* in English (par. 4)
3. *Proponents* say that even with *bilingual* education (par. 5)
4. Opponents see total *immersion* as a *euphemism* for "the good old days" (par. 8)
5. hired five mothers of immigrant students as *outreach* workers (par. 9)
6. offer *comprehensive* services such as *immunizations* (par. 10)
7. provide a *nurturing* atmosphere for a year (par. 10)
8. project director for an *advocacy* group (par. 10)

WRITER'S WORKSHOP ———————

Critical Thinking in Writing

1. Write a paragraph describing what you think would be the best way to bring a student who is not a native speaker of English into the U.S. education system.

2. In a one-page essay, explain why you believe bilingual education, total immersion, or ESL instruction is the best general approach to educating immigrant children.
3. In one paragraph, describe the diversity of nationalities and language experiences of children in a school that you or someone you know attended.

Connecting Ideas

Write a few paragraphs comparing how the programs described in "Classrooms of Babel" would try to overcome or otherwise deal with the kinds of pressures on immigrant children described by Margaret A. Gibson in "Cultural Barriers and the Press to Americanize" (page 65). In what ways do the different programs create a bridge between cultures or erect new barriers that students must overcome on their own?

Minority, Racial, and Ethnic Groups

Richard T. Schaefer

Richard T. Schaefer, dean of the College of Arts and Sciences and professor of sociology at Western Illinois University, provides sociological definitions of minority, race, ethnicity, *and other terms.*

KEY WORDS

intermingling (par. 9)   blending together.

buffoons (par. 12)   fools.

deviant (par. 13)   abnormal, not in keeping with community standards.

innate (par. 16)   possessed at birth.

categorization (par. 20)   assignment of a place in some order.

stratification (par. 20)   arrangement according to status from highest to lowest.

---

1   SOCIOLOGISTS FREQUENTLY DISTINGUISH BETWEEN racial and ethnic groups. The term *racial group* is used to describe a group which is set apart from others because of obvious physical differences. Whites, blacks, and Asian Americans are all considered racial groups within the United States. Unlike racial groups, an *ethnic group* is set apart from others primarily because of its national origin or distinctive cultural patterns. In the United States, Puerto Ricans, Jews, and Polish Americans are all categorized as ethnic groups.

Minority Groups

2   A numerical minority is a group that makes up less than half of some larger population. The population of the United States includes

thousands of numerical minorities, including television actors, green-eyed people, tax lawyers, and descendants of the Pilgrims who arrived on the *Mayflower*. However, these numerical minorities are not considered to be minorities in the sociological sense; in fact, the number of people in a group does not necessarily determine its status as a social minority (or dominant group). When sociologists define a minority group, they are primarily concerned with the economic and political power, or powerlessness, of that group. A *minority group* is a subordinate group whose members have significantly less control or power over their own lives than the members of a dominant or majority group have over theirs.

3   In certain instances, a group which constitutes a numerical majority can still be a minority group in sociological terms. For example, the city of Gary, Indiana, has a majority black population (71 percent in 1980) and has had black mayors since 1968. Yet it would be incorrect to conclude that this industrial city is genuinely controlled by its black majority. Lawyer Edward Greer (1979) has convincingly shown that Gary remains ruled by outside, white-dominated organizations such as U.S. Steel, financial institutions, and chain stores. Thus, in terms of their degree of power, Gary's black citizens continue to function as a minority group.

4   Sociologists have identified five basic properties of a minority group—physical or cultural traits, unequal treatment, ascribed status, solidarity, and in-group marriage (M. Harris, 1958: 4–11):

1. Members of a minority group share physical or cultural characteristics that distinguish them from the dominant group. Each society has its own arbitrary standard for determining which characteristics are most important in defining dominant and minority groups.
2. Members of a minority experience unequal treatment and have less power over their lives than members of a dominant group have over theirs. For example, the management of an apartment complex may refuse to rent to blacks, Hispanics, or Jews. Social inequality may be created or maintained by prejudice, discrimination, segregation, or even extermination.
3. Membership in a dominant (or minority) group is not voluntary; people are born into the group. Thus, race and ethnicity are considered *ascribed* statuses.
4. Minority group members have a strong sense of group solidarity. William Graham Sumner, writing in 1906, noted that individuals make distinctions between members of their own group (the *in-group*) and everyone else (the *out-group*). When a group is

the object of long-term prejudice and discrimination, the feeling of "us versus them" can and often does become extremely intense.

5. Members of a minority generally marry others from the same group. A member of a dominant group is often unwilling to join a supposedly inferior minority by marrying one of its members. In addition, the minority group's sense of solidarity encourages marriages within the group and discourages marriages to outsiders.

Race

5 As already suggested, the term *racial group* is reserved for those minorities (and the corresponding dominant groups) set apart from others by obvious physical differences. But what is an "obvious" physical difference? Each society determines which differences are important while ignoring other characteristics that could serve as a basis for social differentiation. In the United States, differences in both skin color and hair color are generally quite obvious. Yet Americans learn informally that differences in skin color have a dramatic social and political meaning, while differences in hair color are not nearly so socially significant.

6 When observing skin color, Americans tend to lump people rather casually into such general racial categories as "black," "white," and "Asian." More subtle differences in skin complexion often go unnoticed. However, this is not the case in other societies. In Brazil, numerous categories are used to classify and identify people on the basis of skin color. An individual can be called *branco, cabra, moreno, mulato, escuro,* and so forth (van den Berghe, 1978:71). As a result, Americans must recognize that what we see as "obvious" differences are subject to each society's social definitions.

7 The largest racial minorities in the United States are blacks, American Indians, Japanese Americans, Chinese Americans, and other Asian peoples. Information about the population and distribution of racial groups in this country is presented in Table 1.

8 **Biological Significance of Race**   Biologically, race has a very precise meaning. A *race* is a category of people who, through many generations of inbreeding, have developed common physical characteristics that distinguish them from other humans. Contrary to popular belief, there are no "pure races." Nor are there physical traits—whether skin color or baldness—that can be used to describe one group to the exclusion of all others. If scientists examine a smear of

TABLE 1   Racial and Ethnic Groups in the United States, 1980

Classification	Number in Thousands	Percent of Total Population	Geographical Distribution, %
Racial groups			
Native whites	155,844	76.7	
Blacks	26,488	11.7	South, 53
American Indians	1,418	0.6	West, 49
Chinese	806	0.4	California, 40
Filipinos	775	0.3	California, 46; Hawaii, 31
Japanese	701	0.3	California, 37; Hawaii, 34
Asian Indians	362	0.2	New York, 17; California, 16
Koreans	355	0.2	California, 29
Vietnamese	262	0.1	California, 34; Texas, 11
Hawaiians	167	0.1	Hawaii, 69
Samoans/Guamanians	74	0.01	California, 51
Ethnic groups			
White ancestry			
Germans	17,160	7.9	
British and Scottish	13,116	6.1	
Irish	9,760	4.5	
Italians	6,110	2.8	
Poles	3,498	1.6	
French	3,047	1.4	
Jews	5,925	2.6	
Hispanics	13,244	5.8	
Mexican Americans	7,932	3.5	
Puerto Ricans	1,823	0.8	
Cubans	831	0.4	
Total (all groups)	226,505		

NOTE: Percentages do not total 100 percent, and subheads do not add up to figures in major heads, since overlap between groups exists (e.g., Polish American Jews). Therefore, numbers and percentages should be considered approximations. Data on white ancestry are for 1979.
SOURCES: Bureau of the Census, 1981a, 1981b: 55–56, 1981c: 32; Himmelfarb and Singer, 1981. Racial and ethnic groups vary in number and distribution. Some groups, such as Japanese Americans, are highly concentrated in particular regions of the United States.

human blood under a microscope, they cannot tell whether it came from a Chinese or a Navajo, a Hawaiian or a black.

9   Migration, exploration, and invasion have further compromised the maintenance of pure races and led to increased racial intermingling. Scientific investigations suggest that the proportion of North American blacks with white ancestry ranges from 20 percent to as much as 75 percent (Herskovits, 1930:15; D. Roberts, 1975). Such statistics undermine a fundamental assumption of American life: that we can accurately categorize individuals as "white" or as "black."

10   Some people wish to find biological explanations which would help us to understand why certain peoples of the world have come to dominate others. Given the absence of pure racial groups, there can be no satisfactory biological answers for such social and political questions.

11   **Social Significance of Race**   One of the most crucial aspects of the relationship between dominant and subordinate groups is the ability of the dominant or majority group to define a society's values. American sociologist William I. Thomas (1923: 41–44), an early critic of theories of racial and gender differences, saw that the "definition of the situation" could mold the personality of the individual. To put it another way, Thomas, writing from the interactionist perspective, observed that people respond not only to the objective features of a situation or person but also to the meaning that situation or person has for them. Thus we can create false images or stereotypes that become real in their consequences. *Stereotypes* are unreliable generalizations about all members of a group which do not recognize individual differences within the group.

12   In the last 20 years, there has been growing awareness of the power of the mass media to introduce stereotypes into everyday life. As one result, stereotyping of racial and ethnic minorities in Hollywood films and on television has come under increasing fire. For example, Asian American community groups in several American cities led picketing and boycotts of a 1985 film, *Year of the Dragon*, which portrayed Chinese Americans as violent killers and dope peddlers (Butterfield, 1985; Fong-Torres, 1986; Hwang, 1985). Hispanics recall that Hollywood has traditionally presented them as vicious bandits, lazy peasants, or humorous buffoons (Beale, 1984; Lichter et al., 1987). Similarly, Jack Shaheen (1984:52, 1988) is critical of prime-time television for perpetuating four myths about Arabs: "They are fabulously wealthy; they are barbaric and uncultured; they are sex maniacs with a penchant for white slavery; and they are prone to terrorist acts." While the use of stereotyping can promote in-group solidarity, conflict theorists point out that stereotypes contribute to prejudice and thereby assist the subordination of minority groups (Schaefer, 1988:65–68).

13   In certain situations, we may respond to stereotypes and act on them, with the result that false definitions become accurate. This is known as the *self-fulfilling prophecy*. A person or group is described as having particular characteristics and then begins to display the very traits that were said to exist. In assessing the impact of self-fulfilling prophecies, we can refer back to labeling theory, which em-

phasizes how a person comes to be labeled as deviant and even to accept a self-image of deviance.

14   Self-fulfilling prophecies can be especially devastating for minority groups (see Figure 1). Such groups often find that they are allowed to hold only low-paying jobs with little prestige or opportunity for advancement. The rationale of the dominant society is that these members of a minority lack the ability to perform in more important and lucrative positions. Minority group members are then denied the training needed to become scientists, executives, or physicians and are locked into society's inferior jobs. As a result, the false definition has become real: in terms of employment, the minority has become inferior because it was originally defined as inferior and was prevented from achieving equality.

15   Because of this vicious circle, talented people from minority groups may come to see the worlds of entertainment and professional sports as their only hope for achieving wealth and fame. Thus, it is no accident that successive waves of Irish, Jewish, Italian, black, and Hispanic performers and athletes have made their mark on American society. Unfortunately, these very successes may convince

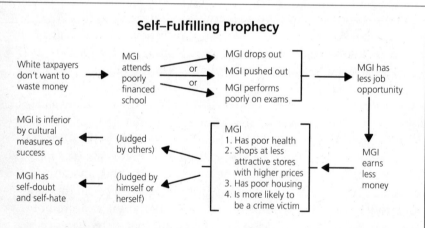

Self–Fulfilling Prophecy

NOTE: MGI stands for "minority group individual." Arrows represent direction of negative cumulative effect.
SOURCE: Schaefer, 1988: 25; see also Daniels and Kitano, 1970:21.

Figure 1 *The self-validating effects of definitions made by the dominant group are shown in this figure. A minority-group person attends a poorly financed school and is left unequipped to perform jobs which offer high status and pay. He or she then gets a low-paying job and must settle for a lifestyle far short of society's standards. Since the person shares these standards, he or she may begin to feel self-doubt and self-hatred. This aspect of the cycle has been called into question in recent research.*

the dominant group that its original stereotypes are valid—that these are the only areas of society in which minorities can excel. Furthermore, athletics and the arts are well known in our society as highly competitive arenas. For every Fernando Valenzuela, Bill Cosby, or Oprah Winfrey who "makes it," many, many more will end up disappointed (Allport, 1979:189–205; Merton, 1968:475–490; Myrdal, 1944:75–78, 1065–1070; M. Snyder, 1982).

16   Sociologist Harry Edwards (1984:8–13)—appointed in 1987 by baseball commissioner Peter Ueberroth to assist in the hiring of more minorities for high-level jobs—agrees that the self-fulfilling prophecy of "innate black athletic superiority" can have damaging consequences. Edwards points out that although this perception of athletic prowess may cause many black Americans to be channeled into sports, at best, only about 2500 of them currently make a living in professional sports as players, coaches, trainers, team doctors, and executives. In his view, blacks should no longer "put playbooks ahead of textbooks," and the black community should abandon its "blind belief in sport as an extraordinary route to social and economic salvation."

17   Blacks and other minorities are not always passive victims of harmful stereotypes and self-fulfilling prophecies. In the 1960s and 1970s, many subordinate minorities in the United States rejected traditional definitions and replaced them with feelings of pride, power, and strength. "Black is beautiful" and "red power" movements among blacks and American Indians were efforts to take control of their own lives and self-images. However, although a minority can make a determined effort to redefine a situation and resist stereotypes, the definition that remains most important is the one used by a society's most powerful groups. In this sense, the historic white, Anglo-Saxon, Protestant norms of the United States still shape the definitions and stereotypes of racial and ethnic minorities (Baughman, 1971:37–55).

18   **Ethnicity**   An ethnic group, unlike a racial group, is set apart from others because of its national origin or distinctive cultural patterns. Among the ethnic groups in the United States are peoples referred to collectively as *Hispanics,* such as Puerto Ricans, Mexican Americans, Cubans, and other Latin Americans (see Table 1). Other ethnic groups in this country include Jewish, Irish, Polish, Italian, and Norwegian Americans.

19   The distinction between racial and ethnic minorities is not always clear-cut. Some members of racial minorities, such as Asian Americans, may have significant cultural differences from other

groups. At the same time, certain ethnic minorities, such as Hispanics, may have obvious physical differences which set them apart from other Americans.

20   Despite such problems of categorization, sociologists continue to feel that the distinction between racial and ethnic groups is socially significant. In most societies, including the United States, physical differences tend to be more visible than ethnic differences. Partly as a result of this fact, stratification along racial lines is less subject to change than stratification along ethnic lines. Members of an ethnic minority sometimes can, over time, become indistinguishable from the majority—though it may take generations and may never include all members of the group. By contrast, members of a racial minority find it much more difficult to blend in with the larger society and gain acceptance from the majority.

EXERCISES

Details and Their Meanings

1. According to Richard T. Schaefer, what is the key difference between racial groups and ethnic groups? Does the writer identify Hispanics as a racial or an ethnic group? Why?
2. What do sociologists mean when they use the expression *minority group*? Distinguish between a numerical minority and a minority group of interest to sociologists.
3. If Gary, Indiana, is at least 71 percent black, why aren't blacks considered the dominant group in that city? What are the major features that define a minority group?
4. Which groups are the largest racial minorities in the United States? If a scientist analyzed blood samples from different racial groups, which groups could he or she correctly identify? What makes the identification possible or stands in its way?
5. According to the writer, what defines an individual in the United States as black? How does the classification of skin color in Brazil differ from that in the United States?
6. Which group in the United States is historically dominant? What role does the majority group serve in a nation? What roles do stereotypes play in keeping groups dominant?

7. According to the writer, why do some racial or ethnic groups seem to excel in some areas, such as sports or entertainment, but not in other areas?

Reading and Critical Thinking

1. Why does the writer suggest that prejudice and discrimination are necessary ingredients to the creation of a minority group? What do you think happens to minorities who are not discriminated against?
2. Why do people tend to marry within their own ethnic or racial groups? What happens when they do not? Do you think it is possible for society to change the way it views intermarriage? Why or why not? What view do you or your friends and relatives hold about intermarriage?
3. Why do you think there are so few skin-color categories in the United States? Why does Brazil have so many?
4. Why can't biology provide answers to the question of why some groups dominate others? Can you imagine a society without dominant groups? What would it be like?
5. In the past, what impact did Hollywood have on notions of ethnic and racial identity? In what ways (if any) has Hollywood's portrayal of racial and ethnic groups changed in recent years?
6. What advice would the writer give to a young minority man or woman who is planning a career in sports? What is misleading about the apparent domination of some sports by certain ethnic groups?
7. What is a fair conclusion about the absence of some minority groups among the ranks of scientists or business executives? If you could, would you attempt to change this situation? Why or why not?
8. Why is it reasonable to predict that some Hispanics will assimilate into the majority faster than will some members of other groups?

The Writer's Strategies

1. What is the thesis of this selection? What primary rhetorical strategy does Shaefer use to advance his point?
2. Who do you think is the audience for this selection? How can you tell?

3. What is the writer's purpose in including Table 1 (page 182)? What is his purpose in including Figure 1 (page 184)? How do the table and figure differ?
4. Why does the writer cite other authors, such as van den Berghe in paragraph 6? Where else does he cite others?
5. How much of this piece is the writer's opinion? Where do you find examples of opinion?
6. Where does Schaefer state his main purpose in writing this selection? What is his purpose? Who is the intended audience? How can you tell?
7. Where does the writer state his conclusion? What is it?

Thinking Together

Schaefer says that sometimes ethnic or racial stereotypes are adopted by minority groups in a sort of self-fulfilling prophecy. Working with two to four of your classmates, discuss whether you agree with this observation. How can stereotypes become self-fulfilling? Do you accept Schaefer's explanation that ethnic and racial stereotypes are the inventions of dominant groups and are ascribed to minorities as a means of keeping them subordinate? Discuss your group's answers with your other classmates.

Vocabulary

The following terms are used in the text. Write a definition of each.

1. dominant group (par. 2)
2. subordinate group (par. 2)
3. ascribed status (par. 4)
4. in-group (par. 4)
5. out-group (par. 4)
6. stereotype (par. 11)
7. self-fulfilling prophecy (par. 13)
8. stratification (par. 20)

WRITER'S WORKSHOP ────────────

Critical Thinking in Writing

1. Write a summary of this selection by Schaefer. Once you have the main points clearly on paper write a short essay about the is-

sues as if you were explaining them to elementary school children—sixth graders, say.

2. Schaefer says that replacing negative stereotypes with power,
   pride, and strength is a good way to overcome self-fulfilling
   prophecies. Write an essay in which you describe your ethnic or
   racial group in terms of things that you take pride in. What
   about your group is admirable, noble, and notable?

3. Choose a term from the vocabulary list given above—in-group,
   out-group, stereotype, subordinate group—or choose any other
   interesting term from the selection, and write your own definition paper. Draw on your own experiences or on what you have
   read.

Connecting Ideas

Read Marcus Maybry's "Confronting Campus Racism" (page 350).
How does Schaefer's definition of prejudice apply in Maybry's
essay? Who are the in-groups and out-groups in Maybry's piece?
How are the in-groups trying to ascribe behavior to the out-groups?
What information in the Schaefer selection might help campus
groups to understand each other better?

Women's Language

Robin Lakoff

*Robin Lakoff, professor of linguistics at the University of California
at Berkeley, has written both scholarly and general-interest works,
including* Abstract Syntax, Language and Woman's Place, *and*
Face Value: The Politics of Beauty. *In this selection, she describes
the problems imposed on women by the English language.*

KEY WORDS

elicit (par. 7)   to bring out.
subliminal (par. 10)   repressed or intuitive.
requisite (par. 10)   necessary, required by circumstances.
idiosyncrasies (par. 12)   quirks, peculiarities.
derogatory (par. 13)   belittling, insulting.
denigrates (par. 20)   slanders, brings down.
paramour (par. 23)   lover.
consummate (par. 23)   complete, total.
faux pas (par. 25)   French expression meaning a mistake, a
   false step.

1   "WOMEN'S LANGUAGE" IS THAT pleasant (dainty?), euphemistic, never-
aggressive way of talking we learned as little girls. Cultural bias
was built into the language we were allowed to speak, the subjects
we were allowed to speak about, and the ways we were spoken of.
Having learned our linguistic lesson well, we go out in the world,
only to discover that we are communicative cripples—damned if
we do, and damned if we don't.

2   If we refuse to talk "like a lady," we are ridiculed and criticized
for being unfeminine. ("She thinks like a man" is, at best, a left-
handed compliment.) If we do learn all the fuzzy-headed, unasser-
tive language of our sex, we are ridiculed for being unable to think
clearly, unable to take part in a serious discussion, and therefore un-
fit to hold a position of power.

3   It doesn't take much of this for a woman to begin feeling she de-
serves such treatment because of inadequacies in her own intelligence and education.

4   "Women's language" shows up in all levels of English. For example, women are encouraged and allowed to make far more precise discriminations in naming colors than men do. Words like
mauve, beige, ecru, aquamarine, lavender, and so on, are unremarkable
in a woman's active vocabulary, but largely absent from that of most
men. I know of no evidence suggesting that women actually *see* a
wider range of colors than men do. It is simply that fine discriminations of this sort are relevant to women's vocabularies, but not to
men's; to men, who control most of the interesting affairs of the
world, such distinctions are trivial—irrelevant.

5   In the area of syntax, we find similar gender-related peculiarities of speech. There is one construction, in particular, that women
use conversationally far more than men: the tag-question. A tag is
midway between an outright statement and a yes-no question; it is
less assertive than the former, but more confident than the latter.

6   A *flat statement* indicates confidence in the speaker's knowledge
and is fairly certain to be believed; a *question* indicates a lack of
knowledge on some point and implies that the gap in the speaker's
knowledge can and will be remedied by an answer. For example, if,
at a Little League game, I have had my glasses off, I can legitimately
ask someone else: "Was the player out at third?" A *tag-question*, being intermediate between statement and question, is used when the
speaker is stating a claim, but lacks full confidence in the truth of
that claim. So if I say, "Is Joan here?" I will probably not be surprised
if my respondent answers "no"; but if I say, "Joan is here, isn't she?"
instead, chances are I am already biased in favor of a positive answer, wanting only confirmation. I still want a response, but I have
enough knowledge (or think I have) to predict that response. A tag-
question, then, might be thought of as a statement that doesn't demand to be believed by anyone but the speaker, a way of giving lee-
way, of not forcing the addressee to go along with the views of the
speaker.

7   Another common use of the tag-question is in small talk when
the speaker is trying to elicit conversation: "Sure is hot here, isn't
it?"

8   But in discussing personal feelings or opinions, only the speaker
normally has any way of knowing the correct answer. Sentences
such as "I have a headache, don't I?" are clearly ridiculous. But there
are other examples where it is the speaker's opinions, rather than

perceptions, for which corroboration is sought, as in "The situation in Southeast Asia is terrible, isn't it?"

9   While there are, of course, other possible interpretations of a sentence like this, one possibility is that the speaker has a particular answer in mind—"yes" or "no"—but is reluctant to state it baldly. This sort of tag-question is much more apt to be used by women than by men in conversation. Why is this the case?

10   The tag-question allows a speaker to avoid commitment, and thereby avoid conflict with the addressee. The problem is that, by so doing, speakers may also give the impression of not really being sure of themselves, or looking to the addressee for confirmation of their views. This uncertainty is reinforced in more subliminal ways, too. There is a peculiar sentence intonation-pattern, used almost exclusively by women, as far as I know, which changes a declarative answer into a question. The effect of using the rising inflection typical of a yes-no question is to imply that the speaker is seeking confirmation, even though the speaker is clearly the only one who has the requisite information, which is why the question was put to her in the first place:

(Q) When will dinner be ready?
(A) Oh . . . around six o'clock . . . ?

11   It is as though the second speaker were saying, "Six o'clock—if that's okay with you, if you agree." The person being addressed is put in the position of having to provide confirmation. One likely consequence of this sort of speech-pattern in a woman is that, often unbeknownst to herself, the speaker builds a reputation of tentativeness, and others will refrain from taking her seriously or trusting her with any real responsibilities, since she "can't make up her mind," and "isn't sure of herself."

12   Such idiosyncrasies may explain why women's language sounds much more "polite" than men's. It is polite to leave a decision open, not impose your mind, or views, or claims, on anyone else. So a tag-question is a kind of polite statement, in that it does not force agreement or belief on the addressee. In the same way a request is a polite command, in that it does not force obedience on the addressee, but rather suggests something be done as a favor to the speaker. A clearly stated order implies a threat of certain consequences if it is not followed, and—even more impolite—implies that the speaker is in a superior position and able to enforce the order. By couching wishes in the form of a request, on the other hand, a speaker implies that if the request is not carried out, only the speaker will suffer; noncompliance cannot harm the addressee. So the deci-

sion is really left up to the addressee. The distinction becomes clear in these examples:

> Close the door.
> Please close the door.
> Will you close the door?
> Will you please close the door?
> Won't you close the door?

13   In the same ways as words and speech patterns used *by* women undermine their image, those used *to describe* women make matters even worse. Often a word may be used of both men and women (and perhaps of things as well); but when it is applied to women, it assumes a special meaning that, by implications rather than outright assertion, is derogatory to women as a group.

14   The use of euphemisms has this effect. A euphemism is a substitute for a word that has acquired a bad connotation by association with something unpleasant or embarrassing. But almost as soon as the new word comes into common usage, it takes on the same old bad connotations, since feelings about the things or people referred to are not altered by a change of name; thus new euphemisms must be constantly found.

15   There is one euphemism for *woman* still very much alive. The word, of course, is *lady. Lady* has a masculine counterpart, namely *gentleman*, occasionally shortened to *gent*. But for some reason *lady* is very much commoner than *gent(leman)*.

16   The decision to use *lady* rather than *woman*, or vice versa, may considerably alter the sense of a sentence, as the following examples show:

> (a) A woman (lady) I know is a dean at Berkeley.
> (b) A woman (lady) I know makes amazing things out of shoelaces and old boxes.

17   The use of *lady* in (a) imparts a frivolous, or nonserious, tone to the sentence: the matter under discussion is not one of great moment. Similarly, in (b), using *lady* here would suggest that the speaker considered the "amazing things" not to be serious art, but merely a hobby or an aberration. If *woman* is used, she might be a serious sculptor. To say *lady doctor* is very condescending, since no one ever says *gentleman doctor* or even *man doctor*. For example, mention in the San Francisco *Chronicle* of January 31, 1972, of Madalyn Murray O'Hair as the *lady atheist* reduces her position to that of scatterbrained eccentric. Even *woman atheist* is scarcely defensible: sex is irrelevant to her philosophical position.

18   Many women argue that, on the other hand, *lady* carries with it overtones recalling the age of chivalry: conferring exalted stature on the person so referred to. This makes the term seem polite at first, but we must also remember that these implications are perilous: they suggest that a "lady" is helpless, and cannot do things by herself.

19   *Lady* can also be used to infer frivolousness, as in titles of organizations. Those that have a serious purpose (not merely that of enabling "the ladies" to spend time with one another) cannot use the word *lady* in their titles, but less serious ones may. Compare the *Ladies' Auxiliary* of a men's group, or the *Thursday Evening Ladies' Browning and Garden Society* with *Ladies' Liberation* or *Ladies' Strike for Peace*.

20   What is curious about this split is that *lady* is in origin a euphemism—a substitute that puts a better face on something people find uncomfortable—for *woman*. What kind of euphemism is it that subtly denigrates the people to whom it refers? Perhaps *lady* functions as a euphemism for *woman* because it does not contain the sexual implications present in *woman:* it is not "embarrassing" in that way. If this is so, we may expect that, in the future, *lady* will replace *woman* as the primary word for the human female, since *woman* will have become too blatantly sexual. That this distinction is already made in some contexts at least is shown in the following examples, where you can try replacing *woman* with *lady:*

   (a) She's only twelve, but she's already a woman.
   (b) After ten years in jail, Harry wanted to find a woman.
   (c) She's my woman, see, so don't mess around with her.

21   Another common substitute for *woman* is *girl*. One seldom hears a man past the age of adolescence referred to as a boy, save in expressions like "going out with the boys," which are meant to suggest an air of adolescent frivolity and irresponsibility. But women of all ages are "girls": one can have a man—not a boy—Friday, but only a girl—never a woman or even a lady—Friday; women have girlfriends, but men do not—in a nonsexual sense—have boyfriends. It may be that this use of *girl* is euphemistic in the same way the use of *lady* is: in stressing the idea of immaturity, it removes the sexual connotations lurking in *woman. Girl* brings to mind irresponsibility: you don't send a girl to do a woman's errand (or even, for that matter, a boy's errand). She is a person who is both too immature and too far from real life to be entrusted with responsibilities or with decisions of any serious or important nature.

22   Now let's take a pair of words which, in terms of the possible relationships in an earlier society, were simple male-female equivalents, analogous to *bull:cow*. Suppose we find that, for independent reasons, society has changed in such a way that the original meanings now are irrelevant. Yet the words have not been discarded, but have acquired new meanings, metaphorically related to their original senses. But suppose these new metaphorical uses are no longer parallel to each other. By seeing where the parallelism breaks down, we discover something about the different roles played by men and women in this culture. One good example of such a divergence through time is found in the pair, *master:mistress*. Once used with reference to one's power over servants, these words have become unusable today in their original master-servant sense as the relationship has become less prevalent in our society. But the words are still common.

23   Unless used with reference to animals, *master* now generally refers to a man who has acquired consummate ability in some field, normally nonsexual. But its feminine counterpart cannot be used this way. It is practically restricted to its sexual sense of "paramour." We start out with two terms, both roughly paraphrasable as "one who has power over another." But the masculine form, once one person is no longer able to have absolute power over another, becomes usable metaphorically in the sense of "having power over *something*." *Master* requires as its object only the name of some activity, something inanimate and abstract. But *mistress* requires a masculine noun in the possessive to precede it. One cannot say: "Rhonda is a mistress." One must be *someone's* mistress. A man is defined by what he does, a woman by her sexuality, that is, in terms of one particular aspect of her relationship to men. It is one thing to be an *old master* like Hans Holbein, and another to be an *old mistress*.

24   The same is true of the words *spinster* and *bachelor*—gender words for "one who is not married." The resemblance ends with the definition. While *bachelor* is a neuter term, often used as a compliment, *spinster* normally is used pejoratively, with connotations of prissiness, fussiness, and so on. To be a bachelor implies that one has the choice of marrying or not, and this is what makes the idea of a bachelor existence attractive, in the popular literature. He has been pursued and has successfully eluded his pursuers. But a spinster is one who has not been pursued, or at least not seriously. She is old, unwanted goods. The metaphorical connotations of *bachelor* generally suggest sexual freedom; of *spinster*, puritanism or celibacy.

25   These examples could be multiplied. It is generally considered a *faux pas*, in society, to congratulate a woman on her engagement,

while it is correct to congratulate her fiancé. Why is this? The reason seems to be that it is impolite to remind people of things that may be uncomfortable to them. To congratulate a woman on her engagement is really to say, "Thank goodness! You had a close call." For the man, on the other hand, there was no such danger. His choosing to marry is viewed as a good thing, but not something essential.

26   The linguistic double standard holds throughout the life of the relationship. After marriage, bachelor and spinster become man and wife, not man and woman. The woman whose husband dies remains "John's widow"; John, however, is never "Mary's widower."

27   Finally, why is it that salesclerks and others are so quick to call women customers "dear," "honey," and other terms of endearment they really have no business using? A male customer would never put up with it. But women, like children, are supposed to enjoy these endearments, rather than being offended by them.

28   In more ways than one, it's time to speak up.

EXERCISES

Details and Their Meanings

1. At what age do women begin to learn a distinct form of speech?
2. What kinds of sentences are women most likely to use? What impression are these sentences likely to give?
3. According to Robin Lakoff, what is the purpose of euphemisms in forms of address for women? Why are new euphemisms constantly needed?
4. According to the writer, why have originally parallel words like *master* and *mistress* or *spinster* and *bachelor* evolved into distinct, gender-specific words? How do they now convey different meanings?
5. In polite society, which sex is to be congratulated for getting engaged? What is the reasoning behind this distinction?
6. What does the writer mean by the phrase "linguistic double standard"?

Reading and Critical Thinking

1. Who is responsible for teaching women the rules of speaking "like a lady"? Where does the writer give you this information?

2. According to the writer, how does "women's language" reinforce negative images of women? What do women conclude about themselves on the basis of language? What aspects of "men's language" that you have heard reinforce negative images of women?
3. What reason can you give for "women's language" sounding more "polite" than men's. Is politeness more necessary for women than for men? Why or why not?
4. How does the use of the world *girl* deprive women of status? What other words also reduce a woman's power? Are there similar words that reduce men's power? What are they?
5. According to the writer, why is it inappropriate to call Sandra Day O'Connor "a woman Supreme Court justice"? Why is that use of *woman* condescending?

The Writer's Strategies

1. What is the thesis of this selection? Where is it stated?
2. What is Lakoff's attitude toward her topic? How can you tell?
3. Why does the writer list sample sentences in paragraphs 12, 16, and 20?
4. Where does the writer give examples of euphemisms?
5. Where does Lakoff state facts? Where does she express conclusions?
6. What is the conclusion of this essay? What new idea is introduced in the conclusion?

Thinking Together

Go to a place in which you can overhear men and women speaking. Likely places are your school's cafeteria, hallways, or quad, but any social situation will do. Listen to differences in the ways men and women speak. Make a list of how often you hear tag-questions and flat statements; also list the forms of address men and women use when speaking to each other. Then in class compare your results. What valid conclusions can you draw from your observations? Which of your conclusions support Lakoff's?

Vocabulary

The following terms from the selection relate to speech. Some are defined in the text, but others you may need to look up. Write a definition of each.

1. euphemistic (par. 1)
2. left-handed compliment (par. 2)
3. tag-question (par. 5)
4. flat statement (par. 6)
5. intonation-pattern (par. 10)
6. declarative answer (par. 10)
7. overtones (par. 18)
8. metaphorical (par. 22)
9. neuter (par. 24)
10. pejoratively (par. 24)

WRITER'S WORKSHOP ━━━━━━━━━━━━━

Critical Thinking in Writing

1. Do you feel that words like *dear, girl,* and *lady* really have a negative impact on women, or is their use harmless? Write a letter to Robin Lakoff in which you present your ideas on terms of address and the ways in which they influence how men and women think about themselves and each other.
2. The current generation of college students has been called "the post-feminist generation," by which is meant that young women today no longer feel a pressing need to assert their equality. Does that label imply that women have given up the fight for equal rights or that the major battles for equality have been won? Defend your answer in a well-detailed essay.
3. Write a narrative essay about an occasion in which you were called an offensive name. How did this experience affect the way you thought about yourself?

Connecting Ideas

Read Elizabeth Wong's "The Struggle to Be an All-American Girl" (page 32). How are the issues of language that Wong raises similar to or different from the issues raised by Lakoff? How would Lakoff feel about the use of the word *girl* in Wong's title? Why?

If Black English Isn't a Language . . . What Is?

James Baldwin

From the 1950s until his death in 1988, James Baldwin was one of the most eloquent voices on the subject of race relations. He made important contributions in fiction and essay-writing, including Gio-vanni's Room (1956) and The Fire Next Time (1963). In this essay, he defends the status of black English, maintaining that it is more than simply a dialect of standard English.

KEY WORDS

diaspora (par. 7)   group migration.
chattel (par. 7)   disposable property.
tabernacle (par. 7)   a place of worship.

━━━━━━━━━━

1   THE ARGUMENT CONCERNING THE use, or the status, or the reality, of black English is rooted in American history and has absolutely nothing to do with the question the argument supposes itself to be posing. The argument has nothing to do with language itself but with the *role* of language. Language, incontestably, reveals the speaker. Language, also, far more dubiously, is meant to define the other—and, in this case, the other is refusing to be defined by a language that has never been able to recognize him.

2   People evolve a language in order to describe and thus control their circumstances, or in order not to be submerged by a reality that they cannot articulate. (And, if they cannot articulate it, they *are* submerged.) A Frenchman living in Paris speaks a subtly and crucially different language from that of the man living in Marseilles; neither sounds very much like a man living in Quebec; and they would all have great difficulty in apprehending what the man from Guadeloupe, or Martinique, is saying, to say nothing of the man from Senegal—although the "common" language of all these areas is French. But each has paid, and is paying, a different price for this

"common" language, in which, as it turns out, they are not saying, and cannot be saying, the same things: They each have very different realities to articulate or control.

3   What joins all languages, and all men, is the necessity to confront life, in order, not inconceivably, to outwit death: The price for this is the acceptance, and achievement, of one's temporal identity. So that, for example, though it is not taught in the schools (and this has the potential of becoming a political issue) the south of France still clings to its ancient and musical Provençal, which resists being described as a "dialect." And much of the tension in the Basque countries, and in Wales, is due to the Basque and Welsh determination not to allow their languages to be destroyed. This determination also feeds the flames in Ireland for among the many indignities the Irish have been forced to undergo at English hands is the English contempt for their language.

4   It goes without saying, then, that language is also a political instrument, means, and proof of power. It is the most vivid and crucial key to identity: It reveals the private identity, and connects one with, or divorces one from, the larger public, or communal identity. There have been, and are, times, and places, when to speak a certain language could be dangerous, even fatal. Or, one may speak the same language, but in such a way that one's antecedents are revealed, or (one hopes) hidden. This is true in France, and is absolutely true in England: The range (and reign) of accents on that damp little island make England coherent for the English and totally incomprehensible for everyone else. To open your mouth in England is (if I may use black English) to "put your business in the street": You have confessed your parents, your youth, your school, your salary, your self-esteem, and, alas, your future.

5   Now, I do not know what white Americans would sound like if there had never been any black people in the United States, but they would not sound the way they sound. *Jazz*, for example, is a very specific sexual term, as in *jazz me, baby*, but white people purified it into the Jazz Age. *Sock it to me*, which means, roughly, the same thing, has been adopted by Nathaniel Hawthorne's descendants with no qualms or hesitations at all, along with *let it all hang out* and *right on! Beat to his socks*, which was once the black's most total and despairing image of poverty, was transformed into a thing called the Beat Generation, which phenomenon was, largely, composed of *uptight*, middle-class white people, imitating poverty, trying to *get down*, to get *with it*, doing their *thing*, doing their despairing best to be *funky*, which we, the blacks, never dreamed of doing—we *were* funky, baby, like *funk* was going out of style.

6   Now, no one can eat his cake, and have it, too, and it is late in the day to attempt to penalize black people for having created a language that permits the nation its only glimpse of reality, a language without which the nation would be even more *whipped* than it is.

7   I say that this present skirmish is rooted in American history, and it is. Black English is the creation of the black diaspora. Blacks came to the United States chained to each other, but from different tribes: Neither could speak the other's language. If two black people, at that bitter hour of the world's history, had been able to speak to each other, the institution of chattel slavery could never have lasted as long as it did. Subsequently, the slave was given, under the eye, and the gun, of his master, Congo Square, and the Bible—or, in other words, and under these conditions, the slave began the formation of the black church, and it is within this unprecedented tabernacle that black English began to be formed. This was not, merely, as in the European example, the adoption of a foreign tongue, but an alchemy that transformed ancient elements into new language: *A language comes into existence by means of brutal necessity, and the rules of the language are dictated by what the language must convey.*

8   There was a moment, in time, and in this place, when my brother, or my mother, or my father, or my sister, had to convey to me, for example, the danger in which I was standing from the white man standing just behind me, and to convey this with a speed, and in a language, that the white man could not possibly understand, and that, indeed, he cannot understand, until today. He cannot afford to understand it. This understanding would reveal to him too much about himself, and smash that mirror before which he has been frozen for so long.

9   Now, if this passion, this skill, this (to quote Toni Morrison) "sheer intelligence," this incredible music, the mighty achievement of having brought a people utterly unknown to, or despised by "history"—to have brought this people to their present, troubled, troubling, and unassailable and unanswerable place—if this absolutely unprecedented journey does not indicate that black English is a language, I am curious to know what definition of language is to be trusted.

10   A people at the center of the Western world, and in the midst of so hostile a population, has not endured and transcended by means of what is patronizingly called a "dialect." We, the blacks, are in trouble, certainly, but we are not doomed, and we are not inarticulate because we are not compelled to defend a morality that we know to be a lie.

11   The brutal truth is that the bulk of the white people in America never had any interest in educating black people, except as this could serve white purposes. It is not the black child's language that is in question, it is not his language that is despised: It is his experience. A child cannot be taught by anyone who despises him, and a child cannot afford to be fooled. A child cannot be taught by anyone whose demand, essentially, is that the child repudiate his experience, and all that gives him sustenance, and enter a limbo in which he will no longer be black, and in which he knows that he can never become white. Black people have lost too many black children that way.

12   And, after all, finally, in a country with standards so untrustworthy, a country that makes heroes of so many criminal mediocrities, a country unable to face why so many of the non-white are in prison, or on the needle, or standing, futureless, in the streets—it may very well be that both the child, and his elder, have concluded that they have nothing whatever to learn from the people of a country that has managed to learn so little.

━━━━━━━━━━

EXERCISES

Details and Their Meaning

1. Give some examples of languages that have the same name but are nevertheless distinct.
2. In paragraph 3, what does Baldwin say is the true purpose of language? In what way is language political?
3. What do "Jazz" and "sock it to me" refer to in black English? How did white America modify their meaning?
4. Why didn't Africans speak their own language when they were brought to America?
5. Where did black English begin? What institution is responsible for originating it? What purpose was served by the development of a separate tongue understood by black Americans but not by white people?
6. What does Baldwin say black children will lose if they are cut off from their language?

Reading and Critical Thinking

1. Who says Provençal is a dialect of French? Who says it is not? How does this discussion relate to black American English?
2. What do you infer is the result of speaking improper English in England?
3. Who is Nathaniel Hawthorne? Why does Baldwin refer to him in paragraph 5? What is Baldwin implying?
4. What is the Beat Generation? What were the beatniks pretending to be, according to Baldwin? What were they really? How is the Beat Generation similar to its 1990s counterpart?
5. Why does Baldwin suggest that black people with a common language would not have tolerated slavery for long? How might a common language unify people against oppression?
6. What is a dialect? Why does Baldwin consider the description of black English as a dialect to be patronizing? Do you agree or disagree? Why?
7. What does Baldwin mean by "we are not compelled to defend a morality that we know to be a lie" (paragraph 10)? Do you agree? Why or why not?
8. How does the concluding paragraph turn the question of language and truth around? What implied challenge to education do you see in paragraph 12? How might this challenge be met?

The Writer's Strategies

1. What is Baldwin's thesis? Where does he state it?
2. In which paragraphs does Baldwin give examples of dialects that are really distinct languages?
3. What is Baldwin's purpose in including many examples of black English? How does the use of these terms strengthen his argument?
4. What is Baldwin assuming that his audience knows about the black English debate? Is his assumption justified in your case?
5. Why does Baldwin put the last sentence of paragraph 7 in italics?
6. Why does Baldwin include a quotation from Toni Morrison in paragraph 9? Who is she?
7. Why is "dialect" put in quotation marks in paragraph 10? What emotion is Baldwin conveying by the use of this punctuation?

Thinking Together

Break into groups and brainstorm to produce a list of qualities of the language "white English." What linguistic elements define "white English"? How do these elements compare and contrast to the qualities of black English?

Vocabulary

James Baldwin uses the following italicized words in this selection. Write a definition of each one, using clues from the context of the sentence in which the word appears below.

1. We asked the dean to *articulate* her position on off-campus housing more clearly.
2. The continental United States is divided into four *temporal* zones: Eastern, Central, Mountain, and Pacific.
3. Our professor told us that the adding machine and the calculator were *antecedents* of the computer.
4. Although Martin was nervous about many things, he had no *qualms* about skydiving.
5. The Chicago Bulls *transcended* many problems this season and won the championship.
6. By giving us study guides that included every exam question, the professor made the test *patronizingly* simple.
7. Sunlight is essential to the *sustenance* of most plant life.
8. The gangster decided to *repudiate* his criminal past and join a monastery.
9. After auditioning dozens of *mediocrities*, the director decided to hold another day of tryouts for talent night.

WRITER'S WORKSHOP ————————————

Critical Thinking in Writing

1. Write an essay describing the qualities of the English you use. How does your language reveal social and cultural factors in your life? How does it reveal political factors?
2. Although Baldwin doesn't address this point directly, implied in his essay is the suggestion that black students should be taught in their own language in schools. If this were done, how would it change the nature of education? Take a position on this issue, and write an essay supporting your argument.

3. As Baldwin says, language divides as much as it unites. Should we retain our current concept of standard English, or should each segment of American culture teach and write in its own idiom? Can the same argument Baldwin makes for black English be applied to Spanglish, American Sign Language, and Cajun as well? Or, do you see merit in elements of the "English only" argument—English should be the exclusive language of discourse in America, particularly its schools and courts?

Connecting Ideas

Read Stephen Carter's "I Am an Affirmative Action Baby" (page 89). How do you think Carter would respond to Baldwin's contention that a black child who does not understand black English "will no longer be black"?

Of Mice and Men— and Morality

David Gelman

This selection about a minor event in a laboratory seems at first to be about animal rights. But David Gelman is really writing about the power of language to influence how we think about each other and how we act toward each other. Notice how the simple story at the beginning gains more and more meaning and significance and finally raises major moral issues.

KEY WORDS

scrupulous (par. 2)   extremely careful.
pathogens (par. 3)   disease-causing organisms.
lethal (par. 4)   deadly.
subsist (par. 5)   to live off of.
predator (par. 5)   a creature that lives by eating another.
imbroglio (par. 6)   a confused tangle.

1   IT WON'T SETTLE THE argument—probably nothing could. But it is something to be pondered in the never-ending wrangle over animal rights. It is a story of "good mice" and "bad mice," and how animal researchers make judgments about them.

2   The University of Tennessee's Walters Life Sciences Building is a model animal facility, spotlessly clean, scrupulous in obtaining prior approval for experiments from an animal-care committee. Of the 15,000 mice housed there in a typical year, most give their lives for humanity. These are "good" mice and, as such, warrant the protection of the animal-care committee.

3   At any given time, however, some mice escape and run free. These mice are pests. They can disrupt experiments with the pathogens they carry. They are "bad" mice, and must be captured and destroyed. Usually, this is accomplished by means of "sticky" traps, a kind of flypaper on which they become increasingly stuck. Mice that are not dead by morning are gassed.

4   But the real point of this cautionary tale, says animal behaviorist Harold A. Herzog Jr., writing in the June issue of *American Psychologist*, is that the labels we put on things can skew our moral responses to them. Using sticky traps or the more lethal snap traps would be deemed unacceptable for good mice. Yet the killing of bad mice requires no prior approval. "Once a research animal hits the floor and becomes an escapee," writes Herzog, "its moral standing is instantly diminished."

5   In Herzog's own home, there was a more ironic example. When his young son's pet mouse, Willie, died recently, it was accorded a tearful, ceremonial burial in the garden. Yet even as they mourned Willie, says Herzog, he and his wife were setting snap traps to kill the pest mice in their kitchen. With the bare change in labels from "pet" to "pest," the kitchen mice attained a totally different moral status. Something of the sort happens with so-called feeders—mice raised to be eaten by other animals. At the Walters facility, no approval is needed for feeding mice to laboratory reptiles that subsist on them. But if a researcher wants to film a mouse defending itself against a predator, the animal-care committee must review the experiment, even though the mouse will often survive. The critical factor in the moral regard of the mouse is whether it is labeled "subject" or "food."

6   **Beyond the Laboratory**   Although it is hard to come near the issue without inflaming it, Herzog insists he has no desire to touch off yet another animal-rights imbroglio. In writing about labeling he was also thinking beyond the laboratory: how politicians or governments use labels, for instance. "A contra is a freedom fighter to the Reagan administration," he says, "but in Nicaragua, a contra may be a terrorist." The moral "numbing" that American GI's experienced in Vietnam resulted in part from their calling the enemy "gooks" and "dinks."

7   Labels can be dehumanizing, a way of disposing of things. Calling ghetto minorities the "underclass" helps identify a problem, but also puts it at an impersonal distance. The "Third World" designation reminds us there is more to our world than the Western and Eastern countries, but it lumps the teeming millions of Asia and Africa into a faceless mass. "Labels," says Herzog, "are a fundamental part of how we interact with people." Not to mention mice.

EXERCISES

Details and Their Meanings

1. Where is the laboratory in which the animal experiments are carried out? How does David Gelman describe it? What point is he making by the description? What kinds of mice are in the laboratory? How are they treated?
2. Who is Harold Herzog? What is the importance of his role? What is his interest in how the mice are treated? Where did he publish his article about the mice? Why is his article appropriate for a journal in psychology?
3. In the opening paragraph, what labels are given to two kinds of mice? How does the writer explain and expand on these labels in the following paragraphs? How do the labels influence the treatment received by the mice?
4. How is the concept "escapee" similar to and different from the concept "bad"? What does the term *escapee* imply about a mouse's former condition and about the mouse's desires? In actual practice, is a mouse treated any differently if it is called "bad" or "escapee"? How does the use of the term *escapee* make you rethink the meaning of the categories "good" and "bad."
5. In what way is the story of the pet mouse and pest mice in Herzog's home ironic?
6. What is the laboratory distinction between feeders and mice used in studies of predators? Is the fate of the mice the same in both cases? For whom is there a difference? What is the meaning of this difference?
7. In the last two paragraphs, the writer mentions labels given to humans. Which labels are paired with their opposites? What is the significance of using these labels or their opposites? Which labels are not paired with an opposite? What do you think their opposite might be?
8. Do any of the labels applied to humans have a positive intention but partly negative result? How?

Reading and Critical Thinking

1. Gelman begins by mentioning the controversy over animal rights. What is the animal-rights issue? Why is it said to be volatile? Why does the writer say that Herzog's article does not settle the issue? What does Herzog's article contribute to the discussion?

2. Why don't Gelman and Herzog actually state where they stand on the protection of animal rights? What do you think their position is?

3. In what ways are the examples of mice at home or in the laboratory making the same point? In what ways do they develop slightly different aspects of the same idea?

4. How do you evaluate the practice of treating mice in different ways depending on the labels they are given? Is the difference in treatment silly and absurd, or does it make a certain kind of sense? Explain your opinion.

5. How does the need to do good science and the need to create a pleasant family life stand behind the distinctions made between mice? Are the distinctions warranted? Are the distinctive labels given to humans, described in paragraphs 6 and 7, justifiable? Is it fair to label others because of your own needs? How can you express your needs without labeling others?

The Writer's Strategies

1. What issues does Gelman refer to in the opening paragraph? What is his thesis? What issues does he refer to in the closing paragraph? How does he get from the opening issues to the closing issues?

2. In the middle paragraphs, how many incidents does the writer relate? What point does he make with each of these incidents? How do these incidents work together to raise an important issue overall?

3. What phrases does the writer use to highlight the point of each incident? What phrases does he use to tie the ideas of the separate incidents together?

4. How do the points made by the incidents establish an idea that is developed in the last two paragraphs? What phrases tie the discussion about animal rights to the discussion about human relationships?

5. Each paragraph is built around a contrast of labels. In each paragraph what labels are contrasted? What is the final overall contrast or comparison between mice and humans?

6. What is the purpose of this essay? Who is the audience?

Thinking Together

Form a small group and select one member to read aloud the last paragraph of this essay to the rest of the group. Then discuss the validity of the points raised in the last paragraph. Does your group agree with Gelman? Why? What instances in your own experience support or challenge his conclusions? Finally, report back to the class at large on what your group concluded.

Vocabulary

In this selection, several words and phrases gain special meaning from the way the writer uses them. Give the usual meaning of the following words and phrases. Then find where each item appears in the selection, and define the special meaning created by the context.

1. wrangle (par. 1)
2. warrant (par. 2)
3. cautionary (par. 4)
4. behaviorist (par. 4)
5. skew (par. 4)
6. moral responses (par. 4)
7. moral standing (par. 4)
8. feeders (par. 5)
9. moral regard (par. 5)

WRITER'S WORKSHOP ━━━━━━━━━━

Critical Thinking in Writing

1. Where do you stand on the issues of animal rights? How did Gelman's article influence your thinking on the issue? Write an essay in which you respond to these questions.
2. In one paragraph, describe a positive label that turned out to have negative consequences.
3. Write several paragraphs describing how people use labels to define people they dislike or people who disagree with their beliefs. Include several appropriate examples.

Connecting Ideas

Write a paragraph comparing the effect of the distinctions created by the labels described in this article with the effect of the distinctions created by the terms described in the next piece, Charles Berlitz's "Racial Slurs" (page 211).

Racial Slurs: The Etymology of the International Insult

Charles Berlitz

Charles Berlitz is a descendant of the founder of the famous international language schools. In this selection he traces our uses of negative terms for racial, religious, and ethnic groups.

KEY WORDS

opprobrious (par. 3) scornful, disgraceful.
fancied (par. 3) imagined.
appellations (par. 4) names, labels.
effete (par. 10) decadent, snobbish.
diminutive (par. 11) shortened form of a name.
physiognomy (par. 12) facial features.
sanctified (par. 15) made holy or sacred.

1 "WHAT IS A KIKE?" Disraeli once asked a small group of fellow politicians. Then, as his audience shifted nervously, Queen Victoria's great Jewish Prime Minister supplied the answer himself. "A kike" he observed, "is a Jewish gentleman who has just left the room."

2 The word kike is thought to have derived from the ending *-ki* or *-ky* found in many names borne by the Jews of Eastern Europe. Or, as Leo Rosten suggests, it may come from *kikel*, Yiddish for a circle, the preferred mark for name signing by Jewish immigrants who could not write. This was used instead of an X, which resembles a cross. Kikel was not originally pejorative, but has become so through use.

3   Yid, another word for Jew, has a distinguished historic origin, coming from the German *Jude* (through the Russian *zhid*). *Jude* itself derives from the tribe of Judah, a most honorable and ancient appellation. The vulgar and opprobrious word "Sheeny" for Jew is a real inversion, as it derives from *shaine* (Yiddish) or *schön* (German), meaning "beautiful." How could beautiful be an insult? The answer is that it all depends on the manner, tone or facial expression or sneer ... with which something is said. The opprobrious Mexican word for an American—*gringo*, for example, is essentially simply a sound echo of a song the American troops used to sing when the Americans were invading Mexico—"Green Grow the Lilacs." Therefore the Mexicans began to call the Americans something equivalent to "los green-grows" which became Hispanized to *gringo*. But from this innocent beginning to the unfriendly emphasis with which many Mexicans say *gringo* today there is a world of difference—almost a call to arms, with unforgettable memories of past real or fancied wrongs, including "lost" Texas and California.

4   The pejorative American word for Mexicans, Puerto Ricans, Cubans and other Spanish-speaking nationals is simply *spik*, excerpted from the useful expression "No esspick Englitch." Italians, whether in America or abroad, have been given other more picturesque appellations. *Wop,* an all-time pejorative favorite, is curiously not insulting at all by origin, as it means, in Neapolitan dialect, "handsome," "strong" or "good looking." Among the young Italian immigrants some of the stronger and more active—sometimes to the point of combat—were called *guappi,* from which the first syllable, "wop," attained an "immediate insult" status for all Italians.

5   "Guinea" comes from the days of the slave trade and is derived from the African word for West Africa. This "guinea" is the same word as the British unit of 21 shillings, somehow connected with African gold profits as well as New Guinea, which resembled Africa to its discoverers. Dark or swarthy Italians and sometimes Portuguese were called *Guineas* and this apparently spread to Italians of light complexion as well.

6   One of the epithets for Negroes has a curious and tragic historic origin, the memory of which is still haunting us. The word is "coons." It comes from *baracoes* (the o gives a nasal *n* sound in Portuguese), and refers to the slave pens or barracks (*"baracoons"*) in which the victims of the slave trade were kept while awaiting transshipment. Their descendants, in their present emphasizing of the term "black" over "Negro," may be in the process of upgrading the very word "black," so often used pejoratively, as in "black-hearted,"

"black day," "black arts," "black hand," etc. Even some African languages use "black" in a negative sense. In Hausa "to have a black stomach" means to be angry or unhappy.

7   The sub-Sahara African peoples, incidentally, do not think that they are black (which they are not, anyway). They consider themselves a healthy and attractive "people color," while whites to them look rather unhealthy and somewhat frightening. In any case, the efforts of African Americans to dignify the word "black" may eventually represent a semantic as well as a socio-racial triumph.

8   A common type of national insult is that of referring to nationalities by their food habits. Thus "Frogs" for the French and "Krauts" for the Germans are easily understandable, reflecting on the French addiction to *cuisses de grenquilles* (literally "thighs of frogs") and that of the Germans for various kinds of cabbage, hot or cold. The French call the Italians *"les macaronis"* while the German insult word for Italians is *Katzenfresser* (cateaters), an unjust accusation considering the hordes of cats among the Roman ruins fed by individual cat lovers—unless they are fattening them up? The insult word for an English person is "limey," referring to the limes distributed to seafaring Englishmen as an antiscurvy precaution in the days of sailing ships and long periods at sea.

9   At least one of these food descriptive appellations has attained a permanent status in English. The word "Eskimo" is not an Eskimo word at all but an Algonquin word unit meaning "eaters-of-flesh." The Eskimos naturally do not call themselves this in their own language but, with simple directness, use the word *Inuit*—"the men" or "the people."

10   Why is it an insult to call Chinese "Chinks"? Chink is most probably a contraction of the first syllables of *Chung-Kuo-Ren*—"Middle Country Person." In Chinese there is no special word for China, as the Chinese, being racially somewhat snobbish themselves (although *not* effete, according to recent reports), have for thousands of years considered their land to be the center or middle of the world. The key character for China is therefore the word *chung* or "middle" which, added to *kuo*, becomes "middle country" or "middle kingdom"—the complete Chinese expression for "China" being *Chung Hwa Min Kuo* ("Middle Flowery People's Country"). No matter how inoffensive the origin of "Chink" is, however, it is no longer advisable for everyday or any-day use now.

11   Jap, an insulting diminutive that figured in the last national U.S. election (though its use in the expression "fat Jap" was apparently meant to have an endearing quality by our Vice President) is a sim-

ple contraction of "Japan," which derives from the Chinese word for "sun." In fact the words "Jap" and "Nip" both mean the same thing. "Jap" comes from Chinese and "Nip" from Japanese in the following fashion: *Jihpen* means "sun origin" in Chinese, while *Nihon* (Nip-pon) gives a like meaning in Japanese, both indicating that Japan was where the sun rose. Europeans were first in contact with China, and so originally chose the Chinese name for Japan instead of the Japanese one.

12   The Chinese "insult" words for whites are based on the observations that they are *too* white and therefore look like ghosts or devils, *fan kuei* (ocean ghosts), or that their features are too sharp instead of being pleasantly flat, and that they have enormous noses, hence *ta-bee-tsu* (great-nosed ones). Differences in facial physiognomy have been fully reciprocated by whites in referring to Asians as "Slants" or "Slopes."

13   Greeks in ancient times had an insult word for foreigners too, but one based on the sound of their language. This word is still with us, though its original meaning has changed. The ancient Greeks divided the world into Greeks and "Barbarians"—the latter word coming from a description of the ridiculous language the stranger was speaking. To the Greeks it sounded like the "baa-baa" of a sheep —hence "Barbarians!"

14   The black peoples of South Africa are not today referred to as Negro or Black but as Bantu—not in itself an insult but having somewhat the same effect when you are the lowest man on the totem pole. But the word means simply "the men," *ntu* signifying "man" and *ba* being the plural prefix. This may have come from an early encounter with explorers or missionaries when Central or South Africans on being asked by whites who they were may have replied simply "men"—with the implied though probably unspoken follow-up question, "And who are you?"

15   This basic and ancient idea that one's group are the only people —at least the only friendly or non-dangerous ones—is found among many tribes throughout the world. The Navajo Indians call themselves *Diné*—"the people"—and qualify other tribes generally as "the enemy." Therefore an Indian tribe to the north would simply be called "the northern enemy," one to the east "the eastern enemy," etc., and that would be the *only* name used for them. These ancient customs, sanctified by time, of considering people who differ in color, customs, physical characteristics and habits—and by enlargement all strangers—as potential enemies is something mankind can no longer afford, even linguistically. Will man ever be able to rise

above using insult as a weapon? It may not be possible to love your neighbor, but by understanding him one may be able eventually to tolerate him. Meanwhile, if you stop calling him names, he too may eventually learn to dislike *you* less.

EXERCISES

Details and Their Meanings

1. Who is Leo Rosten? What is his field of specialty?
2. What song did Americans sing when they first visited Mexico? How did that song become the basis of an insulting expression?
3. Identify some insults that began as complimentary expressions. How did they change in meaning?
4. What are *baracoes*? How did they figure in the formation of an insult?
5. What insulting words are derived from the foods people eat?
6. What does *Eskimo* mean? What language is the word taken from?
7. What expression do most groups in the world use to describe themselves? How do many groups describe people who are not of their group?
8. What is a *fan kuei*? On what basis do people in China make fun of white people?

Reading and Critical Thinking

1. Who was Benjamin Disraeli? Why do you think Disraeli was permitted to tell a joke about Jews? What purpose do you think he expected the joke to serve? Ethnic jokes are very popular even today. How do you account for their popularity?
2. What sources does Charles Berlitz cite to support his derivations? On what basis should you accept his etymologies as accurate?
3. What country is Berlitz from? What clues help you answer this question?
4. Which group enjoyed better relations with whites, the Algonquins or the Eskimos? How can you tell?

5. What generalization can you draw about the way most groups describe people who are different from themselves? What insults have you heard used for your ethnic group? What insults have you or your friends used for other ethnic groups?
6. Why might an Inuit be insulted to be called an Eskimo? Why might a Japanese person prefer to be called Nipponese?
7. In what way does dignifying the word *black* represent a triumph for black Americans?

The Writer's Strategies

1. Where does the writer state the thesis of this essay? What is it? How does the first paragraph serve as an effective introduction?
2. Who is the primary audience for this selection? What assumptions is the writer making about his audience? Are those assumptions justified in your case?
3. How does Berlitz organize this essay? Why does he use so many examples? What do all his examples have in common?
4. How does Berlitz make sure that he does not offend his readers with ethnic slurs?
5. Where does the writer use definitions? In which paragraph does he define the term *national insult*?
6. How does the writer make transitions from one paragraph to another? What examples of effective transitions can you give?
7. What new idea does the writer introduce in the final paragraph?

Thinking Together

Working in small groups, brainstorm to develop a list of places and situations in which one is likely to experience ethnic and racial slurs and a list of places and situations in which they are unlikely.

What can you conclude from the different lists? Discuss your findings with the class. How are insults used as a form of political or social control?

Vocabulary

The following foreign expressions are defined in the text. Write the definitions you find for them there.

1. kikel (par. 2)
2. shaine (par. 3)

3. guappi (par. 4)
4. cuisses de grenquilles (par. 8)
5. Katzenfresser (par. 8)
6. Inuit (par. 9)
7. Chung Hwa Min Kuo (par. 10)
8. Jihpen (par. 11)
9. Diné (par. 15)

WRITER'S WORKSHOP

Critical Thinking in Writing

1. Write a well-detailed essay about how you can reconcile the positive need to identify with people who are like you with the negative tendency to belittle people who are different from you. What steps can you take to make sure that pride in your culture or heritage does not lead you to create negative stereotypes and slurs about others?
2. In the final paragraph, Berlitz asks, "Will man ever be able to rise above using insult as a weapon?" Write an argumentative essay in which you attempt to answer this question.
3. If the basis of prejudice is fear, suggest some ways to help people to overcome their fear of others. In a detailed essay, discuss your suggestions.

Connecting Ideas

Read Richard T. Schaefer's "Minority, Racial, and Ethnic Groups" (page 179). How is the labeling of groups related to the establishing of dominant and minority groups in society? How do insults isolate and minimize the qualities of groups?

Macho and *Machismo* as Loan Words

Constance Sullivan

Constance Sullivan examines how the Spanish words macho *and* machismo *have been taken over by American English in recent years. These words do not carry a narrow meaning but are associated with a range of attitudes and actions. The words' popularity in English depends on the political and intellectual needs of individuals and groups who are looking to label an attitude that they either admire or oppose.*

KEY WORDS

loan words (title)   words borrowed from one language by another.
adjectival (par. 1)   used as an adjective to describe a noun or pronoun.
semantic (par. 1)   meaning.
linguistic (par. 3)   referring to the systematic study of language.
bilingualism (par. 3)   fluency in two languages.
burgeoning (par. 4)   rapid growth.

1   IN THE UNITED STATES of the late 1970s and early 1980s, it became very difficult to listen to the radio, watch television, see a film, or read a newspaper, magazine, or book without frequent encounters with the words *macho* and *machismo* or variants thereof. One of the hits of disco music in 1979 was "Macho Man" by the Village People, a New York group, although perhaps not all those in the central heartland of America were aware of the record's basis in the East Coast homosexual lifestyle and militancy. And on October 6, 1980, then–President Carter, in an attack on his Republican opponent's foreign policy stance as warmongering and jingoistic, called it one that would "push everybody around and show them the macho of

the United States." Obviously the incumbent presidential candidate believed that his audience would recognize the term and would share his view that to be *macho* is unacceptable behavior. Even Carter's nominative use of the adjectival form, which differs from the Spanish language's rules, represented English-speaking North America's linguistic freedom with the word. *Macho*, and its companion term *machismo*, are so current in today's English that they are rarely italicized as belonging to another language when printed. They have been adopted as valid and expressive semantic items into English, and most speakers and writers who use the words appear not to connect them with Hispanic culture but to regard them as descriptive of patterns in their own.

2   The appearance in North American English of *macho* and *machismo* on a broad scale dates from the 1970s and was usually seen prior to that decade in reference to Latin American culture only. A formal tracing of these words in dictionaries of American English reveals no reference to either *macho* or *machismo* prior to 1973. In that year, *The Random House Dictionary of the English Language* (p. 859) has "*ma-chis-mo* (mä chiz' mo), n. (in Hispanic cultures) maleness or virility; male domination. [Sp *macho* male, he-man]," and *Webster's New Collegiate Dictionary* (p. 689) has "*ma-chis-mo* mä-chez-(,)mo,-' chiz- n [Mex Sp, from Sp *macho* male]: a strong sense of masculine pride; an exaggerated awareness and assertion of masculinity." It should be noted that these early entries clearly relate the words to Hispanic culture and languages. By 1975 the latter dictionary added items on *macho* as well (p. 689): "[1]*ma-cho* mä-, cho adj. [Sp, male, fr L. *masculus*—more at MALE]; aggressively virile. [2]*macho*, n. 1: MACHISMO 2: one who exhibits machismo." Also in 1975, *The Harper Dictionary of Contemporary Usage* (p. 381) states: "*machismo*. Borrowed from the Spanish word meaning 'masculinity,' *machismo* is a vogue word for an excessive display of actions and attitudes which are supposed to demonstrate masculinity and virility, such as boldness, aggressiveness, physical courage, and domination over women." All American dictionaries after 1975 provide definitions of both terms in new editions or supplements to earlier editions; they no longer limit application to Spanish, and they include the American English definition of *macho* as *machismo*.

3   Hispanic peoples, principally from Puerto Rico, Cuba, and Mexico, were already a significant presence in the United States before this recent linguistic loan occurred. In the 1970s Hispanics came close to representing the largest minority group in the United States and Hispanic-Americans gained high visibility not merely because of their numbers but from the effects of civil rights and ethnic pride

movements (particularly of Chicanos), increasing pressures for bilingualism in schools and governmental matters, and large concentrations of Hispanics in the communities of the Southwest and large
Eastern cities, particularly. To an extent, the origins of English adoption of *macho* and *machismo* may be ascribed to the Hispanic cultural
presence in the United States, and Anglo-American contact with
Hispanic linguistic and cultural patterns.

However, the simultaneous burgeoning of feminism in the late
1960s and 1970s has to be regarded as another and more essential
factor in the adoption into English of *macho* and *machismo*. Feminist
consciousness and popularization of gender role stereotyping and
the process of socialization into those stereotypes within the United
States and, more broadly, Western society, provided the basis for taking these words from Spanish and using them as new English
words. Feminist discussion of and protests against what has been
variously called male authoritarianism, male hegemony, patriarchy,
and male dominance based on physical, psychological, and economic violence or aggressiveness, raised the issue of sexism and
maintained it before a national public. In other words, awareness of
the existence of the "male chauvinist (pig)" and the ideology of sexism predated the last decade's new choice of *macho* and *machismo* as
a better descriptive term for the concept.

EXERCISES

Details and Their Meanings

1. Who are the various groups and individuals, mentioned in the
   first paragraph, who use the Spanish terms *macho* and *machismo*?
   In each case, when do they use the terms? What are they trying
   to express? Do they view the terms positively or negatively?
   Why?
2. What does the last sentence of the first paragraph mean? Do you
   agree with the statement? Why or why not?
3. When did *macho* and *machismo* first start appearing in North
   American English? What evidence does Constance Sullivan use
   to establish the dates?
4. How do different dictionaries define *macho* and *machismo*? To
   what extent are the definitions consistent or different?

5. When did Hispanic people first come to North America? To what extent can the popularity of the terms be related to a large Hispanic presence in the United States?
6. Why did *macho* and *machismo* start appearing in English when they did? What is the relation between these terms and feminist views of the world? How do feminists view *machismo*? Why?
7. In the last paragraph, what is the meaning of the phrase "gender role stereotyping and the processes of socialization into those stereotypes"? How do the concepts in this phrase explain the feminist interest in the terms *macho* and *machismo*?

Reading and Critical Thinking

1. In what ways are the various uses of *macho* and *machismo* by English-speakers in the United States similar to and different from each other? Does a single consistent set of meanings arise out of these uses? Would it be accurate to use just one set of terms for all these different uses? Support your opinion.
2. How do the needs and attitudes of the various English-speakers influence their use of the terms?
3. Are the ways in which the English-speakers use the terms similar to or different from the way in which the terms are used by Spanish-speakers? To what extent do you believe the terms have a positive meaning in Hispanic culture?
4. Overall, do you view *machismo* as a positive or a negative concept or as a nonjudgmental descriptive concept? Do you believe *machismo* itself reflects an actual set of attitudes and behaviors? Why or why not? Do you believe that a Spanish word ought to be used to describe this concept? What alternative terms would you suggest?
5. From the information in this selection what inferences can you make about tensions between the feminist movement and Hispanic culture? What do you know of how the feminist movement has developed within Hispanic communities?

The Writer's Strategies

1. What is the main point made by Constance Sullivan in this selection? Is the thesis ever stated directly? If so, where?
2. How many examples are presented in the opening paragraph? How are these examples related to the opening sentence? Does each of these examples make the exact same point or a slightly different one?

3. Why does Sullivan quote dictionaries in the second paragraph? What kind of authority and information does she establish with these dictionary quotations?
4. What is the effect of ending this selection with a discussion of the feminist use of the terms?

Thinking Together

Divide the class into small groups, each of which should pick a language spoken by a minority in the United States. Each group should then make a list of all the terms they can think of that American English has borrowed from that language. Then in examining this list the group should discuss how those terms have joined American English and what kinds of contributions these words have made to American English. Each group should then summarize its findings and present them to the entire class.

Vocabulary

In this selection, the writer uses the following words to describe attitudes and behaviors that are part of *machismo*. Define each word, and explain how it relates to the concept of *machismo*.

1. militancy (par. 1)
2. warmongering (par. 1)
3. jingoistic (par. 1)
4. domination (par. 2)
5. aggressiveness (par. 2)
6. virility (par. 2)
7. authoritarianism (par. 4)
8. hegemony (par. 4)
9. patriarchy (par. 4)
10. violence (par. 4)

WRITER'S WORKSHOP ⎯⎯⎯⎯⎯⎯⎯⎯

Critical Thinking in Writing

1. Write a paragraph describing a loan word that has become part of American English. Discuss how that word came into English and how it is used. Compare the usage in English with the way the word is used in the original language.

2. Write one paragraph defining what you think *macho* or *machismo* means. Write another paragraph giving an example of a *macho* person or behavior. Write a final paragraph giving your opinion of *machismo*.
3. Do you think your behavior and attitudes toward gender roles are influenced by stereotypes captured in words such as *machismo?* If you do, describe the influence of one or more such stereotyping terms. If you do not, discuss why you think this is not the case.

Connecting Ideas

Here, Constance Sullivan tries to redefine *macho* and *machismo*. Richard Rodriguez, in his essay (page 455), tries to define *minority student*. What similarities in essay construction do you see in Sullivan's and Rodriguez's selections? How does the Latino base of both essays contribute to their meaning? What elements of *machismo* can you relate to minority students?

SIDE BY SIDE

1. In the early part of this century, linguists created an artificial language called Esperanto, which they hoped would become the common language of everyone on Earth one day. Esperanto failed to gain widespread acceptance. Today few people remember it, and even fewer can speak it.

   Would the world be a better place if everyone spoke a common language? How would a common language make the world an easier place in which to live? What would people lose by giving up their national languages in favor of a universal language? Write an argumentative essay drawing on the readings in this unit and support or oppose the idea of giving up national languages for an artificial one.

2. Do you think the number of loan words, such as *macho* and *jazz*, in American English is a sign of the language's strength or weakness? What does American English gain by adopting words from other languages? What are some drawbacks from borrowing words? Write a detailed essay in which you consider this issue.

3. The United States Supreme Court recently has ruled that laws aimed to stop hateful speech are unconstitutional and that freedom of speech is an absolute right, not to be restricted even if people say terrible and insulting things. Do you agree with the Supreme Court's position? Why or why not? Which essays in this section would help you support the argument of absolute free speech? Which would help you oppose it?

UNIT 4

Jobs: Dollars and Dreams

INTRODUCTION ────────────────────────────────

Regardless of our status or origin, nearly all of us share a belief in the American Dream. In a way, the promise of America is that anyone, no matter how humble or poor, anyone who works and studies hard, anyone with talent, skills, or just plain luck can turn ability into financial success and, ultimately, happiness. We all want to be more successful than our parents, and we expect our children to be more successful than we have been.

But dreams sometimes come up against the hard realities that not everyone can rise to the heights of his or her talents, that the dreams and aspirations of some people are "deferred" (to use Langston Hughes's word). Not having a job means not having money, not participating in the economy, not swimming in the mainstream of society. Jobs are essential to fulfilling dreams, sharing in the common life, and gaining the money to live. Yet through persistence, hard work at often menial jobs, and spirited responses to seemingly unyielding obstacles, many people succeed and move ahead in American society.

In this unit, writers share experiences about the struggle to survive and succeed in the world of work. Gary Soto, in "Looking for Work," shows how people strive to connect the reality of their own lives with the images presented on television. Douglas Martin, in "Blind Commuter," tells how Alberto Torres finds dignity and fulfillment despite enormous personal setbacks. In "A Cafe Reopens," William E. Schmidt describes the impact a lunchroom has on the workday life of a Minnesota farming town, and in "Mexicans Come to Work but Find Dead Ends," Roberto Suro shows how a Texas neighborhood has changed over time to reflect the prospects of post-industrial economy. In "Green Frog Skin," John Lame Deer, a Native American medicine man, challenges the cash values that support the American Dream.

What kind of future do you see for yourself as you take your place in the work force after you leave college? These readings will provide a fascinating look at the interconnections among race, gender, ethnicity, jobs, and economic realities and will help place in perspective your personal efforts to unify dollars and dreams.

PREREADING   JOURNAL

1. Write about the best and the worst jobs you ever had. What were they? What about them made them good or bad for you? How did those experiences point you toward the career path that you wish to pursue?

2. Describe the experiences you and your family have had working in the American economy. Has the American economy been a friendly place for your family and you? Have you or your family found satisfying work that will provide an income to allow for a decent way of life? What obstacles or frustrations have you and your family encountered as you tried to find a place in the American economy? To what extent have gender, racial, or ethnic factors influenced the work experiences of your family and yourself?

3. Write a journal entry about where you expect to be in twenty years. What sort of career will you have? What steps will you have to take to achieve your career goals? What career ambitions will you have achieved? What kind of lifestyle will your chosen career enable you to have?

Looking for Work

Gary Soto

Gary Soto is an award-winning poet and author who teaches Eng-
lish and Chicano studies at the University of California at Berkeley.
An American of Mexican descent, Soto quickly grasped the differ-
ence between Anglo and Chicano culture, as this excerpt from his
Living Up the Street (1985) shows.

KEY WORDS

egg candler (par. 4)   someone who examines chicken eggs to
  determine whether they have been fertilized.
muu-muu (par. 5)   a loose-fitting housedress.
feigned (par. 12)   pretended.
chavalo (par. 25)   an informal Spanish word meaning "boy."

1   ONE JULY, WHILE KILLING ants on the kitchen sink with a rolled newspaper, I had a nine-year-old's vision of wealth that would save us
from ourselves. For weeks I had drunk Kool-Aid and watched
morning reruns of *Father Knows Best*, whose family was so uncom-
plicated in its routine that I very much wanted to imitate it. The
first step was to get my brother and sister to wear shoes at dinner.

2   "Come on, Rick—come on, Deb," I whined. But Rick mimicked
me and the same day that I asked him to wear shoes he came to the
dinner table in only his swim trunks. My mother didn't notice, nor
did my sister, as we sat to eat our beans and tortillas in the stifling
heat of our kitchen. We all gleamed like cellophane, wiping the
sweat from our brows with the backs of our hands as we talked
about the day: Frankie our neighbor was beat up by Faustino; the
swimming pool at the playground would be closed for a day because the pump was broken.

3   Such was our life. So that morning, while doing-in the train of
ants which arrived each day, I decided to become wealthy, and right
away! After downing a bowl of cereal, I took a rake from the garage
and started up the block to look for work.

4   We lived on an ordinary block of mostly working class people: warehousemen, egg candlers, welders, mechanics, and a union plumber. And there were many retired people who kept their lawns green and the gutters uncluttered of the chewing gum wrappers we dropped as we rode by on our bikes. They bent down to gather our litter, muttering at our evilness.

5   At the corner house I rapped the screen door and a very large woman in a muu-muu answered. She sized me up and then asked what I could do.

6   "Rake leaves," I answered, smiling.

7   "It's summer, and there ain't no leaves," she countered. Her face was pinched with lines; fat jiggled under her chin. She pointed to the lawn, then the flower bed, and said: "You see any leaves there—or there?" I followed her pointing arm, stupidly. But she had a job for me and that was to get her a Coke at the liquor store. She gave me twenty cents, and after ditching my rake in a bush, off I ran. I returned with an unbagged Pepsi, for which she thanked me and gave me a nickel from her apron.

8   I skipped off her porch, fetched my rake, and crossed the street to the next block where Mrs. Moore, mother of Earl the retarded man, let me weed a flower bed. She handed me a trowel and for a good part of the morning my fingers dipped into the moist dirt, ripping up runners of Bermuda grass. Worms surfaced in my search for deep roots, and I cut them in halves, tossing them to Mrs. Moore's cat who pawed them playfully as they dried in the sun. I made out Earl whose face was pressed to the back window of the house, and although he was calling to me I couldn't understand what he was trying to say. Embarrassed, I worked without looking up, but I imagined his contorted mouth and the ring of keys attached to his belt— keys that jingled with each palsied step. He scared me and I worked quickly to finish the flower bed. When I did finish Mrs. Moore gave me a quarter and two peaches from her tree, which I washed there but ate in the alley behind my house.

9   I was sucking on the second one, a bit of juice staining the front of my T-shirt, when Little John, my best friend, came walking down the alley with a baseball bat over his shoulder, knocking over trash cans as he made his way toward me.

10   Little John and I went to St. John's Catholic School, where we sat among the "stupids." Miss Marino, our teacher, alternated the rows of good students with the bad, hoping that by sitting side-by-side with the bright students the stupids might become more intelligent, as though intelligence were contagious. But we didn't progress as

she had hoped. She grew frustrated when one day, while dismissing class for recess, Little John couldn't get up because his arms were stuck in the slats of the chair's backrest. She scolded us with a shaking finger when we knocked over the globe, denting the already troubled Africa. She muttered curses when Leroy White, a real stupid but a great softball player with the gift to hit to all fields, openly chewed his host when he made his First Communion; his hands swung at his sides as he returned to the pew looking around with a big smile.

11   Little John asked what I was doing, and I told him that I was taking a break from work, as I sat comfortably among high weeds. He wanted to join me, but I reminded him that the last time he'd gone door-to-door asking for work his mother had whipped him. I was with him when his mother, a New Jersey Italian who could rise up in anger one moment and love the next, told me in a polite but matter-of-fact voice that I had to leave because she was going to beat her son. She gave me a homemade popsicle, ushered me to the door, and said that I could see Little John the next day. But it was sooner than that. I went around to his bedroom window to suck my popsicle and watch Little John dodge his mother's blows, a few hitting their mark but many whirring air.

12   It was midday when Little John and I converged in the alley, the sun blazing in the high nineties, and he suggested that we go to Roosevelt High School to swim. He needed five cents to make fifteen, the cost of admission, and I lent him a nickel. We ran home for my bike and when my sister found out that we were going swimming she started to cry because she didn't have the fifteen cents but only an empty Coke bottle. I waved for her to come and three of us mounted the bike—Debra on the cross bar, Little John on the handle bars and holding the Coke bottle which we would cash for a nickel and make up the difference that would allow all of us to get in, and me pumping up the crooked streets, dodging cars and pot holes. We spent the day swimming under the afternoon sun, so that when we got home our mom asked us what was darker, the floor or us? She feigned a stern posture, her hands on her hips and her mouth puckered. We played along. Looking down, Debbie and I said in unison, "Us."

13   That evening at dinner we all sat down in our bathing suits to eat our beans, laughing and chewing loudly. Our mom was in a good mood, so I took a risk and asked her if sometime we could have turtle soup. A few days before I had watched a television program in which a Polynesian tribe killed a large turtle, gutted it, and then

stewed it over an open fire. The turtle, basted in a sugary sauce, looked delicious as I ate an afternoon bowl of cereal, but my sister, who was watching the program with a glass of Kool-Aid between her knees, said, "Caca."

14   My mother looked at me in bewilderment. "Boy, are you a crazy Mexican. Where did you get the idea that people eat turtles?"

15   "On television," I said, explaining the program. Then I took it a step further. "Mom, do you think we could get dressed up for dinner one of these days? David King does."

16   "*Ay, Dios,*" my mother laughed. She started collecting the dinner plates, but my brother wouldn't let go of his. He was still drawing a picture in the bean sauce. Giggling, he said it was me, but I didn't want to listen because I wanted an answer from Mom. This was the summer when I spent the mornings in front of the television that showed the comfortable lives of white kids. There were no beatings, no rifts in the family. They wore bright clothes; toys tumbled from their closets. They hopped into bed with kisses and woke to glasses of fresh orange juice, and to a father sitting before his morning coffee while the mother buttered his toast. They hurried through the day making friends and gobs of money, returning home to a warmly lit living room, and then dinner. *Leave It to Beaver* was the program I re-played in my mind:

17   "May I have the mashed potatoes?" asks Beaver with a smile.

18   "Sure, Beav," replies Wally as he taps the corners of his mouth with a starched napkin.

19   The father looks on in his suit. The mother, decked out in ear-rings and a pearl necklace, cuts into her steak and blushes. Their conversation is politely clipped.

20   "Swell," says Beaver, his cheeks puffed with food.

21   Our own talk at dinner was loud with belly laughs and marked by our pointing forks at one another. The subjects were common-place.

22   "Gary, let's go to the ditch tomorrow," my brother suggests. He explains that he has made a life preserver out of four empty deter-gent bottles strung together with twine and that he will make me one if I can find more bottles. "No way are we going to drown."

23   "Yeah, then we could have a dirt clod fight," I reply, so happy to be alive.

24   Whereas the Beaver's family enjoyed dessert in dishes at the table, our mom sent us outside, and more often than not I went into the alley to peek over the neighbor's fences and spy out fruit, apri-cots or peaches.

25   I had asked my mom and again she laughed that I was a crazy *chavalo* as she stood in front of the sink, her arms rising and falling with suds, face glistening from the heat. She sent me outside where my brother and sister were sitting in the shade that the fence threw out like a blanket. They were talking about me when I plopped down next to them. They looked at one another and then Debbie, my eight-year-old sister, started in.

26   "What's this crap about getting dressed up?"

27   She had entered her profanity stage. A year later she would give up such words and slip into her Catholic uniform, and into squealing on my brother and me when we "cussed this" and "cussed that."

28   I tried to convince them that if we improved the way we looked we might get along better in life. White people would like us more. They might invite us to places, like their homes or front yards. They might not hate us so much.

29   My sister called me a "craphead," and got up to leave with a stalk of grass dangling from her mouth. "They'll never like us."

30   My brother's mood lightened as he talked about the ditch—the white water, the broken pieces of glass, and the rusted car fenders that awaited our knees. There would be toads, and rocks to smash them.

31   David King, the only person we knew who resembled the middle class, called from over the fence. David was Catholic, of Armenian and French descent, and his closet was filled with toys. A bear-shaped cookie jar, like the ones on television, sat on the kitchen counter. His mother was remarkably kind while she put up with the racket we made on the street. Evenings, she often watered the front yard and it must have upset her to see us—my brother and I and others—jump from trees laughing, the unkillable kids of the very poor, who got up unshaken, brushed off, and climbed into another one to try again.

32   David called again. Rick got up and slapped grass from his pants. When I asked if I could come along he said no. David said no. They were two years older so their affairs were different from mine. They greeted one another with foul names and took off down the alley to look for trouble.

33   I went inside the house, turned on the television, and was about to sit down with a glass of Kool-Aid when Mom shooed me outside.

34   "It's still light," she said. "Later you'll bug me to let you stay out longer. So go on."

35   I downed my Kool-Aid and went outside to the front yard. No one was around. The day had cooled and a breeze rustled the trees.

Mr. Jackson, the plumber, was watering his lawn and when he saw me he turned away to wash off his front steps. There was more than an hour of light left, so I took advantage of it and decided to look for work. I felt suddenly alive as I skipped down the block in search of an overgrown flower bed and the dime that would end the day right.

EXERCISES

Details and Their Meanings

1. How old is the narrator? In what decade does this piece take place? What suggests the time frame to you?
2. What kind of neighborhood does the narrator live in? What is its ethnic composition? What details give you clues about the family's economic status?
3. What are some jobs that the narrator does to earn money?
4. Where does the narrator go to school? What group does he belong to? What is his teacher's hope in placing students in class?
5. Who is Little John? Where is he from? Who is David King? Why is he an important figure to the narrator?
6. What does the narrator want his family to do at dinner? Why do they reject this proposal?

Reading and Critical Thinking

1. What evidence is there of the narrator's ethnic identity? How does that identity influence the point of view?
2. How do distinctions between different classes of people show up in this piece?
3. Why is the mother angry when the children come home from the pool? Is she justified? Why or why not?
4. What does the request for turtle soup convey about the differences between the narrator and the rest of his family? How do you think these differences might have developed?
5. What attitude toward television is expressed in this narrative? Do you agree or disagree with it? Why or why not?
6. What does Gary Soto mean when he says that the poor children in the neighborhood were "unkillable"? In what sense is he using the word?

The Writer's Strategies

1. What is the main point that Soto is trying to make?
2. Why has the writer chosen to tell this narrative in the first person?
3. How do details help make this piece effective? Which details do you find appealing? What kinds of sensory descriptions does Soto use? Which sense predominates in this narrative?
4. Why is this piece titled "Looking for Work"? Did the title prepare you for the narrative? Why or why not?
5. What ordering or organizing principle keeps the selection moving despite the sidetracks from the main narrative?
6. Why does the selection end the same way it began, with the narrator looking for work? What effect does this full circle achieve?
7. Where does this selection reach the climax, the decisive point of resolution? How has the piece been building toward this point?
8. Why does Soto refer to profanity without using any? How would this piece be different if he had used profane language?

Thinking Together

The two television shows referred to in this selection, *Father Knows Best* and *Leave It to Beaver*, showed idealized suburban families and in a sense gave people who grew up in the 1950s and 1960s a romantic view of how a normal family behaved. What television shows represent family life today? Brainstorm in groups about shows like *Beverly Hills 90210*, *The Simpsons*, *Family Ties*, *Roseanne*, and any others that deal with family life. What kinds of problems do the shows address? How do they give a true or false picture of family life?

Vocabulary

The writer creates some vivid images in this selection. Restate the following images in your own words.

1. gleamed like cellophane (par. 2)
2. the train of ants (par. 3)
3. her face was pinched with lines (par. 4)
4. runners of Bermuda grass (par. 8)
5. palsied step (par. 8)
6. blows . . . whirring air (par. 11)
7. toys tumbled from their closets (par. 16)
8. breeze rustled the trees (par. 35)

WRITER'S WORKSHOP ━━━━━━━━━━━━

Critical Thinking in Writing

1. Write a short essay entitled "Looking for Work."
2. Gary Soto describes himself as the only member of his family who aspired to rise above "the commonplace." Which member of your family or of some family you know has similar aspirations? In what ways does this person try to be different? How do other people in the family treat this person?
3. Write an essay in which you explain some of the special problems facing teenagers who seek to join America's work force. What workplace conditions affect a young worker's attitudes most, do you think?

Connecting Ideas

Read "Kiss of Death," Armando Rendón's account of growing up as a Chicano in a predominantly Anglo environment (page 91). How much of Soto's account agrees with Rendón's? What are some major differences in their experiences? What can you conclude about what life was like for a Chicano growing up in Northern California?

Why Black Men Have Lost Ground

Peter Passell

In this selection, Peter Passell, an economist and professor at Columbia University, examines recent studies of employment trends over the past twenty years.

KEY WORDS

stagnating (par. 4)   stuck in the same place.
spectrum (par. 13)   the entire range of something.

1   IT IS NO GREAT puzzle why young male workers have had to run so hard over the last 15 years simply to stay in place. They are the first generation to compete with women workers on a nearly equal basis. More important, they are the first postwar generation to enter the labor market when labor productivity was barely growing.

2   The mystery is why, in spite of the triumphs of the civil rights movement, young black men have lost ground to their white counterparts during the period.

3   Economists like simple explanations—especially ones that point toward simple policy fixes. But in this case, argue John Bound of the University of Michigan and Richard Freeman of Harvard, simplicity is the enemy of truth.

4   No single cause stands out in their analysis of stagnating employment opportunities for black men, published last month in a National Bureau of Economic Research working paper. Anything that could go wrong, it seems, has gone wrong, damaging the job prospects of black college graduates as well as high school dropouts.

5   There is no disputing that the drive for racial equality in the workplace ran out of steam in the mid-1970's. Adjusted for educa-

tion levels, the gap in weekly earnings for black men and white men with less than 10 years of work experience fell from 35 percent in 1963 to just 11 percent in 1975. But since then, it has crept back up to 18 percent.

6   Young black men face parallel problems in getting jobs. In 1973 the black-white gap in employment rates was 9 percentage points; by 1989 it had widened to 15.

7   What happened? Many small things rather than one big thing.

8   The researchers divided black men by region (Northeast, Midwest, South) and by education (college graduates, high school graduates, dropouts). All of these sub-groups lost ground on wages and (with one modest exception) on employment rates as well. But the differences in the rate of loss are striking.

9   College graduates did especially badly on wages. The white-black differences for college graduates widened three times faster than the gap for high school graduates and six times faster than the gap for dropouts. Midwestern blacks were also particularly big losers, losing far more ground than their Southern counterparts.

10   The pattern is somewhat different on rates of employment. Dropouts' prospects deteriorated far more rapidly than the prospects for all young male blacks. And in contrast to Southerners and Midwesterners, young male blacks in the Northeast actually gained a little on whites.

11   Using statistical regression techniques to dig deeper, the economists found that blacks had the misfortune of being in the wrong places and the wrong occupations at the wrong time. For example, relatively more depend on minimum-wage jobs for a living. The erosion of the minimum wage as a fraction of average wages is all that is needed to explain 17 percent of the ground lost by young male blacks. Similarly, a disproportionate number were union members. Thus as union wages fell relative to wages in general, blacks lost more than whites—a phenomenon that explains 5 percent of the change in the earnings gap.

12   Then there are the twin problems of occupation and industry. More blacks wore blue collars and more worked in manufacturing. Both groups suffered heavily in the early 1980's, when foreign competition savaged the Rust Belt. This one-two punch accounts for 29 percent of the relative decline in the wages of young blacks.

13   Slippage in employment rates is largely a problem at the unskilled end of the job spectrum. And here, Mr. Bound and Mr. Freeman look to crime and punishment for the explanation: Between 1980 and 1989 the proportion of black high school dropouts in jail or

on probation has grown by one-fifth. This explains fully 71 percent of the downward trend in black dropouts at work.

14   These results should depress people who look to government to promote equality of result as well as equality of opportunity. The great forces of history that have exposed the American economy to global competition and have led to a restructuring of industry probably cannot be stopped. Even if they could, few policy makers would be inclined to reverse course solely to keep black workers out of harm's way.

15   By the same token, Americans already have very good reasons to end the plague of urban street crime. The fact that crime leaves so many young black men effectively unemployable is not, in itself, likely to move public policy.

About the best that can be said here is that the worst is probably over. The regional economic shifts that worked to the disadvantage of blacks have apparently ended. So, too, have the shifts in labor demand that made blue-collar workers such a drag on the market during the 1980's. With a little luck, future trends will prove colorblind —or even work to the advantage of racial minorities.

EXERCISES

Details and Their Meanings

1. What new segment added to the labor force fifteen years ago altered the prospects of employment for young male workers?
2. What is the National Bureau of Economic Research? Who are John Bound and Richard Freeman? How did they contribute to this selection?
3. What was the difference between wages for black men and white men with equivalent experience in 1963? What happened to that gap by 1973? What has happened to it since then?
4. Which group of black men by region and education level suffered the greatest decline in wages? Which group fared best?
5. What is the present gap between blacks and whites with respect to employment? How has that figure changed since the 1960s?

6. What happened to union jobs since the 1970s? Why was this development bad for blacks?
7. How did foreign competition hurt blacks? Why didn't it hurt white workers in the same way?
8. What connection does Peter Passell suggest between crime and unemployment?

Reading and Critical Thinking

1. What is the writer's attitude toward the civil rights movement? Do you agree with his position? Why or why not?
2. Is this essay based on fact or opinion? How do you know?
3. What conclusion can you draw from the changes between white and black salaries over the last twenty years? What could be done to improve matters?
4. How do you explain the writer's report that the smallest gap in wages was between black and white male high school dropouts?
5. What conclusion does Passell come to about the job prospects of young black men who commit crimes?
6. In paragraph 16, what is Passell's reason for saying "the worst is probably over"? What support does he give for this statement? Do you agree with his assessment? Why or why not?

The Writer's Strategies

1. What is the thesis of this selection? How does it relate to the introductory paragraph?
2. Comment on the length of Passell's paragraphs. Could any paragraphs be combined?
3. What is the function of paragraph 7? Why is it only one sentence in length?
4. What transitional words or phrases does Passell use?
5. What is the purpose of dividing the piece into three sections? How does each section contribute to the whole?
6. Where does the writer offer his opinion?

Thinking Together

Each student brings in a different article on the economy from a newspaper or a news magazine. After forming groups of four or five, present the findings to the class. The class prepares a list of responses that address some of these questions: What is the state of the economy? What trends are good? What trends could be better? What indicators do economists use to measure the health of the economy? What is hard to understand about the economy?

Vocabulary

A.   Determine the meanings of the following words by using the essay context. Write definitions in your own words.

1. counterparts (par. 2)
2. sub-groups (par. 8)
3. deteriorated (par. 10)
4. restructuring (par. 14)

B.   Write definitions for these familiar figurative phrases from the essay.

5. ran out of steam (par. 5)
6. being in the wrong places . . . at the wrong time (par. 11)
7. ground lost (par. 11)
8. Rust Belt (par. 12)
9. one-two punch (par. 12)

WRITER'S WORKSHOP

Critical Thinking in Writing

1. One of the basic beliefs of American society is that education is the key to success. In what ways does Passell's essay support or challenge this belief? What is your position on the benefits of education for job success? Write a short essay to address these questions.
2. It is clear from this essay that American industry still does not always follow the doctrine of equal pay for equal work. Imagine that you are writing a letter to the owner of an American company. What arguments can you give in support of the owner's responsibility to promote, and encourage equality on the job.
3. Passell ends his essay with this sentence: "With a little luck, future trends will prove colorblind—or even work to the advantage of racial minorities." Do you agree? What is the basis of Passell's optimism?

Connecting Ideas

Read Stephen Carter's "I Am an Affirmative Action Baby" (page 89). In light of the statistics presented here by Peter Passell, do you consider Carter's position on opportunity for black men as a realistic assessment? Why or why not?

Blind Commuter

Douglas Martin

Douglas Martin, a reporter for the metropolitan section of the New York Times, *examines the life of Alberto Torres, an X-ray developer at Bronx Municipal Hospital.*

KEY WORDS

labyrinthine (par. 7)   like a complicated maze.
invariably (par. 9)   without fail, always the same way.
interminably (par. 9)   endlessly.
rehabilitating (par. 11)   repairing, fixing for further use.
arduous (par. 12)   extremely difficult.
transcends (par. 17)   rises above.

---

1 YOU COULD FEEL SORRY for Alberto Torres, who is blind. The last thing he remembers seeing was his daughter, Lauren, being born 13 years ago. Then the world went blank; he can only imagine what his only child looks like as a cheerleader and honor student.

2 Total darkness came as a result of an inflammation of his optic nerve—a condition that was unrelated to the retinal disease that had obscured his vision since birth. "I went to sleep and woke up with nothing," he said.

3 Bad luck is no stranger to this warm and thoughtful 37-year-old man. His mother died of cancer when he was 4, and Mr. Torres's ailing father had to give him up to foster care when he was 11. He later worked for 19 years in a workshop assembling mops and other household goods, mind-numbing stuff.

4 Earlier this month, Alberto Torres's wife, Idalia, who had just been laid off from her job as a receptionist, had a radical mastectomy and now faces a year of chemotherapy and radiation treatments. Things seemed always to go from almost unbelievably bad to worse. Even Mr. Torres's good luck has a dark side: Five years ago, his be-

245

loved seeing-eye dog, Gambler, got him out of the path of a truck. Mr. Torres was unharmed, Gambler died.

5   But know this and know it well: Mr. Torres does not feel sorry for himself. "These are just little bumps you have to go over in your life," he said.

6   At 5 A.M. on a recent morning, we caught up with Mr. Torres at the Nassau Avenue subway stop in Greenpoint, Brooklyn, where he lives in a third-floor walkup. He had been up since 3, feeding Greg, his new dog, making coffee, getting ready. "When you're blind, it takes a little longer to do things," he said.

7   Mr. Torres was beginning the labyrinthine two-hour trip to his job developing film in the X-ray department of the emergency room of the Bronx Municipal Hospital Center. He would take the G train to Queens Plaza where he would walk up a set of stairs and down another to the Manhattan-bound R train. he would then ride the R to 59th Street where he would walk upstairs to switch to the No. 6.

8   At one point along the journey, he might chat with a stranger. At another, someone would pat Greg, calling him by name. People offered assistance, even seats.

9   At 125th Street, Mr. Torres would transfer to the No. 4 by crossing the platform. At 149th Street, he would descend to the No. 2. He would take that to East 180th Street where he invariably waits interminably for his final train, the Dyre Avenue shuttle to Pelham Parkway. Then he and Greg would walk 20 minutes to the hospital.

10   "They shouldn't make any special provisions for me," Mr. Torres said. "It's a job, and I should be on time."

11   It was a hard job to come by. Before he got the job, Mr. Torres was determined to escape the workshop run by the Lighthouse, an organization dedicated to rehabilitating the visually impaired, and to try to make it on his own. He wanted a job developing X-ray film, something that everyone must do in the dark. The Lighthouse called many hospitals, to no avail, even though they offered to pay his first three months' salary and provide training.

12   The Lighthouse people would have much preferred something closer to his home. But they believed he could handle the arduous trip, as well as the work. "Our philosophy here is that blind people can do just about anything besides drive buses," said Marianne Melley, who tries to help place blind people in jobs.

13.   And that, as it turned out, was also the thinking about disabled people at the Bronx hospital. "We find what a person can do rather than what he can't do," said Noel McFarlane, the hospital's associate executive director.

14   "The point is that it works," Pamela Brier, executive director, said.

15   One day a while ago marked the first anniversary of Mr. Torres's hiring. He will likely develop 150 or so X-rays, his usual output, to celebrate. The cards with names and other data will be folded on the upper right hand corner so he can photograph them right-side-up. That is the only concession to blindness.

16   Mr. Torres works by himself in a small, chemical-scented dark-room. He cannot wear protective gloves, because he needs to feel. It is exacting work, and, since this is an emergency room, lives can be at stake. His immediate supervisor, Alcides Santambrosio, says he trusts him 100 percent.

17   Mr. Torres makes $20,000 a year. He could be pocketing more than $12,000 from disability payments. But his motivation tran-scends money. "If I start feeling like a victim, that makes me bitter," he said. "And why be bitter? That makes you go into a hole and stay there."

18   Just then, a technician rushed in undeveloped X-rays of a teen-ager who had jumped from a window and was in critical condition.

19   "I'm not doing anything out of the ordinary," insisted Mr. Torres as he briskly completed the task.

EXERCISES

Details and Their Meanings

1. Who is Alberto Torres? How did he go blind? When did it hap-pen? What was the last thing he remembers seeing?
2. What other hardships has Torres overcome? Where does he work now? How long has he been working there?
3. What kind of job did Torres have previously? How long was he there? Why did he want to leave this job?
4. Where does Torres live? How does he get to work? What time does he have to get up every morning in order to be at work on time?
5. What is the Lighthouse? How did the Lighthouse help Torres?
6. In what ways has Torres's job been modified to accommodate his visual impairment?

Reading and Critical Thinking

1. Why does Douglas Martin list all the troubles Alberto Torres has endured? How do you think you would have responded to these troubles? What steps can society take to cut down on problems faced by differently abled people?
2. Why is it so hard for Torres to get to work? Would all of his commuting problems vanish if his vision were normal? Why or why not?
3. Where does the writer criticize the subway system? Are his complaints valid? How can other forms of mass transit—buses, planes, and trains—make it easier for the differently abled to use travel facilities?
4. Why is Torres's job a good one for a blind person? What other kinds of jobs are well suited to visually impaired people?
5. Why does Martin mention how much money Torres could receive in disability payments? Why do you think Torres has not chosen this option? If you could advise Torres about taking disability pay, what would you tell him? Why?
6. How does Martin describe Alberto Torres? How does Torres describe himself? How do the descriptions differ? With which description do you agree? Why?

The Writer's Strategies

1. What is the thesis of this selection? Where is it expressed?
2. Why does Martin take four paragraphs to tell how Torres gets to work?
3. What writing strategies is Martin primarily using—description, narration, example? Support your answer with specific references to the text.
4. Identify a paragraph in which Martin uses details.
5. What is the concluding quotation intended to show?
6. Why does the writer quote both the executive director and the associate executive director of the hospital? Why isn't one quotation enough?

Thinking Together

Imagine how your journey to classes or work would be changed if you lost your sight. What things would you have to do differently? What adjustments would you need to make at school, at work, and at home? In small groups, develop responses to these questions.

Vocabulary

The effective use of adjectives and adverbs can heighten the meaning of sentences. Explain why the italicized adjectives and adverbs from the selection make each phrase more forceful.

1. *unbelievably* bad (par. 4)
2. waits *interminably* (par. 9)
3. *arduous* trip (par. 12)
4. *exacting* work (par. 16)
5. *briskly* completed (par. 19)

WRITER'S WORKSHOP ━━━━━━━━━━━

Critical Thinking in Writing

1. Some people argue that providing equal access to differently abled Americans would be too expensive and that the costs of installing ramps, Braille signs and buttons on elevators, and so on are not justified. Do you agree? Present your views in an argumentative essay.
2. *Ableism* is a belief that physically challenged people are in some sense inferior to the majority of people who have no special challenges. Sometimes ableism takes the form of pity or celebrating the ordinary achievements of differently abled people as if they were heroic deeds. Is Douglas Martin's essay ableist? Should Alberto Torres be seen as a hero or as an average man? Write a paragraph to respond to these questions.
3. Alberto Torres believes that everyone has "bumps" to get over in life, although the word *bump* seems to minimize Torres's physical challenges. What bumps have you overcome? How do they compare with Torres's? Describe, narrate, and give examples of adversity that you faced and overcame.

Connecting Ideas

Read "Looking Forward, Looking Backward" by Robert DeBlois (page 434). In what ways are Torres's and DeBlois's views of life similar, especially in the way they face physical challenges? How are their perspectives different? Which one would you say is more optimistic, more hopeful about the future? How do you account for this difference?

Mexicans Come to Work but Find Dead Ends

Roberto Suro

Newspaper correspondent Roberto Suro examines the United States's fastest-growing ethnic group and the struggles of many people in this group to achieve the American Dream.

KEY WORDS

assimilated (par. 1)   integrated into the whole.
faltering (par. 2)   hesitating, stumbling.
enticing (par. 5)   attracting.
accoutrements (par. 25)   additional items or features.
surreptitiously (par. 27)   secretly.
robust (par. 33)   strong.
menial (par. 38)   lowly, servile.

1   BORDERED BY FACTORIES AND docks, the Magnolia Park neighborhood [of Houston, Texas] has long been a beacon for generations of Mexican immigrants seeking sturdy homes and steady wages. Over time, most found jobs, assimilated and moved on to a better life.

2   But that is much less the case nowadays. The neighborhood is as much a place to stay poor as it is to start poor. Upward mobility among the 14 million people of Mexican descent in the United States —the nation's fastest-growing major ethnic group—is faltering, and on Magnolia Park's shady streets the signs of trouble are everywhere: high-school dropouts, teen-age mothers, families doubled and tripled up in bungalows, and day-laborers who gather at street corners hoping to sell their services.

3   Raul Jimenez, a 62-year-old machinist, remembers better days in Magnolia, as the neighborhood is commonly known. "I arrived

on Saturday, rested on Sunday and found a machinist's job on Monday," he said. "That was 1956, and Magnolia was a place where people could work hard for good money."

A Bleaker Job Market

4   The neighborhood's troubles started with the oil bust of the early 1980's and continued as the nation's labor market underwent vast changes, shifting more and more from a blue-collar, manufacturing base to high-technology and service industries. With the loss of those jobs went the traditional stepping stones that Mexican immigrants had long used to get ahead. Now, the immigrant networks that once helped new arrivals like Mr. Jimenez find factory work mostly lead nowhere.

5   Immigrants still receive lots of help from relatives and friends in finding work, but they usually end up in dead-end, low-paying service jobs—cleaning offices, mowing lawns, baby-sitting or sewing. Because wages in Mexico are even worse, rapid growth in this sector of the economy keeps drawing people across the Rio Grande, both legally and illegally. And the ready availability of such jobs is enticing teen-agers to drop out of school, often to help support their families.

6   Hugo del Moral came to Magnolia five years ago. He had several years more education than Mr. Jimenez and substantially more work experience as a machinist. But working mostly at odd jobs, the closest he has come to a factory floor is the one he has swept as a janitor.

7   "It's been hard to keep our dignity sometimes, but we still have our hopes," said his wife, Maria.

Economy Down, Population Up

8   The story is much the same in other big cities where people of Mexican descent are concentrated, in neighborhoods like East Los Angeles and the Pilsen area of Chicago. While the upheaval in the labor market hurt urban working-class neighborhoods of all ethnic or racial groups in the 1980's, because it occurred just as the Mexican-American population was exploding, the neighborhoods where they live suffered particularly.

9   During the 1980's the number of people of Mexican origin in this country grew at five times the rate of the national average. Nationwide, this group accounts for about two-thirds of the entire Hispanic population.

10   The surge in growth was mainly fueled by two factors. The first was a wave of immigration from Mexico that numbered at least 4

million in the decade when estimates of illegal aliens are included—
the largest such influx by any national group in American history
and about 45 percent of the total of 9 million people who immigrated
to the United States in the 1980's.

11   The second factor was a high birth rate. In Mexican neighborhoods like Magnolia, at least one out of every three residents is under the age of 16.

12   These numbers alone insure that the nation will have to be increasingly concerned with the future of people in places like Magnolia. At issue is whether America can still assimilate poor and unskilled immigrants and make them a source of economic vitality.

Neighborhood Declines: Immigrants Find Downward Mobility

13 Most Mexican communities have so far avoided the tailspin that carried many black and Puerto Rican neighborhoods into a seemingly
permanent state of economic despair. But locked in their own peculiar dynamic, the Mexican neighborhoods, too, have begun to fall.

14   If current trends continue, at the turn of the century young people of Mexican descent will be second only to young whites as
the largest source of new entrants into the labor force. But some experts are pessimistic about the prospects for these young Mexican-
Americans, fearing that many will be high school dropouts and
young unwed mothers at a time when the country will need highly
skilled workers to compete globally.

15   It was a different world when Mr. Jimenez, the machinist, came
to Magnolia in the 1950's. Post-war industry was booming and factory jobs required little education. "I always found work," Mr. Jimenez said, his large gnarled fingers stained black by lubricating oil. "If
I changed jobs, it was because I went for something better."

16   Although Mr. Jimenez and his wife have learned only a little
English, their four children finished high school and three went to
college. Such generational advances have not been unusual among
Mexican immigrant families that arrived before 1982. Historically,
the first-generation immigrant has begun the process of becoming
an American and the second has completed it, making notable economic gains.

17   But leaders in many Mexican-American communities now
worry that this pattern has been broken.

'Eyes No Longer Sparkle'

18 "I can tell by looking in their eyes how long they've been here," said
the Rev. Virgil Elizondo, rector of San Fernando Cathedral in San

Antonio. "They come sparkling with hope, and the first generation finds that hope rewarded." But he added: "Their children's eyes no longer sparkle. They have learned only to want jobs and money they can't have, and thus to be frustrated."

19   In many ways Magnolia, Houston's oldest Mexican neighborhood, is a profile in miniature of America's large and scattered population of Mexican descent.

20   Starting in 1916, refugees from the Mexican Revolution settled in Magnolia, a swampy area named for its big-blossomed trees, and helped build the Houston Ship Channel that borders it. Except during the Depression, it offered a stable home for those content with their industrial jobs and served as a stepping stone for immigrants with higher aspirations.

21   "Magnolia was the heart of all the colonias," said Mr. Jimenez, speaking in Spanish and using an old term for Mexican immigrant neighborhoods.

22   Magnolia still acts as a springboard for some. Austin High School, which serves the neighborhood, has an enrollment that is 94 percent Hispanic, and last year 68 percent of the graduating seniors went on to college. But only 400 seniors made it to graduation out of a class that began with 1,500 freshmen.

23   Across the country, dropout rates of 60 percent or more are common in schools with large numbers of Hispanic students. Many of the dropouts are teen-age parents. Every year in Magnolia out of a population of about 20,000, nearly 90 percent of whom are of Mexican descent there are about 400 new teen-age mothers.

The Signs Are Everywhere

24   Signs of economic decay and diminished opportunities are everywhere. In the middle of a residential area sits an equipment yard for a once-thriving manufacturing plant. But now it is nothing more than rusting piles of metal and chest-high weeds. Nearby, the huge doors of a warehouse are open, revealing an abandoned interior.

25   Yet a certain degree of economic vitality is also visible. On the commercial streets are a new Taco Bell and several other fast-food restaurants as well as a new shopping center serving the low end of the retail market. They now coexist with dozens of old cantinas, small, dark places where men drink beer with salt and have been known to draw pistols, and yerberías, crowded shops that sell herbal teas, statues of saints and sticks from ebony and mesquite trees—accoutrements favored by spiritualist cults.

26   "There has been a two-part restructuring of the work force in Magnolia," said Nestor P. Rodriguez, a sociologist at the University

of Houston. "The old, industrial jobs disappeared, which caused many people to change work or retire or move cities. And at the same time low-wage service sector jobs boomed. The net effect is that you still have a lot of economic activity, but it is at the bottom of the ladder."

27   Despite the prohibition on hiring illegal aliens in the Immigration Reform and Control Act of 1986, several recent studies have shown that people continue to enter the country surreptitiously and readily find service-sector jobs by using false documents. Many of the low-wage jobs are also filled by former illegal aliens who are among the 1.9 million Mexicans granted amnesty under the 1986 law.

28   "They may not earn much individually, but there are enough immigrants with two or three jobs to a household that they are keeping the neighborhood alive," said Mr. Rodriguez.

Economy Changes: Different Workers in a Different World

29   Magnolia's troubles can be traced to the Texas oil bust of 1982 to 1987, when plunging oil prices set in motion an economic collapse in Houston, the center of the industry, that some economists have compared in severity to the Great Depression. The empty office buildings and abandoned, half-built housing subdivisions appeared all the more jolting because the oil bust followed boom years that had made Houston among the most prosperous and fastest-growing cities in the country.

30   The changes in the local labor market brought on by the bust and the city's subsequent recovery are a stark version of what is happening more gradually nationwide. The number of jobs in manufacturing in Houston dropped from 163,200 in 1981 to a low of 74,000 in 1987. Since then the number of manufacturing jobs has risen to 176,400, but many are now in high-technology fields requiring skills that few immigrants have. Across the country the number of manufacturing jobs dropped by nearly 6 percent during the 1980's while the number of jobs in the service sector grew by more than 27 percent.

31   Roger Waldinger, a professor of sociology at the University of California–Los Angeles, found in a study that nearly 36 percent of the native born Hispanic workforce was employed in construction or manufacturing in Houston in 1980 but that by 1987 the number had dropped to 14 percent. Meanwhile, the proportion of Hispanic residents working in the service sector climbed to about 50 percent.

32   This tidal shift in employment helped bring a sudden end to a long period of upward mobility.

33   Gregory DeFreitas, an economist at Hofstra University on Long Island, said income for workers of Mexican origin across the nation rose from the 1950's through the 1970's. They were concentrated in areas experiencing robust growth, especially Texas, the Southwest and California. Meanwhile, blacks and Puerto Ricans increasingly suffered from the decline of manufacturing in the Midwest and the Northeast. In the 1970's family income for people of Mexican origin rose by 7 percent, compared with about 3 percent for whites and blacks.

34   But in the 1980's a national recession, the restructuring of the labor market and competition from new immigrants all took their toll. Mr. DeFreitas found that real family income for people of Mexican origin fell by more than 13 percent between 1979 and 1987. During that time, the earnings of whites remained comparably flat and those of blacks fell by almost 7 percent.

35   To make matters worse, having never recovered from the last recession, neighborhoods like Magnolia are now enduring another one, and some of the new economic losses look permanent.

Numbers Rise: Old Job Networks Lead to Nowhere

36   The oil bust also dealt a potentially long-lasting setback to the network built up over decades in Houston's Mexican neighborhoods that had helped thousands of people find work.

37   Such a network is typical of all immigrant communities, and access to it can determine an immigrant's success. But with manufacturing jobs scarce, the network in Magnolia is now leading mainly to dead ends.

38   "We came because my sister was here and we had friends here who told us that they would help us find work in the port, in the factories, with the oil companies," said Maria del Moral. Indeed, she and her husband, Hugo, a janitor, received plenty of help, but they were led to menial jobs.

39   Even when networks still connect to good jobs, they cannot serve their purpose if the job seekers are unqualified. The Flores Motor Company, for example, an auto-repair shop in Magnolia, has long been a stepping stone for a number of employees who went on to open businesses of their own. But these days the company's president, Roy Flores, is frustrated.

40   "I still have good jobs that'll feed a family," he said, "but I'm going to have to open my own school soon if I want to fill them. The

Mexican people coming up these days just know old-fashioned technology, and the kids coming out of school here don't know any. Men will come in here who have been working in a body shop in Mexico and they won't have any idea what we're doing."

41   Although the good jobs that once propelled the upward mobility of Houston's Mexican-Americans are ever harder to find, the city continues to draw large numbers of immigrants in search of work, many of them crossing the border illegally and many now coming from Central America. Census figures show a 72 percent increase in the Hispanic population of the Houston area during the 1980's.

42   Driven by political turmoil or the kind of economic crisis that saw real per capita income in Mexico drop by more than half since 1982, the new arrivals readily accept low-paying service jobs that do not offer the wages, benefits, security or chances for advancement of the old manufacturing jobs.

43   Ana H., who spoke only on the condition that her full name not be used because she lives here illegally, said she had been able to get started in Magnolia because so many minimum wage jobs were available.

44   For a time she lived in a small two-bedroom apartment that was home for as many as six adults, all working cleaning offices, washing dishes and doing other menial jobs. Now Ana has a job as a maid, has married a gardener and, she said, has no regrets about her move to America. "I didn't expect it to be easy here," she said. "But it is better than what I had."

EXERCISES

Details and Their Meanings

1. Where is Magnolia Park? What kind of a place is it? When did it begin to be a haven for Mexican Americans? How is it a typical neighborhood?
2. What are some signs that there is trouble in Magnolia Park?
3. When did the neighborhood's troubles start? What key industry declined? What else went wrong? What happened to the number of manufacturing jobs in Houston?

4. What other American cities have large concentrations of Mexican Americans? How does their experience differ from that of the Mexican Americans in Texas?
5. What two factors account for the surge in the numbers of Mexican immigrants?
6. What is the Immigration Reform and Control Act? What was its purpose? How did it change employment for Mexicans?
7. Who are Robert Waldinger and Gregory DeFreitas? What does their work indicate about life today for Mexican Americans?

Reading and Critical Thinking

1. Why are so many Mexican immigrants attracted to Magnolia Park? If you were a recent Mexican immigrant, would you go there? Why or why not? What needs do you think the neighborhood fulfills? How has it changed for Mexicans in recent years? Why do they keep coming?
2. What can you infer is the relation between the economies of Mexico and the United States? What advantage do you see in their relation? What is the disadvantage? Which nation benefits more?
3. How do you think the fortunes of Mexican Americans have changed in comparison to the fortunes of other Hispanics? of blacks? of whites?
4. What does the writer suggest are some reasons besides the economy that account for Mexican Americans' trouble in finding work? Do you find the reasons valid?
5. Why would an employer risk hiring illegal aliens? According to paragraph 40, what are the implied benefits for owners of companies? What advice would you give to someone who employs illegal aliens?
6. What can you infer from Ana H.'s remark at the end? How does her statement effectively conclude the article?

The Writer's Strategies

1. What is the thesis of this selection? Where does Roberto Suro express it? What subpoints does it raise?
2. What was Suro's purpose in choosing Magnolia Park, a specific neighborhood, as the focus of an article about Mexican Americans?

3. Where does the writer use statistics to back up his points? Where does he express opinions?
4. Where does Suro use descriptions? What evidence is there to suggest that he has visited Magnolia Park?
5. Where does the writer use quotations to support his points? What two kinds of testimony are used?
6. What does the writer suggest is in store for Mexican Americans?

Thinking Together

Conduct a survey of your classmates to find out who is working now and who held a job in the past. How many have or had white-collar jobs, blue-collar jobs, service jobs, menial jobs? What kind of work do your classmates expect to have in the future? What does the employment profile of your class tell you about the state of the American economy today?

Vocabulary

The following economic terms appear in the selection. Look up definitions of each in a dictionary or book about the economy.

1. upward (downward) mobility (par. 2)
2. boom (par. 29)
3. bust (par. 29)
4. day-laborers (par. 2)
5. service jobs (par. 5)
6. dead-end jobs (par. 5)
7. recession (par. 34)
8. depression (par. 20)
9. real family income (par. 34)
10. per capita income (par. 42)
11. high-technology fields (par. 30)
12. retail market (par. 25)

WRITER'S WORKSHOP

Critical Thinking in Writing

1. Some politicians have advocated using the army to close the Mexican border to illegal immigration and enforcing severe penalties on Mexicans who are caught working in the United

States illegally. Is this a workable idea? What would it accomplish if it worked? Present your response in the form of a letter to the editor of your local newspaper.

2. Looking for work is an experience shared by many Americans. Write a narrative or descriptive essay in which you tell about a job-hunting experience that you or someone you know (a friend or relative) had. What successes, challenges, and (or) failures did you find? How do you explain them?

3. From your reading here, what recommendation would you make for improving the prospects of American minorities in the coming decades? What can minority citizens do to enhance their levels of employment and prosperity?

Connecting Ideas

Look at Peter Passell's report on changes in employment for black men in "Why Black Men Have Lost Ground" (page 239). What similar conclusions do Passell and Roberto Suro reach about changes in the American economy? What is Passell saying that is somewhat different from Suro's points?

Like Mother, Like Daughter

Lloyd Gite

Lloyd Gite points to a variation on an old business tradition as women bring their daughters into the family firm. With this new development come new challenges.

1 ANDREA, CHERYL AND DERYL McKissack were barely out of diapers when their father started teaching them the family business. William McKissack, the late owner and president of McKissack & McKissack, the nation's oldest black-owned architectural and engineering firm, used to bring his daughters to the company's job sites every Saturday, giving them an "inside look" into how the architecture business works. Moses McKissack II, William's father and the man who founded McKissack & McKissack in 1905, used to give his son that same up-close-and-personal look into the company.

2 Andrea McKissack, now 40, still remembers those Saturdays spent at various job sites. "The three of us started at the architectural drawing board early on," she admits. "I remember going to my father's office when I was 6 years old, and I remember drawing architectural plans for my father when I was 13. By the time I got to high school, all of us were designing our own structures."

3 Today, these "designing women" are doing more than just blueprinting structures in their spare time. In 1983, when a stroke forced William into retirement, his wife, Leatrice, a former high-school math teacher with a master's degree in psychology, took over the Nashville, Tenn.–based firm and became its chairman and CEO. Five years later, when her husband passed away, she asked her daughters to join the company. "I didn't have any fears about bringing my daughters into the firm," recalls the 60-year-old Leatrice, whose company has designed more than 4,000 structures over the past 86 years, including facilities at Howard University and Tennessee State University. "I just decided that this was family. It was a legacy."

4   Cheryl, who at the time was a consultant for Weidlinger Associates, a New York–based engineering consulting firm, vividly remembers how her mother made the offer. "She said, 'I have all this work and I don't know what to do. I need some help.'"

5   Cheryl immediately came to her mother's rescue. For nearly two years, she commuted from New York to Nashville, where she served as the company's vice president of marketing. Cheryl, 30, also opened McKissack & McKissack branch offices in Memphis and New York. (She manages the latter.) In November 1989, Deryl McKissack-Cappell followed in Cheryl's footsteps. The 30-year-old twin sister joined the firm and opened a Washington, D.C., office. Andrea, who has a degree in architectural engineering from Tennessee State University, recently came on board at the New York office where she handles marketing, contract negotiations and consulting.

6   So far, bringing her daughters into the family business has paid off handsomely for Leatrice—and McKissack & McKissack. When Leatrice took over, McKissack & McKissack was designing projects totaling $30 million. Last year, the 28-employee company handled $75 million worth of projects, 10% of which the company received as fees.

7   Since taking over, Leatrice has won over a multitude of fans. "I like the low-key, highly professional way in which Leatrice goes about business," says Benjamin F. Payton, president of Tuskegee University (McKissack & McKissack has designed several of the school's buildings.) "Her husband was a real professional—someone who cared deeply about the work he did. Leatrice is the same. She has demonstrated to us that she can carry out major architectural work."

All In The Family

8   According to the Small Business Administration (SBA), the number of family-owned companies—many of which are run by mothers and daughters—are on the rise. In 1988 of the nearly 19 million companies in the United States, more than 13 million were sole proprietorships. Most of those were described as family-owned businesses with two or more related individuals who were working together. While there are no hard numbers of how many mother-daughter companies exist, experts agree that more mothers and daughters are going into business together.

9   "About 90% of American businesses are family-owned and/or controlled," says Marta Vago, Ph.D., a Los Angeles family business consultant. "People still prefer, whenever possible, to work with people they know."

10   Experts say that during the go-go '80s, many children of business owners shied away from working in their parents' companies. Instead, many elected to get their advanced degrees and to cut their teeth in corporate America. But now with the problems in the economy and the realization of the proverbial "glass ceiling," many women are returning to the entrepreneurial fold.

11   "Family members are going into business together, because of their disenchantment with the corporate world," says Dennis T. Jaffe, Ph.D., author of *Working with the Ones You Love: Conflict Resolution & Problem Solving Strategies for a Successful Family Business* (Conari Press: Berkeley, Calif.), and co-owner with his wife, Cynthia, of The Heartwork Group, a San Francisco consulting firm specializing in family business. "Many women who want to get to the top think, 'Why don't I just join the family business or form a company with my mother.'"

12   Daughters who become partners with their mothers in business will face many challenges that traditional father-son or father-daughter companies won't. For starters, it's more difficult for women-owned firms to get start-up capital to launch their businesses. And for black women, the chase is even tougher.

13   Sexism often poses another major hurdle. Says Deryl McKissack: "We only deal with men. Most of the presentations I go to, I'm the only woman in the room and I'll get wisecracks like, 'Deryl, all you have to do is show your legs.' I usually just smile and continue the presentation. It goes with the territory."

14   Renee Ferrell, president of sales and operations for Bennie Ferrell Catering Co., says that many of the men in her company used to give her, her sister and her mother a hard time. "Initially, the men in our company—especially some of the white men who worked for us —didn't want to listen to anything that we had to say because we were women," says Renee, who runs the 32-year-old Houston catering company with her mother, Norma, and her sister, Cynthia. "They figured that we didn't know what we were doing. But we had no problems getting rid of those men."

15   And the Ferrells didn't have any problems deciding that Bennie Ferrell Catering would have to be more aggressive in the '90s if it was going to remain competitive. In May, the Ferrells opened a new retail outlet in River Oaks, a fashionable upper-middle-class neighborhood in Houston.

16   "We were dying in the area where we were," says Renee of the company's other location in West Houston, a heavily industrialized

area of the city. The move marked a new beginning for the $1.2 million business that was launched in 1959 by the late Bennie Ferrell and his wife, Norma.

17   During the downturn in Houston's oil-based economy in the mid-'80s, Bennie Ferrell Catering, which has 12 full-time employees and 150 part-time workers, took a severe financial beating. In 1982, the company posted sales of $800,000. Three years later, revenues plummeted to $400,000.

18   In an effort to boost sagging sales, the Ferrells opened Catering Supplies, a company that sells such items as tablecloths, linens, silverware and serving trays. They also teach gourmet cooking classes and sell cooking accessories. The Ferrells believe that diversification will help lift the company's sales to $5 million—an ambitious projection—by 1994. Says Renee of the new thrust, "We needed to breathe new life into our company."

Making It Work

19   Breathing life into a mother-daughter business venture won't be easy. Marta Vago says that if the mother and daughter have had a dysfunctional relationship throughout the years, that kind of relationship will also be taken into the business. She advises that if you're thinking about going into business with your mother, ask yourself the following questions:

- How uncomfortable am I with disagreeing with my mother openly?
- Are we able to respect each other's differences of opinion?
- Can we find common ground even if we don't agree on everything?
- How do we solve problems?
- Will I have a tendency to go along with my mother so I won't hurt her feelings, or am I going to be more outspoken about what I really think and feel?

20   Author Dennis Jaffe suggests that mothers and daughters work together in some informal setting before forming a business partnership. And that's just what Sharon Pryor did before she joined Cluttered Corners, her mother's 16-year-old, Detroit-based antique store. "As a child, I always worked with my mother on projects," says Sharon, the company's 36-year-old marketing and public relations manager. "We've always had a good working relationship."

What Are the Drawbacks?

21   That old saying, "mothers will always be mothers" certainly applies here. Many daughters say that one of the major drawbacks to successfully running a mother-daughter company can be the inability of the mother to respect the daughter's professional skills. Some mothers still treat their daughters as "mommy's little girl"—despite the fact that they're adult business owners. That thinking can cripple a mother-daughter operation.

22   "Did I have reservations about working with my mother? Sure I did," says Cheryl McKissack. "Mom still likes to exert a certain amount of control over me. That's the biggest issue. My most difficult challenge is weaning myself from my mother. Her challenge is to look at her children more as trained professionals."

23   As in any company, it's also important to clearly define the roles and responsibilities of each employee. Cheryl McKissack remembers getting upset while she and her mother were making a presentation. "Mom answered a question that I should have answered because it was of a technical nature. Did that bother me? Yes. But, she has the savvy in dealing with people, and nobody seemed concerned about it but me," she says.

24   Objective job performance standards should also be adopted to apply to all employees, including family members. "Everyone in the company, including the daughters, should go through a period of evaluation and performance review," says Vago. "The more objective those standards are, the more objective the judgments can be. Either you performed or you didn't perform. The less objective these job performances are, the greater the likelihood that the mother will either play favorites or will treat the daughter uncommonly harsh."

25   If it's difficult for mothers and daughters to deal with problems, Jaffe recommends using a mediator. "They might need somebody who can help them talk," he says. "It could be another family member involved in the company. But I think the best mediators are people outside the company—somebody they both trust."

26   Mother-daughter businesses can be very rewarding ventures. Just ask the McKissacks, the Ferrells, and the Pryors. "There are many advantages to working with my mother and sisters," says Deryl McKissack. "There are fewer restrictions placed on my professional growth. And we have strong relationships that make things work."

EXERCISES

Details and Their Meanings

1. Who founded the architectural business of McKissack and McKissack? When? How many generations of the family have been in the family business? Until recently, what was the gender of the principals of the company? Who was the first woman to take a major role in the company? When and why did she do so?
2. How did Andrea, Cheryl, and Deryl first learn about the architectural business? Did they learn in the same way as their father? What training did they receive? Why and when did they return to the family business after having other jobs? Was their professional success dependent on joining the family business? What have been the results of their partnership with their mother?
3. How widespread are family-owned businesses in the United States? How are children's attitudes toward working in family businesses changing? Why are they changing?
4. What special challenges face female-led companies, challenges not faced by companies with males in leadership roles? Are these challenges attributable to the women themselves or to the surrounding society? How does the Ferrell family company illustrate these challenges? How has Bernie Ferrell Catering overcome these and other challenges?
5. What advice do experts give to women thinking of running a business? What does that advice suggest about the problems such companies may have?

Reading and Critical Thinking

1. Of the problems that mother-daughter businesses are likely to face, which ones are father-son or any other family business also likely to face? What problems do you think are peculiar to mother-daughter businesses?
2. Lloyd Gite suggests that good personal relations are important to the success of any business. In what ways might family businesses have advantages or disadvantages over other small businesses in this respect?
3. How strong a force is sexism in the business world, according to the writer? In what ways does it influence the careers and companies described here? How does sexism draw daughters into

family businesses? How do families protect daughters from sexist discrimination? How does sexism present obstacles to company growth? Do you believe that sexism is a stronger or a weaker force in the workplace than is described here?

4. After reading this article, do you think it would be a good idea to go into a family business? In what ways would this article help you to do so?

5. Evaluate the questions that Marta Vargo suggests daughters ask themselves if they are thinking about going into business with their mothers. Would the questions really help? Why or why not? Would the questions also serve sons seeking to go into business with their fathers? What questions might you add to the list?

The Writer's Strategies

1. What is the thesis of this selection? In what paragraph is the thesis most directly expressed? Why doesn't the thesis appear at the beginning of the piece? How does the direct presentation of the thesis change the level of discussion?

2. How much of the piece and what part of the piece is devoted to the McKissack family? Do the McKissacks reappear later in the piece? What point is made by their first appearance? by their later appearance? How does the example of this family tie the selection together?

3. What other examples are used beside the McKissacks? What do these additional examples add?

4. How does the focus of the last part of the article change, beginning with paragraph 18? What purpose might this section serve for some readers?

5. How does the last paragraph sum up the main point? What does that ending suggest about the writer's overall purpose?

Thinking Together

In small groups, discuss family-owned businesses that you are familiar with. Discuss the kinds of opportunities, problems, and temptations that are likely to arise in family businesses.

Vocabulary

Embedded in the following words from the selection are root words. Identify each root word, and then define both the root and the larger term.

1. architectural (par. 1)
2. diversification (par. 18)
3. dysfunctional (par. 19)
4. industrialized (par. 16)
5. mediator (par. 25)

WRITER'S WORKSHOP

Critical Thinking in Writing

1. In a few paragraphs, describe instances that you have observed or experienced in which sexism in the workplace slowed the careers of women or limited the success of women-led companies.
2. From what you know of relations between mothers and daughters and between fathers and sons, explain the advantages and disadvantages of family business partnerships. Which—father-son or mother-daughter—might be more likely to succeed in what circumstances? You may also consider father-daughter, mother-son, brother-sister, and any other family combination.
3. Choose one activity that you have successfully carried out with a member of your family. Write one page of advice about how to get along and work well with family members in this activity and what to watch out for.

Connecting Ideas

Jesus Sanchez's "Era Passes from the Landscape" (page 294) also describes the career choices of different generations. Write a few paragraphs comparing how and why the choices described by Sanchez differ from the choices described here by Lloyd Gite.

Green Frog Skin

John Lame Deer

John Lame Deer is writer, lecturer, and shaman of the Sioux tribe. In this essay, he critiques the values related to money in white American society.

KEY WORDS

gally-hooting (par. 2)   racing.
buffalo chips (par. 3)   dried manure used as fuel.

1   THE GREEN FROG SKIN—that's what I call a dollar bill. In our attitude toward it lies the biggest difference between Indians and whites. My grandparents grew up in an Indian world without money. Just before the Custer battle the white soldiers had received their pay. Their pockets were full of green paper and they had no place to spend it. What were their last thoughts as an Indian bullet or arrow hit them? I guess they were thinking of all that money going to waste, of not having had a chance to enjoy it, of a bunch of dumb savages getting their paws on that hardearned pay. That must have hurt them more than the arrow between their ribs.

2   The close hand-to-hand fighting, with a thousand horses gally-hooting all over the place, had covered the battlefield with an enormous cloud of dust, and in it the green frog skins of the soldiers were whirling around like snowflakes in a blizzard. Now, what did the Indians do with all that money? They gave it to their children to play with, to fold those strange bits of colored paper into all kinds of shapes, making them into toy buffalo and horses. Somebody was enjoying that money after all. The books tell of one soldier who survived. He got away, but he went crazy and some women watched him from a distance as he killed himself. The writers always say he must have been afraid of being captured and tortured, but that's all wrong.

3   Can't you see it? There he is, bellied down in a gully, watching what is going on. He sees the kids playing with the money, tearing it

268

up, the women using it to fire up some dried buffalo chips to cook on, the men lighting their pipes with green frog skins, but mostly all those beautiful dollar bills floating away with the dust and the wind. It's this sight that drove that poor soldier crazy. He's clutching his head, hollering, "Goddam, Jesus Christ Almighty, look at them dumb, stupid, red sons of bitches wasting all that dough!" He watches till he can't stand it any longer, and then he blows his brains out with a six-shooter. It would make a great scene in a movie, but it would take an Indian mind to get the point.

4   The green frog skin—that was what the fight was all about. The gold of the Black Hills, the gold in every clump of grass. Each day you can see ranch hands riding over this land. They have a bagful of grain from their saddle horns, and whenever they see a prairie-dog hole they toss a handful of oats in it, like a kind little old lady feeding the pigeons in one of your city parks. Only the oats for the prairie dogs are poisoned with strychnine. What happens to the prairie dog after he has eaten this grain is not a pleasant thing to watch. The prairie dogs are poisoned, because they eat grass. A thousand of them eat up as much grass in a year as a cow. So if the rancher can kill that many prairie dogs he can run one more head of cattle, make a little more money. When he looks at a prairie dog he sees only a green frog skin getting away from him.

5   For the white man each blade of grass or spring of water has a price tag on it. And that is the trouble, because look at what happens. The bobcats and coyotes which used to feed on prairie dogs now have to go after a stray lamb or a crippled calf. The rancher calls the pest-control officer to kill these animals. This man shoots some rabbits and puts them out as bait with a piece of wood stuck in them. That stick has an explosive charge which shoots some cyanide into the mouth of the coyote who tugs at it. The officer has been trained to be careful. He puts a printed warning on each stick reading, "Danger, Explosive, Poison!" The trouble is that our dogs can't read, and some of our children can't either.

6   And the prairie becomes a thing without life—no more prairie dogs, no more badgers, foxes, coyotes. The big birds of prey used to feed on prairie dogs, too. So you hardly see an eagle these days. The bald eagle is your symbol. You see him on your money, but your money is killing him. When a people start killing off their own symbols they are in a bad way.

7   The Sioux have a name for white men. They call them *wasicun*—fat-takers. It is a good name, because you have taken the fat of the land. But it does not seem to have agreed with you. Right now you don't look so healthy—overweight, yes, but not healthy. Americans

are bred like stuffed geese—to be consumers, not human beings. The moment they stop consuming and buying, this frog-skin world has no more use for them. They have become frogs themselves. Some cruel child has stuffed a cigar into their mouths and they have to keep puffing and puffing until they explode. Fat-taking is a bad thing, even for the taker. It is especially bad for Indians who are forced to live in this frog-skin world which they did not make and for which they have no use.

EXERCISES

Details and Their Meanings

1. What term does John Lame Deer use for *dollars*?
2. Why did white people want to possess the Black Hills? What valuable substance was there?
3. What about the Black Hills was valuable to Native Americans?
4. Why do cowboys throw oats into prairie dog holes? Which animals feed on prairie dogs?
5. What does Lame Deer say will eventually happen to the prairie?
6. What do the Sioux call white men? According to Lame Deer, what is the function of white people?

Reading and Critical Thinking

1. Is Lame Deer's description of the aftermath of the Battle of Little Bighorn a matter of fact or an invention? How can you be sure? Why does Lame Deer conclude that the last surviving soldier killed himself over money?
2. What does Lame Deer find especially troubling about the possible extinction of the American eagle? Do you agree with him?
3. Why did the Sioux give money to their children to play with?
4. How can you tell from the piece what tribe John Lame Deer belongs to?
5. Why are prairie dogs considered pests?
6. What do you infer is Lame Deer's attitude toward modern culture? Do you agree or disagree with him? Why?
7. What do you think Lame Deer would like to see happen to Native American peoples?

The Writer's Strategies

1. What do you think is Lame Deer's thesis? Comment on the introduction. Is it effective? Why or why not?
2. How much of this essay is based on opinion? How much is based on direct observation?
3. What emotions does the writer express toward white people? What words best convey these emotions?
4. Where does Lame Deer offer examples in this essay? Where does he offer analysis?
5. Where does Lame Deer use generalizations? How valid are they?
6. Is Lame Deer writing for an audience of Native Americans or others? How can you tell?

Thinking Together

Most of the people who settled the American prairie and displaced the Indians were poor immigrants fleeing from oppression and poverty in Europe. Break into groups to discuss this question: When people's rights are in conflict, how can you decide what decisions are appropriate? Then as a whole class, discuss the findings of the groups.

Vocabulary

Lame Deer uses the following informal words to make his points. Write a definition of each one in your own words.

1. paws (par. 1)
2. bellied (par. 3)
3. gully (par. 3)
4. hollering (par. 3)
5. dough (par. 3)
6. crazy (par. 2)

WRITER'S WORKSHOP ━━━━━━━━━

Critical Thinking in Writing

1. Do you think Lame Deer's critique of white society is valid? Are you yourself or are your friends, for instance, motivated in your

job goals primarily by the pursuit of money and the consumption of material goods? Write a reply to Lame Deer in which you discuss the validity of his conclusions.

2. Lame Deer raises critical questions about the relation between capitalism and the environment, earning money and its potential dangers to nature. Write a short essay exploring those issues. In the light of human financial need just how much should we put our environment at risk?

3. Suppose you could speak with a Native American who never had experienced contemporary culture as you know it in America today. What would you tell this person about American values—especially money values?

Connecting Ideas

Read "The Man to Send Rain Clouds," by Leslie Marmon Silko (page 104). What generalizations, based on Silko's and John Lame Deer's selections, can you make about the culture and values of Native Americans? What kinds of things are important to them? How does their society differ from the dominant culture?

A Cafe Reopens: Lunch Returns to the Prairie

William E. Schmidt

Reporter William E. Schmidt tells about the reopening of a cafe in a small farming town. He also tells about the changing way of life in rural America.

KEY WORDS

refuge (par. 2)   safe place, away from difficulties.
progeny (par. 12)   offspring, children, descendants.
plight (par. 14)   unhappy fate.
facade (par. 21)   front exterior of a building.
circuit box (par. 23)   a metal box in which the main electrical line for a house or building is split into separate circuits; often contains fuses or circuit-breakers.

1   WHEN LOUISBURG'S LAST CAFE closed its doors in 1988, Keith Hansen and John Lund and the other men who farm the rich, rolling prairies of western Minnesota found themselves confronting a new and lonely challenge: lunch.

2   Not only had they lost their midday refuge in town, a place to gather over coffee and talk prices and politics, but they had no one back at the house to cook for them either.

3   "My wife's got a job now," Mr. Lund said. "So does Keith Hansen's and Spence's and Elmo's. You want to keep your farm these days, you need two incomes."

4   **$4,500 to Reopen the Doors**   So a few months ago, Mr. Lund and his neighbors near Louisburg did what seemed natural. Nearly 50 of them got together, raised about $4,500 in contributions and reopened the little cafe that has served this remote town of 60 residents since the turn of the century.

5   For the farmers in Louisburg and other small towns across America, the cafe represents more than just a yearning for hearty home-cooked meals at noon, which the men say they do not have the time or the skills to make for themselves.

6   The campaign to reopen the cafe is a measure of the way in which the rhythms of rural life have changed.

7   More and more farm women now have jobs off the farm, forcing their husbands and their children to adapt to life in families in which both parents are wage-earners just as their counterparts have in the cities.

8   **Creation of the Railroad**   What has happened in Louisburg also reflects the concerns that are shared by residents of many small towns who have watched their communities wither away, bled by declining populations and failing businesses along Main Street.

9   "There is not much left here in Louisburg, but we're not ready just yet to let go of it," said Mr. Hansen, surveying the afternoon crowd in the cafe, where Emily Hansen, who is no relation, and her husband, Harold, were busy filling coffee cups and chatting up the customers. "At least we managed to bring a little bit of action back to town."

10   Like most places in the far reaches of western Minnesota and the Dakotas and Montana, Louisburg was a creation of the railroad, one of hundreds of small towns built at regular intervals along rail lines during the late 19th century so that nearby farmers could deliver a horse-drawn wagon of grain to the rail siding and be back home again by nightfall.

11   The grain elevator is still the town's biggest enterprise, and its most imposing structure. Its tin-sided towers dominate the long, low prairie horizon, and it is easily seen from several miles away.

12   But Louisburg, almost straight west from Minneapolis and close to the South Dakota border, is not on the railroad's main line. It is not even on some highway maps, since it is several miles from the nearest state road. Although the population nearly reached 100 in the 1950's, mostly the progeny of the Scandinavian and German farmers who first settled the area, it began slipping in the 1960's.

13   In the mid-1970's the farm implement dealership closed, and the town's only gasoline station shut its doors a decade later, along with the last grocery store. Except for two soda machines on the sidewalk in front of empty storefronts, the only retail commerce conducted along the main street these days is at the cafe.

14   Steve Padgitt, a sociologist at Iowa State University who specializes in rural areas, said residents of Louisburg were confronting a

plight common to farm people throughout the region: as small communities and their populations have shrunk, services have been concentrated in fewer and more distant places.

15   "From the house where I was raised, I could always see the smoke from two or three other chimneys," Mr. Padgitt said. "Now the countryside has thinned out so that people have to drive 10 miles to get their mail, or 30 miles to find a restaurant."

16   When the old cafe closed in 1988, Mr. Lund said, it meant that he was traveling 10 miles to Madison, the closest town, to buy lunch. It was either that or make do alone at home. "You can only eat Campbell's soup for so long," said Mr. Lund, whose wife, Nancy, works as a bank teller in Appleton, about 12 miles to the east.

17   As farm profits have declined in recent years, particularly among the operators of small family farms, both husbands and wives have been forced to seek work off the farm. A 1988 Agriculture Department survey estimated that 50 percent of all farm households had someone in the family who was working off the farm. As often as not it is the wife, as most farms are operated by men. In farm communities closest to urban areas, Mr. Padgitt said, some studies suggest that more than half the farm wives now hold jobs off the farm. In any case, sociologists say the number has been growing slowly but steadily over the years.

18   **Offer from Former Resident**   The idea of reopening Louisburg's cafe took root last December, when Catherine Wiese, who grew up in Louisburg but now lives in California, came home to visit her father. Since the cafe had closed her father, Arnold, an elderly widower, had lost a place to go for meals and companionship. She said she would help buy the cafe if others in the town could help fix it up and find someone to run it.

19   Mr. Lund and the men down at the elevator started taking up a collection, asking for donations of $50 or $100. "The names on the list just kept coming and coming," Mr. Lund said. Some nearby banks and businesses contributed, too, and the local power company offered three months of free electricity.

20   Most of the work was done by Harlan Wiese, who is Ms. Wiese's cousin. Along with helpers, he tore out the interior of the old cafe, a one-story storefront, and put up plywood paneling and installed floor tiles and new kitchen equipment. Dining tables were ordered and a new menu board was mounted on the wall for notice of the dinner special, which costs $3.50 and changes daily. Today it was roast beef with mashed potatoes.

21   Then they painted the facade and put out an American flag and a sign that reads: "Louisburg Cafe: Service with a Friendly Smile." At least that is what it was supposed to say: on one side the painter misspelled service as "sevrice."

22   The restaurant had its formal opening in mid-April. Toby Haug and His Playmores, a polka band from Madison, performed on the street out front, and most of the town turned out to dance and drink a little beer. Radio station KQLP from Madison broadcast live from the scene. So many people showed up to sample Mrs. Hansen's swiss steak that they had to wait in line for tables.

23   Since then, there have been some problems. The roof started leaking and the farmers had to go $4,000 into debt to replace it. Then the electrical system blew. Now they say they are going to have to install a new circuit box.

24   But Emily Hansen, who was managing a convenience store in Madison when she was asked to take on the cafe, says she and her husband, who had been laid off from his job, will stay on as long as they can. They work every day as it is, including Sunday, when the church crowd comes in for coffee.

25   "Even if we don't get rich, it's such a great feeling just to be here," said Mrs. Hansen, who had just finished baking a fresh batch of homemade doughnuts. "Whatever else, we feel like we're helping to hold this little community together."

———————

EXERCISES

Details and Their Meanings

1. When did the last cafe in Louisburg close? What kind of problem did this closing create for the men of Louisburg? Why do you think that the writer describes lunch as a "new and lonely challenge" (paragraph 1)?

2. Where is Louisburg located? How big is it? How do the location and size of the town affect the significance of the cafe? Who helped pay for the reopening of the cafe? Why did it seem the "natural" thing to do?

3. What forces and events led to the growth of Louisburg over the last century? How is the history of the town related to major

landmarks still in the town? Is Louisburg like other neighboring towns in its origin and design? How do you know?

4. What led to the closing of Louisburg's previous cafe? Did other businesses close? How is what happened in Louisburg related to what happened in other farming communities?

5. Where do the residents of Louisburg (and small towns like it) go to shop, do business, and work? How do you think this affects the pace of their lives?

6. Who decided to rebuild the cafe? Which people and organizations got involved and in what ways? Do businesses usually start in that way? What is the significance of such wide involvement?

7. Who has taken over management of the cafe? What were their personal reasons for taking on the job? Did they have any other reasons? What satisfaction do they expect to get from the job? Why do you think it might not matter to Mrs. Hansen or to the town whether the cafe makes a profit?

8. From the information provided by the writer, what future would you predict for the Louisburg cafe? What further information would you need to more accurately predict its future?

Reading and Critical Thinking

1. In what ways do you believe the process of reopening the cafe benefited the community? In what ways do you think the residents of Louisburg will benefit from being able to have lunch together?

2. From the descriptions of Louisburg and the surrounding area, what do you think some of the daily "hardships" faced by the residents might be (besides not having a cafe)?

3. What can you infer from this piece about how settlement patterns in the United States are changing?

4. What can you infer from this selection about the farming industry in general? How do you believe the occupation of farming is changing?

5. Find at least two quotations from the selection that indicate a resident's positive feelings about both the cafe and the town of Louisburg. Speculate about why people might want to live in a place like Louisburg. How does it compare to where you live now?

The Writer's Strategies

1. What issues does William E. Schmidt mention in the first three short paragraphs? From these three paragraphs, what seems to be the main focus of the selection? Do you think that this in fact is the overall idea? If it is not, which paragraph contains the best statement of the thesis?

2. What is the tone of the selection—that is, the writer's attitude toward the topic he is writing about? How does the writer create this tone?

3. Explain the figurative language in this quotation from paragraph 8: "What has happened in Louisburg also reflects the concerns that are shared by residents of many small towns who have watched their communities wither away, bled by declining populations and failing businesses along Main Street." How does the language help create an image in your mind of what is happening to this town? What are some of the images you have as a result of this sentence? Find two more sentences from the piece that contain figurative language. What images do they give you?

4. How does the writer support his claims about changes in rural life? What are the sources of his evidence? Do you find the evidence convincing? Why or why not?

5. What kind of information do paragraphs 8 through 17 give about Louisburg? What pattern does the writer use to present the case of the Louisburg cafe? How does the background information broaden the significance of the cafe's history?

6. In the last four paragraphs, do you think the writer indicates a particular hope for what happens to the cafe? If he does, what is that hope, and how do you think the order of the information at the end affects what you decided?

Thinking Together

Discuss with a small group the popular gathering places in your hometown or on your campus. What do people do in these places, and how are the places important to people's lives? Are they associated with eating, sports, or some other activity? How do these places foster a spirit of community? Each student should write a paragraph description of his or her community's most important meeting place and explain how it serves to bring people together.

Vocabulary

In the space next to each definition, write the letter of the appropriate term from the essay.

_____ 1. strong desire

_____ 2. things given

_____ 3. a coordinated operation, like an army's maneuvers

_____ 4. make fit, get used to

_____ 5. storehouse for grain

_____ 6. project

_____ 7. rule over, take up a large part

_____ 8. far off

_____ 9. dry up, lose liveliness

_____ 10. one who studies society and the ways in which people interact in groups

a. remote (par. 4)

b. sociologist (par. 14)

c. grain elevator (par. 11)

d. contributions (par. 4)

e. campaign (par. 6)

f. wither (par. 8)

g. yearning (par. 5)

h. adapt (par. 7)

i. enterprise (par. 11)

j. dominate (par. 11)

WRITER'S WORKSHOP ━━━━━━━━━━

Critical Thinking in Writing

1. Write a brief essay on what your daily life would be like if you lived in Louisburg. Imagine what would be different from your present life and what would be the same. Would you like your new life?

2. Explain in a brief essay some of the changes that the residents of Louisburg, Minnesota, have experienced in the last twenty years. How do these changes compare and contrast with the changes that residents in your community have experienced? How does community change affect people's lives?

3. Should communities take steps to preserve a known, comfortable way of life in the face of social and technological changes? Or is change inevitable and desirable even if old familiar places must vanish? Take a position on these questions in an argumentative essay.

Connecting Ideas

In a few paragraphs, compare the role of the cafe in the town of Louisburg with the role of the family kitchen in Rosemarie Santini's "An American Dream" (page 24) or in Gary Soto's "The Jacket" (page 52). End by thinking about the ways in which food and eating places bring people together.

Easy Job, Good Wages

Jesus Colon

Jesus Colon describes how unpleasant work can be. The disparity be-
tween his hopes and the realities of the job he finds raises questions
about the promises of the workplace.

KEY WORDS

galvanized (par. 2)   made of sheet metal covered with zinc.
mucilage (par. 4)   a type of glue for paper.

1   THIS HAPPENED EARLY IN 1919. We were both out of work, my brother and I. He got up earlier to look for a job. When I woke up, he was already gone. So I dressed, went out and bought a copy of the *New York World* and turned its pages until I got to the "Helped Wanted Unskilled" section of the paper. After much reading and re-reading the same columns, my attention was held by a small advertisement. It read: "Easy job. Good wages. No experience necessary." This was followed by a number and street on the west side of lower Manhattan. It sounded like the job I was looking for. Easy job. Good wages. Those four words revolved in my brain as I was travelling toward the address indicated in the advertisement. Easy job. Good wages. Easy job. Good wages. Easy . . .

2   The place consisted of a small front office and a large loft on the floor of which I noticed a series of large galvanized tubs half filled with water out of which I noticed protruding the necks of many bottles of various sizes and shapes. Around these tubs there were a number of workers, male and female, sitting on small wooden benches. All had their hands in the water of the tub, the left hand holding a bottle and with the thumb nail of the right hand scratching the labels.

3   The foreman found a vacant stool for me around one of the tubs of water. I asked why a penknife or a small safety razor could not be used instead of the thumb nail to take off the old labels from the bottles. I was expertly informed that knives or razors would scratch

281

the glass thus depreciating the value of the bottles when they were to be sold.

4   I sat down and started to use my thumb nail on one bottle. The water had somewhat softened the transparent mucilage used to attach the label to the bottle. But the softening did not work out uniformly somehow. There were always pieces of label that for some obscure reason remained affixed to the bottles. It was on those pieces of labels tenaciously fastened to the bottles that my right hand thumb nail had to work overtime. As the minutes passed I noticed that the coldness of the water started to pass from my hand to my body giving me intermittent body shivers that I tried to conceal with the greatest of effort from those sitting beside me. My hands became deadly clean and tiny little wrinkles started to show especially at the tip of my fingers. Sometimes I stopped a few seconds from scratching the bottles, to open and close my fists in rapid movements in order to bring blood to my hands. But almost as soon as I placed them in the water they became deathly pale again.

5   But these were minor details compared with what was happening to the thumb of my right hand. For a delicate, boyish thumb, it was growing by the minute into a full blown tomato colored finger. It was the only part of my right hand remaining blood red. I started to look at the workers' thumbs. I noticed that these particular fingers on their right hands were unusually developed with a thick layer of corn-like surface at the top of their right thumb. The nails on their thumbs looked coarser and smaller than on the other fingers—thumb and nail having become one and the same thing—a primitive unnatural human instrument especially developed to detach hard pieces of labels from wet bottles immersed in galvanized tubs.

6   After a couple of hours I had a feeling that my thumb nail was going to leave my finger and jump into the cold water of the tub. A numb pain imperceptibly began to be felt coming from my right thumb. Then I began to feel such pain as if coming from a finger bigger than all of my body.

7   After three hours of this I decided to quit fast. I told the foreman so, showing him my swollen finger. He figured I had earned 69 cents at 23 cents an hour.

8   Early in the evening I met my brother in our furnished room. We started to exchange experiences of our job hunting for the day. "You know what?" my brother started, "early in the morning I went to work where they take labels off old bottles—with your right hand thumb nail. . . . Somewhere on the west side of lower Manhattan. I only stayed a couple of hours. 'Easy job . . . Good wages . . .' they said. The person who wrote that ad must have had a great sense of

humor." And we both had a hearty laugh that evening when I told my brother that I also went to work at that same place later in the day.

9   Now when I see ads reading, "Easy job. Good wages," I just smile an ancient, tired, knowing smile.

––––––––––

EXERCISES

Details and Their Meanings

1. What words in the ad appealed to young Jesus Colon? Why? What was his attitude toward work?
2. What did Colon see at the workplace? What did that indicate about the work?
3. What instructions was Colon given? What did the instructions suggest about the concerns of the employers and their attitude toward the workers?
4. What happened to Colon's right thumb as he worked? What had happened to the thumbs of the other workers? What does the condition of their thumbs suggest about how long they had been employed and what they had been putting up with?
5. How much did Colon earn? What was the year? Did he view his earnings as a decent wage for the time? Do you think he was paid a decent wage?
6. What was Colon's brother's experience? How does it relate to the writer's experience?

Reading and Critical Thinking

1. The incident described by the writer took place over seventy years ago. Do similar work circumstances still exist? With what kinds of jobs and workers?
2. What attitudes about work does the writer develop as a result of this incident? What does the last paragraph indicate about his new attitude? Does that attitude reflect an appropriate generalization?
3. Do the bosses in this narrative seem to show concern for what happens to the workers? Do you think such an attitude is typical of bosses? Why or why not? How do these employers compare with those you or someone you know has worked for?

4. Do any of the workers seem to have been at the job for a long time? How do you know? Why do you think they stayed? Do you think they liked the work? What do you suspect their attitude was? Would you have stayed? What would have been your attitude?
5. Why does Jesus talk with his brother about his experiences? How does the brother's view reinforce his own? What point is the writer making?

The Writer's Strategies

1. What is the thesis of this piece? State it in your own words.
2. What mood does Colon convey at the start of the selection? What details help build that mood?
3. In what order does the writer present the details? Does any idea or perspective build up as the piece continues?
4. How does Colon increase the reader's sense of his pain? What details does he give about his discomfort and that of the other workers? How do the descriptions of hands, fingers, and nails change as the narrative progresses?
5. Where does the title of the narrative come from? Where do the words of the title appear in the selection? Do you think the title is appropriate? Why or why not? How is the title ironic—in other words, is the writer suggesting something opposite to what he says? How do you become aware of the irony? What helps to build the sense of irony?
6. What is the effect of the last sentence? Why does the writer use the words *ancient, tired,* and *knowing* to describe his own smile?

Thinking Together

In small groups, share your experiences of your first days on a recent job. What surprised you? What did you like and dislike? How did you relate to your supervisor?

Vocabulary

Locate the following words in the narrative, and then write a definition that fits the context in which the word is used.

1. loft (par. 2)
2. protruding (par. 2)

3. depreciating (par. 3)
4. uniformly (par. 4)
5. tenaciously (par. 4)
6. intermittent (par. 4)
7. immersed (par. 5)
8. imperceptibly (par. 6)

WRITER'S WORKSHOP

Critical Thinking and Writing

1. Write a few paragraphs describing how you came to learn that work is hard.
2. Jobs and careers are rarely what you imagine them to be. Write one page describing how one job you are familiar with is not the same as the employer made it sound or you thought it would be.
3. Write an essay in which you define the perfect job from your point of view. What does the job have to offer? What makes it perfect?

Connecting Ideas

Compare and contrast the realities and expectations about job experiences in this piece and in Gary Soto's "Looking for Work" (page 231). Describe a conversation that might take place between the narrators of these selections.

Running from Racists

Suzanne Seixas

Many African-Americans are haunted by continuing racist attacks. As Suzanne Seixas shows, racism has direct economic consequences for a family that wants to protect its children. The economic costs of racism, just like any other expense, must be calculated into the family budget.

KEY WORDS

paramilitary (par. 1)   similar to an army.
Down's syndrome (par. 6)   a genetic condition that results in mental retardation.
heinous (par. 12)   vile, hatefully wicked.
galvanized (par. 13)   shocked into action.

1   JOANN LONG THOUGHT IT was a prank at first. At 2:45 P.M. on December 18, 1989, her son Ray Jr.—then a 14-year-old 10th-grader at Barry Goldwater High in Phoenix—came pounding on the back door, shouting, "Let us in! The skinheads are after us!" When Joann slid open the bolt, Ray and a black school mate darted past her to the front window, obviously terrified. Peering over their shoulders, Joanne saw about 30 white youths, some carrying baseball bats and many sporting the shaved scalps and paramilitary dress of neo-Nazi "skinheads," advancing on the Longs' three-bedroom stucco home in the mostly white, middle-class neighborhood of Deer Valley. The mob kept yelling, "We're gonna get you niggers!" as it searched yard to yard for the teens.

2   Breathlessly, Ray Jr. explained that the gang had ambushed them after he challenged one of the "skins" for making fun of a planned rally marking the Rev. Dr. Martin Luther King Jr.'s birthday. After quickly locking the doors and closing the drapes, Joann phoned the police and then her husband Ray, a $41,900-a-year sales manager for the cellular-telecommunications equipment maker Celwave. "I

drove like a bat out of hell," recalls Ray, now 45. "But by the time I got home, the skinheads had been scared off by the police sirens." Although no one was hurt, the Longs were deeply shaken.

3 They are not alone: bias crimes are on the rise nationwide. Klanwatch, an arm of the Southern Poverty Law Center in Montgomery, Ala., recorded 291 race-related incidents in 41 states last year, ranging from threats to arson, bombing and even murder (the count includes only crimes where bias is known to be the main motive and thus understates the problem). The total was up 20% from the year before and fully five times higher than in 1986.

4 Five of the 20 murders, the biggest fraction attributed to any single group, were committed by skinheads—loosely organized gangs with 3,000 members across the country that ape the style and sometimes the racist politics of Great Britain's immigrant-bashing youths of the 1970s. In Arizona, skins have been active in the state's emotional debate on whether to become the 49th state to honor King's Jan. 15 birthday with a holiday. Some skins joined an anti-King rally last January, for example, to celebrate the defeat of the proposal by Arizona's 81%-white electorate two months earlier.

5 For their part, the Longs found that though their son escaped from the mob, the incident left financial scars as well as emotional ones. Specifically, they were so unsettled by the harassment that they felt compelled to move last August, even though the decision left their finances in shambles. They had to spend all their $2,300 savings to buy an $88,000, three-bedroom house in another section of Deer Valley three miles from their old home. And now their $840 monthly mortgage payment alone is 34% higher than their old $625-a-month rent.

6 On the emotional side, they want to repair the fragile sense of belonging that the attack shattered. The Longs have always prided themselves on being black pioneers: they were one of the first African-American families in Deer Valley, and Ray Jr., now 16, and sister Tasha, 18, were among only three dozen blacks in the 2,045-student Barry Goldwater High School. But the family had no desire to contend with racist toughs—especially since their third child, 12-year-old Reggie, is so profoundly retarded by Down's syndrome that he cannot read, write or even talk. Ray and Joann, 39, worried that Reggie might wander away from home and run into a group of violent skinheads.

7 The Longs now need advice on how to budget, boost savings and provide for Reggie's future. "He'll be with Joann and me all our lives," says Ray. "But what happens after we're dead?" In addition,

they need to build a solid base of diversified investments so that if they cannot flee from racism entirely, they at least won't go broke along the way.

8   Ray Long already has much to be proud of. Born the eighth of nine children on a family farm outside Houston, he finished high school and spent four years in the Navy before enrolling at Laney College in Oakland, Calif. in 1968. When his widowed mother fell ill two years later, he headed back to Houston and got a $12,000-a-year job as a moving-company salesman. After his mother's death, Ray married Joann Rogers, a teacher's aide from Brenham, Texas. And in 1975, the couple put $1,000 down and borrowed $18,500 at 8.5% to buy a three-bedroom house in northeast Houston.

9   Ray held a succession of sales jobs for local firms until he was hired by Marlboro, N.J.–based Celwave for $25,000 a year in 1984. Celwave moved the Longs to Phoenix and put Ray in charge of developing accounts in the western half of the U.S. ("Not bad for a black farm boy who never finished college," he jokes.) But since Houston's housing market was already headed downhill, Ray and Joann rented out their old home rather than sell it at a loss. The strategy worked. The roughly $3,600 annual rent more than covers the $2,400 a year they pay on the mortgage, and the property has doubled in value to about $40,000.

10   In Phoenix, the Longs moved into Deer Valley at the suggestion of one of Ray's white co-workers. All seemed to go well. Tasha became the first black cheerleader in the local Pop Warner Football League. Ray Jr. integrated marching bands as a drummer and won a roomful of softball trophies. Best of all, Reggie entered the district's highly regarded program for the mentally handicapped.

11   As more blacks moved into Deer Valley, though, racial tensions surfaced at Barry Goldwater High. At least two students proclaimed themselves skinheads. And four black youths began dressing in the trademark reds and blues of the Bloods and the Crips, the ghetto-bred Los Angeles street gangs that have been spreading nationwide.

12   The incident involving Ray Jr. began when one of the skinheads gave Tasha a "Heil, Hitler!" salute after hearing her mention an upcoming King rally. "I was shocked," she remembers. "I knew the skinheads were at school, but we'd never had much trouble from them." Ray Jr. confronted the white youth in the schoolyard at lunch. Name-calling swiftly escalated into threats, reinforcements arrived on both sides, and finally security guards hauled the chief antagonists off to assistant principal Wayne Kindall. "I issued warnings and thought that was the end of it," Kindall says. "But later that day

the police called to say Ray Jr. had been chased." Ray could identify many of his attackers, and Kindall gave one baldpated white student a two-week suspension the following day. The police subsequently took the same boy into custody briefly but then released him, saying the case was not serious enough to warrant formal charges. "He had not committed a particularly heinous crime," explains Sgt. Kevin Robinson, "and we didn't think he was a danger to himself or others."

13   Galvanized into action, Joann organized a group of 20 black parents that urged the school board to ban organized gangs. The board wouldn't go that far. But in May 1990, it called for a program to encourage sensitivity to minorities (7.2% of the district's 16,000 pupils are either black or Hispanic). A black social worker directs the effort, which has since sponsored five weekend retreats attended by a total of 200 students, parents and staffers.

14   Still, the Longs continued to feel uncomfortable at home—especially since several of Ray Jr.'s assailants lived less than a block away. "It scared the hell out of me to hear them hanging out until 2 A.M. in their backyards," admits Ray Sr. "For a while there, I wouldn't even let our kids go to the store." So as soon as their lease expired, the Longs put $4,000 down—$2,300 in savings plus $1,700 from Ray's earnings—and assumed an $84,000, 9.5% fixed-rate mortgage to buy the home they now inhabit. Moving and closing costs totaled $1,200 and Joann spent another $1,100 on bedroom furniture.

15   Those outlays tightened a family budget that was already stretched by $300-a-month payments on their '83 Toyota, bought used in the spring of 1990, and the $5,400 they had spent in the previous 12 months to travel to Houston and keep up the property there. And Ray will make that budget even tighter if he goes ahead with his plan to buy a second car after his current auto loan is paid off this fall. Already, he can only afford to pay about $25 a month on outstanding charge-card balances of $900, and add a scant $150 in paycheck deductions to the $4,000 in his 401(k). That $4,000, the family's only savings, is spread among stock, fixed-income and government-obligation funds.

16   Considering the Longs' lack of cash, it's fortunate that both Tasha and Ray Jr. have their eyes on inexpensive Glendale Community College near Phoenix, where the tuition is only $650 a year. Tasha plans to enroll this fall, and her brother will be ready to join her in 1992.

17   Racial tension at Goldwater, meanwhile, has mostly dropped out of sight. "I may overhear the word nigger when I pass some

white kids," says Ray Jr., "but it's not directed at me." Yet his mother worries her son may be downplaying the situation. "When I organized the black parents," says Joann, "my kids told me, 'Hey, Ma, the teachers tell us you're causing trouble.' Now my son won't say anything, because he doesn't want me going up to school and raising a ruckus." But she hasn't forgotten that day in December 1989. "As long as we live in this district and pay taxes, I'll watch the schools. We've run as far as we're going to go."

EXERCISES

Details and Their Meanings

1. What happens in the incident that opens the selection? What attitudes does the incident reveal? What effect did the incident have on the Longs? What did they do as a result? What were the economic consequences of the action they took?
2. What part of the mob was made up of skinheads? What do the skinheads represent? What is especially troubling about skinhead involvement in the incident? What does the skinheads' involvement suggest about whether the incident was isolated and unplanned?
3. What is the controversy in Arizona over Martin Luther King's birthday? Why does this controversy evoke racist feelings? What decision was made by the voters? What can you infer from this piece about racial attitudes in the state as a result of that vote? Do you believe the inferences are valid? Why or why not?
4. What is the father's personal history? What does that history indicate about his motivation, character, concerns, and lifestyle?
5. What are the basic facts of the family's economic condition? How does the skinhead incident affect the Longs' economic condition?
6. Did the authorities ever prosecute the attackers? Why or why not? How has the family had to protect itself? How do the Longs' economic concerns relate to their desire for self-protection? Does the family seem to expect protection by public agencies, or do the Longs feel the responsibility is primarily their own?

Reading and Critical Thinking

1. What do you think is the main purpose of this selection? the secondary purpose? How do you know? Do these two purposes work with each other or against each other?
2. What attitude do the Longs take toward the causes of the incident, the persons responsible for it, and the need to protect themselves? What position does Suzanne Seixas take on each of these? Do you agree that her attitude is appropriate or realistic?
3. How do the Longs react emotionally to the incident immediately and in the long term? Do you think that is how you would react in similar circumstances? Explain.
4. Does the move seem to have worked for the Longs? Have they escaped racism? Do you think moving was the right solution?
5. What does the family's concern for budgeting indicate? What role does money play in the lives of the Longs? Do you think money does or does not help them solve their problems? Do you think money can protect one's family from general social problems? Do you think the best strategy for protecting yourself and your family is to focus on personal economic goals? Explain.

The Writer's Strategies

1. What is the thesis of this selection? Does the writer express it directly anywhere?
2. Why does the selection open with the racist incident? Is this incident the most important point in the essay? How does it relate to and dramatize the main point?
3. The writer mixes details of racial incidents and family finances. How do these two types of details fit together to make the overall point? How do the combined details create a portrait of the family's concerns, character, and life? How does this combination of details create a general impression of racial tensions in the country?
4. In what ways do the racial incidents highlight the Longs' minority status? In what ways do the financial details highlight their majority, middle-class status? Overall, who appears most all-American in this narrative and who appears to be the fringe outsiders?
5. The narrative contains flashbacks into the history of the Long family members. Identify the flashbacks. What do they show? How do they enrich the ideas of the selection?

6. Comment on the transitional elements Seixas uses. How does she connect thoughts within paragraphs? between paragraphs? Which transitions help her achieve smooth connections between ideas? What is the purpose of the final quotation? What outlook does it leave you with? Does this piece have a simple, happy ending? Explain.

Thinking Together

In small groups, discuss any racially motivated incidents you have observed, read about, or seen on television. What stimulated them? What economic consequences can you see in those actions?

Vocabulary

Define in your own words the italicized words in the following phrases from the selection.

1. *sporting* the shaved scalps (par. 1)
2. *bias* crimes (par. 3)
3. unsettled by *harassment* (par. 5)
4. repair the *fragile* sense of belonging (par. 6)
5. a solid base of *diversified* investments (par. 7)
6. a *succession* of sales jobs (par. 9)
7. *proclaimed* themselves skinheads (par. 11)
8. swiftly *escalated* into threats (par. 12)
9. hauled the chief *antagonists* off (par. 12)
10. *outlays* tightened a family budget (par. 15)

WRITER'S WORKSHOP ━━━━━━━━━━━

Critical Thinking in Writing

1. Write a short essay explaining the extent to which middle-class life has or has not protected the Long family from some of the effects of racism. To what extent are they or are they not better off for having achieved a moderate degree of financial success?
2. Write a one-page essay agreeing or disagreeing with this statement: "Middle class life is much the same whatever race or eth-

nicity you are. The basic concerns and lifestyles are the same, even though some problems may be different."

3. Write a one-page essay describing the pressures on your financial situation and how you manage your budget to meet those pressures.

Connecting Ideas

Write a few paragraphs comparing the kinds of concerns expressed in Peter Passell's "Why Black Men Have Lost Ground" (page 239) to the kinds of concerns expressed in this selection. Are the two sets of concerns totally separate, or are they related? How do they together reinforce an overall pattern?

Era Passes from the Landscape

Jesus Sanchez

Jesus Sanchez considers the passing tradition of Japanese-American gardeners in Southern California, the forces of economics and prejudice that originally led Japanese Americans to take on the job, and the forces that are leading a new ethnic group to take over the work.

KEY WORDS

dormant (par. 3)   asleep.
flourished (par. 6)   grew well and thrived.
indignity (par. 7)   humiliating experience.

1   UP ALONG WINDING BELFAST Drive, amid a lushly planted terrace in the Hollywood Hills, the last Japanese gardener on the block prepared for a change of seasons.

2   Ted Koseki plopped flower bulbs into freshly dug holes beneath blooming rose bushes that seemed to dance in the stiff breeze on a recent morning.

3   When the bushes lie dormant in late winter, Dutch irises, daffodils and tulips will bloom in their place, said Koseki.

4   And who will replace the gray-haired Koseki—already semi-retired after more than 45 years in the business—as caretaker of this hillside garden one day? Probably not another Japanese-American gardener.

5   "I used to talk shop with them, and I would see them on the road," the gravelly-voiced Koseki said of his fellow Japanese-American gardeners. "But I don't see them anymore."

6   The former legions of Japanese-American gardeners, whose profession flourished amid prosperity and prejudice in Southern California, are fast disappearing from the suburban landscape they

mowed, trimmed and pruned with renowned skill and pride for nearly a century.

7   Most of the gardeners have reached retirement age and are giving up their routes or selling them—many to Latinos and other recent immigrants. The vast majority of younger Japanese-Americans want nothing to do with the physically-demanding profession that brought their fathers indignity despite the care they brought to their work.

8   "There is no new blood to follow," said Takeshi Kotow, general manager of the Southern California Gardeners' Federation, whose 3,000 members are predominantly Japanese-American men in their 60s. "The Japanese gardener—their quality, their pride—it's soon going to be lost. Most of today's gardening is just cut and blow."

9   The end of an era—when a Japanese gardener attired in khaki work clothes and pith helmet was a suburban status symbol—meets with mixed emotions among Japanese-Americans, who recall the racism that forced so many men to labor under the sun six days a week.

10   Japanese began gardening in California at the turn of the century, another ethnic minority for whom manual labor was the entry point into the U.S. economy.

11   Though gardening offered a decent living to men who couldn't speak English—about $2 a day—there were other, less benign reasons why so many immigrants entered the trade. California's Alien Land Laws forced many Japanese farmers to abandon their property; widespread discrimination severely limited job opportunities.

12   "Somehow, the public has a romantic notion that the Asian immigrant has a special skill that makes them gravitate to agriculture or horticulture," said Ronald Tadao Tsukashima, a sociology professor at Cal State Los Angeles and the son of a gardener. "That's not necessarily true. It was not their first choice. It was more of a matter of necessity, because of the barriers erected around them."

13   Still, it was not till after World War II—after thousands of Japanese-Americans were stripped of their livelihoods and herded into relocation camps—that they came to dominate the gardening trade.

14   Leaving the camps with little money and few opportunities, the Japanese-Americans found a refuge in gardening, where they still were held in high esteem by West Coast homeowners and it did not take a lot of cash to get started. As a result, college graduates and former businessmen turned to the skin-toughening work, making as little as $5 a month per customer for once-a-week service.

15   In the Japanese-American neighborhoods of Los Angeles, it seemed as if everyone's father was a gardener. A study shortly after the war estimated that seven of 10 adult Japanese-American males in West Los Angeles worked as gardeners.

16   "When we came out of the camps, we were all in the same boat—we had to make a living," said James Kawaguchi, who scrapped his prewar plans to attend college to take up gardening. "I had other dreams. But I had to be realistic."

17   The gardeners played a major role in rebuilding Japanese-American communities from San Diego to Seattle that were up-rooted during the war, and they paved the way for the next generation to enter the professional class. Even as late as 1970, about 8,000 gardeners supported an estimated 20% of Japanese-American households in Southern California, according to an analysis of U.S. Census statistics by historian Nobuya Tsuchida.

18   "The Japanese gardener is the unsung or unrecognized hero of the Japanese ethnic community," said Tsukashima. "After the war, they represented the economic backbone of the Japanese community."

19   Despite their hard work, many skilled gardeners felt their profession never got the respect it deserved. One gardener recalled the formation of a Japanese-American service club for professionals. There were doctors and lawyers, but no gardeners—even though some made it big, earning $250,000 a year and directing groups of 10 or more helpers.

20   For most, though, the rewards were more modest—enough to buy homes and raise children.

21   "When Japanese-Americans are asked about a prominent individual or occupation, Japanese gardeners are often left out," said Tsukashima. "It was hard work that did not confer very much status in the larger community of things."

22   The children of the gardeners grew up with mixed feelings about their fathers' profession.

23   "Most of my friends growing up had fathers who were gardeners," said John Tateishi, now a 52-year-old public affairs consultant in Los Angeles. "We sort of compared notes on whose father had what movie stars. My dad was the gardener for Marilyn Monroe. He was the gardener when she died."

24   But Tateishi has other childhood memories—like spending long, weary Saturdays helping his father at Bel-Air and Brentwood homes so big it took hours just to hand mow the lawns.

25   "You looked at some of your Caucasian friends, they went out on Saturday and played," said Tateishi. "That gave you a notion that

there were other ways to make a living. I don't think any kid whose father was a gardener ever considered it as a career option."

26   Bryan Yamasaki is one of the rare young Japanese-Americans who has followed his father into gardening.

27   As a teen-ager, the 29-year-old Yamasaki, a third-generation gardener, said he viewed the work as tedious and dirty when he would help his father on weekends.

28   But when the Los Angeles man started college, he began working a gardening route to finance his studies in landscape architecture. Eventually, his plan is to offer his clients landscape design, construction and maintenance, all from one source.

29   "I'm very picky about who my clients are," said Yamasaki, who charges at least $150 a month. "To be my client, one has to listen to my suggestions to improve the yard. The customers look to me for input as to how to solve landscape problems."

30   Yamasaki is the exception. Most gardeners these days are young Latinos, not young Japanese-Americans.

31   Mas Nishikawa, 70, who began gardening in 1950 and is now semi-retired, has passed along some of his former clients to an apprentice, Antonio Betancourt. "They will ask for a Japanese gardener," said Nishikawa. "But I tell them I know a Latino fellow that is just as good."

32   Betancourt performed house and yard work for a Los Feliz homeowner who also employed Nishikawa as gardener. After a while, Nishikawa began to entrust his gardening know-how—as well as customers—to Betancourt.

33   While the work is hard and the competition stiff, Betancourt enjoys working outdoors, and his route generates a sufficient income to support his wife and two daughters. But Betancourt—like the Japanese-Americans before him—vows no child of his will ever work as a gardener.

34   "If I had a son, I don't think I would want him to have a job like this," said Betancourt, who added he had never even thought of his daughters as future gardeners. "I believe they could get a better education and a better job."

35   These days, Latino gardeners tend to most of the yards along Belfast Avenue where Ted Koseki has worked for nearly 25 years. Like most other Japanese-American gardeners, Koseki never encouraged his only child, Calvin, to enter the field. And his son never showed any interest.

36   "When he saw me doing this kind of work, he said, 'I want to be something else,'" Koseki recalled.

37   "He wanted me to go to college," said Calvin Koseki, a 44-year-old father of two young children. "When you go to college, you start to see how other kids' parents make a living."

38   Comparing his own generation to that of his father, Koseki said: "We just had more opportunity than they did."

39   Calvin Koseki is an optometrist in San Diego. He takes care of his own yard, sometimes with the help of his father.

———————

EXERCISES

Details and Their Meanings

1. What is Ted Koseki's ethnic background? What is his work? For whom does he work? At what point is he in his career? In what way is he typical of a group of people?

2. What is the primary ethnicity and average age of members of the Southern California Gardeners' Federation? Why don't younger Japanese Americans want to enter the business? Who is taking over from the Japanese Americans?

3. Why and when did Japanese Americans first turn to gardening as a career? What happened during World War II that led to Japanese-American domination of the gardening trade? How widespread was Japanese-American participation in gardening at its height? What was the effect of this group of workers on the Japanese-American community as a whole?

4. Were gardeners given much respect in the Japanese-American community? Were they considered professionals? Was the Japanese-American view of them fair? Explain your answers.

5. What relation did the gardeners have with clients? What was the effect of the fathers' work on their children? Were the children's feelings simply positive or negative? Why?

6. Who is Bryan Yamasaki? What does he do for a living? In what way is he unusual? How does his special way of doing business set him apart from the traditional Japanese-American gardener? What does he demand from clients that his parents' generation wasn't in a position to demand?

7. Who is taking over the gardening routes? Why? In what ways are the new gardeners like the previous generation of Japanese-American gardeners? Do you think their children will follow in their footsteps? Why or why not?

Reading and Critical Thinking

1. Why do you think gardening flourished as a career for Japanese Americans? How did the Japanese workers bring dignity, quality, and pride to hard manual labor? In what ways do first generation laborers pave the way for a different kind of work for their second generation offspring?
2. In what ways, all other things being equal, was gardening a good career choice and in what ways a bad one? Consider the particular circumstances of Japanese Americans earlier in this century. In what ways was the choice good or bad in that light?
3. What does the Yamasaki story reveal about what was missing in the experience of the previous generation? What does it say about the lives of current Hispanic-American gardeners?
4. Is it better to adopt a lesser job and survive or to fight against unfair conditions? Explain your response.
5. In what ways does the writer look back nostalgically at the experience of the Japanese-American gardeners? In what way might the memories be fond ones for the employers? for the gardeners? Who do you think is more likely to be nostalgic? Why?
6. What idea and attitude does the title of the selection reflect? Is it good or bad that the era is passing away? Will the new era be any different? For whom?

The Writer's Strategies

1. What is the thesis of the selection? How do the introductory paragraphs help set the stage for the thesis?
2. Where and with whom does the selection end in the last paragraph? How does the discussion of Ted Koseki at the end contrast with the opening? What points are made by the contrast? How does the last anecdote tie the themes of the piece together?
3. Who is the audience for this piece? How can you tell? How might the various ethnic groups represented here react to Jesus Sanchez's point?
4. What are the various ways in which the writer shows that there was another, less pleasant, side to the job? How is the comparison with the children's career choices used to highlight the shortcomings of a career in gardening? How are the children's choices related to the passing of the era?
5. What specific connections are made between the Japanese-American and the Hispanic-American gardeners? How do these connections shed light on the conditions of the new generation

of gardeners, and how do they predict the future? What does the writer's name suggest about his ethnicity? What do you think his interest in the issues might be?

6. Explain the introduction in this piece. How is it related to the closing? How do they both relate to the title?

Thinking Together

In small groups, discuss the ways in which the experience of the Japanese-American gardeners may or may not be similar to the work experience of other immigrant groups in the United States. Compare the experiences described here with what you know of your own family's history. Also consider the effect of the United States being at war with the country of origin. Do you think German Americans suffered similar difficulties in entering the American economy? Why or why not?

Vocabulary

Write definitions for the following words, which appear in the selection.

1. lushly (par. 1)
2. caretaker (par. 4)
3. pruned (par. 6)
4. gravitate (par. 12)
5. horticulture (par. 12)

WRITER'S WORKSHOP ─────────────────

Critical Thinking in Writing

1. Describe a time when you made the best of a bad situation and were able to feel a sense of achievement and take some pleasure in your handling of some painful choices.
2. Write a paragraph describing whether and in what ways your career goals and choices parallel or differ from those of your parents. Explain why you think they do or do not do so.

3. Are you familiar with any immigrant or ethnic group that has been limited to a narrow range of careers or has found its best opportunities within a single career? Write a few paragraphs describing the career experience of this group and the forces that directed group members toward their careers.

Connecting Ideas

In what ways might the gardeners presented here agree or disagree with Jesus Colon's feelings about his work experience in "Easy Job, Good Wages" (page 281)?

SIDE BY SIDE

1. Drawing on the information and examples presented in the selections in this unit, write an essay evaluating whether America is the land of opportunity.
2. Recalling what you have learned from the selections in this unit, write a letter to a college-age student from any country and of any ethnic background. This student is thinking of immigrating to the United States and has asked for your advice about where and how he or she might successfully enter the American economy. Before writing the letter, write a brief paragraph describing the background of the student you are writing to.
3. Write an essay comparing how the different people described in the selections of this unit confront the obstacles and frustrations they find in the workplace and economy. What traits of character help them deal with difficulties? What strategies do they use to gain some place in the economy? What attitudes do they develop to deal with their situations?

UNIT 5

Prejudices:
Tears in the
Rainbow Fabric

INTRODUCTION ──────────────────────────────

No one can make a special claim for his or her group as the "true" Americans because, in fact, no human beings are indigenous to this continent. Everyone, even the intrepid Native Americans who first discovered this land thousands of years ago, came from somewhere else. Some people who came to North America chose to leave their homes in search of better lives; others were brought as prisoners or slaves. But each wave of immigrants has come to view the next group as outsiders. Fear and competition for land, jobs, and spouses often breed conditions in which newcomers are excluded and considered dangerous. In this way prejudices develop, grow, and overwhelm.

In this unit you will read about the experiences of people who come up squarely against discrimination, either because of their race or because of their heritage. In "Nazi Hate Movies Continue to Ignite Fierce Passions," Rebecca Lieb recounts the continuing controversy surrounding hate films made in Germany by the Nazis in the 1940s. In "Zoot Suit Riots," Albert Camarillo examines the anger and violence that erupt when people find themselves excluded from the benefits of American life. Hisaye Yamamoto in "Wilshire Bus," looks at the hurt of modern-day prejudices in Los Angeles. James M. Freeman in "Hearts of Sorrow," describes the often bitter experiences of Vietnamese immigrants trying to make their way in America. In "A Hanging," the only essay in this book to show a clash of cultures outside America, George Orwell takes us to the execution of a Burmese man during the British occupation of the man's country. Ellen Goodman in "The Great Divide," and Marcus Mabry in "Confronting Campus Racism," explore growing concerns about racism on college campuses and the incidents of bias that sometimes arise in the shadow of the ivory tower.

A fundamental element in the promise of America is both its open invitation to immigrants of all lands and its support for assimilation into the American way. Nevertheless human behavior has many dark sides, and none perhaps is so unreasonable and without validity as prejudging other human beings because of how they look or what they believe. Prejudice tears at the rainbow fabric of equity and fairness that should tie together the people of a nation.

PREREADING JOURNAL

1. Write a journal entry about an experience in which you or someone you know was the victim of discrimination. When did it take place? What were the circumstances? What characteristic of you or the other person—appearance, sex, age, race, or something else—made you or that person a victim? What was the outcome of this event? How did it change you or the other person?

2. How do you think prejudices develop? Do you think people learn prejudices or are prejudices innate? If your parents or neighbors harbor prejudices against some group, do you think you will inevitably develop the same beliefs?

3. Imagine you are a stranger to this country. You do not speak the language or know the customs. The food is strange, and many people seem unfriendly. Write a journal entry in which you describe how you would feel in these circumstances. What steps will you take to become comfortable in your new surroundings? How will you work to overcome the potential or apparent hostility of people toward you?

Wilshire Bus

Hisaye Yamamoto

In this selection, a Japanese-American woman riding on a bus witnesses a racist incident and realizes something disturbing about herself and society as a whole.

KEY WORDS

somatotonic (par. 5)   aggressive, physical personality type associated with a muscular body.
metaphor (par. 8)   word or phrase that compares two things.
diatribe (par. 9)   abusive speech.
coolies (par. 12)   unskilled, poorly paid Chinese laborers.
gloating (par. 15)   delighting in someone else's misfortune.
desolate (par. 17)   deserted, joyless.
craw (par. 22)   stomach.

1   WILSHIRE BOULEVARD BEGINS SOMEWHERE near the heart of downtown Los Angeles and, except for a few digressions scarcely worth mentioning, goes straight out to the edge of the Pacific Ocean. It is a wide boulevard and traffic on it is fairly fast. For the most part, it is bordered on either side with examples of the recent stark architecture which favors a great deal of glass. As the boulevard approaches the sea, however, the landscape becomes a bit more pastoral, so that the university and the soldiers' home there give the appearance of being huge country estates.

2   Esther Kuroiwa got to know this stretch of territory quite well while her husband Buro was in one of the hospitals at the soldiers' home. They had been married less than a year when his back, injured in the war, began troubling him again, and he was forced to take three months of treatments at Sawtelle before he was able to go back to work. During this time, Esther was permitted to visit him twice a week and she usually took the yellow bus out on Wednesdays because she did not know the first thing about driving and because her friends were not able to take her except on Sundays. She

309

always enjoyed the long bus ride very much because her seat companions usually turned out to be amiable, and if they did not, she took vicarious pleasure in gazing out at the almost unmitigated elegance along the fabulous street.

3   It was on one of these Wednesday trips that Esther committed a grave sin of omission which caused her later to burst into tears and which caused her acute discomfort for a long time afterwards whenever something reminded her of it.

4   The man came on the bus quite early and Esther noticed him briefly as he entered because he said gaily to the driver, "You robber. All you guys do is take money from me every day, just for giving me a short lift!"

5   Handsome in a red-faced way, greying, medium of height, and dressed in a dark grey sport suit with a yellow-and-black flowered shirt, he said this in a nice, resonant, carrying voice which got the response of a scattering of titters from the bus. Esther, somewhat amused and classifying him as a somatotonic, promptly forgot about him. And since she was sitting alone in the first regular seat, facing the back of the driver and the two front benches facing each other, she returned to looking out the window.

6   At the next stop, a considerable mass of people piled on and the last two climbing up were an elderly Oriental man and his wife. Both were neatly and somberly clothed and the woman, who wore her hair in a bun and carried a bunch of yellow and dark red chrysanthemums, came to sit with Esther. Esther turned her head to smile a greeting (well, here we are, Orientals together on a bus), but the woman was watching, with some concern, her husband who was asking directions of the driver.

7   His faint English was inflected in such a way as to make Esther decide he was probably Chinese, and she noted that he had to repeat his question several times before the driver could answer it. Then he came to sit in the seat across the aisle from his wife. It was about then that a man's voice, which Esther recognized soon as belonging to the somatotonic, began a loud monologue in the seat just behind her. It was not really a monologue, since he seemed to be addressing his seat companion, but this person was not heard to give a single answer. The man's subject was a figure in the local sporting world who had a nice fortune invested in several of the shining buildings the bus was just passing.

8   "He's as tight-fisted as they make them, as tight-fisted as they come," the man said. "Why, he wouldn't give you the sweat of his . . ." He paused here to rephrase his metaphor, ". . . wouldn't give you the sweat off his palm!"

9   And he continued in this vein, discussing the private life of the famous man so frankly that Esther knew he must be quite drunk. But she listened with interest, wondering how much of this diatribe was true, because the public legend about the famous man was emphatic about his charity. Suddenly, the woman with the chrysanthemums jerked around to get a look at the speaker and Esther felt her giving him a quick but thorough examination before she turned back around.

10   "So you don't like it?" the man inquired, and it was a moment before Esther realized that he was now directing his attention to her seat neighbor.

11   "Well, if you don't like it," he continued, "why don't you get off this bus, why don't you go back where you came from? Why don't you go back to China?"

12   Then, his voice growing jovial, as though he were certain of the support of the bus in this at least, he embroidered on this theme with a new eloquence, "Why don't you go back to China, where you can be coolies working in your bare feet out in the rice fields? You can let your pigtails grow and grow in China. Alla samee, mama, no tickee no shirtee. Ha, pretty good, no tickee no shirtee!"

13   He chortled with delight and seemed to be looking around the bus for approval. Then some memory caused him to launch on a new idea. "Or why don't you go back to Trinidad? They got Chinks running the whole she-bang in Trinidad. Every place you go in Trinidad . . ."

14   As he talked on, Esther, pretending to look out the window, felt the tenseness in the body of the woman beside her. The only movement from her was the trembling of the chrysanthemums with the motion of the bus. Without turning her head, Esther was also aware that a man, a mild-looking man with thinning hair and glasses, on one of the front benches, was smiling at the woman and shaking his head mournfully in sympathy, but she doubted whether the woman saw.

15   Esther herself, while believing herself properly annoyed with the speaker and sorry for the old couple, felt quite detached. She found herself wondering whether the man meant her in his exclusion order or whether she was identifiably Japanese. Of course, he was not sober enough to be interested in such fine distinctions, but it did matter, she decided, because she was Japanese, not Chinese, and therefore in the present case immune. Then she was startled to realize that what she was actually doing was gloating over the fact that the drunken man had specified the Chinese as the unwanted.

16   Briefly, there bobbled on her memory the face of an elderly Oriental man whom she had once seen from a streetcar on her way home from work. (This was not long after she had returned to Los Angeles from the concentration camp in Arkansas and been lucky enough to get a clerical job with the Community Chest.) The old man was on a concrete island at Seventh and Broadway, waiting for his streetcar. She had looked down on him benignly as a fellow Oriental, from her seat by the window, then been suddenly thrown for a loop by the legend on a large lapel button on his jacket. I AM KOREAN, said the button.

17   Heat suddenly rising to her throat, she had felt angry, then desolate and betrayed. True, reason had returned to ask whether she might not, under the circumstances, have worn such a button herself. She had heard rumors of I AM CHINESE buttons. So it was true then; why not I AM KOREAN buttons, too? Wryly, she wished for an I AM JAPANESE button, just to be able to call the man's attention to it, "Look at me!" But perhaps the man didn't even read English, perhaps he had been actually threatened, perhaps it was not his doing— his solicitous children perhaps had urged him to wear the badge.

18   Trying now to make up for her moral shabbiness, she turned towards the little woman and smiled at her across the chrysanthemums, shaking her head a little to get across her message (don't pay any attention to that stupid old drunk, he doesn't know what he's saying, let's take things like this in our stride). But the woman, in turn looking at her, presented a face so impassive yet cold, and eyes so expressionless yet hostile, that Esther's overture fell quite flat.

19   Okay, okay, if that's the way you feel about it, she thought to herself. Then the bus made another stop and she heard the man proclaim ringingly, "So clear out, all of you, and remember to take every last one of your slant-eyed pickaninnies with you!" This was his final advice as he stepped down from the middle door. The bus remained at the stop long enough for Esther to watch the man cross the street with a slightly exploring step. Then, as it started up again, the bespectacled man in front stood up to go and made a clumsy speech to the Chinese couple and possibly to Esther. "I want you to know," he said, "that we aren't all like that man. We don't all feel the way he does. We believe in an America that is a melting pot of all sorts of people. I'm originally Scotch and French myself." With that, he came over and shook the hand of the Chinese man.

20   "And you, young lady," he said to the girl behind Esther, "you deserve a Purple Heart or something for having to put up with that sitting beside you."

21   Then he, too, got off.

22   The rest of the ride was uneventful and Esther stared out the window with eyes that did not see. Getting off at last at the soldiers' home, she was aware of the Chinese couple getting off after her, but she avoided looking at them. Then, while she was walking towards Buro's hospital very quickly, there arose in her mind some words she had once read and let stick in her craw: People say, do not regard what he says, now he is in liquor. Perhaps it is the only time he ought to be regarded.

23   These words repeated themselves until her saving detachment was gone every bit and she was filled once again in her life with the infuriatingly helpless, insidiously sickening sensation of there being in the world nothing solid she could put her finger on, nothing solid she could come to grips with, nothing solid she could sink her teeth into, nothing solid.

24   When she reached Buro's room and caught sight of his welcoming face, she ran to his bed and broke into sobs that she could not control. Buro was amazed because it was hardly her first visit and she had never shown such weakness before, but solving the mystery handily, he patted her head, looked around smugly at his roommates, and asked tenderly, "What's the matter? You've been missing me a whole lot, huh?" And she, finally drying her eyes, sniffed and nodded and bravely smiled and answered him with the question, yes, weren't women silly?

EXERCISES

Details and Their Meanings

1. During what years do you assume the selection is taking place? What important events occurred in this time period? In general, why do you think it might be important to know the time period reflected in a written selection?

2. How is Wilshire Boulevard described by the narrator? What is her usual experience of the bus ride to see her husband? What does this information have to do with what happens to Esther Kuroiwa?

3. Identify the ethnic origins of Esther Kuroiwa, the elderly woman who is holding a bunch of chrysanthemums, the drunk somatotonic man on the bus, and the sympathetic man who speaks to the elderly woman after the drunk man gets off the bus. Why do you think the writer mentions all these different ethnic groups?

4. What do you know about Esther Kuroiwa's husband, Buro? How does his role in World War II contribute to what you think the overall point of the selection might be? Where was Esther Kuroiwa during World War II? What does this detail have to do with the other bus ride that she remembers?

5. How does Esther feel at first about the drunk man's comments? By the time she gets to her husband's room, how does she feel? How have Esther's attitudes about racial issues changed by the end of the piece?

6. Is Esther's reaction to the drunk man's racism clearly known to the other riders? Why do you think her reaction upsets her so much?

Reading and Critical Thinking

1. What is the significance of the "I am Korean" button? Why do you think Esther remembers it on this particular bus ride? How did Esther's racism differ from that of the man she observed wearing the "I am Korean" button? What kind of racism has Esther experienced?

2. In what ways did Esther's and Buro's experience during World War II contrast? How does the contrast contribute to the overall meaning of the narrative?

3. Why do you think Esther repeats the saying: "do not regard what he says, now he is in liquor" and then thinks to herself, "Perhaps it is the only time he ought to be regarded"? What does her analysis have to do with the feeling that she has committed a grave sin of omission?

4. In what ways does this selection intend to change stereotypic expectations of what racism is? Has the piece helped you see racism in a new light? How?

5. Do you think "grave sin of omission" describes what Esther "did"? What did she omit? How might you word what she "did" in a different way?

6. How do you think your knowledge of history or different cultures affects your reading of this piece?

The Writer's Strategies

1. How does Yamamoto open the selection? What do the first two paragraphs have to do with the event that the narrative discloses?
2. From whose point of view are the events told? In what ways could the narrative be different if told from another character's perspective? Discuss several different possibilities.
3. The point of the selection is announced in paragraph 3, but it is not really understood until approximately paragraph 15. What effect does this have on the reader? What is the purpose of the second half of the story after Esther's realization?
4. Pick out several descriptions, lines of dialogue, or thoughts that give you an idea of what Esther is feeling. How does the writer make Esther's thoughts and feelings real to you?
5. Why do you think the writer included the man of Scotch and French background? If this character were not present, how would the meaning of the selection change?

Thinking Together

In small groups, discuss whether you or someone you know has been in a situation similar to that of any of the people in the selection. Discuss what you did in the situation and how you felt. Then discuss with the group if you wish you had responded differently. If you do, think about how you could respond differently in the future in a similar situation. As a group, discuss what sort of thinking has to change for the Wilshire bus "scene" to disappear.

Vocabulary

The following adjectives and adverbs describe characters, places, objects, and ideas mentioned in the selection. Define each word.

1. stark (par. 1)
2. pastoral (par. 1)
3. amiable (par. 2)
4. vicarious (par. 2)
5. unmitigated (par. 2)
6. grave (par. 3)
7. acute (par. 3)
8. resonant (par. 5)

9. jovial (par. 12)
10. detached (par. 15)
11. benignly (par. 16)
12. solicitous (par. 17)
13. infuriatingly (par. 23)
14. insidiously (par. 23)

WRITER'S WORKSHOP ━━━━━━━━━━━

Critical Thinking in Writing

1. Suppose you are invited to speak to a group of third grade children about racist attitudes. What would you tell the children about how to develop positive relations with people no matter what their backgrounds? What would you say about the causes of racism and how to avoid it.
2. What effects do you think racism has on people to whom it is directed? Write a short essay on this question. If you want, use this selection or other selections, as well as your own experiences and knowledge, as evidence to support your main point.
3. Write a short piece about the different forms of racism that exist in your community. Like Hisaye Yamamoto does in this piece, use scenes of people and places to illustrate the kinds of racism that you identify.

Connecting Ideas

In this piece, the narrator at first distances herself from the fate of other people being discriminated against but then makes an imaginative leap to understand sympathetically how another person's situation might be just as real as hers.

Compare that process of sympathetic imagination to the one that occurs in George Orwell's "A Hanging" (page 332) or to one occurring in any other selection in this anthology.

White Guilt

Shelby Steele

Shelby Steele is the author of The Content of Our Character: A New Vision of Race in America *and an associate professor of English at San Jose State University. In this essay, he explores the relation between guilt and action in racial issues.*

KEY WORDS

palpable (par. 2)   able to be felt.
denigration (par. 3)   putting down, belittling.
bestowed (par. 3)   gave.
recalcitrant (par. 3)   unwilling to cooperate.
mundane (par. 5)   common, ordinary.
parity (par. 5)   equality.
regression (par. 5)   moving backward.
subjugation (par. 7)   conquest.
anathema (par. 7)   a hateful thing.
inadvertently (par. 10)   not intentionally.
paradigm (par. 12)   an example, model.
visceral (par. 13)   felt in a deep way.

1   I DON'T REMEMBER HEARING the phrase "white guilt" very much before the mid-1960s. Growing up black in the 1950s, I never had the impression that whites were much disturbed by guilt when it came to blacks. When I would stray into the wrong restaurant in pursuit of a hamburger, it didn't occur to me that the waitress was unduly troubled by guilt when she asked me to leave. I can see now that possibly she was, but then all I saw was her irritability at having to carry out so unpleasant a task. If there was guilt, it was mine for having made an imposition of myself. I can remember feeling a certain sympathy for such people, as if I was victimizing them by drawing them out of an innocent anonymity into the unasked for role of racial policemen. Occasionally they came right out and asked me to feel sorry for them. A caddymaster at a country club

317

told my brother and me that he was doing us a favor by not letting us caddy at this white club and that we should try to understand his position, "put yourselves in my shoes." Our color had brought this man anguish and, if a part of that anguish was guilt, it was not as immediate to me as my own guilt. I smiled at the man to let him know he shouldn't feel bad and then began my long walk home. Certainly I also judge him a coward, but in that era his cowardice was something I had to absorb.

2   In the 1960s, particularly the black-is-beautiful late 1960s, this absorption of another's cowardice was no longer necessary. The lines of moral power, like plates in the earth, had shifted. White guilt became so palpable you could see it on people. At the time what it looked like to my eyes was a remarkable loss of authority. And what whites lost in authority, blacks gained. You cannot feel guilty about anyone without giving away power to them. Suddenly, this huge vulnerability had opened up in whites and, as a black, you had the power to step right into it. In fact, black power all but demanded that you do so. What shocked me in the late 1960s, after the helplessness I had felt in the fifties, was that guilt had changed the nature of the white man's burden from the administration of inferiors to the uplift of equals—from the obligations of dominance to the urgencies of repentance.

3   I think what made the difference between the fifties and sixties, at least as far as white guilt was concerned, was that whites underwent an archetypal Fall. Because of the immense turmoil of the civil rights movement, and later the black-power movement, whites were confronted for more than a decade with their willingness to participate in, or comply with, the oppression of blacks, their indifference to human suffering and denigration, their capacity to abide evil for their own benefit and in the defiance of their own sacred principles. The 1964 Civil Rights Bill that bestowed equality under the law on blacks was also, in a certain sense, an admission of white guilt. Had white society not been wrong, there would have been no need for such a bill. In this bill the nation acknowledged its fallenness, its lack of racial innocence, and confronted the incriminating self-knowledge that it had rationalized for many years a flagrant injustice. Denial is a common way of handling guilt, but in the 1960s there was little will left for denial except in the most recalcitrant whites. With this defense lost there was really only one road back to innocence—through actions and policies that would bring redemption.

4   In the 1960s the need for white redemption from racial guilt became the most powerful, yet unspoken, element in America's social-policy-making process, first giving rise to the Great Society and then

to a series of programs, policies, and laws that sought to make black equality and restitution a national mission. Once America could no longer deny its guilt, it went after redemption, or at least the look of redemption, and did so with a vengeance. Yet today, some twenty years later, study after study tells us that by many measures the gap between blacks and whites is widening rather than narrowing. A University of Chicago study indicates that segregation is more entrenched in American cities today than ever imagined. A National Research Council study notes the "status of blacks relative to whites (in housing and education) has stagnated or regressed since the early seventies." A follow-up to the famous Kerner Commission Report warns that blacks are as much at risk today of becoming a "nation within a nation" as we were twenty years ago, when the original report was made.

5   I think the white need for redemption has contributed to this tragic situation by shaping our policies regarding blacks in ways that may deliver the look of innocence to society and its institutions but that do very little actually to uplift blacks. The specific effect of this hidden need has been to bend social policy more toward reparation for black oppression than toward the much harder and more mundane work of black uplift and development. Rather than facilitate the development of blacks to achieve parity with whites, these programs and policies—affirmative action is a good example—have tended to give blacks special entitlements that in many cases are of no use because blacks lack the development that would put us in a position to take advantage of them. I think the reason there has been more entitlement than development is (along with black power) the unacknowledged white need for redemption—not true redemption, which would have concentrated policy on black development, but the appearance of redemption, which requires only that society, in the name of development, seem to be paying back its former victims with preferences. One of the effects of entitlements, I believe, has been to encourage in blacks a dependency both on entitlements and on the white guilt that generates them. Even when it serves ideal justice, bounty from another man's guilt weakens. While this is not the only factor in black "stagnation" and "regression," I believe it is one very potent factor.

6   It is easy enough to say that white guilt too often has the effect of bending social policies in the wrong direction. But what exactly is this guilt, and how does it work in American life?

7   I think white guilt, in its broad sense, springs from the knowledge of ill-gotten advantage. More precisely, it comes from the juxtaposition of this knowledge with the inevitable gratitude one feels for

being white rather than black in America. Given the moral instincts of human beings, it is all but impossible to enjoy an ill-gotten advantage, much less to feel at least secretly grateful for it, without consciously or unconsciously experiencing guilt. If, as Kierkegaard writes, "innocence is ignorance," then guilt must always involve knowledge. White Americans *know* that their historical advantage comes from the subjugation of an entire people. So, even for whites today for whom racism is anathema, there is no escape from the knowledge that makes for guilt. Racial guilt simply accompanies the condition of being white in America.

8   I do not believe that this guilt is a crushing anguish for most whites, but I do believe it constitutes a continuing racial vulnerability—an openness to racial culpability—that is a thread in white life, sometimes felt, sometimes not, but ever present as a potential feeling. In the late 1960s almost any black could charge this vulnerability with enough current for a white person to feel it. I had a friend who had developed this activity into a sort of speciality. I don't think he meant to be mean, though certainly he was mean. I think he was, in that hyperbolic era, exhilarated by the discovery that his race, which had long been a liability, now gave him a certain edge—that white guilt was the true force behind black power. To feel this power he would sometimes set up what he called "race experiments." Once I watched him stop a white businessman in the men's room of a large hotel and convince him to increase his tip to the black attendant from one to twenty dollars.

9   My friend's tactic was very simple, even corny. Out of the attendant's earshot he asked the man simply to look at the attendant, a frail, elderly, and very dark man in a starched white smock that made the skin on his neck and face look as leathery as a turtle's. He sat listlessly, pathetically, on a straight-backed chair next to a small table on which sat a stack of hand towels and a silver plate for tips. Since the attendant offered no service whatever beyond the handing out of towels, one could only conclude the hotel management offered his lowly presence as flattery to their patrons, as an opportunity for that easy noblesse oblige that could reassure even the harried and weary traveling salesman of his superior station. My friend was quick to make this point to the businessman and to say that no white man would do in this job. But when the businessman put the single back in his wallet and took out a five, my friend only sneered. Did he understand the tragedy of a life spent this way, of what it must be like to earn one's paltry living as a symbol of inferiority? And did he realize that his privilege as an affluent white businessman (ironically he had just spent the day trying to sell a printing

press to the Black Muslims for their newspaper *Mohammed Speaks*) was connected to the deprivation of this man and others like him?

10   But then my friend made a mistake that ended the game. In the heat of argument, which until then had only been playfully challenging, he inadvertently mentioned his father. This stopped the victim cold and his eyes turned inward. "What about your father?" the businessman asked. My friend replied, "He had a hard life, that's all." "How did he have a hard life?" the businessman asked. Now my friend was on the defensive. I knew he did not get along with his father, a bitter man who worked nights in a factory and demanded that the house be dark and silent all day. My friend blamed his father's bitterness on racism, but I knew he had not meant to exploit his own pain in this silly "experiment." Things had gotten too close to home, but he didn't know how to get out of the situation without losing face. Now, caught in his own trap, he did what he least wanted to do. He gave forth the rage he truly felt to a white stranger in a public men's room. "My father never had a chance," he said with the kind of anger that could easily turn to tears. "He never had a freakin' chance. Your father had all the goddam chances, and you know he did. You sell printing presses to black people and make thousands and your father probably lives down in Fat City, Florida, all because you're white." On and on he went in this vein, using— against all that was honorable in him—his own profound racial pain to extract a flash of guilt from a white man he didn't even know.

11   He got more than a flash. The businessman was touched. His eyes became mournful, and finally he simply said, "You're right. Your people got a raw deal." He took a twenty dollar bill from his wallet and walked over and dropped it in the old man's tip plate. When he was gone my friend and I could not look at the old man, nor could we look at each other.

12   It is obvious that this was a rather shameful encounter for all concerned—my friend and I, as his silent accomplice, trading on our racial pain, tampering with a stranger for no reason, and the stranger then buying his way out of the situation for twenty dollars, a sum that was generous by one count and cheap by another. It was not an encounter of people but of historical grudges and guilts. Yet, when I think about it now twenty years later, I see that it had all the elements of a paradigm that I believe has been very much at the heart of racial policy-making in America since the 1960s.

13   My friend did two things that made this businessman vulnerable to his guilt—that brought his guilt into the situation as a force. First he put this man in touch with his own knowledge of his ill-gotten advantage as a white. The effect of this was to disallow the

man any pretense of racial innocence, to let him know that, even if he was not the sort of white who used the word *nigger* around the dinner table, he still had reason to feel racial guilt. But, as disarming as this might have been, it was too abstract to do much more than crack open this man's vulnerability, to expose him to the logic of white guilt. This was the five-dollar, intellectual sort of guilt. The twenty dollars required something more visceral. In achieving this, the second thing my friend did was something he had not intended to do, something that ultimately brought him as much shame as he was doling out: He made a display of his own racial pain and anger. (What brought him shame was not the pain and anger, but his trading on them for what turned out to be a mere twenty bucks.) The effect of this display was to reinforce the man's knowledge of ill-gotten advantage, to give credibility and solidity to it by putting a face on it. Here was human testimony, a young black beside himself at the thought of his father's racially constricted life. The pain of one man evidenced the knowledge of the other. When the businessman listened to my friend's pain, his racial guilt—normally only one source of guilt lying dormant among others—was called out like a neglected debt he would finally have to settle. An ill-gotten advantage is not hard to bear—it can be marked up to fate—until it touches the genuine human pain it has brought into the world. This is the pain that hardens guilty knowledge.

14   Such knowledge is a powerful influence when it becomes conscious. What makes it so powerful is the element of fear that guilt always carries, the fear of what the guilty knowledge says about us. Guilt makes us afraid for ourselves, and thus generates as much self-preoccupation as concern for others. The nature of this preoccupation is always the redemption of innocence, the reestablishment of good feeling about oneself.

EXERCISES

Details and Their Meanings

1. When did Shelby Steele grow up? What important social movement did he witness.
2. When was the Civil Rights Bill proposed? What did this legislation bestow?

3. What was the Great Society? What social problems did it try to solve? How much did it accomplish?
4. What research groups have reported on the status of blacks? What have they reported?
5. What is *Mohammed Speaks*? Who publishes it?

Reading and Critical Thinking

1. What do you infer is the writer's class and educational background? What details give you this information? How do his class and education influence his opinions, do you think?
2. What does the writer believe entitlement programs do to the black community? Who is responsible for this situation? Do you agree or disagree with his position? For what reasons?
3. What does the writer believe was the force behind black power? How did the black power movement change civil rights legislation?
4. How does the story about the twenty-dollar tip relate to black power?
5. What can we infer from this selection about how white Americans feel toward blacks? Is this feeling conscious or unconscious?
6. According to the writer, does social legislation uplift blacks? Why or why not?
7. What does the writer imply that blacks who exploit white guilt are trading? Is it a fair trade?
8. What is the writer's opinion about black separatism? What does he suggest is the real motivation behind it?

The Writer's Strategies

1. What part of this essay deals with the writer's personal experience? How much of this selection is drawn from his direct knowledge?
2. What is the writer's purpose for writing this essay? Where does he establish his purpose?
3. What major rhetorical strategies appear here? How does Steele order the details?
4. What is Steele's thesis? How does it relate to the introduction? Which paragraphs make up the introduction?
5. In which paragraph does the writer express an opinion? Where does he advance his argument through facts? Which paragraphs use interpretation?
6. Who is the intended audience for this essay? How can you tell?

Thinking Together

Conduct a survey, and make a list of sports teams, sororities, clubs and other organizations on your campus that are separatist—only open to certain people on the basis of gender, race, religion, or ethnic heritage. Brainstorm to develop a list of reasons for and against exclusionary organizations.

Vocabulary

The following phrases appear in the text. Define each phrase in your own words. Identify the ones that are examples of figurative language—that is, poetical expressions that suggest more than the literal meaning of the words themselves.

1. obligations of dominance (par. 2)
2. urgencies of repentance (par. 2)
3. archetypal Fall (par. 3)
4. incriminating self-knowledge (par. 3)
5. flagrant injustice (par. 3)
6. special entitlements (par. 5)
7. ill-gotten advantage (par. 7)
8. racial culpability (par. 8)
9. hyperbolic era (par. 8)
10. easy noblesse oblige (par. 9)

WRITER'S WORKSHOP

Critical Thinking in Writing

1. Describe and analyze an experience you or someone you know has had with guilt about another individual or group. Did your guilt stem from a sense of injustice or from having taken unfair advantage of a situation?
2. Considering the other readings you have looked at or your own experience, do you believe that any particular groups—black people, Hispanics, women, specially-abled—have suffered more than any other people? What explanation can you give for your answer?
3. If Steele is right and entitlement is not a satisfactory cure for institutional racism, then what is? Write a process essay in which you spell out how to eliminate obstacles confronting various ethnic groups in America.

Connecting Ideas

Read "Fighting the Failure Syndrome," by Susan Tifft (page 46). How would Steele feel about separate classrooms for black men? Would he think that separate classrooms can help improve opportunities or that they are just another example of segregation as a means of avoiding real change? Explain your response.

Nazi Hate Movies Continue to Ignite Fierce Passions

Rebecca Lieb

Rebecca Lieb, a correspondent for Variety, *a magazine devoted to show business, lives and works in Berlin, Germany. In this essay, she considers the propaganda films made by Adolf Hitler in the 1930s and 1940s.*

KEY WORDS

anti-Semitic (par. 1)   prejudice against Jews.
rabidly (par. 2)   extremely; literally, foaming at the mouth like a mad dog.
inure (par. 3)   to accustom.
vitriolic (par. 3)   corrosive like acid.
avaricious (par. 3)   incredibly greedy.
usurp (par. 3)   to steal someone else's place.
diatribe (par. 3)   long critical speech, harangue.

1   DO THE PROPAGANDA FILMS made by the Nazis to inspire anti-Semitic prejudice still have the power to stir up hate? Are they dangerous or should they be shown? If they are to be shown, who will show them and under what circumstances? Is there anything to be learned from them or are they too horrifying even to contemplate?

2   Some 1,400 films were made under the supervision of Joseph Goebbels, Hitler's minister of propaganda. At least three ("Jud Süss," "The Rothschilds" and "The Eternal Jew") were rabidly anti-Semitic. Widely shown, they were used to turn Germans against their Jewish neighbors and to inure them to the march of the Holocaust.

3   The most vitriolic of the films is the pseudo-documentary "The Eternal Jew," shot in the Warsaw ghetto in 1940. Jews are portrayed as a lice-infested, lazy and avaricious people, who disguise them-

selves in European garb to infiltrate and usurp Western civilization. Jewish migration is compared visually to a plague of rats. Prominent individuals are attacked, including the "deadly enemy" Charlie Chaplin and "the relativity Jew" Albert Einstein. Graphic scenes of kosher butchering, showing Jews as bloodthirsty and sadistic, climax the diatribe.

4   Whether "The Eternal Jew" and the other Nazi films should now be seen is stirring debate in the United States and Germany. In the United States, a major archive for films about Jewish life is restricting access to the movies. In Germany, the state-appointed custodian of the films has launched a campaign against an American who has distributed videocassettes of the films. Those believing they are dangerous, including the German Government and some Jewish groups in the United States, demand that the films be kept in vaults, inaccessible to all but a scholarly few. Arguments over morals, censorship, freedom of speech and copyright are raging over whether the films should be seen by the public, historians or film scholars.

5   The major archive, the National Center for Jewish Film at Brandeis University, obtained prints of "The Eternal Jew" and other anti-Semitic films from the German Government in 1988. Sharon Rivo, the executive director of the center, is opposed to allowing the films to be shown to the public and will only permit scholars to see them after a panel has reviewed their applications.

6   "This is not a First Amendment issue," says Ms. Rivo. "We are protecting the rights of the dead." She likens the portrayal in "The Eternal Jew" of the Warsaw ghetto, whose detainees were later deported to concentration camps, to the videos of Iraqi-held American hostages televised during the gulf war.

7   Jeffrey Abramson, a professor of politics at Brandeis who was chairman of a recent forum on the validity of showing "The Eternal Jew," disagrees. "If this film isn't a test case for the First Amendment, then I don't know what is." But he calls the film "the ultimate snuff movie" because it was made to inspire Nazis to kill Jews, and the Jews who appeared in it were killed.

8   While Mr. Abramson cautiously asserts that there may be social benefits to allowing "The Eternal Jew" to be shown, Ms. Rivo says that without a study to measure the impact of the film on audiences, the center will continue to severely restrict access. The National Center for Jewish Film has twice applied for and been denied a Federal grant for the study, and now its plans for the film are in limbo. Ms. Rivo recently denied a request from Bill Moyers to use clips from the film in a PBS special on hate. The move fanned allegations of censorship.

9   The center's efforts to control "The Eternal Jew" are also frustrated by legalities. Ms. Rivo asserts that her archive is the only legally authorized distributor of the films in the United States. The center struck an agreement with the German Government to disallow transfer of the films to video to hinder piracy and dissemination. But videos of the films have been in the United States for a long time, and despite the center's claim on exclusive rights, most legal experts agree that the films are in the public domain. Anyone can purchase or rent video and film copies from four or five mail-order sources.

10   Both Ms. Rivo and Karl Wörner, president of Transit Film, a German Government–owned distributor that claims to control world rights to the films, allege that any distribution in the United States other than by the Jewish film center or German Government is illegal. (In Germany, showing any Nazi propaganda film is prohibited, including Leni Riefenstahl's 1935 documentary of the rise of Nazism, "Triumph of the Will," which is widely available in the United States.) Mr. Wörner has launched a campaign in the German press against Americans who sell the films or videos. Peter Bernotas, president of International Historic Films, a Chicago-based company that has distributed Nazi videos since the early 1980's, has been the target of criticism. His activities have led Mr. Wörner to publicly call him a Nazi sympathizer who supplies hate groups with propaganda material.

11   Mr. Bernotas makes no reply to the contention. He declines to address the moral issues that others raise about his business affairs. He says that it is company policy never to sell Nazi films to hate organizations, and that his cassettes carry disclaimers warning viewers that the films are "extremely prejudicial in nature." Mr. Bernotas says his market for the films is Jewish groups and Holocaust study centers, adding that hate groups already have the films.

12   Mr. Bernotas's activities were called into question when it was discovered that his company advertised Nazi films in *The Spotlight*, a magazine published by the Liberty Lobby, described by the Anti-Defamation League of B'nai B'rith as "the wealthiest and most active anti-Semitic organization in the United States." Mr. Bernotas says the ads were placed by an advertising agency, which described the paper to him only as "conservative and anti-Communist." Although the ads stopped, the revelation was damning. Lawrence Grossman, an advocate of free access to Nazi films, which he obtained from Mr. Bernotas for his company, the Jewish Video Library, severed business contacts with Mr. Bernotas after the disclosure.

13   The Anti-Defamation League does not support blocking Nazi films. The league's research director, Alan Schwartz, said the group is "opposed to censorship and keeping films under lock and key." Mr. Schwartz calls for responsible handling of the material.

14   Others, like the documentarian Frederick Wiseman, call for a ban on any restrictions. "I can't believe anyone with an ounce of intelligence could take that film seriously," he said of "The Eternal Jew." But a viewer who considers himself a free-speech absolutist, seeing "The Eternal Jew" for the first time, found the film's fierce racism extreme to a degree of near absurdity. "The real danger," said Andrew Horn, a director, "is that this could become a cult film."

EXERCISES

Details and Their Meanings

1. How many of Hitler's propaganda films still exist? Where are they kept?
2. Who was Joseph Goebbels? What was his connection to the propaganda movies?
3. What is *The Eternal Jew*? Where and when was it made? What is the film about?
4. Who is Peter Bernotas? Why is he a controversial figure? How is he connected to *The Spotlight*?
5. Which films are banned in Germany but available in the United States?
6. What is the First Amendment? What does it say that may have a bearing on the Nazi films?

Reading and Critical Thinking

1. What was the purpose of the Nazi films? How were they effective? How do you think you would feel watching one of them?
2. Why is control of the films a point of disagreement between the United States and Germany? What makes the issue difficult to resolve? Which side do you think is right? Why?

3. What danger do the films represent to Jews? Who else besides Jews are concerned about the subject of the films? Are those who oppose the films raising valid points in your opinion?
4. Why were the Jews who appeared in *The Eternal Jew* killed? How do we know the reason for their death?
5. Which groups are in favor of allowing the films to be shown? How do the motives of the various groups differ?
6. Why hasn't the German government simply destroyed the films? Who would criticize it if it did so?
7. Where does the writer defend the films' use? Do you find their use defensible?

The Writer's Strategies

1. What is the thesis of this selection? Where does the writer state it most clearly? What is stated in the introduction? in the conclusion?
2. What is Rebecca Lieb's purpose in writing this article? Where does she state her position? Which audience do you think she is trying to reach?
3. Where does Lieb use description? What other strategies for essay development does she use?
4. Where does the writer state people's opinions or beliefs? Where does she draw on facts?
5. Why does Lieb use rhetorical—that is, unanswered—questions? Identify two questions that she raises but does not answer, and explain their effects.
6. Is this a balanced article, or does it come down on one side of the issue? Support your response.

Thinking Together

In a group, develop a list of attributes for some culture or group about which you have no direct, personal knowledge but which have been portrayed on television or in the movies. You might choose to focus on Iraqis, Australian aborigines, white South Africans, Vietnamese, or any other group. Then discuss how the way the people have been represented on film or television affects your feelings about them or would influence you to experience them in a certain way if you ever met them.

Vocabulary

The following names are important in history. Use an encyclopedia or a historical dictionary to identify them.

1. Joseph Goebbels (par. 2)
2. the Rothchilds (par. 2)
3. the Holocaust (par. 2)
4. Charlie Chaplin (par. 3)
5. Albert Einstein (par. 3)
6. Leni Riefenstahl (par. 10)

WRITER'S WORKSHOP ━━━━━━━━━━

Critical Thinking in Writing

1. Do you believe that Nazi films can still fan the flames of prejudice? In the years since World War II ended in 1945, have people changed sufficiently so that anti-Semitism is no longer a concern? Address these questions in a well-reasoned essay.
2. What kinds of issues do you feel that actors, producers, and directors should not be permitted to address in the movies or on television? Do you favor censorship of any kind? Write an essay about your views on censorship.
3. Pretend that you are speaking to a group of educated foreign visitors to America. Your topic is freedom of speech, one of America's important contributions to world culture. How strong are your feelings on this subject? Does a person have the right to express a view even if others find that view objectionable, prejudiced or even hateful? Would you defend the right to free speech of someone whose views are critical of you and potentially harmful to your group?

Connecting Ideas

Read Marcus Mabry's "Confronting Campus Racism" (page 350). How does Mabry raise issues about the conflict between freedom of speech and thought, and the dangers that free speech presents to members of oppressed minorities.

A Hanging

George Orwell

George Orwell, author of Animal Farm *(1945) and* Nineteen
Eighty-four *(1949), was one of England's most important writers
in the middle of the twentieth century. In this essay, he describes an
experience he had while serving as a police officer in Burma. Orwell
was not American, nor does he write here of America; yet he is to
this day one of the best chroniclers of social and cultural issues.*

KEY WORDS

sodden (par. 1) soaked with water.
pariah (par. 6) an outcast.
timorously (par. 15) timidly, fearfully.
refractory (par. 22) stubborn.

---

1   IT WAS IN BURMA, a sodden morning of the rains. A sickly light, like
yellow tinfoil, was slanting over the high walls into the jail yard.
We were waiting outside the condemned cells, a row of sheds
fronted with double bars, like small animal cages. Each cell measured about ten feet by ten and was quite bare within except for a
plank bed and a pot of drinking water. In some of them brown
silent men were squatting at the inner bars, with their blankets
draped round them. These were the condemned men, due to be
hanged within the next week or two.

2   One prisoner had been brought out of his cell. He was a Hindu,
a puny wisp of a man, with a shaven head and vague liquid eyes. He
had a thick, sprouting moustache, absurdly too big for his body,
rather like the moustache of a comic man on the films. Six tall Indian
warders were guarding him and getting him ready for the gallows.
Two of them stood by with rifles with fixed bayonets, while the others handcuffed him, passed a chain through his handcuffs and fixed
it to their belts, and lashed his arms tight to his sides. They crowded
very close about him with their hands always on him in a careful,
caressing grip, as though all the while feeling him to make sure he

was there. It was like men handling a fish which is still alive and may jump back into the water. But he stood quite unresisting, yielding his arms limply to the ropes, as though he hardly noticed what was happening.

3   Eight o'clock struck and a bugle call, desolately thin in the wet air, floated from the distant barracks. The superintendent of the jail, who was standing apart from the rest of us, moodily prodding the gravel with his stick, raised his head at the sound. He was an army doctor, with a grey toothbrush moustache and a gruff voice. "For God's sake hurry up, Francis," he said irritably. "The man ought to have been dead by this time. Aren't you ready yet?"

4   Francis, the head jailer, a fat Dravidian in a white drill suit and gold spectacles, waved his black hand. "Yes sir, yes sir," he bubbled. "All iss satisfactorily prepared. The hangman iss waiting. We shall proceed."

5   "Well, quick march, then. The prisoners can't get their breakfast till this job's over."

6   We set out for the gallows. Two warders marched on either side of the prisoner, with their files at the slope; two others marched close against him, gripping him by arm and shoulder, as though at once pushing and supporting him. The rest of us, magistrates and the like, followed behind. Suddenly, when we had gone ten yards, the procession stopped short without any order or warning. A dreadful thing had happened—a dog, come goodness knows whence, had appeared in the yard. It came bounding among us with a loud volley of barks, and leapt round us wagging its whole body, wild with glee at finding so many human beings together. It was a large woolly dog, half Airedale, half pariah. For a moment it pranced round us and then, before anyone could stop it, it had made a dash for the prisoner, and jumping up tried to lick his face. Everyone stood aghast, too taken aback even to grab at the dog.

7   "Who let that bloody brute in here?" said the superintendent angrily. "Catch it, someone!"

8   A warder, detached from the escort, charged clumsily after the dog, but it danced and gambolled just out of his reach, taking everything as part of the game. A young Eurasian jailer picked up a handful of gravel and tried to stone the dog away, but it dodged the stones and came after us again. Its yaps echoed from the jail walls. The prisoner, in the grasp of the two warders, looked on incuriously, as though this was another formality of the hanging. It was several minutes before someone managed to catch the dog. Then we put my handkerchief through its collar and moved off once more, with the dog still straining and whimpering.

9   It was about forty yards to the gallows. I watched the bare brown back of the prisoner marching in front of me. He walked clumsily with his bound arms, but quite steadily, with that bobbing gait of the Indian who never straightens his knees. At each step his muscles slid neatly into place, the lock of hair on his scalp danced up and down, his feet printed themselves on the wet gravel. And once, in spite of the men who gripped him by each shoulder, he stepped slightly aside to avoid a puddle on the path.

10   It is curious, but till that moment I had never realised what it means to destroy a healthy, conscious man. When I saw the prisoner step aside to avoid the puddle, I saw the mystery, the unspeakable wrongness, of cutting a life short when it is in full tide. This man was not dying, he was alive just as we were alive. All the organs of his body were working—bowels digesting food, skin renewing itself, nails growing, tissues forming—all toiling away in solemn foolery. His nails would still be growing when he stood on the drop, when he was falling through the air with a tenth of a second to live. His eyes saw the yellow gravel and the grey walls, and his brain still remembered, foresaw, reasoned—reasoned even about puddles. He and we were a party of men walking together, seeing, hearing, feeling, understanding the same world; and in two minutes, with a sudden snap, one of us would be gone—one mind less, one world less.

11   The gallows stood in a small yard, separate from the main grounds of the prison, and overgrown with tall prickly weeds. It was a brick erection like three sides of a shed, with planking on top, and above that two beams and a crossbar with the rope dangling. The hangman, a grey-haired convict in the white uniform of the prison, was waiting beside his machine. He greeted us with a servile crouch as we entered. At a word from Francis the two warders, gripping the prisoner more closely than ever, half led, half pushed him to the gallows and helped him clumsily up the ladder. Then the hangman climbed up and fixed the rope round the prisoner's neck.

12   We stood waiting, five yards away. The warders had formed in a rough circle round the gallows. And then, when the noose was fixed, the prisoner began crying out on his god. It was a high, reiterated cry of "Ram! Ram! Ram! Ram!", not urgent and fearful like a prayer or a cry for help, but steady, rhythmical, almost like the tolling of a bell. The dog answered the sound with a whine. The hangman, still standing on the gallows, produced a small cotton bag like a flour bag and drew it down over the prisoner's face. But the sound, muffled by the cloth, still persisted, over and over again: "Ram! Ram! Ram! Ram! Ram!"

13   The hangman climbed down and stood ready, holding the lever. Minutes seemed to pass. The steady, muffled crying from the prisoner went on and on, "Ram! Ram! Ram!" never faltering for an instant. The superintendent, his head on his chest, was slowly poking the ground with his stick; perhaps he was counting the cries, allowing the prisoner a fixed number—fifty, perhaps, or a hundred. Everyone had changed colour. The Indians had gone grey like bad coffee, and one or two of the bayonets were wavering. We looked at the lashed, hooded man on the drop, and listened to his cries—each cry another second of life; the same thought was in all our minds: oh, kill him quickly, get it over, stop that abominable noise!

14   Suddenly the superintendent made up his mind. Throwing up his head he made a swift motion with his stick. "Chalo!" he shouted almost fiercely.

15   There was a clanking noise, and then dead silence. The prisoner had vanished, and the rope was twisting on itself. I let go of the dog, and it galloped immediately to the back of the gallows; but when it got there it stopped short, barked, and then retreated into a corner of the yard, where it stood among the weeds, looking timorously out at us. We went round the gallows to inspect the prisoner's body. He was dangling with his toes pointed straight downwards, very slowly revolving, as dead as a stone.

16   The superintendent reached out with his stick and poked the bare body; it oscillated, slightly. "*He's* all right," said the superintendent. He backed out from under the gallows, and blew out a deep breath. The moody look had gone out of his face quite suddenly. He glanced at his wristwatch. "Eight minutes past eight. Well, that's all for this morning, thank God."

17   The warders unfixed bayonets and marched away. The dog, sobered and conscious of having misbehaved itself, slipped after them. We walked out of the gallows yard, past the condemned cells with their waiting prisoners, into the big central yard of the prison. The convicts, under the command of warders armed with lathis, were already receiving their breakfast. They squatted in long rows, each man holding a tin pannikin, while two warders with buckets marched round ladling out rice; it seemed quite a homely, jolly scene, after the hanging. An enormous relief had come upon us now that the job was done. One felt an impulse to sing, to break into a run, to snigger. All at once everyone began chattering gaily.

18   The Eurasian boy walking beside me nodded towards the way we had come, with a knowing smile: "Do you know, sir, our friend (he meant the dead man), when he heard his appeal had been dismissed, he pissed on the floor of his cell. From fright—Kindly take

one of my cigarettes, sir. Do you not admire my new silver case, sir? From the boxwallah, two rupees eight annas. Classy European style."

19   Several people laughed—at what, nobody seemed certain.

20   Francis was walking by the superintendent, talking garrulously: "Well, sir, all hass passed off with the utmost satisfactoriness. It wass all finished—flick! like that. It iss not always so—oah, no! I have known cases where the doctor wass obliged to go beneath the gallows and pull the prisoner's legs to ensure decease. Most disagreeable!"

21   "Wriggling about, eh? That's bad," said the superintendent.

22   "Ach, sir, it iss worse when they become refractory! One man, I recall, clung to the bars of hiss cage when we went to take him out. You will scarcely credit, sir, that it took six warders to dislodge him, three pulling at each leg. We reasoned with him. 'My dear fellow,' we said, 'think of all the pain and trouble you are causing to us!' But no, he would not listen! Ach, he wass very troublesome!"

23   I found that I was laughing quite loudly. Everyone was laughing. Even the superintendent grinned in a tolerant way. "You'd better all come out and have a drink," he said quite genially. "I've got a bottle of whisky in the car. We could do with it."

24   We went through the big double gates of the prison, into the road. "Pulling at his legs!" exclaimed a Burmese magistrate suddenly, and burst into a loud chuckling. We all began laughing again. At that moment Francis's anecdote seemed extraordinarily funny. We all had a drink together, native and European alike, quite amicably. The dead man was a hundred yards away.

―――――――――

EXERCISES

Details and Their Meanings

1. What is the setting for this essay? What sort of day is it? What time of day is it? Why is the time unusual?
2. Who is about to be hanged? What crime is he convicted of?
3. What is George Orwell's function at the prison? Why is he there?
4. Whose dog wanders into the action? Why is the dog tolerated?
5. Why are the other prisoners eager to see the man hanged?
6. What event makes Orwell realize the absurdity of this situation?

Reading and Critical Thinking

1. What is Orwell's attitude toward the Burmese? toward the British? Where does this attitude become clear? What significance do you see in the fact that the British, in a country not their own, are executing an Indian Hindu?
2. Why are so many people needed to execute one man? What other function do they serve?
3. Why does the condemned man step around the puddle? Why is this detail so important for explaining Orwell's position on what is about to take place?
4. What quality do human beings have that lower animals do not have? How does your answer reveal an irony about capital punishment?
5. Why are the witnesses so tense? How would their answer to that question differ from Orwell's? Why does everyone laugh at the end? What are they laughing about?

The Writer's Strategies

1. What is the thesis of the essay? Which paragraph best suggests Orwell's thesis?
2. What kinds of details does Orwell use to make this writing effective? What mood do these details create?
3. Where does Orwell use comparison and contrast as a development strategy? What other rhetorical strategies does he use?
4. Does this piece appeal more to reason or to emotion? What helps you to answer this question?
5. What is the function of the dog? Why does Orwell include him?
6. Who is the audience for this essay? What action does Orwell wish his readers to take?
7. Which paragraphs represent the introduction, body, and conclusion? What is the purpose of the last sentence?

Thinking Together

Supporters of capital punishment say it deters murderers in society. In an almanac, look up the American states that have reinstated capital punishment since the 1970s. How many people are on death row? How many have actually been executed? In the same book, you can also look up the number of murders each year in the United States. Does what you find surprise you? Discuss in class your interpretation of the data—the relation between homicide and capital punishment.

Vocabulary

Use context clues to determine the meaning of the following italicized words from the selection, and then write a definition of each.

1. a bugle call *desolately* thin in the wet air (par. 3)
2. moodily *prodding* the gravel with his stick (par. 3)
3. Everyone stood *aghast*, too taken aback even to grab at the dog. (par. 6)
4. the dog . . . danced and *gambolled* just out of his reach (par. 8)
5. He greeted us with a *servile* crouch as we entered. (par. 11)
6. It was a high, *reiterated* cry of "Ram! Ram! Ram! Ram!" (par. 12)
7. stop that *abominable* noise! (par. 13)
8. the bare body . . . *oscillated*, slightly. (par. 16)
9. Francis was walking by the superintendent, talking *garrulously*. (par. 20)
10. We all had a drink together . . . quite *amicably*. (par. 24)

WRITER'S WORKSHOP ————————————

Critical Thinking in Writing

1. According to surveys, most Americans favor capital punishment. Why? Are you personally in favor of it? On what grounds? Write an argument to defend your views.
2. Is it possible to exercise control without violence? Must a society discipline and punish its citizens in order to ensure law and order? What alternatives can you suggest?
3. Some people argue that life in prison is actually a worse punishment than death. If you were forced to choose between these alternatives for yourself, which one would you pick and why?

Connecting Ideas

Read Douglas Martin's "Blind Commuter" (page 245). What support do you find there for Orwell's views on the sanctity of life, on the connection between life and hope, and on the human capacity to cling to life in difficult circumstances?

The Great Divide

Ellen Goodman

Ellen Goodman is a syndicated newspaper columnist whose work is seen by millions of readers. In this essay, she discusses segregation on American college campuses.

KEY WORDS

apartheid (par. 1)   racial separation.
camaraderie (par. 3)   friendship.
shantytown (par. 4)   a neighborhood of shacks and hovels.
transversed (par. 5)   moved across at an angle.
volatile (par. 9)   likely to blow up.

---

1   THE MAN WAS TALKING about what he calls the "resegregation" of American life. He was a veteran of the civil-rights movement, and went South as a student in the '60s when whites and blacks fought American apartheid together.

2   The man went on to make his life in a Midwestern university, where he was my guide one spring day. Indeed he taught about race in America until he felt discredited on account of his skin color—white—and went into administration.

3   Walking me into the student union, he said: "Look." The tables were nearly as segregated as a lunch counter in the Alabama of the 1960s. There was just one table where black and white undergraduates ate in noisy camaraderie. They, my guide explained, were members of the varsity team.

4   Pausing, he counted on one hand the number of places where blacks and whites interact on his campus these days: in sports, the arts or, he added ironically, in race-relations class. A few years back there was a shantytown on campus, a makeshift protest against investing in South Africa. Now he was almost sorry the university divested because it had been one of the few actions that brought students together.

5   I brought this story home to a woman who disputed only one phrase: resegregation. We never desegregated, she says. An academic and black, she knows few people who ever had social lives that easily transversed the color lines.

6   As a mother, she sees her grade-school kids with friends of all hues, but her college students subdivided by skin color. So she also wonders when it happens and why. Many of her black students believe they can only integrate on white terms and turf. Many of her white students feel unwelcome by blacks. Many feel unwelcoming.

7   Who was defensive and who was racist and who was just uncomfortable? And why this great silence today between blacks and whites about race relations in America?

8   Both of these academics, now enjoying the summer that is their chief professional perk, can cite incidents over the past year. Graffiti, hostility, tension. Yet they would agree that these are by no means the worst days on campus or the worst years. They remember the KKK, Mississippi, legal segregation.

9   But they also know that nearly every campus holds a volatile mix of attitudes that in no way resembles a melting pot. In some places, whites believe that their black classmates were admitted because of their race. In others, blacks believe that whites believe that.

10   On many universities, the black search for identity—their own place on a white campus—can end up fusing blackness with victimization. In many universities, white classmates resent the racist label brushing them indiscriminately.

11   There is today a high degree of racial consciousness and a sorry lack of a language, of a forum, of a common ground where people can talk honestly about race. These two facts have given many campuses the look and sound of two cultures. And in these segregated places, there may not even be faith anymore in the value of integration.

12   Neither of my guides believes that campuses are unique in their sharp segregations. Quite the opposite is true, they say. Look around the office. Look around town.

13   In Washington, it is still almost impossible for blacks and whites to talk about the trial of Mayor Barry. To most whites in the nation's capital, the case was "about" the mayor and his alleged use of drugs. To most blacks the case was "about" the entrapment of a black leader. Across the great divide of the race, the words defied interpretators.

14   Even in journalism, bylines often come color-coded. White journalists are awkward writing about blacks as if race were a qualification. Black journalists are often both required and discredited for writing about "their own."

15   And in our cities, there are neighborhoods as separated by race as ever in our history. There are people who speak for the "black community" and the "white community" as if their apartness was an accepted and permanent reality.

16   But universities have often thought of themselves as models, communities of scholars. At best, they are expected to uphold their own values. At a minimum, they are places where we are to think and talk deeply about what troubles the "real world."

17   The universities are re-opening. They start each new year with a fresh curriculum. But what troubles the real world as much as anything these days is race relations. It's a problem that exists on a scale as large as a city. But it can also be seen—and changed—on a scale as small as a dining-room table.

EXERCISES

Details and Their Meanings

1. What signs of racism on campus does Ellen Goodman report?
2. What is the KKK? Why is it mentioned in this essay?
3. Who is Marion Barry? Why is his case a good barometer of race relations in the United States?
4. In what places on campus do blacks and whites interact? What grounds are there for mistrust between blacks and whites on campus?
5. What future hope does Goodman hold out in paragraph 6? What other paragraph is hopeful?
6. How are lunch counters in Alabama in the 1960s relevant to this selection?

Reading and Critical Thinking

1. How in paragraphs 1 through 4 does Goodman establish the administrator's right to speak?
2. What made Goodman choose college campuses as the focus of this essay? Are college campuses more segregated than other areas of American life? How are race relations on your campus?

3. What forums for dialogue between and among races are there in American society? What would you propose to improve communication?
4. How does Goodman define the work *resegregation*? Is it a real word?
5. What does Goodman mean in paragraph 14 when she says that journalism is "color-coded"? Do you agree or disagree? Why?
6. What can you infer from the author's statement that blacks and whites interpret the Marion Barry case differently?
7. Goodman suggests that blacks on campus fuse blackness with victimization. What support does she give for this observation? Do you agree with her? Why or why not?
8. Why is this article titled "The Great Divide"?

The Writer's Strategies

1. Where does the writer state her thesis? Why does it come so late in the essay?
2. What is the connection between the title and the thesis?
3. Why are the paragraphs so short, often only one or two sentences long?
4. Why is this essay based more on facts than on opinions?
5. What is the primary writing strategy that the writer uses to develop this essay?
6. Why doesn't Goodman mention the names of the administrator and the black academic?

Thinking Together

Conduct a survey in your class. How many people have good friends who are from different races? How many have acquaintances, people they interact with on a daily basis, from other races? How many live in racially mixed neighborhoods? From the results, is it fair to conclude that you and your classmates live in a segregated or in an integrated society?

Vocabulary

The following words have prefixes. Separate each prefix from its root word, and write a definition.

1. resegregation (par. 1)
2. discredited (par. 2)

3. interact (par. 4)
4. divested (par. 4)
5. disputed (par. 5)
6. desegregated (par. 5)
7. integrate (par. 6)
8. unwelcome (par. 6)
9. indiscriminately (par. 10)
10. entrapment (par. 13)

WRITER'S WORKSHOP

Critical Thinking in Writing

1. Write an essay about befriending someone from a racial or ethnic group different from your own. What steps would you take to establish and nurture the friendship? Would you have to take any special steps? Which? Why?
2. Do colleges have a responsibility to talk deeply about the problems of the real world? Is college supposed to be a place where people receive training for future employment, or is it supposed to be a model community intended to address social ills? Explain your position.
3. Write an essay in which you suggest how you could create "a forum, . . . a common ground where people can talk honestly about race," as Goodman suggests.

Connecting Ideas

Read "White Guilt," by Shelby Steele (page 317). What do you see in Goodman's essay that speaks to similar concerns expressed by Steele about the failure of entitlement programs to achieve real integration?

Crossing a Boundary

Athlone G. Clarke

*Athlone G. Clarke describes how racial barriers are subtly main-
tained even when nobody seems to be taking an openly racist position. Notice how the writer, a middle-class and moderate African
American, gradually comes to feel like an outsider.*

KEY WORD

Bensonhurst (par. 6)   a neighborhood in Brooklyn where a
well-known racial incident occurred.

1   THERE WAS A BIG sign that warned of a NEIGHBORHOOD WATCH
IN PROGRESS and then there were the less obvious ones. Placed
strategically at the entrances of mile-long driveways bordering
multi-acre lawns were smaller signs emblazoned with the names
of some of America's finest security companies. Something told
me I had strayed from the beaten path.

2   Being a creature of habit, I have always jogged a path that takes
me under a certain bridge into a recreational park for a breathtaking
three-mile run. I've stuck to this path like a bus route. This particular evening, I accepted the challenge of trying a new route. Brad,
a white middle-aged jogging acquaintance with the stamina and
speed of a Derby winner, thought it would break the monotony. As
usual, 10 minutes into the run he chose to quicken his pace, while I
chose to continue living. It wasn't long before he disappeared. I remembered his directions and instead of going under the bridge, I
crossed over it and made a few extra turns. Twilight Zone it must
have been because within minutes, I was in unfamiliar territory
where homes boasted titles like "chateau," "estate" and "villa." The
vegetation was orderly and even the light breeze seemed to cooperate. There were signs with pictures of dogs baring their fangs and
words like "patrol and protection."

3   The way I figured it, the warnings were meant for those harbor-
ing criminal motives or acting suspiciously. Being a clean-shaven

344

black male in broad daylight, wearing no bulky attire to hide weapons, no suspicious bag, no dark glasses (and not being in South Africa where they have the Group Areas Act), I had nothing to worry about. Wrong! I started to get an eerie feeling. A lot of expensive cars were suddenly slowing down, almost as if there were a visibility problem. I assumed I was it. A silver-haired older lady, who oozed power from every pore, abruptly halted her Jaguar and sweetly inquired whether I worked for the McArthurs. On hearing "No," she sped off in apparent concern. Still, I reassured myself that this was America. I would not retreat, even while drowning in sweat and adrenaline.

4   I thought back to the media depiction of a white middle-class suburbanite who gets lost in the heart of a tough inner-city neighborhood and takes leave of his nerves. At that moment if I could have had my choice, I would have chosen the inner city. It wasn't long before a police car cruised by and I noticed the driver adjusting his rear-view mirror. As he didn't stop I knew trouble was stalking me.

5   I saw a few other blacks in the neighborhood but they wore the working clothes of gardeners, nannies and utility technicians. I wore a spandex running outfit, headphones and an ingratiating smile. The teeth of the black man have been known to get him out of some tight spots, and my father did not raise a fool. There were a few fellow joggers and some walkers who moved with impressive alacrity as they crossed the street and responded to my nervous nod with furtive glances. It was not hard to imagine that to come face to face with a stranger the same color as Willie Horton must have been, for them, a terrifying experience.

6   I tried to quicken my pace, hoping that through some miracle I could catch up with Brad or at least keep him in sight. Experience has taught me that a little ethnic buffering serves the politics of acceptance and at the very least lessens the shock factor. However, it seemed decreed that I would do this journey alone. I kept reminding myself that this was not Bensonhurst and there was little chance of a mob-induced fracas. These people obviously had class and believed in maintaining secure borders.

7   I sensed I was being followed and looked around. My fears were confirmed. Driving about 150 yards behind me at funeral-procession speed was a lone police car. As it pulled alongside my flank, a portly white police officer in the trademark sunglasses ordered me to pull over. "Do you live around here, sir?" he asked. "May I see some kind of ID?" As I never go jogging with my driver's license, or my wallet for that matter, I knew this would make "Bull

Connor" a little upset. I explained my predicament. He then said something I was not ready to hear. "That's OK sir," he said, "I've been watching you for the last 15 minutes and you do seem like a runner going about his business. The problem I'm having, and I hope you'll try to understand, is that some of these people think their snot can make cole slaw; fact is, I still have to do my job." He went on the explain that the police had gotten a flood of phone calls about a suspicious black man roaming the area.

8   We spoke for another two minutes. I went on to point out that in my own neighborhood, I had witnessed a few white strangers running by in the name of exercise and wondered if maybe I ought to start calling the police. As he got back into his car he removed his glasses. His weary eyes appeared to plead for some kind of tacit understanding: in the future, he would be counting on me not to make his life more difficult by running through this forbidden stretch. I sensed a conspiracy to cooperate with the forces of bigotry.

9   Later I recounted my journey to Brad and wasn't surprised when he said the only problem he'd had was his hamstring acting up again. He also thought I was being a little sensitive. On reflection, I think I can see Brad's point. Yet where would we be today if Rosa Parks's "sensitivity" hadn't gotten her into all that mess in Montgomery 35 years ago?

EXERCISES

Details and Their Meanings

1. What signs did Athlone G. Clarke notice in the neighborhood he was passing through? Whom did he think the signs were for? What message did he get from the signs? In light of what happened later, what further meanings do the signs convey?

2. What activity and sequence of events brought the writer to this neighborhood? How was he dressed? Was it unusual for someone dressed as he was to go jogging in this neighborhood? Did he think he looked dangerous? Did others think he looked dangerous? Why or why not?

3. Who stopped the writer or otherwise took notice of him? What were their reactions? Who did they think he might be? How did these responses to his presence make him feel?

4. Did Clarke see any other blacks in the neighborhood? Who were they, and what were they doing? Would passers-by think he was one of them? Which would, and which would not?

5. What questions did a police officer ask Clarke? What attitude did the officer have? Did he think Clarke was dangerous? Why was the officer following him? What was the effect of the police officer's stopping him? Did the officer's attitude influence the consequences of the writer's being stopped?

6. What happened to Brad, the friend Clarke was jogging with, once he and Clarke were separated? Why did Clarke think that rejoining Brad would be a good idea? Did Brad undergo experiences similar to Clarke's? How did Brad react when he heard Clarke's story?

7. Who was Rosa Parks? Why is she mentioned? In what way did Clarke act like Rosa Parks? In what ways did he not act like her? What meaning does the writer wish to convey by making the comparison to Rosa Parks?

Reading and Critical Thinking

1. What was the attitude of the neighborhood residents to Clarke? Why were they upset at Clarke's presence? Is their reaction a form of racism? How would members of your community react to an informal visitor from a racial group different from those groups represented in your neighborhood?

2. Why does Clarke say that the police were part of a conspiracy? Did the policeman treat him badly or think poorly of him? Whom did the officer think more poorly of? What should have been the policeman's attitude?

3. How did Clarke feel in this neighborhood? How do his feelings of anger and injustice build throughout the narrative? Why did Brad think Clarke was being too sensitive? Did you think he was being too sensitive? Why or why not?

4. What other blacks does Clarke mention? What roles does he suggest are available to blacks who wish to move freely about all neighborhoods?

5. Do you think the white people described in this piece consider themselves racists? Do you consider them racists? Why or why not?

The Writer's Strategies

1. What is the writer's thesis? How do the introduction and conclusion support the thesis? the title?
2. Why does Clarke begin the essay by describing the signs in the neighborhood? What is he trying to convey about the messages sent from the neighborhood to people who pass through?
3. Why does the writer compare his feelings to those of a white suburbanite lost in an inner-city neighborhood? What various meanings can you take from this comparison? How is the comparison-contrast strategy particularly useful here?
4. The narrative ends with a discussion of the writer's sensitivity and a comparison to Rosa Parks. How does this ending contrast with the opening no-trespassing signs? What attitude is the writer expressing by this shift?
5. Who is the audience for this piece? How can you tell?

Thinking Together

In small groups, discuss a time that you felt out of place and other people viewed you suspiciously. What did you think they were thinking about you? What category were they putting you in? Is there anything you could have done to change their minds? How did their categorization influence your behavior?

Vocabulary

Find words in the selection with the following meanings. The definitions are listed in the order in which the words appear in Clarke's essay.

1. in a planned, goal-directed manner
2. written in bold letters
3. three fancy names for home
4. carefully hiding
5. a bodily chemical that heightens emotions
6. designed to appear friendly
7. secret
8. fight or riot
9. a shared plan to do wrong
10. a muscle in the lower leg

WRITER'S WORKSHOP ───────────────

Critical Thinking in Writing

1. Write an essay describing how racist actions can result from subtle suspicions and quiet signals as well as from overt hostile behavior.
2. Describe how a group or neighborhood that you belong to takes notice of and views someone from outside. Which kinds of outsiders (if any) are welcomed with wholehearted gestures? Which kinds of outsiders are treated more cautiously?
3. Write an essay in which you analyze the title "Crossing a Boundary." What are the various boundaries being crossed here? Include you own definition of the word *boundary*.

Connecting Ideas

In one paragraph, compare the subtle racism presented by Athlone G. Clarke with the subtle racism presented by Shelby Steele in "White Guilt" (page 317).

Confronting Campus Racism

Marcus Mabry

Marcus Mabry, an associate editor of Newsweek, *lives and works in Washington, D.C. In this piece, he discloses the tense racial climate on college campuses and describes a few attempts to increase understanding.*

KEY WORDS

blatant (par. 3)   obvious.
deluge (par. 3)   flood.
epithets (par. 7)   names.
egregious (par. 7)   glaringly bad.
explicitly (par. 8)   with clarity and precision.
abridgements (par. 10)   shortenings, contractions.

1 IT WAS SUPPOSED TO be a day for "Bridging the Gap," a program on interracial understanding sponsored by African-American and white fraternities at George Mason University. But instead of building bridges, they were being burned, as African-American students and whites clashed over one of the most recent racial incidents on America's college campuses. The women of Gamma Phi Beta sorority had decided it would be funny to put a wig and charcoal black face on a Sigma Chi man during an "ugliest girl" contest, sponsored by the fraternity. Not surprisingly, African-American students (and a lot of whites) were not amused. The black face incident touched off a wave of racial tensions that left one fraternity suspended and most students hurt and angry. The Virginia college is not alone: from anti-Black and anti-Jewish graffiti to hate notes slipped under students' doors, racial episodes are as much a part of college life these days as fraternity parties and football.

2 Timothy Maguire, a third-year student at Georgetown Law Center set off another racial tempest with an article saying African

Americans didn't belong at Georgetown. In an opinion piece titled "Admissions Apartheid" Maguire used LSAT test scores and grade point averages to argue that lesser qualified African Americans are admitted. Although Maguire used hard data on grades and test scores, he wrapped them in racist rhetoric. For instance, he argues that on one African-American student's transcript: "There alongside a C+ in Shakespeare, C in Macroeconomics, and F in Calculus were 8 A's in African-American courses," leaving the implications unstated. At one point he concludes, "The biggest problem is that in every area and at every level of postsecondary education, Black achievements are inferior to those of whites." Really? And, if so, Therefore? Maguire later apologized for much of the article, not only to the Georgetown Law community but to the press as well when reporters asked him to clarify or prove many of his points.

3   Although no one keeps hard statistics on racial incidents on college campuses (the FBI only this year started doing it for the nation), the National Institute Against Prejudice & Violence at the University of Maryland–Baltimore County says racial episodes have been reported at over 300 colleges and universities over the past five years. Moreover, "Surveys indicate that one in five minority (students) have been victimized. We have seen an increase in the number of reports of racial incidents—and only the most blatant get reported," says Adele Terrell, program director. When the incidents of tense race relations are added to the recent deluge of articles and broadcasts condemning colleges' efforts to confront these problems as "political correctness" or a "tyranny of minorities," an African-American student victimized by racism might ask, "Is there nowhere to turn?"

4   Actually, there is. An increasing number of African-American students are deciding that an education at a predominantly white school isn't worth the racial hassle, and they're heading for historically Black colleges where the atmosphere isn't hostile. The United Negro College Fund's member schools reported 1990–91 enrollment was up 21 percent over the previous school year to 49,397—and applications were up 39 percent. But African-American students don't have to flee predominantly white schools. Most colleges and universities recognize racial harassment as a serious breach of student conduct and offer a range of options for students who have been harassed.

5   A simple first step for an offended student is to let the victimizer know that you're hurt. That might sound close to sophomoric once you have been slighted through an off-hand comment about how Blacks don't do this . . . or Blacks always do that . . . but based on the

philosophy (not always true) that hurtful or offensive acts of prejudice are often committed out of ignorance, communication can be your most effective weapon.

6   Nichet Smith and three other African-American women at Arizona State University took this approach last year. They were walking through a dorm when they saw a leaflet posted on a door with the heading "Simplified Form of a job application. Form for minority applicants." The flier went on to insult people of color by asking "Sources of income: (1) theft, (2) welfare, (3) unemployment"; "Marital Status: (1) common law, (2) shacked up, (3) other," and "Number of legitimate children (if any)." The women were angry, so they knocked on the door. They explained how they felt about the poster and one of the roommates (not the one who put it up apparently) took it down. The women then organized dorm meetings to discuss the poster and its underlying assumptions. From there, feelings and suspicions that had been stewing under the surface at Arizona State were brought into the open where they could be dismissed or discussed and wounds could be healed, or at least exposed to the fresh air. John Singsank, the president of Sigma Chi fraternity at George Mason, says the university never tried to educate Sigma Chi; instead they placed the group on probation for two years, dictating that they cannot meet or socialize as a chapter.

7   Clearly, just talking is not always the solution to a racial confrontation, even though it is likely to be a good step. Although ignorance can be a root cause of much unconscious prejudice, it cannot explain many of the grotesquely offensive actions that have recently plagued college campuses. Students at the University of Texas surely knew that the epithets spray-painted on a car in front of the fraternity were racist. Likewise, whoever scribbled "NIGGERS" across the poster advertising a Black Greek party at Stanford knew exactly what he was doing. In cases of egregious racism or when you feel your own safety might be threatened by trying to talk to the offender, you can usually turn to the college or university for help.

8   Almost all colleges and universities have student codes of conduct or a "fundamental standard" that requires students to behave themselves with a basic sense of civility at all times. Cheating, stealing, and harassing others generally fall under these age-old codes. But many schools, including the University of Georgia, finding that these codes did not condemn racist actions explicitly enough, now have speech codes that forbid students from using racially offensive language. At Stanford University, students and faculty can say whatever they please in a public forum or a classroom. But, they are not allowed to address a racial or ethnic epithet to a

specific individual. So while a white student could give a speech in the middle of the Quadrangle arguing that Blacks are inferior, he is not allowed to come up to an African-American student and call him "nigger."

9   If you are offended and your school has a speech code like Stanford's—and more and more colleges do—you generally file a complaint with a student-faculty judiciary board that oversees violations of the student code of conduct, including offenses like plagiarism. The committee will listen to both sides of the story, assess whether one party broke the school's rules and if so, how he should be punished. Penalties can run the gamut, from attending a racial-sensitivity seminar to suspension from university housing (where people from all different backgrounds have to live in close proximity to one another) to expulsion from school. At the University of Texas' Austin campus an offended student and the offending party hash out their differences before any disciplinary process goes into motion. "It's a two-tier system," says Curtis Polk, race relations counselor at U.T. Austin. "The first part is education and mediation. The second part is penalties. Often the offended party doesn't want anything more than the offender to be more racially sensitive."

10   Some speech codes, like the University of Wisconsin's and the University of Connecticut's, are being challenged in court as unconstitutional abridgements of students' First Amendment rights to free speech. The University of Michigan was forced to modify its code when it was ruled unconstitutional. But universities are in a bind. They have to strike a balance between all students' right to free speech and the rights of students of color to an equal education under the Fourteenth Amendment.

11   While these codes and standards are useful if you have been racially harassed by another student, most schools have Affirmative Action Equal Education Opportunity programs that cover faculty and staff as employees of the university. These codes are meant to guide the university in hiring and promotion, and to prevent discrimination against people of color, but they also demand that discrimination be brought up before a school administrator whenever a faculty or staff member has launched a racial incident.

12   This impressive body of regulation, for all its might, is reactive —it only springs into effect after much of the damage has been done. A lot of schools—and many students—are deciding that they can't wait until the dam breaks to address racial tensions. They are going after the problems before they erupt through seminars, courses, and workshops aimed at helping us to better understand our differences and to talk about them.

13   The most common university practice is to have programs in the dorm that address racial differences. Student resident assistants, or R.A.s, often lead the sessions which can include films like "Still Burning . . . Confronting Ethnoviolence on Campus" distributed by the University of Maryland–Baltimore County or workshop materials from the International Committee Against Racism, a New York City group. In a common version of a dorm racial-sensitivity seminar, all residents are lined up on one side of a room, a facilitator (often an R.A.) calls out a category like "Black or African American" or even "tall." All the people who place themselves in that group walk to the other side of the room. Then they look back at the students they are separated from, usually the "majority"—and tell them "all the things I never want to hear again," that they have heard people say about their group. The majority is not allowed to ask why or to criticize. Later all the individuals come back into one group and talk about how each of them is, in some way or another, a member of a group discriminated against—and how each of them has been told things they don't want to be told again.

14   Another method of achieving racial sensitivity is through curricular coursework. Many colleges are redesigning their required curricula and including more works from people of color and women. Educators have argued that teaching African Americans and whites, for instance, about the contributions of people of color to human civilization and to the United States will foster greater respect of people of color today, as well as present a more accurate picture of human endeavor and achievement.

15   Other colleges, like Cornell University, offer specific racial-sensitivity courses. James Turner, associate professor of Africana Studies and founder of the Africana Studies and Research Center, has taught "Racism in American Society" for four years. For the first three years, student enrollment tripled each year. In this course, students from different races confront their fellow students' prejudices and their own. "Our job in the classrooms is to provide an analysis of the historical sociology, the development of racism," says Turner. "We show how patterns of relationships have developed along racial lines . . . individual attitudes and ideas derive from the historical development of racism in society." As individual students learn about the perspectives in our society that are subtly racist, they can identify the subtle racism in their own thoughts and behavior. And they can work to alleviate it or at least be more sensitive to it.

16   And what if you don't feel it's your job to educate others—all you want to do is get an education? That's all right, too. If you are victimized in a racial incident and you just seek healing from the

pain, there are usually many resources on campus that can help. Student counseling or psychological services usually have at least one counselor who can aid racial harassment victims. His goal is usually to remind you of your own self-worth. In addition to your friends, the Black student union is often a valuable support network as well.

17   Even though African-American students should not feel obligated to instruct their white peers in how to care about the feelings of others, every community member has an obligation to work for greater understanding. That means talking to students of other races in and out of class in your dorm. Students who want to decrease racial tensions on campus can have a positive effect by getting involved before the problems surface. You can take the initiative by organizing workshops in your dorm, sponsoring films aimed at stimulating cross-cultural discussion or sponsoring inter-Greek activities between Black and white fraternities and sororities. Before things get to the raw level of insults and slurs, try to personally (and in the African-American organizations you're a part of) foster interaction with different kinds of students and create an atmosphere of mutual education rather than mutual suspicion. Students of color have more to gain than anyone else from greater sensitivity on campus. There are many Americans who would like to see the world's grandest experiment in multiculturalism fail. If we give them victory, then we lose.

EXERCISES

Details and Their Meanings

1. What happened at George Mason University on "Bridging the Gap" day? What incident sparked the trouble? What punishment did the offending group receive?
2. Who is Timothy Maguire? What did he write that caused a stir at Georgetown?
3. How many colleges have reported racial incidents over the past five years? What proportion of minority students has been victimized? When did the FBI start keeping records?
4. What impact are racial incidents having on enrollment at predominantly black schools?

5. How are some colleges trying to increase dialogue between the races? Which schools have adopted speech codes to suppress racist epithets?
6. Which colleges are offering courses to promote understanding? What kinds of courses are they offering?

Reading and Critical Thinking

1. What conclusion can you draw from the enrollment changes in historically black colleges?
2. Where in the selection does Marcus Mabry suggest that racial incidents stem from ignorance? Where does he suggest other causes? Which causes do you find most valid? Why?
3. What distinction is Stanford University making about the difference between classroom speech and personal attacks? Do you believe this distinction is valid? Why or why not?
4. Why are colleges in a bind when it comes to outlawing racist speech?
5. What does the writer criticize about the new body of regulations? Do you support his criticisms? Why or why not?
6. What does Mabry suggest is at stake if campus racism cannot be overcome? What other consequences can you see?

The Writer's Strategies

1. Where does the thesis of this essay appear? What is it? Who is the audience for this piece? Is Mabry writing primarily for a black audience? How can you tell?
2. What is Mabry's purpose in writing this essay?
3. Why do you think the writer encloses the phrases "political correctness" and "tyranny of minorities" in quotation marks in paragraph 3?
4. What is your reaction to the lengths of the paragraphs? Why do you think they are so long?
5. What words does Mabry use to make transitions from one paragraph to another?
6. In what sense is this a how-to essay? What process does Mabry explain?

Thinking Together

Divide up your class according to height. Have all the tall people go to one side of the room and the short people go to the other side. If everyone is nearly the same height, pick some other superficial physical attribute as a means of separation—eye or hair color, for example. Once the class has separated, each group brainstorms to produce a list of annoying things that the other group might do to you, say about you, or assume about you. The groups then compare lists. What did you discover?

Vocabulary

The following terms are relatively new and are the subject of discussion on college campuses and in the media. Write an appropriate definition of each.

1. political correctness (par. 3)
2. ethnoviolence (par. 13)
3. racial-sensitivity courses (par. 15)
4. multiculturalism (par. 17)

WRITER'S WORKSHOP ━━━━━━━━━━

Critical Thinking in Writing

1. Write a narrative about an experience you have had with a member of another racial group. What did you expect beforehand? What did your experience teach you?
2. When the rights of free speech and equal opportunity are in conflict, which right should be upheld? Which right is more important to the well-being of society? Write an essay in which you compare and contrast the two rights.
3. Write an essay called "How to Create Interracial Understanding." In it, explain the process that you would put into place to address racism on your own campus or other campuses that you know.

Connecting Ideas

Read Ellen Goodman's "The Great Divide" (page 339). What in Mabry's piece confirms Goodman's observations? How does the Mabry selection suggest a solution to the problems that Goodman sees?

Zoot Suit Riots

Albert Camarillo

Albert Camarillo is a historian. In this selection from his book
Chicanos in California: A History of Mexican Americans in
California, *he highlights an overlooked episode in Los Angeles history during World War II.*

1   NOTHING HAS COME TO symbolize more dramatically the racial hostility encountered by Chicanos during the 1930s and 1940s than the Sleepy Lagoon case and the Zoot Suit Riots. Both involved Chicano youth in Los Angeles city and county, local police departments, and the judicial system.

2   At the heart of these conflicts was the growing attention paid to Chicano youth by the local media. The press focused on *pachucos*, members of local clubs or neighborhood gangs of teenagers (both male and female). They separated themselves from other barrio youth by their appearance—high-pompadoured ducktail haircuts, tattoos, and baggy zoot suits for boys; short skirts, bobby sox, and heavy make-up for girls—and by their use of *caló*, a mixture of Spanish and English. Their characteristics, according to the press, included unflinching allegiance to neighborhood territories, clannish-

ness, and bravado. Though other teenagers in cities such as Detroit, Chicago, and New York dressed like their counterparts in wartime Los Angeles, *pachuquismo* became popularly identified with Chicano youth who came of age during the 1930s and 1940s in the Los Angeles area. Predominantly children of immigrant parents, these youths matured in an environment in which they saw themselves as neither fully Mexican nor American. Raised in impoverished barrios and alienated from a society that discriminated against Mexicans, they identified only with others of their age and experience. Pachucos constituted a minority among Chicano youth, and they set themselves apart by their disdain of the public schools, skipping classes and drawing together into neighborhood gangs where they found companionship and camaraderie. To outsiders who relied on the local media for their information, pachucos were perceived not only as marijuana-smoking hoodlums and violence-prone deviants, but also as un-American. These stigmas during the early 1940s, particularly during the first two years of a frustrating war for Americans, helped create a climate of repression for pachucos and, by extension, to others in the Chicano community.

3   In the hot summer days of August 1942, most Los Angeles residents had wearied of newspaper reports of setbacks against the Japanese forces in the Pacific. Japanese Americans on the home front had already been relocated to internment camps, thereby temporarily silencing Californians embittered by Pearl Harbor. Many xenophobic citizens also did not like Mexicans, especially the "foreign, different-looking" pachucos arrested following an incident at Sleepy Lagoon.

4   Sleepy Lagoon, a swimming hole frequented by Chicano youth of east Los Angeles, soon became the symbol of both popular outrage and repression. At a home near the lagoon, where the night before two rival gangs had confronted one another, the body of a young Chicano was discovered. Though no evidence indicated murder, the Los Angeles Police Department summarily arrested members of the 38th Street Club, the teenage group that had crashed a party the prior evening and precipitated the fighting.

5   The grand jury indicted twenty-two members of the club for murder and, according to Carey McWilliams, "to fantastic orchestration of 'crime' and 'mystery' provided by the Los Angeles press seventeen of the youngsters were convicted in what was, up to that time, the largest mass trial for murder ever held in the country." Reflecting on the treatment of the Sleepy Lagoon defendants, the aroused McWilliams stated:

For years, Mexicans had been pushed around by the Los Angeles police and given a very rough time in the courts, but the Sleepy Lagoon prosecution capped the climax. It took place before a biased and prejudiced judge (found to be such by an appellate court); it was conducted by a prosecutor who pointed to the clothes and the style of haircut of the defendants as evidence of guilt; and was staged in an atmosphere of intense community-wide prejudice which had been whipped up and artfully sustained by the entire press of Los Angeles. . . . From the beginning the proceedings savored more of a ceremonial lynching than a trial in a court of justice.

Concerned Anglo and Chicano citizens, headed by McWilliams, sharply criticized violations of the defendants' constitutional and human rights (such as beatings by police while the youths were being held incommunicado and the courtroom improprieties indicated above by McWilliams). They organized the Sleepy Lagoon Defense Committee and, with the support of such groups as the Congreso and UCAPAWA, faced down intimidation by the media and accusations of being "reds" by state senator Jack Tenney and his Committee on Un-American Activities. In 1944 they succeeded in persuading the District Court of Appeals to reverse the convictions, declare a mistrial, and release the defendants from San Quentin prison.

6   The Sleepy Lagoon case served as a prelude to an even more discriminatory episode in wartime Los Angeles—the so-called Zoot Suit Riots of 1943. Racial tensions intensified after the Sleepy Lagoon case as police continued to arrest large numbers of Chicano youth on a variety of charges. Adding to the unrest were confrontations between military servicemen and Chicano zoot suiters on city streets. Then on June 3, 1943, rumors circulated that Chicanos had beaten sailors over an incident involving some young Mexican women. The newspapers seized on the rumor and soon sailors and marines from nearby bases converged on the downtown area and on Chicano neighborhoods. There they attacked Chicano youth, regardless of whether they wore zoot suits, beat them, stripped off their clothes, and left them to be arrested by the police who did nothing to interfere with the "military operations." A virtual state of siege existed for Chicanos in Los Angeles as hundreds of servicemen in "taxicab brigades" looked for Mexicans on whom to vent their anger. "I never believed that I could see a thing like that," recalled Josephine Fierro de Bright.

I went downtown and my husband and I were standing there and we saw all these policemen hanging around . . . and hundreds of taxis with sailors hanging on with clubs in their hands, bullies just beating Mexicans on Main Street. And we went up and asked a cop to stop it: he says, "You better shut up or I'll do the same to you." You can't do a thing when you see people and the ambulances coming to pick them up and nobody is stopping the slaughter. It's a nightmare. It's a terrible thing to see.

The local press continued to feed the hysteria with headlines announcing the sailors' "war" against zoot-suited pachucos. After five days of beatings, mass arrests, and rampant fear in Chicano communities, military authorities—ordered by federal officials at the request of the Mexican consulate—quelled the riots by declaring downtown Los Angeles off limits to all naval personnel.

7   In the wake of the riots, which also occurred in San Diego and several other communities but with much less violence than in Los Angeles, the Chicano community remained paralyzed with fear of another occurrence. The Mexican government and many local citizens protested the outrages, and Governor Earl Warren appointed a committee composed of clergy, public officials, and other well-known citizens to investigate the incident. Even so, Chicano relations with the police remained tense for many years. Jesse Saldana, a Los Angeles resident who witnessed the riots, articulated the sentiment of many Chicanos: "Justice is blind; she can't see the Mexicans."

8   The Zoot Suit Riots climaxed an era of overt hostility against Chicanos in California. Beginning with mass deportations during the early years of the depression and the violent suppression of unionization efforts, the 1930s and early 1940s witnessed much sadness and frustration for Chicanos who struggled to keep family and neighborhood from moral and physical deterioration. The irony was that tens of thousands of Mexican fathers and sons were fighting overseas with the U.S. armed forces as their families on the home front were experiencing bigotry and persecution. But this period of depression and repression also aroused in Chicanos a desire to gain the equality that eluded them. The post–World War II decades witnessed a new upsurge of activity and a sense of hope within the Mexican community.

EXERCISES

Details and Their Meanings

1. What time period is Albert Camarillo examining? What event of national importance was also taking place? In which state, city and neighborhood did the Zoot Suit Riots take place?
2. Why did some young Chicanos separate themselves from mainstream society? In what ways did they make themselves distinct?
3. Who is Carey McWilliams? Why does he play an important role in this selection?
4. Why were twenty-two Chicanos arrested for murder? Why were they convicted? What eventually happened to them?
5. What event touched off the Zoot Suit Riots? How long did the riots last? When did they end? Why did they end?
6. What was the long-term political result of the Zoot Suit Riots?

Reading and Critical Thinking

1. What does the writer suggest is the relation between the barrio and the pachucos? Is his point well made? Do you agree or disagree with him? Why or why not?
2. What kinds of people do you think wore zoot suits in other American cities? How were the zoot suits a kind of costume or emblem?
3. How would you characterize the court's treatment of the 38th Street Club?
4. Why do you think that sailors indiscriminately attacked young Chicanos? Do indiscriminate attacks on ethnic groups take place today? Where?
5. What can you conclude is the reason that the police didn't enforce the law? How do you think the police today would react to the events presented in this selection?
6. Which group does the writer suggest is responsible for prolonging the conflict between Chicanos and sailors? Do you agree? Why or why not?
7. What is a fair inference to draw about the Anglo community in Los Angeles at the time of the Zoot Suit Riots? How would you characterize that community today?
8. Why might you consider the conclusion of this piece ironic?

The Writer's Strategies

1. What is Camarillo's thesis? How does the introduction contribute to his main point?
2. What is Camarillo's purpose in writing this piece? Who is his audience?
3. With which group does the writer sympathize? What clues give away his position?
4. Why does Camarillo mention the internment of the Japanese Americans in California at a similar period? Is the introduction of this issue a good rhetorical strategy? Why or why not?
5. What is the tone of this selection?
6. How much of this selection is the result of Camarillo's direct experience? In which paragraphs does the writer express his own opinion? Where does he quote the opinions of others?
7. Was this piece written during the 1940s, shortly after, or long after? What clues tell you the answer to this question?

Thinking Together

Many people believe that relations between law enforcement officers and minority youths have improved in the last fifty years. Can you support this conclusion from your own experience, the experience of your friends, or information you've read or heard about? Are there gangs in your town? What kinds of youngsters join gangs? Are there still gangs in Los Angeles and other large cities? How do young people get along with the police in large cities? Make an outline of the steps to take in order to investigate these questions. Working in small groups try to get some answers. After your research is finished, make a group report to the class.

Vocabulary

Items 1 through 5 are period or historical references. Look them up in a dictionary or an encyclopedia. Items 6 through 12 are Spanish or Chicano in origin. Look them up in a Spanish/English dictionary. Write definitions of all twelve items in your own words.

1. zoot suit (par. 2)
2. ducktail haircuts (par. 2)
3. bobby sox (par. 2)
4. internment of Japanese Americans (par. 3)

5. Pearl Harbor (par. 3)
6. Chicano (par. 1)
7. pachucos (par. 2)
8. barrio (par. 2)
9. caló (par. 2)
10. incommunicado (par. 5)
11. camaraderie (par. 2)
12. Congreso (par. 5)

WRITER'S WORKSHOP ────────────

Critical Thinking in Writing

1. Prepare a brief—that is, a lawyer's argument—summarizing the reasons Camarillo gives for granting the 38th Street gang a new trial.
2. Each generation chooses its own fashions and hairstyles to show alienation and rebellion. Today, teenagers do not wear bobby sox, zoot suits, or ducktail haircuts. Write an essay to describe how a rebellious teenager today is likely to dress, wear his or her hair, and behave in order to show disaffection. Draw an illustration if you'd like.
3. The Los Angeles riots of 1992, which produced scorching fires in some areas of the city, in large part resulted from simmering tensions between minorities and the police. What steps can urban communities take to reduce those tensions? Write an essay to explain the process you would put in place if you could.

Connecting Ideas

Gary Soto, in "Looking for Work" (page 231) and Armando Rendón, in "Kiss of Death" (page 91), are the sons of Chicanos who experienced discrimination during the 1930s and 1940s. Look at the parents and other grown-ups in Soto's and Rendón's pieces to see what you can discover about those adults' attitudes and expectations. Would they probably agree with the remark made by Jesse Saldana in paragraph 7 of the Camarillo selection: "Justice is blind; she can't see the Mexicans"?

Hearts of Sorrow

James M. Freeman

The narrator of this selection, a Vietnamese teacher, tells his story to writer, James Freeman. The teacher was driven from his home after a long and painful war.

1   MY FAMILY ARRIVED IN America in October 1976. At that time I spoke a little English; my wife spoke none. I had not had any intention of coming to America, but since I had a relative here, the International Rescue Committee contacted the American Embassy, and we were brought into this country.

2   I remember our first misunderstanding. We saw lots of people waving to each other in greeting. My wife said, "Oh, how do they know us like a friend, that they're calling us to go over to them?" For us, the gesture signified "Come here."

3   We were sent to a place in the South where the people were quite friendly, but the climate was too cold for us in the winter, and much too hot in the summer. There were mosquitoes and flies all over. It was not pleasant.

4   Although white people were friendly with us, we saw discrimination against blacks. I asked a black friend to go with me while I visited a friend. When he saw that I was about to enter the house of a white man, he said, "I'll stay outside and wait."

5   "Why not go inside?" I asked.

6   He replied, "My mother told me not to go to white people."

7   I tried one more time. I took a white man to a black man's house. The white man wouldn't go in. "Why?" I asked.

8   "My mother told me not to visit black people."

9   One day I went to the store and selected lots of oranges, apples, and vegetables. I had only ten dollars in my pocket. The girl at the checkout counter added up the cost of the items and said, "You owe fifteen dollars."

10   I replied, "I've only got ten, so I'll put back some oranges. Give me ten dollars' worth. Tomorrow I'll buy more."

11   A black woman standing behind me said, "Let him get everything; I'll pay the rest for him."

12   That was the first time something like that happened; I'll never forget it.

13   On another occasion, when I had moved to another state, an old man saw me buy a hamburger but nothing else at a hamburger stand. He asked, "Why did you buy only a hamburger, and nothing to drink?"

14   I replied, "I don't have enough money, only a little over a dollar."

15   The old man said, "I'll buy another hamburger for you."

16   "No, no," I said. "It's too much for me."

17   He bought me another hamburger and some orange juice. We sat down and ate together.

18   Some people are good, but others are not friendly. Where we live now, we cannot ride a bicycle, for young people shout loudly as they drive by in cars. I don't care what they say, but they startle me when they drive right behind me, pass me close by, on the narrow road, and then shout in my ear.

19   Sometimes my wife and I walk along the sidewalk. Even that we cannot do, for the young people shout out at us as they drive by. My wife feels bad when she hears this; she does not want to go out. I care about that. I say to her, "Let's drive to the park; then we can walk there." But walking nearby is better because we do not need a car.

20   My wife often feels so lonely here in America because she cannot walk near her home, for she is afraid that people will shout at her. She has friends around here, but if she wishes to visit them, she asks me to accompany her. So her behavior in America is quite different from how she lived in Vietnam, where she'd leave the house alone two, three, or four times a day, visiting the market, her parents, and her friends. She used to walk a lot and enjoyed it very much; now she fears to do it. I don't know, the old people in America are very nice, but young people are rude and destructive. At the rear of my apartment stands a large wheeled garbage bin. It is real dirty and has a bad smell that attracts lots of flies. Many people also go there to drink beer and smoke cigarettes. The manager of the apartment put up a sign to keep out of private property; still, two to three carloads of dirty young people with long hair gather around the garbage bin; they make so much noise, even at night. Often they are drunk. They throw cans and empty bottles on the roof; the clatter is terrible. Even though the manager calls the police, these people often return. And they end the evening by urinating on the fence.

21   Although some other Vietnamese people live near here, we do not see them often. They work all day, eat, sleep, watch television, but don't go out much except to work. Like my wife, they have stopped walking in the neighborhood because the youths shout at

them. In Vietnam, the old people used to walk a lot, stopping along the way at restaurants, where they would meet friends, talk, and drink coffee. Sometimes they would go fishing or swimming, and at other times they would visit friends. All of that is gone for them in America, and it is no longer possible in Vietnam either.

22   My wife says, "I feel so lonely when you and the children are away from the house." She stays home and cooks and does house-work. The children too are lonely. I tell them to take the car and visit friends, but they say, "That's a waste of gas and money." They un-derstand our situation, that with my low-paying job, which may stop at any moment, we do not have enough money to support us. A couple of my children attend one of the colleges nearby; I drive them there before going to work, and I pick them up after work. But my wife remains alone all day. For companionship, I bought her two birds in a large cage. From time to time, one of the birds sings. Be-cause she has poor eyesight, my wife cannot watch television. Her days are long. I work five days a week. On those days, I am tired. All I want to do is relax, eat, drink, and go to sleep. On the weekends, I take her to the market, and we go to the laundromat. Sometimes we write letters to our relatives and friends. But our life is a lonely one in America. That's why lots of old people want to return to Vietnam. Religion here won't help them; that's only for a few hours on Sunday. People still remain lonely. They dream of fighting the Com-munists, throwing them out, and returning to live out their days peacefully in their homeland. But this is only a dream.

23   Sometimes my friends call me on the telephone. We talk about our lives here and what other people are doing. We sometimes invite one another to come by and take some food. This is different from Vietnam, where we used to just arrive at the door of our friend, and they'd invite us in. We'd say, "We've got some food ready; why don't you stay and have some." We'd travel around a lot and visit friends, more than here in America. We'd help our friends get jobs, and we'd share room, clothes, food. A friend might stay with us for months; we don't care about that. During holidays, maybe four or five people will come by and stay. That's how we do it.

24   For my wife, adjustment in America is very hard. For me and my children, adjustment is not that difficult. I had some experience in dealing with Westerners before I left Vietnam. My children are young enough to adapt to new customs. Within three days of our ar-rival in America, I had enrolled them in school; within four months, they were speaking English.

25   Somewhat difficult for us was learning to cope with American food, which contains too much salt and sugar, and very peculiar sea-

soning. We dislike it, and I still eat mostly Vietnamese-style food. At my place of work, I eat food that I have taken from home. My daughters have learned to tolerate American food, but prefer Vietnamese.

26   Also hard for us is the speaking of English. Often we can read well, but because of our pronunciation people think we are not well educated. We find it quite difficult to ask for information over the telephone, so we may drive 20 or 30 miles to get the information. Yesterday, I tried to call a pet shop where I had bought two finches. I said to the man, "The mother bird has laid five eggs, but after they hatched, she kicked them out of her nest area, and they died. What should I do to prevent that?"

27   The man at the pet shop said, "Sorry, I cannot understand what you said."

28   I asked an American friend to call for me. He received the information and relayed it to me.

29   That's not the only language problem. One morning I was cleaning our floor with a vacuum cleaner that made a lot of noise. The people who live below us pounded on the ceiling with something. They were angry, I guess. I went next door to an American lady and asked her to explain to the people below that I was cleaning with a vacuum cleaner. She did that, and the people said it was okay.

30   In 1979, I enrolled in a technical training institute where I received nine months of instruction. I started out in one field, but a friend persuaded me to try another. It turned out I had quite a bit of skill for it, so my counselor at the institute let me switch. After completing my training, I went out to look for work. My friend, who was younger, was hired immediately; I had more difficulty, for when people saw that I was in my fifties, they were not anxious to hire me. After two months, one company offered me a job. The man who hired me said, "Take five dollars an hour."

31   I replied, "No, six."

32   "Okay," the man said. "I'll hire you."

33   In Vietnam, a man of my age would have retired. I would have been able to support my family to the end of my life. But not in America. I tell my children to work hard, because I will not be able to help them forever; one day they will be on their own. I have no security of any kind here; I must keep working as long as I have a job, and it might end at any moment.

34   I liked my job in Vietnam much more. I talked with people of a higher class, and people treated me with respect. I had three months of paid summer vacation every year. The status of my job in Vietnam was much higher than the factory labor I do here. That is very difficult, not only for me, but for many other Vietnamese men. We have

lost our country. We are making a new life in another country. We don't care about our second life in a new country, that we are lower in status. Even though it is difficult, many of us are happy because our children have a chance here. I'm at the end of my life; I'm happy simply to sacrifice for my children. I'll take any job to help them. I do know some Vietnamese people who are unable to adjust to the loss of their status.

35   I am happy that I was able to change my life and start a new job in America. At least I showed I could make the adjustment. But if you ask me what life is like for me here in America, I have to tell you: Terrible! I say that because all the money I get from my new job is gone. Almost all of it goes for rent, which is increased too much. We have no money for heating. In the winter, we keep warm by wrapping blankets around ourselves, and we cover the windows with sheets. We can buy a blanket for seven dollars and use it for a year. We have no need for heat. We never use our big oven, but boil all of our food to keep down the costs. For food, we don't pay too much. If food increases in price, we decrease how much we eat. If rent increases, there is no way to decrease. Rent is a major problem for us. I have some health coverage at my place of work, but it is so inadequate that when I am ill, I try to avoid doctors and hospitals because they are so expensive. I use home remedies; my wife uses herbal medicines. That's why we are able to survive on so much less than other Americans.

36   I often wonder what will happen to my family. The future of my children is bright, for they work hard and have talent. They know they must work hard, for I will not be able to help them much longer. The work I do requires good hand-and-eye coordination. One day I will lose that. What will happen to me then? Sometimes I worry about my future; at other times I don't care.

EXERCISES

Details and Their Meanings

1. Why did the narrator and his family come to America? What effect do you think this reason has on his feelings about his new home?

2. In what region of the country does the narrator first live, and what are his experiences there? What can you infer about the narrator's racial attitudes?

3. Why do the narrator and his wife have problems walking or riding bicycles where they now live? How does this difficulty affect their lives? How do you think it might remind them of what they have given up?

4. How is the narrator's work different from the work he did in Vietnam? How would his work life be different if he had stayed in Vietnam?

5. What cultural differences (besides language) does the narrator mention between Vietnam and America? Which of these differences does he indicate are the biggest problems for him and his family?

6. What kinds of problems do the narrator and his family have in communicating in English? How do they cope with these problems?

7. In what ways does the narrator find himself supported by other people in America? How do these people seem to differ from those who harass him and his family?

Reading and Critical Thinking

1. How do the narrator and his family socialize in America? How could this situation contribute to their having a hard time getting established in this country? How would things be different in Vietnam?

2. Why does the narrator say that life in America is terrible but the future of his children is bright? Do you agree with his observation? Why or why not?

3. Which individuals in the narrator's family do you think are adjusting more quickly to American life? What are the reasons given here for how one becomes accustomed to a new culture? What seem to be the greatest barriers to adjusting from the point of view of the narrator? What other barriers do you see?

4. What picture do you get of America from the narrator? What are his attitudes toward young people in America? From the account of his experiences, do you think his attitudes are justified? Why or why not? How might his attitudes change?

5. What are the causes of the narrator's and his family's loneliness? How might some of their loneliness be soothed? What causes of their loneliness can never be removed?

6. What problems that the narrator and his family have to deal
   with do people who were born in America take for granted?
   How do these problems make the narrator feel? How do they
   seem to make his wife feel? In what ways can you generalize
   from this essay about how other immigrants might feel?

The Writer's Strategies

1. The narrator's story was told to James M. Freeman, who wrote it
   down. How would you describe the language used in this essay?
   Does the language more closely represent Freeman's language
   or the language of the Vietnamese teacher? How does the language contribute to the overall effect of the piece?
2. Do you think that withholding the narrator's name is an effective strategy? Why or why not? What might the writer have had
   in mind by leaving out the narrator's name? Does the absence of
   the name give the selection any special meaning?
3. What information given by the narrator tells you about his personality? How does the last line of the piece both agree with and
   contradict what you know about the narrator's personality?
4. Why do you think the writer uses dialogue? What other points
   of view emerge besides the narrator's? Why do you think the
   narrator is the dominant voice? How does his dominance affect
   the meaning of the selection?
5. Why do you think the writer chose the title "Hearts of Sorrow"?
   How does the title affect the message you get from the essay?
   Think of another, more positive, title for the essay. How does
   your new title affect how the essay will be read? What different
   passages might become more important?

Thinking Together

In small groups, discuss your experiences of going to a different
town, city, state, or country. Were there times when you felt out of
place, when you did not understand what was being said to you, or
when you did not know the customs or practices of the place you
were visiting? How did these feelings affect your sense of yourself?
Did you become confused or frustrated, or did you adapt quickly
and enjoy yourself? After discussing these questions for a while, the
group should develop a list of the things that would upset group
members most if they had to relocate.

Vocabulary

Define the following italicized words from the selection.

1. the gesture *signified* "Come here." (par. 2)
2. they *startle* me (par. 18)
3. a friend *persuaded* me (par. 3)
4. health coverage . . . is so *inadequate* (par. 35)
5. my wife uses *herbal* medicines. (par. 35)

WRITER'S WORKSHOP ━━━━━━━━━━━

Critical Thinking in Writing

1. Find out what first-generation immigrant populations live in your town or city. Write a paper identifying the countries and cultures these new immigrants come from and explaining some of their reasons for coming to America.
2. Imagine that you are leaving your home forever to live in a strange country. You cannot take anything you enjoy with you. Write an essay on the things in your home that you would miss most. Include a discussion of what you would miss most about your town or about American culture.
3. After war or a serious disagreement countries often try to normalize relations with each other. The countries, for example, encourage their former enemies to visit as tourists. Do you think Americans should befriend countries against whom we have fought or had major disagreements? Write an essay in favor of forging a new friendship with this country or in opposition to embracing a former enemy. Support your argument with background information from the library.

Connecting Ideas

Compare the loneliness and dislocation felt by the Vietnamese teacher's family and by the Punjabi families described in Margaret A. Gibson's "Cultural Barriers and the Press to Americanize" (page 65). Are there any similarities or differences in the conditions under which the families have to adjust to America? Does the essay about the Punjabi students suggest some of the difficulty the children of the Vietnamese family might be having? Explore these comparisons in a short essay.

Uncaring Women's Health Care

Leonard Abramson

Leonard Abramson is president of U.S. Healthcare, a company that operates health maintenance organizations in several states. In this essay, he finds fault with the medical system for not being attentive enough to the special needs of women.

KEY WORDS

disparity (par. 5)   difference.
expedient (par. 7)   efficient method.
mammogram (par. 7)   an X-ray of the breast.
Pap smears (par. 8)   medical tests to detect cancer in a woman's reproductive system.
fulcrum (par. 9)   the supporting point.
prenatal (par. 10)   before birth.
Caesarean sections (par. 11)   the surgical delivery of infants.
hysterectomies (par. 11)   surgical removals of the uterus.

---

1   .A WOMAN VISITS HER doctor for a yearly checkup. Aware of heart trouble in her family's history, and knowing that heart disease is the number-one killer of women, she asks the doctor whether she should begin taking one aspirin a day, as her husband does, to decrease the risk of heart attack.

2   What does the physician advise? If the doctor is honest, he will admit that he doesn't know. Most of the research on the protective qualities of aspirin was performed on 22,071 men and, like so many medical studies, *no* women. And a study measuring the links among high cholesterol, lack of exercise, smoking and heart disease likewise featured 12,866 men—and no women.

3   Researchers argue that members of a sample group must be as alike as possible to test the hypothesis. But if only one sex is to be used, why not use women?

373

4   Recently in Los Angeles, a team of doctors found that women who need heart bypass surgery usually exhibit more severe symptoms of coronary disease than men before doctors take their condition seriously. As a result, many women who undergo bypass surgery face a greater risk of dying from it.

5   This disparity in research and treatment—the National Institutes of Health reported that, in 1987, they spent only 13.5 percent of their research budget on women's health—is important for its own sake and also as a symbol of the larger neglect of women in our health care delivery system. Women spend more on health care than men, and yet a disproportionate amount of medical attention goes to men.

6   Consider that every day, tourists stream past the Vietnam veterans' memorial in Washington, remembering the war that cost 58,000 American lives. Yet breast cancer takes 40,000 American lives every year, a tragic and unnecessary toll that is increasing steadily.

7   Almost a fifth of those deaths are preventable by the simple expedient of a timely mammogram. Yet, according to the Centers for Disease Control, as many as 9 out of 10 doctors do not follow the American Cancer Society's guidelines on recommending mammograms.

8   Nor can doctors assure women that other threats are guarded against adequately. Studies have shown that Pap smears, which test for cervical cancer, are inconclusive almost half the time because of poor sampling and interpretation methods. And, scandalously, it was just discovered in New York City that the Department of Health has a year's backlog of 2,000 unanalyzed Pap tests. Untold numbers of women who relied on the city's health care services now may die from a treatable disease.

9   Our nation's health care system must move to redress the inadequate attention paid to women's health concerns. There is no better way, I believe, to practice true "family medicine," for women are often the fulcrum of family life.

10   It is impossible to estimate the annual cost of poor prenatal care for women. Premature and low-birth-weight babies put immense pressure on the health care system; the care of one such baby costs as much as $1 million in the first year of life. And children who are inadequately nourished during pregnancy are known to have greater developmental difficulties than well-nourished babies—difficulties that can persist throughout life.

11   Studies also show that women are undergoing more Caesarean sections and other procedures than are medically appropriate. There is a need for an aggressive monitoring program to prevent un-

necessary hysterectomies, a continuing problem in many regions of the country.

12   Medicine is not a perfect science, by any means. But when thousands of American women are dying from diseases we *can* treat, when thousands more succumb to diseases that more research might prevent, and when thousands of babies are born with unnecessary handicaps because their mothers' medical care was inadequate, then something is deeply wrong.

13   Women are reaching equality in earnings, in education and in employment. They must achieve equality in health care.

———

EXERCISES

Details and Their Meanings

1. What do doctors know about the effect of aspirin on heart disease in men? in women? Why is there a difference in knowledge?

2. In what other medical areas is there a difference in knowledge about men and women? What pattern do the differences suggest about research? How is this pattern reflected in the research budget of the National Institutes of Health?

3. How many women die of breast cancer each year? How many breast cancers are easily preventable by early detection through mammograms? What percentage of doctors does not follow the American Cancer Society's guidelines on mammograms? What does this overall pattern suggest? What other facts indicate a similar pattern?

4. What can be the costs of caring for a premature or low-weight baby? What other problems result from prematurity and low-weight birth? How can prenatal care of women reduce these problems?

5. What do studies indicate about Caesarean sections and hysterectomies? What do these patterns suggest about attitudes in the health care system?

6. What does the writer believe must be done to improve women's health care? What specific suggestions does he make to achieve that end?

Reading and Critical Thinking

1. What is the writer's overall belief about the health care system's different attitudes toward men and women? Has that difference been evident to you? On what specific occasions was it apparent?
2. Some of the medical problems that Abramson refers to may be similar for men and women. What are these problems? Where do the male-female differences in health care research and treatment of these problems come from?
3. What medical issues described here are specific to women? Do you think the writer presents an accurate picture of these issues? Why or why not?
4. In what way do you see the arguments presented here as connected to or separate from the feminist movement?
5. This piece was written in 1990. In the years since Leonard Abramson wrote it, have you seen any changes? What are they? What further changes could be made to improve women's health care?

The Writer's Strategies

1. What is Abramson's thesis? State it in your own words. How does the introduction help set up the thesis?
2. Is the opening incident actual or imagined? Is it realistic or exaggerated? What point is the writer making with the opening incident? How does that incident make you feel about the health care system?
3. How does the attitude established in the opening set the tone for the whole essay? What is the writer's attitude toward his subject? What techniques does he use to establish the tone?
4. What facts, statistics, and cases does the writer present to support his position? Which do you find most specific? Why?
5. Comment on the last two paragraphs. Are they an effective conclusion for the essay? Why or why not? Why is the last paragraph only two sentences long?
6. Leonard Abramson is president of U.S. Healthcare, a private company that operates health maintenance organizations. How does that fact influence you in interpreting what he says, the stand he takes, and the reasons he takes it?

Thinking Together

In small groups, discuss occasions in which the health care delivery system has been or has not been sensitive to your needs or to the needs of someone close to you. Then discuss the characteristics that would make up an ideal health care system.

Vocabulary

Among the key words listed at the beginning of the selection are a number of medical terms: *mammogram, Caesarean sections, hysterectomies, Pap smears,* and *prenatal.* Find as many other medical terms as you can in the selection, and define each.

WRITER'S WORKSHOP ━━━━━━━━━━━━━━━━

Critical Thinking in Writing

1. Write a narrative of an experience you had with a doctor or hospital. Express your feelings about how helpful the medical system was to you.
2. Women are only one particular group served by medicine. Write a few paragraphs from the perspective of any other group, evaluating how well medicine serves its needs.
3. Leonard Abramson raises questions about the insensitivity of institutions to women's needs. Write a one-page essay describing how an institution, agency, or profession has or has not been sensitive to women's needs.

Connecting Ideas

In "Momma" (page 39), Dick Gregory tells how his family was treated by a city hospital. Compare that account with this one. Do you see any similarities or differences in how Gregory's family was treated by the health care system and how Leonard Abramson suggests women are treated? What conclusions can you draw from the comparison? Write several paragraphs exploring this comparison.

S I D E   B Y   S I D E

1. Drawing on the incidents and issues described in this unit, write an essay evaluating the state of race relations in the United States and discussing what can be done to create a better future.
2. Write an essay examining what you have learned about prejudice from the selections in this unit. Are there any activities or attitudes that you now, for the first time, understand are prejudicial? Have any of your attitudes changed? Do you now better understand the behaviors and attitudes of any other people? Is there anything you will do or say in a different way? In each instance of change that you can identify, specify exactly what in the readings led to this new thought.
3. One of the root causes of prejudice is the competition between groups for limited resources. Does society as a whole have a responsibility to remedy the unequal distribution of resources? What new policies, if any, would you adopt to help groups that have suffered from discrimination and exclusion? Argue your position in a well-detailed essay.

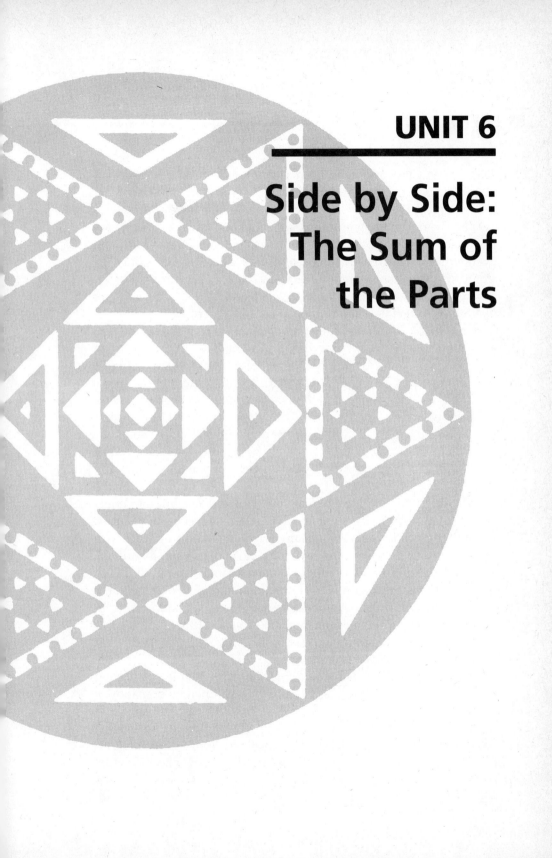

UNIT 6

Side by Side:
The Sum of
the Parts

INTRODUCTION ────────────────────────────────────

Many of the innovations that Americans have helped develop—the telephone, air travel, the mass-produced automobile, television, recorded music, the computer—have changed the nature of this country and the rest of the world. Physical distances between people are no longer significant. Information moves so quickly that local and even regional differences shrivel and fade. So powerful is the electronic image and so immediate its visual record that during the Persian Gulf War, Saddam Hussein watched Cable News Network (CNN), not direct field action, to learn how his own troops were doing. In a world where nearly everyone listens to rock music and eats at McDonald's the things that make individuals unique are difficult to identify.

Being part of a diverse society with a shared identity has many rewards: we learn from each other; we adopt notable behaviors and attitudes from the many cultures around us; we connect broadly and deeply with groups different from our own. Indeed, what makes our country great is that so many varied racial, religious, and ethnic groups can live side by side in relative harmony, interacting, sharing, expanding our visions.

Yet, many feel an inevitable trade-off in the leveling of people and communities is the erosion of group-based cultural identity. Certainly, much of who Americans are is the result of where we come from or the feelings we have for a particular place, a heritage, a family background. When one voice rolls into everyone's living room from the television, when one town's mall looks the same as another's, when millions of adolescents around the world dress every day in the required jeans and tee-shirt costume, it is easy to forget cultural connections and past history, to lose the sense of what made each of us unique and special.

The selections in this unit explore the ways people balance the struggle to maintain a unique identity with compelling demands of a dynamic American culture. Alex Haley searches for his roots; and Kathleen Teltsch, in "Scholars and Descendants," describes a group of people who have forgotten theirs. Sheila Rule shares the delightful phenomenon of cultural crossover in "The Men Who Would Be Elvis." Venny Villapando, in "Mail Order Brides," describes the feelings of Asian women who become wives of strangers in a new land.

Robert DeBlois, in "Looking Forward, Looking Backward," his essay on life as a quadriplegic, reveals how fragile our sense of identity is. William Least Heat Moon reminds us in "Wind" how strange and curious a hybrid American culture is.

Together the writers of these selections ask what we lose and gain by becoming part of this country. They are living testimony to how varied perspectives contribute to American culture and to how much we can learn from each other. But even more, the selections say that we are here, together. And they consider how we can live here, together, peacefully, successfully, with lives richly lived and powerfully intertwined.

PREREADING   JOURNAL

1. Describe some aspect of a culture other than your own that appeals to you. Why does it appeal to you? From what cultural community does it come? What values are represented by this cultural practice? How might this practice be related to the entire way of life of that culture? How has your appreciation of this aspect opened your eyes not only to another culture but also to another side of yourself?

2. Write a journal entry in the form of a top-ten list entitled "The Top Ten Most Essential Aspects of American Culture." The items in the list should be the characteristics that you feel best describe America, its culture, its values, and its way of life.

3. Psychologists sometimes describe the human personality by comparing it to an onion with many layers separating the surface from the core. When you look at your own personality or the personality of a friend or family member in this way, what does each level of identity contain? Write a journal entry in which you discuss each level of personality, identifying the levels that are most apparent and closest to the surface and the levels that are deeper. Where does ethnic identity fit in? How apparent is regional or local identity? How has experience added to or modified early layers of personality?

Across Third Avenue: Freedom

Humberto Cintrón

Humberto Cintrón, a writer and television producer, describes childhood attitudes that taught him not to venture forth far into the world but to protect himself.

KEY WORDS

Third Avenue El (par. 1)   an elevated train that ran on tracks above Third Avenue in Manhattan.
oblivious (par. 3)   not aware.
vicarious (par. 3)   experienced imaginatively through the experience of others.
meanderings (par. 3)   wanderings.
P. F.'s (par. 3)   a brand of sneakers.

1   THIRD AVENUE. AS FAR as the eye could see, the cobblestone street was saddled by a great, black, spider-like iron monster called the "Third Ave. El." It cast a checkerboard shadow, alternating with shafts of sunlight like a huge web draped across the wide boulevard waiting for unsuspecting victims. I remember sitting on the curb, staring across to the east side of the street, the ominous, foreboding presence of the "El" weighing on my 8-year-old mind and giving more substance to the taboo that Third Avenue was for the Puerto Rican kid in East Harlem.

2   Across that no man's land was an unknown world filled with exotic delights and adventures not accessible to me except through hearsay. Somewhere beyond was Jefferson Park and an Olympic-sized swimming pool; the Italian festival of Our Lady of Mt. Carmel, complete with Ferris wheel, merry-go-round, pizza pies, cotton candy, multi-flavored ices, and fireworks; there were a live market, fishing piers that extended into the East River, and the Boys Club. That I knew of for certain. The things I didn't know about were endless. My imagination soared as I sat watching the red and gold

trolleys rattle along on the shiny silver tracks embedded in the cobblestones and listened to the roar and clatter of the iron horse overhead, spattering sparks into the air.

3   The traffic wasn't so heavy, and the traffic light was no different from any other. Red meant "stop," green meant "go." And there wasn't any barbed wire or solid wall or alligator-filled moat or any other physical obstacle to keep me sitting on the curb day-dreaming while other people came and went, oblivious to my vicarious meanderings. None of that. The fact is, with my P. F.'s I could probably beat nearly anyone across and back.

4   No, the barrier wasn't one my wiry body couldn't run under, over or through. The barrier was inside my head. Not that it wasn't real. It was real. But it had gotten inside my head the same way the knowledge of Jefferson Pool and the Boys Club had gotten there—through hearsay: stories, rumors, and countless tales that fill the ether, the "stuff" of which tradition is made, transmitted from one person to another over time and distance. It was accepted fact without ever having been experienced. It was self-fulfilling.

5   Puerto Ricans were not to cross Third Avenue; that was Italian territory. Period.

6   Even Danny—"Italian Junior" we called him then—to this day among my closest and most trusted friends, more a brother than a friend, could not offer a solution.

7   Beyond Third Avenue you risked your life. It was a challenge I grew up with. Over the years the Third Avenue "barrier" appears to have crumbled under the steady flow of Puerto Ricans into "El Barrio" and Italians out of East Harlem. Not without a good measure of violence and heartache and bloodshed. Yet although the "Third Avenue El" and the trolleys no longer run on Third Avenue, and although the movement of Puerto Ricans in and around New York seems, on the surface, to have overcome the "barrier," no such thing has ever happened. The wall of "unwelcome" flourishes. As always it is invisible. It came to us through tradition, through institutional behavior—it is the life-style of America. It can be traced back through the various ebbs and flows of waves and waves of immigrants who were nursed on an institutional inferiority syndrome which required them to cast away their cultural values in order to assume the American identity.

8   Nor am I suggesting that this behavior was peculiar to Italians in East Harlem. No such luck—had it been that way it would be easy to deal with. No, they learned it here, as a result of their experience as newcomers. And others had learned it before them, and they in turn

learned from their predecessors. That's what tradition is. That's how social institutions are built.

9   In those days I never questioned the pennies dropped into the church basket or the coins for the poor box that mom gave us ritually on Sunday, though our table seldom saw a chicken or a pork chop. That too was tradition.

10   In the midst of the roar of bricks launched from a rooftop and zip gun blasts in the night, we were learning in school that George Washington never told a lie; Abraham Lincoln freed slaves; and every child in America could grow to be president. We learned it all by rote ("Four score and seven years ago our forefathers brought forth upon this continent a new nation conceived in liberty and dedicated to the proposition that all men are created equal. . . . ."). Those words reverberated through my mind on many occasions; while I heaved a garbage can down hard and heavy on some bastard who I'd knocked to the ground before he got to me; and when I rolled in the gutter tasting blood and dirt while someone's booted foot dug deep into my ribs and spine.

11   But I never grew up bitter.

12   I grew up hauling blocks of ice up five flights for the little old Italian lady who lived next door; and running every conceivable kind of errand for anybody who needed it; and translating for Mrs. Rivera and Mr. Gonzalez to the teacher, insurance agent, welfare investigator, cop, landlord, nurse, truant officer, etc, etc, etc. "What a good boy you have, Maria," all the neighbors said. And I was.

13   And I grew up getting my ass kicked and kicking the next guy's ass up and down the streets of El Barrio.

14   "That's a bad dude, Chino," the reputation went. And I was.

15   I grew up knowing that cruelty and violence and deceit were all part of the personal repertoire of social tools that I needed to be armed with to fend off the merchants of hypocrisy that rule and govern and perpetuate the "traditions" that make America "great." In the vernacular of contemporary American thought it all comes under the category of "being realistic."

16   The idea was never to unleash your weapons until the showdown came. The "good guy," after all, never drew his gun first in the movies. But when he did, look out.

17   A strange ethic when you look at it. In order to be the "good guy" you have to be able to do all the things that characterized the "bad guy" better than they did. Simplistic? Probably so—it's also what the Watergate mess appears to be about. A self-righteous hypocrisy that led some people to think that they, being the "good

guys," could use any means necessary to insure that they could continue to be the "good guys."

18   Bullshit.

19   But it's the American way and it's the system that has been perpetuated in institution after institution, from the church to the Mafia; from government to revolutionary movements; from the suburbs to the central city. From corporations to united funds.

20   I'm not going to judge it. After all, even the "Watergate" came to light; and there may be a remedy for that mess; and someone may say, "It was that same system that weeded out the imperfections and developed a solution"; and certainly the traditions and institutions in America seek to resolve the problems they confront.

21   I won't disagree with that.

22   But history has taught me that the institution which is a solution to one problem quickly becomes, itself, the next problem for which a solution must be found. So it is with churches and armies and police and museums and corporations and labor unions and newspapers and commissions.

23   "Third Avenue" has been with me all my life and I suspect it will be with all Puerto Ricans all of their lives, in one form or another. And it affected and will continue to affect every experience of any significance in my lifetime.

24   It was there in the military when, after four years as an instructor and "Guided Missiles Expert," I was discharged A/2C.

25   It was there in college, which required seven years and three dropouts to complete.

26   It was there in Mississippi when we started "freedom schools" to achieve "equal" education.

27   It was still there in "El Barrio" during the rent strike days and community action days when the anti-poverty program raised hopes and generated dreams of self-help, only to be ground into the dust of yesterday's rhetoric.

28   And it lived on with the experimental school districts and the struggles for "community control" and the vain attempts to wrest control in a neighborhood shared politically by legislators from other communities but served by none.

29   It was there when the publishers sent rejection slip after rejection slip and I finally had to raise the bucks to publish my book myself.

30   It's still there now, when every instrument of mass communications—print and electronic—chooses to ignore the Puerto Rican editorially; or carefully selects the images it presents, thus helping to perpetuate stereotypical negativism or promote a token Puerto Ri-

can personality while systematically denying employment and opportunities to Puerto Ricans exclusive of the mail room. In New York City today you can count on the fingers of your hands the number of Puerto Ricans employed in a professional capacity in all the major television, radio and print media combined.

31   I suppose I'll always sit on the curb somewhere, staring in the Third avenues of the world, wanting to belong. And I suppose too that I'll venture forth into that unknown, seeking and probing and discovering. And I expect too that I'll always have my pennies for the poor box, eager to serve and be "good" in what is likely to be a quixotic adventure. But one thing you can count on as absolutely certain:

32   "Third Avenue" was not and will not be a deterrent to joining the struggle and doing the things that need to be done—or, better said, trying to do what needs to be done. It certainly can not deter me from choosing to put on my P. F.'s and running under, over or through it.

EXERCISES

Details and Their Meanings

1. Why did Third Avenue seem like a barrier? Was it a real barrier? How did Humberto Cintrón come to treat it as a barrier?
2. Does the barrier still exist? For whom? How has it become an institution?
3. What were some of the elements to be found on the other side of Third Avenue? How did Cintrón find out about them? Who lived on the other side of Third Avenue? Did Cintrón know any people from that group? Did he have real reasons to fear those people?
4. What did Cintrón learn in school? How did he behave in school and with adults? How did he behave on the streets? How did those two different places affect who he became? What kinds of values did he develop? In what way are they American values?
5. How did Cintrón's feelings about Third Avenue and his street values carry over to his later life? In which examples is he using Third Avenue thinking? In which ones is it being used against him?

6. How did Cintrón fight prejudices against him? How is he continuing to do so? In what way is his struggle also part of Third Avenue thinking?

Reading and Critical Thinking

1. What was the effect on the writer's growth and attitudes of staying within his own community? Was this pattern of staying among his own inevitable for him? Is this a common pattern in neighborhoods? Why or why not?
2. What does the writer mean in paragraph 22 when he says, "the institution which is a solution to one problem quickly becomes, itself, the next problem for which a solution must be found"? What example does he use to support this point? What other examples can you think of?
3. Do you think the writer has left Third Avenue? In what ways has he not? In what ways is it still a struggle for him to cross over from his home territory?
4. What is the meaning of the title? Do you observe any ironies in it?

The Writer's Strategies

1. What overall point is Humberto Cintrón making? Does he ever argue it directly? How does he use the narrative about his own development to make this point? What audience does he have in mind—that is, whom do you think he is trying to reach with this selection?
2. Where does the narrative start? Where does it end? How do the locale and the ideas change from beginning to end? How are they linked?
3. What rhetorical strategies other than narrative does the writer use?
4. How does the writer relate personal local experiences to general American patterns? Why does he do so? What is he showing about the way he must act in wider American society?
5. What transitions help the writer connect ideas between paragraphs? within paragraphs?
6. Comment on the writer's style. Is it formal or informal? How do the sensory details contribute to the style? How do the short, simple sentences contribute to the style?

Thinking Together

In small groups, compare your experiences of places that were off limits to you as a child. To what places were you not supposed to go? Who established this prohibition? How did you learn you weren't supposed to go to a specific place? What did you think would happen if you went there? Did you accept the limitations to your freedom? When (if ever) did you step beyond the boundaries? Why did you do so, and what was the effect? What do you think now about those limitations?

Vocabulary

Find the context in the selection for the following words. Then define each word as it is used there.

1. boulevard (par. 1)
2. ominous (par. 1)
3. foreboding (par. 1)
4. inferiority syndrome (par. 7)
5. predecessors (par. 8)
6. reverberated (par. 10)
7. repertoire (par. 15)
8. hypocrisy (par. 15)
9. perpetuate (par. 15)
10. vernacular (par. 15)
11. ethic (par. 17)
12. wrest (par. 28)

WRITER'S WORKSHOP ━━━━━━━━━━━━━

Critical Thinking in Writing

1. Describe the values you learned in school, church, or some other adult-led institution; then describe the values you learned in your neighborhood or on the street. Finally, compare the two sets of values, explaining how well they fit together and how you reconciled them.
2. Write a narrative essay to show how you moved beyond some restrictions of your childhood to discover a bigger world.
3. Write a short essay about some value you learned in childhood that has stayed with you or that you changed as you grew older.

Connecting Ideas

Compare Humberto Cintrón's way of dealing with the many cultures in his world with Elizabeth Wong's way of dealing with the many worlds she describes in "The Struggle to Be an All-American Girl" (page 32).

The Business of Selling Mail-Order Brides

Venny Villapando

This selection is a sociological description of an unusual practice: men selecting wives through the mail. The men are usually white, and the women are usually poor Asians from underdeveloped countries.

KEY WORDS

intimidating (par. 6) frightening.
resurgence (par. 6) a return to activity or importance.
exploitation (par. 25) unjust use of another person for advantage.
unabashedly (par. 30) without disguise or embarrassment.
prevail (par. 38) to continue, survive.

▬▬▬▬▬

1 THE PHENOMENON IS FAR from new. Certainly in the Old West and in other frontier situations such as the labor camps at the sugar farms in Hawaii, the colonization of Australia, or even in the early Irish settlements of New York, there were always lonely men who would write to their homeland for a bride. These women would come on the next train or on the next boat to meet their husbands for the very first time.

2 For Japanese immigrants traditional marriages were arranged in Japan between relatives of the man and the prospective bride. Information was exchanged between the two families about the potential union, and photographs were exchanged between the couple. If both parties agreed, then the marriage was legalized in the home country, and the bride came to America.

3 While these marriages occurred in less than ideal situations, a number of them were successful. For example the Japanese sugar worker who once waited on the Honolulu pier for the arrival of his

picture bride, today enjoys the company of a family clan that spans at least two generations. That is indeed an achievement considering the picture bride of yesteryear, just like the contemporary mail-order bride, has always been at a disadvantage. She comes to the marriage from far away, without the nearby support of her family or a familiar culture. The distance that she has traveled is measured not so much in nautical as in emotional miles. She is not quite the happy bride who has been courted and wooed, freely choosing her groom and her destiny.

4   Today's mail-order brides are products of a very complex set of situations and contradictions. They are confronted by far more complicated conditions than the picture brides of years past. They do not quite fit the simple pattern of a marriage between a lonely man stranded in a foreign land and a woman who accepts him sight unseen.

5   In the present matches brides-to-be are generally Asian and husbands-to-be are Caucasians, mostly American, Australian, and Canadian. A majority of the women are poor and because of economic desperation become mail-order brides. Racial, as well as economic, factors define the marriage however. The new wife is relegated to a more inferior position than her picture bride counterpart. Plus the inequity of the partnership is further complicated by the mail-order bride's immigrant status. Consequently she is a foreigner not only to the culture, language, and society, but to her husband's race and nationality as well.

6   **Why Men Choose Mail-Order Brides**   "These men want women who will feel totally dependent on them," writes Dr. Gladys L. Symons of the University of Calgary. "They want women who are submissive and less intimidating." Aged between thirty and forty, these men grew up most likely before the rise of the feminist movement, adds Symons. She partially attributes the resurgence of the mail-order bride to a backlash against the 1980s high-pressure style of dating.

7   Dr. Davor Jedlicka, a sociology professor from the University of Texas, notes in his study of 265 subscribers of mail-order bride catalogues that "very many of them had extremely bitter experiences with divorce or breakups or engagements." His research also shows the median income of these men to be higher than average—65 percent of them had incomes of over $20,000. According to Jedlicka, the average age was thirty-seven, average height five feet seven inches, and most were college educated. Only five percent never finished high school.

8   The Japanese American Citizens League, a national civil rights group, confirms this general profile of the typical male client and adds other findings. According to its recent position paper on mail-order brides, the group found that the men tend to be white, much older than the bride they choose, politically conservative, frustrated by the women's movement, and socially alienated. They experience feelings of personal inadequacy and find the traditional Asian value of deference to men reassuring.

9   In her interview in the Alberta Report, Symons points out that the men are also attracted to the idea of buying a wife, since all immigration, transportation, and other costs run to only about two thousand dollars. "We're a consumer society," says Symons. "People become translated into commodities easily." And commodities they are.

10   **Gold at the End of the Rainbow**   Contemporary traders in the Asian bride business publish lists sold for twenty dollars for a catalogue order form to twenty thousand dollars for a deluxe video-taped presentation. Perhaps the most successful company is Rainbow Ridge Consultants run by John Broussard and his wife Kelly Pomeroy. They use a post office box in Honakaa, Hawaii. Explains Broussard:

> Basically, we just sell addresses. . . . We operate as a pen pal club, not a front for the slave trade, although some people get the wrong idea. We're not a Sears catalogue from which you buy a wife. You have to write and win the heart of the woman you desire.

For providing this service, Broussard and Pomeroy reported a net profit in 1983 of twenty-five thousand dollars, which catapulted to sixty-five thousand in 1984.

11   Rainbow Ridge Consultants distribute three different publications, of which the top two are *Cherry Blossoms* and *Lotus Blossoms*. These differ from the Sears catalogue only because an issue is only twenty-eight pages long, not several hundred, and photos are black and white, not glossy color. A typical entry reads: "If you like 'em tall, Alice is 5'9", Filipina, social work grad, average looks, wants to hear from men 25–40. $4." For the stated dollar amount, interested men can procure an address and a copy of her biographical data.

12   Broussard and Pomeroy's sister publication *Lotus Blossoms* has twice the number of names, but Broussard admits that *Lotus* is a "second string" brochure, offering pictures of women who do not have the same looks as those in *Cherry Blossoms*.

13   Six months of subscription to the complete catalogues of Rainbow Ridge will cost the wife-seeker $250. A special service will engage Broussard and Pomeroy in a wife hunt at the rate of $50 per hour and includes handling all details, even writing letters and purchasing gifts when necessary. Should the match succeed, the business pockets another fee of $1,000.

14   Kurt Kirstein of Blanca, Colorado, runs Philippine-American Life Partners, which offers one thousand pictures of Filipino women looking for American men. Louis Florence of the American Asian Worldwide Service in Orcutt, California, provides men with a similar catalogue for $25; another $630 will permit the bride-seeker to correspond with twenty-four women, of whom any fifteen will be thoroughly investigated by the service. The California business reports an annual gross income of $250,000.

15   Selling Asian women is a thriving enterprise because the number of American men who seek Asian brides continues to grow. Broussard estimates the total number of daily inquiries is five hundred. In 1984 the Gannett News Service reported that seven thousand Filipino women married Australians, Europeans, and Americans. The *Wall Street Journal* noted that in 1970, only 34 Asians were issued fiancée-petitioned visas; while in 1983, the figure jumped dramatically to 3,428.

16   Broussard says that he receives one hundred letters a day from Asian and other women. He publishes about seven hundred pictures every other month in his catalogues. Still, Broussard reports that the chances of a man finding a wife through his service is only about one in twenty.

17   When he receives a letter and the appropriate fees from a prospective groom, Broussard sends off a catalogue. One of his correspondents describes the process: "I selected fourteen ladies to send introductory letters to. To my amazement, I received fourteen replies and am still corresponding with twelve of them." One of the reasons why letters so often succeed is the detailed coaching both parties receive. For instance Broussard and Pomeroy publish a 130-page pamphlet entitled "How to Write to Oriental Ladies." There is also one for women called "The Way to an American Male's Heart."

18   The Japanese American Citizens League points out the disadvantage to women in these arrangements because of the inequality of information disseminated. Under the traditional arranged marriage system, family investigation and involvement insured equal access to information and mutual consent. Now only the women must fill out a personality evaluation which asks very intimate details about their life style and history, and is then shared with the

men. Prospective grooms do not have to submit similar information about themselves. Some companies, in fact, even discourage their male clients from disclosing certain types of personal facts in their correspondence, including such potentially negative characteristics as being black or having physical disabilities.

19   **The Economics of Romance**   Coaching or no coaching, the mail-order brides business succeeds partly because it takes advantage of the economic deprivation faced by women in underdeveloped Asian countries. The Broussard brochure categorically states:

> We hear lots of stories about dishonest, selfish and immature women on both sides of the Pacific. Perhaps women raised in poverty will have lower material expectations and will be grateful to whoever rescues them and offers a better life.

20   One Caucasian man who met his wife through the mail says: "They don't have a whole lot of things, so what they do have they appreciate very much. They appreciate things more than what the average American woman would." In other words, they are properly grateful for whatever the superior male partner bestows on them.

21   "Filipinas come because their standard of living is so low," asserts Pomeroy. In 1984 the per capita income in the Philippines was $640. "Most of the women make no secret of why they want to marry an American: money." An Australian reporter who has studied the influx of Filipino mail-order brides to her country agrees: "Most Filipinas are escaping from grinding poverty." Indeed, most Asian governments that are saddled with chronic unemployment, spiraling cost of living, malnutrition, and political turmoil are faced with the problem of emigration and a diminishing labor force. In contrast, Japan, the economic and technological leader of Asia, has very few women listed in mail-order catalogues.

22   The *Chicago Sun-Times* describes Bruce Moore's visit to the family home of his mail-order bride, Rosie, in Cebu, Philippines:

> "All of a sudden, we were driving through the jungle. There was nothing but little huts. I really started worrying about what I got myself into." . . . The house turned out to be an unpainted concrete building with no doors, plumbing or electricity. . . . Rosie had worked in a factory, eight hours a day, making 75 to 80 cents a day.

23   Because the Filipinas who avail themselves of mail-order bride service may not have much, Broussard's instructional brochures ad-

vise men to use caution in describing their financial status. The woman may turn out to be "a con artist after your money or easy entry into the United States." Despite the poverty, though, many of the women are truly sincere in their responses. The Broussard customer who is still writing to twelve of the fourteen women who wrote him notes:

> They all appeared genuine, and not one has asked me for money or anything else. In fact, in two instances, I offered to help with postage, and in both cases, it was declined. One of the ladies said she could not accept postal assistance, as that would lessen the pleasure she felt in the correspondence.

24   Regardless of the sincerity of the parties involved, one women's rights group in the Philippines has denounced the promotion of relationships through "commerce, industry, negotiation or investment." Their protests, however, do not seem to affect the business.

25   **Racial Images and Romance**   Added to economic exploitation, a major cornerstone of the mail-order bride business, is the prevalence of racial stereotypes. They have a widespread effect on the treatment of women and influence why so many men are attracted to mail-order romance. "These men believe the stereotypes that describe Oriental women as docile, compliant and submissive," says Jedlicka. His 1983 survey showed that 80 percent of the respondents accept this image as true.

26   One Canadian male, who asked not to be identified, was quoted as saying: "Asian girls are not as liberated as North American or Canadian girls. They're more family-oriented and less interested in working. They're old-fashioned. I like that."

27   The California-based American Asian Worldwide Service perpetuates the stereotypes when it says in its brochure: "Asian ladies are faithful and devoted to their husbands. When it comes to sex, they are not demonstrative; however, they are inhibited. They love to do things to make their husbands happy."

28   This company began after owner Louis Florence began his search for a second wife. He says that friends had touted how their Asian wives "love to make their men happy" and finally convinced him to find a wife from Asia.

29   Another mail-order pitch describes Asian women as "faithful, devoted, unspoiled and loving." Broussard confirms this popular misconception by saying these women are "raised to be servants for men in many Oriental countries." Referring to the Malaysian and In-

donesian women who have recently joined his list of registrants, Broussard insists: "Like the Filipinas, they are raised to respect and defer to the male. . . . The young Oriental woman . . . derives her basic satisfaction from serving and pleasing her husband."

30   Virginity is a highly sought virtue in women. Tom Fletcher, a night worker in Ottawa, Canada, who dislikes North American women because they "want to get out [of the house] and work and that leads to break-ups," is especially appreciative of this sign of purity. "These women's virginity was a gift to their husbands and a sign of faithfulness and trust." One mail-order service unabashedly advertises virginity in a brochure with photos, home addresses, and descriptions of Filipino women, some of whom are as young as seventeen. "Most, if not all are very feminine, loyal, loving . . . and virgins!" its literature reads.

31   Many of the Asian countries affected by the revived mail-order bride business have a history of U.S. military involvement. Troops have either fought battles or been stationed in Korea, the Philippines, and countries in Southeast Asia. During their stays, the soldiers have often developed strong perceptions of Asian women as prostitutes, bargirls, and geishas. Then they erroneously conclude that Asian American women must fit those images, too. Consequently, the stereotype of women servicing and serving men is perpetuated.

32   The Japanese American Citizens League objects to the mail-order bride trade for that very reason. "The marketing techniques used by the catalogue bride companies reinforce negative sexual and racial stereotypes of Asian women in the U.S. The negative attitude toward Asian women affects all Asians in the country." Further, the treatment of women as "commodities" adds to the "non-human and negative perception of all Asians."

33   **Romance on the Rocks**   A marriage made via the mail-order bride system is naturally beset by a whole range of problems. In her testimony before the U.S. Commission on Civil Rights, professor Bok-Lim Kim, then with the University of Illinois, noted that negative reactions and attitudes toward foreign Asian wives "exacerbates marital problems," which result in incidences of spouse abuse, desertion, separation, and divorce. In addition, writes an Australian journalist, most of the men they marry are social misfits. "Many of them drink too much; some beat their wives and treat them little better than slaves."

34   The Japanese American Citizens League asserts:

Individually, there may be many cases of couples meeting and marrying through these arrangements with positive results. We believe, however, that for the women, there are many more instances in which the impetus for leaving their home countries and families, and the resulting marriage relationships, have roots and end results which are less than positive.

35   Many of the Caucasian men who marry what they believe are stereotypical women may be in for some surprises. Psychiatry professor Joe Yamamoto of the University of California at Los Angeles says: "I've found many Asian women acculturate rather quickly. These American men may get a surprise in a few years if their wives pick up liberated ways."

36   One legally blind and hard-of-hearing American, married to a Korean woman, was eventually bothered by the same problems that plague other couples: in-laws and lack of money. "She gets frustrated because I don't hear her," complains the man about his soft-spoken Asian wife. In response, she says, "The main problem is [his] parents. I can't adapt to American culture. I was going to devote my life for him, but I can't."

37   Another area which specifically affects foreign-born brides is their immigrant status. According to the Japanese American Citizens League, "these foreign women are at a disadvantage." This civil rights group targets the women's unfamiliarity with the U.S. immigration laws as one of the most disturbing aspects of the business. "As a result [of the ignorance], they may miss an opportunity to become a naturalized citizen, forfeit rights as a legal spouse, or live under an unwarranted fear of deportation which may be fostered by their spouse as a means of control."

38   **Conclusion**   Despite the constant stream of criticism, the mail-order bride system will prevail as long as there are consumers and profit, and as long as underdeveloped countries continue failing to meet the economic, political, and social needs of their people. Indications show the business is not about to collapse now.

39   Erroneous ideas continue to thrive. An Asian woman dreams she will meet and marry someone rich and powerful, someone to rescue her and free her from poverty-stricken bondage. She hopes to live the rest of her life in a land of plenty. An American man dreams he will meet and marry someone passive, obedient, nonthreatening, and virginal, someone to devote her entire life to him, serving him and making no demands. Only a strong women's movement, one tied to the exploited underdeveloped country's struggle for libera-

tion and independence, can challenge these ideas and channel the aspirations and ambitions of both men and women in a more positive and realistic direction.

EXERCISES

Details and Their Meanings

1. What information do Dr. Symons, Dr. Jedlicka, and the Japanese American Citizens League give about the men who use the mail-order service? How does this profile help you understand why these men use the service?
2. What is the profile of the women who use the mail-order service? According to the writer, what is the primary reason they use the service? Do the men and women have equal power in the exchange? Explain.
3. Where do most of the men who use the service come from? Where are most of the women from? What does the economic situation of a man's or woman's country have to do with a person's participation in the mail-order-bride business?
4. How do modern-day mail-order brides compare to the mail-order brides of the past?
5. How is the mail-order-bride business conducted? Describe the differences between the two catalogues, *Cherry Blossoms* and *Lotus Blossoms*. How do the differences highlight some of the sexism involved in this business? How are Asian women described in other brochures and catalogues mentioned in the selection? In what ways do you consider these descriptions sexist and racist?
6. What problems do mail-order marriages have? How do some of these problems reflect an overall problem of racial stereotyping?

Reading and Critical Thinking

1. Why do you think that the men who use the mail-order service believe they will be happy with an Asian woman as a wife? To what extent do the men get what they hope for? In what ways do they get results that they did not expect?

2. Why do you think the "matching" services do not give the women detailed information about the men they are writing to even though the men have detailed information about them? What do you think this difference has to do with Dr. Symons's observation, quoted in paragraph 9: "We're a consumer society. People become translated into commodities easily."

3. What do the Asian women participating expect to gain from the transaction? What do they actually get? What are some of the consequences that they do not expect?

4. In paragraph 10, John Broussard, who runs Rainbow Ridge with his wife, is quoted as saying "Basically, we just sell addresses. . . . We operate as a pen pal club, not a front for the slave trade, although some people get the wrong idea. We're not a Sears catalogue from which you buy a wife. You have to write and win the heart of the woman you desire." Do you agree with this statement? Or do you find the statement contradicted by other facts given about the company and its procedures and services? Explain.

5. Why do you think the writer suggests in her conclusion that "only a strong women's movement, . . . tied to the exploited underdeveloped country's struggle for liberation and independence, can challenge" the mail-order-bride business? Do you agree with her observations? Why or why not?

6. Why do you think the Japanese American Citizens League believes the mail-order-bride system affects all Asians in America?

The Writer's Strategies

1. In the first five paragraphs how does the information about past and present mail-order brides compare? From the comparison, how does the writer seem to want you to feel about present-day mail-order brides? Where in the essay does the thesis first appear? How is the location of this idea related to the comparison?

2. Throughout the piece, the writer uses a variety of language to refer to the practice of selecting wives through the mail. Find as many different words and phrases used as possible. What do they have in common? What is the overall tone that the language conveys about the practice?

3. What kinds of people and organizations does the writer quote? What sorts of patterns do you notice in the kinds of people quoted? For instance, how many professors are quoted? How many mail-order brides are quoted? From the quoted sources,

what kind of information do you receive? Is the picture presented balanced? Is it in any way only a partial picture?

4. How do the details from the catalogues and brochures support the writer's thesis?

5. In what different ways do the quotes from the men who were using the mail-order-bride service advance the writer's main point?

Thinking Together

In small groups, discuss whether the mail-order-bride business bears any similarity to other current social practices concerning relations between the sexes or economic relations between rich and poor nations.

Vocabulary

The words in each of the following groups have similar meanings. Define the words to distinguish their different shades of meaning.

1. submissive (par. 6), deference (par. 8), docile (par. 25), compliant (par. 25)
2. perpetuates (par. 27), reinforce (par. 32), exacerbates (par. 33)

Define the following words, using clues from the context of the passage.

1. prospective (par. 2)
2. procure (par. 11)
3. disseminated (par. 18)
4. deprivation (par. 19)
5. prevalence (par. 25)
6. acculturate (par. 35)
7. naturalized (par. 37)
8. deportation (par. 37)

WRITER'S WORKSHOP ───────────────

Critical Thinking in Writing

1. How do you feel about the existence of a mail-order-bride business in today's world? Would you ban it if you had the opportunity, or would you help it to thrive? Explain your opinion in a short essay.

2. The existence of a mail-order-bride business is directly related to society's view of marriage. What elements in this view of marriage contribute to the success of the mail-order-bride business? How are minority women seen in marriage roles? minority men and majority men? Explore your views in a short essay.
3. Write one page about how this selection changed or reinforced your ideas about romance and marriage, racial stereotypes, and stereotypes of men's and women's roles in society.

Connecting Ideas

Compare the marriage arrangements described by Venny Villapando with those described by Elizabeth Joseph in "My Husband's Nine Wives" (page 120). In an essay of several paragraphs, consider the role of women in both relationships and the overall pattern of gender equality or inequality in each. You may also discuss whether you find either arrangement objectionable or acceptable.

Wind

William Least Heat-Moon

William Least Heat-Moon is a best-selling and award-winning Native American writer who has published a number of works, including Blue Highways *(1982). In this selection, he describes the effects of a tornado.*

KEY WORDS

nonchalance (par. 2)   unconcern.
fatalism (par. 2)   the belief that fate and not action controls human life.
celestial (par. 3)   heavenly.
fulminous (par. 3)   liable to explode.
torquing (par. 4)   twisting.
hunkered (par. 7)   squatted down.

1   WHEN THE KANSA INDIAN people, the South Wind people, were pushed out of the state, they carried with them the last perception of the wind as anything other than a faceless force, a force usually for destruction, that power behind the terrible prairie wildfires, the clout in the blizzards and droughts, and, most of all, in the tornadoes that will take up everything, even the fence posts. But people here know the wind well, and they often speak of it; yet, despite the dozen names in other places for local American winds, in this state (whose name may mean "wind people") it has no identity but a direction, no epithet but a curse. A preacher here once told me, "Giving names to nature is un-Christian." I said that it might help people connect with things, and who knows where that might lead, and he said, "To idolatry." Yet the fact remains: the people are more activated by weather than by religion.

2   Chase County is in the heart of the notorious Tornado Alley of the Middle West, a belt that can average 250 tornadoes a year, more than anywhere else in the world. A hundred and sixty miles from here, Codell, Kansas, got thumped by a tornado every twentieth of

May for three successive years, and five months ago a twister "touched down"—mashed down, really—a mile north of Saffordville at Toledo, a small collecting of houses and trailers, and the newspaper caption for a photograph of that crook'd finger of a funnel cloud was "HOLY TOLEDO!" Years earlier a cyclone wrecked a Friends' meetinghouse there, but this time it skipped over the Methodists' church and went for their houses. In Chase County I've found a nonchalance about natural forces born of fatalism: "If it's gonna get me, it'll get me." In Cottonwood Falls, on a block where a house once sat, the old cave remains, collapsing, yet around it are six house trailers. Riding out a tornado in a mobile home is like stepping into combine blades—trailers become airborne chambers full of flying knives of aluminum and glass. No: if there is a dread in the county, it is not of dark skies but of the opposite, of clear skies, days and days of clear skies, of a drought that nobody escapes, not even the shopkeepers. That any one person in particular will suffer losses from a tornado, however deadly, goes much against the odds, and many residents reach high school before they first see a twister; yet nobody who lives his full span in the county dies without a tornado story.

3   *"Tornado":* a Spanish past participle meaning "turned," from a verb meaning "to turn, alter, transform, repeat," *and* "to restore." Meteorologists speak of the reasons why the midlands of the United States suffer so many tornadoes: a range of high mountains west of a great expanse of sun-heated plains at a much lower altitude, swept by dry and cold northern air that meets warm and moist southern air from a large body of water and combines with a circulation pattern mixing things up—that is to say, the jet stream from Arctic Canada crosses the Rockies to meet a front from the Gulf of Mexico over the Great Plains, in the center of which sits Kansas, where since 1950 people have sighted 1,747 tornadoes. It is a place of such potential celestial violence that the meteorologists at the National Severe Storms Forecast Center, in Kansas City, Missouri, are sometimes called the Keepers of the Gates of Hell. Countians who have smelled the fulminous, cyclonic sky up close, people who have felt the ground shake and heard the earth itself roar and who have taken to a storm cellar that soon filled with loathsome greenish air, find the image apt.

4   Meteorologists speak of thunderstorms pregnant with tornadoes, storm-breeding clouds more than twice the height of Mount Everest; they speak of funicular envelopes and anvil clouds with pendant mammati and of thermal instability of winds in cyclonic vorticity, of rotatory columns of air torquing at velocities up to 300 miles an hour (although no anemometer has survived the eye of a

storm), funnels that can move over the ground at the speed of a strolling man or at the rate of a barrel-assing semi on the turnpike; they say the width of the destruction can be the distance between home plate and deep centerfield and its length the hundred miles between New York City and Philadelphia. A tornado, although more violent than a much-longer-lasting hurricane, has a life measured in minutes, and the meteorologists watch it snuff out as it was born: unnamed.

5   I know here a grandfather, a man as bald as if a cyclonic wind had taken his scalp—something witnesses claim has happened— who calls twisters "Old Nell," and he threatens to set crying children outside for her to carry off. People who have seen Old Nell close, up under her skirt, talk about her colors—pastel pink, black, blue, gray—and a survivor said this: "All at once a big hole opened in the sky with a mass of cherry red, a yellow tinge in the center," and another said, "A funnel with beautiful electric-blue light," and a third person, "It was glowing like it was illuminated from the inside." And the witnesses speak of shapes: formless black masses, cones, cylinders, tubes, ribbons, pendants, dangling lariats, elephant trunks. They tell of ponds being vacuumed dry, eyes of geese sucked out, chickens clean-plucked from beak to bum, water pulled straight up out of toilet bowls, a woman's clothes torn off her, a wife killed after being jerked through a car window, a child carried two miles and set down with only scratches, a Cottonwood Falls woman (fearful of wind) cured of chronic headaches when a twister passed harmlessly within a few feet of her house.

6   Paul and Leola Evans are in their early seventies but appear a decade younger, their faces shaped by the prairie wind into strong and pleasing lines. They have no children. Paul speaks softly and to the point, and Leola is animated, the kind of woman who can take a small, smoldering story and breathe it into bright flame. Paul listens to her in barely noticeable amusement and from time to time tosses tinder to her.

7   Leola says: "It was 1949, May. Paul was home from the Pacific. We'd made it through the war, then this. We were living just across the county line, near Americus, on a little farm by the Neosho River. One Friday night I came upstairs to bed, and Paul gawked at me. He said, '*What* are you doing?' I was wearing my good rabbit-fur coat and wedding rings, and I had a handful of wooden matches. It wasn't cold at all. I said I didn't know but that something wasn't right, and he said, 'What's not right?' and I didn't know. We went to bed and just after dark it began to rain, and then the wind came on

and blew harder, and we went downstairs and tried to open the door but the air pressure was so strong Paul couldn't even turn the knob. That wind had us locked in. We hunkered in the corner of the living room in just our pajamas—mine were new seersucker—and me in my fur coat. The wind got louder, then the windows blew out, and we realized we were in trouble when the heat stove went around the corner and out a wall that had just come down. We clamped on to each other like ticks, and then we were six feet in the air, and Paul was hanging on to my fur coat—for ballast, he says now—and we went up and out where the wall had been, and then we came down, and then we went up again, longer this time, and then came down in a heap of animals: a cow and one of our dogs with a two-by-four through it. The cow lived, but we lost the dog. We were out in the wheat field, sixty yards from the house, and Paul had a knot above his eye that made him look like the Two-Headed Wonder Boy. Splintered wood and glass and metal all over, and the electric lines down and sparking, and here we were barefoot. Paul said to walk only when the lightning flashed to see what we were stepping on. We were more afraid of getting electrocuted than cut. We could see in the flashes that the second story was gone except for one room, and we saw the car was an accordion and our big truck was upside down. The old hog was so terrified she got between us and wouldn't leave all the way up to the neighbors'. Their place wasn't touched. They came to the door and saw a scared hog and two things in rags covered with black mud sucked up out of the river and coated with plaster dust and blood, and one of them was growing a second head. The neighbors didn't know who we were until they heard our voices."

8   Paul says, "That tornado was on a path to miss our house until it hit the Cottonwood and veered back on us. The Indians believed a twister will change course when it crosses a river."

9   Leola: "The next morning we walked back home—the electric clock was stopped at nine-forty, and I went upstairs to the room that was left, and there on the chest my glasses were just like I left them, but our bedroom was gone, and our mattress, all torn up, was in a tree where we'd have been."

10   Paul: "We spit plaster for three weeks. It was just plain imbedded in us."

11   I'm thinking, What truer children of Kansas than those taken aloft by the South Wind?

EXERCISES

Details and Their Meanings

1. Who are the Kansa? What did they believe about the wind?
2. According to the preacher mentioned in paragraph 1, why shouldn't Christians give names to natural objects?
3. Where is Tornado Alley? Why is it so named? What is the difference between a cyclone and a tornado?
4. Where did the word *tornado* come from? What does it mean?
5. What does a tornado look like from the inside? How high can a tornado reach? How wide is one? How far can it travel?
6. What are some things a tornado is capable of doing?
7. How many tornadoes has Kansas suffered since 1950? What nickname has the National Severe Storms Forecast Center been given as a result?

Reading and Critical Thinking

1. Why do you think that tornadoes, unlike hurricanes, are not given names?
2. Why is Kansas such a good place for tornadoes?
3. What implied criticism of non-Native Americans appears in paragraph 1?
4. Why are some people in Chase County fatalists? How do the forces of nature make people of different ethnic groups equal?
5. Why did Leona Evans wear her fur coat to bed? How does this behavior illustrate Least Heat Moon's point about weather?
6. What might *Kansa* mean? Why can't you be sure?
7. What can you conclude from the story of Paul and Leona Evans?
8. Why does the writer conclude that people taken aloft by tornadoes are true children of Kansas?

The Writer's Strategies

1. What primary rhetorical strategy does the writer use to develop this essay?
2. What is the writer's thesis? Who do you think is his audience?
3. In which paragraphs does William Least Heat Moon make use of research? In which paragraphs does he investigate causes and effects?

4. What is the purpose of the sentence "the people are more activated by weather than by religion" in paragraph 1?
5. Why does the writer take six paragraphs to discuss the Evans'
   experience?
6. Where does the writer speak from his own experience? Where
   does he present his own opinions? Is paragraph 5 true? Are the
   examples reliable? Are they the result of facts or conjecture?
7. In which paragraphs does the writer make use of figurative language?

Thinking Together

Brainstorm in small groups to consider the impact of weather on
your immediate community in today's world. Are we victims of natural phenomena? Have our technological advantages given us
power and (or) control over the weather? Support your ideas.

Vocabulary

The following terms are related to weather. Look them up in a dictionary, encyclopedia, or glossary of meteorological terms, and
write definitions in your own words.

1. jet stream (par. 3)
2. funicular envelopes (par. 4)
3. anvil clouds (par. 4)
4. pendant mammati (par. 4)
5. thermal instability (par. 4)
6. cyclonic vorticity (par. 4)
7. anemometer (par. 4)

WRITER'S WORKSHOP ━━━━━━━━━━

Critical Thinking in Writing

1. Write a narrative about a memorable experience that you had
   with weather—snow, rain, hail, heat, and so on.
2. Is William Least Heat-Moon correct when he implies that Americans are usually ignorant about nature? Do you agree that most
   Americans pay no attention to information from the natural
   world? What explanation can you give for this?

3. Native Americans drew many of their social, cultural, and religious activities from natural phenomena and often had to adjust
   their lives to harsh weather conditions. Does his background as
   a Native American give William Least Heat-Moon any special
   insights? Write an essay in which you consider the writer's background in regard to the topic he has chosen here.

Connecting Ideas

Read "Green Frog Skin," by John Lame Deer (page 268). What
points does Lame Deer make about nature that William Least Heat-
Moon would agree with? How are these men's views of the natural
world similar?

The Men Who Would Be Elvis

Sheila Rule

In this piece, news-writer Sheila Rule introduces two unique Elvis pretenders and gives a glimpse of the international appreciation of Elvis and his music.

KEY WORDS

lilt (par. 2)   a light, rhythmic way of speaking.
sari (par. 13)   an Indian woman's garment—one long piece of cloth wrapped around the body, with one end draped over the shoulder.
sedate (par. 20)   calm, quiet, composed.

1   PETER SINGH, AN INDIAN whose Sikh religion requires him to wear a turban, recalled how Elvis Presley came to him in a dream in 1980 to say, "You're the next one."

2   "Elvis said I would entertain millions of people," the 43-year-old Mr. Singh said with a Welsh lilt before a recent performance at a community center in West London, "and that I would be wearing a white suit. Three weeks later, I had the white suit. Now I'm the rocking Sikh. I don't smoke dope. I don't drink bourbon. All I want to do is shake my turban."

3   Paul Chan is not so sure about the possibilities of an Indian Presley. But a Chinese Presley? Well, that's something else entirely.

4   "I think I must be the first Chinese Elvis in the world," said the 40-year-old Mr. Chan, moments before changing out of a dark business suit into a rhinestone-studded white jump suit at Graceland Palace, one of two Chinese restaurants he owns by that name.

5   "Honestly, not too many Chinese people do Elvis. I tell you, I think Elvis—the King—thinks I had the special talent to carry on for him."

Of the Man and His Music

6   Both of these star-struck claimants to the Presley throne are rocking and rolling across cultural boundaries as they try to make a special mark in a field where countless numbers of Presley pretenders come and go. While they're at it, they hope to spread the word about Elvis Presley among their own ethnic groups and instill in them a greater appreciation for the man and his music.

7   For both Mr. Chan and Mr. Singh, whose real name is Narinder, the road to wherever they are heading started at the movies.

8   Mr. Chan saw "Love Me Tender," the first Presley film, made in 1956, when he was 12 years old and living in his native Hong Kong.

9   For Mr. Singh, who was born on the Pakistani side of Punjab, the fever struck at an earlier age, when he was 10. The film was "Jailhouse Rock" in Birmingham, England, in 1957, after his family had immigrated to England.

10   Neither man was ever the same.

11   In Swansea, Wales, where his family eventually settled, Mr. Singh was dancing in a pub one night when a rock-and-roll band leader asked him to sing. Mr. Singh sang "Blue Suede Shoes." Inspired by the response, he said, he produced his own recording of the song and sold all 1,000 copies from his family's clothing stall in a local market.

12   He owns a carry-out food shop, but hopes to hit it big in show business with such original material as "Bhindi Bhaji Boogie" and "Pick Your Turbans," which he plans to release on a record soon.

"Who's Sari Now?"

13   Mr. Singh has also composed "Turbans over Memphis," "Rocking with the Sikh," "My Popadum Told Me," "Who's Sari Now?" and the memorable "Elvis, I'm on the Phone." In that tune, Elvis makes a telephone call to Mr. Singh from heaven to say: "Peter, there's just one thing I wanna know. What's the weather like down there in Swansea?"

14   "I feel that by following the King, I am doing something for my nationality," said Mr. Singh, who has four children and two grandchildren.

15   Mr. Chan said he was a misfit in Hong Kong because he "sang Elvis and everybody else sang the Beatles." He moved to London 16 years ago, worked hard, saved his money and opened his first restaurant two years ago. He wants to own many restaurants, he said, all of them named Graceland. The one in southeast London, where he was performing the other night is, Mr. Chan said, a place "where Elvis's memory will never disappear."

Singing with Supper

16   A sign in a window proclaims: "Elvis is in London." Inside, Presley in various outfits and poses and at various ages and weights stares at diners from dozens of photographs. The restaurant has an "Elvis Night Special" menu featuring Peking, Szechuan and Cantonese cuisine.

17   "The food costs, but my singing is free of charge," said Mr. Chan, who visited Graceland in Memphis every day for two weeks a few months ago. "My dream is to have a big concert and dress up like Elvis so more people would know about the King."

18   For now, Mr. Chan, whose son and daughter are college students, is content to grab the spotlight at his restaurants and sing to the accompaniment of recorded music. There is also recorded applause, perhaps just in case the audience has more Beatles fans than Presley fans.

Curling Lips, Swiveling Hips

19   Both Mr. Chan and Mr. Singh sound more like themselves than like Presley when they sing. That is only fitting, they say, because no one can really take the place of the King. But they have worked hard at mastering the moves. Each one's left leg has a whole lot of shaking going on. Mr. Chan's hands and shoulders also shake a lot.

20   Mr. Singh often passes the microphone under his knee—the left one—and pushes his turban toward the front and then the back of his head. He also curls his lip. Both men practice a decidedly sedate pelvis swivel.

21   "People tell me to keep on rocking," Mr. Singh said as fans gathered around him, asking for autographs. "And I'm going to rock till the day I die, because there is nothing else for me to do. Rock-and-roll is here to stay. We're going to have fun night and day."

EXERCISES

Details and Their Meanings

1. What are the ethnic origins of the two Elvis impersonators in this piece? Where do they live and perform their impersonations? Are these facts surprising in any way? How?
2. What are the typical "moves" or characteristics that an Elvis impersonator needs to have? How well do Peter Singh and Paul Chan imitate these moves or characteristics? Do the men appear to be skilled Elvis imitators?
3. How does each man's ethnic background reveal itself in his impersonation of Elvis? What do you think audiences might gain from each man's performance?
4. How did Singh and Chan become interested in impersonating Elvis? What does their interest tell you about the international boundaries of popular culture?
5. What is Elvis the king of? Is this important to the story of Singh and Chan?
6. What different kinds of musical performances do Singh and Chan take part in? What do the differences tell you about how the men perceive their ethnic background in relation to impersonating Elvis?

Reading and Critical Thinking

1. In what ways are Peter Singh and Paul Chan "rocking and rolling across cultural boundaries" (paragraph 6)? Explain how this phrase could refer to more than just their Elvis performances.
2. Singh has composed songs such as "Rocking with the Sikh," "Elvis, I'm on the Phone," and "Who's Sari Now?" What can you infer from these titles and from other information in the selection about Singh's attitude toward his performances? Does Chan have a similar or different attitude toward his performances? Which of them would you choose to see perform? Why?
3. Do you think Singh and Chan would be able to be Elvis pretenders in their countries of origin? What difficulties might they have if they tried?
4. If you had to state the writer's main point without mentioning anything to do with music, what would you say? In general, why do you think this piece was written?

5. What kind of relation do Singh and Chan feel between themselves and Elvis? How do you think this feeling contributes to how you feel toward them as you read the article?

The Writer's Strategies

1. In the first five paragraphs, Sheila Rule presents several sets of comparisons. Describe as many comparisons as you can find. Why do you think she begins in this way?
2. In which paragraph is the thesis of the selection? Explain how the preceding paragraphs lead up to this main point.
3. Why do you think the writer quotes Singh and Chan so frequently? What subjects are discussed in the quotations? How do the quotations give you a good sense of the men and their performances?
4. Based on the end of the article, how do you imagine the writer intends you to feel about this subject? Has the writer presented a fitting conclusion to the essay? Why or why not?
5. Rudyard Kipling (1865–1936), British author, wrote a famous short story entitled "The Man Who Would Be King." In this story, two white British adventurers are given divine emperor status by the Asian tribal people they have tried to exploit. What points or ironies do you think Sheila Rule was trying to point out by choosing a title so close to that of Kipling's story?

Thinking Together

In small groups, discuss the draw Elvis Presley had and still has on a broad range of cultures throughout the world. How do you account for the Elvis Presley phenomenon? (We now have a United States postage stamp commemorating the singer.) Analyze Elvis' cross-cultural appeal.

Vocabulary

The context of the following italicized words gives good clues about their meaning. Define each italicized word, and then look it up in a dictionary to learn more about its origin.

1. whose *Sikh* religion requires him to wear a turban. (par. 1)
2. *star-struck claimants* to the Presley throne. (par. 6)

3. a *misfit* in Hong Kong because he "sang Elvis and everybody else sang the Beatles." (par. 15)
4. menu featuring Peking, Szechuan and Cantonese *cuisine*. (par. 16)
5. sing to the *accompaniment* of recorded music. (par. 18)
6. a decidedly sedate pelvis *swivel*. (par. 20)

WRITER'S WORKSHOP

Critical Thinking in Writing

1. In one paragraph, describe the main differences and similarities between Paul Chan and Peter Singh.
2. Write a brief essay in which you present an unusual combination of cultures that you know about—perhaps a person engaging in the music or art of a culture different from his or her own.
3. Popular music draws its influences from many sources, including diverse ethnic and cultural influences. Select an area of music—popular, rock, country, classical, or rap—and describe and analyze the effects of diverse cultures and ethnic identities on this musical area.

Connecting Ideas

In a short essay, compare the cultural mixing described by Sheila Rule in this essay with the cultural mixing described by William Least Heat-Moon in "Wind" (page 405). Despite the differences in tone of the two pieces, what similarities do you see in the processes of cultural combination? Do you see any differences?

Scholars and Descendants

Kathleen Teltsch

Kathleen Teltsch is a journalist who writes for the New York Times. *In this selection, she reports on the discovery of a group of people who have been in hiding in New Mexico for five hundred years.*

KEY WORDS

expulsion (par. 1)   exiling, throwing out.
obscurity (par. 1)   the condition of being unknown or un-identified.
cognizance (par. 10)   awareness, recognition.
genealogy (par. 22)   a list of the ancestors who make up one's family tree.
exhilarated (par. 27)   excited, gladdened.
validation (par. 31)   verification, certification.

1   AFTER SEVERAL CENTURIES, SCHOLARS are uncovering the history of Spanish Jews who converted to Catholicism under threat of expulsion by Spain's monarchs in 1492 and then found refuge and obscurity in the mountains of New Mexico.

2   Although most of these early colonizers lived as practicing Catholics, a significant number, often called "conversos," continued to cling secretly to Jewish traditions, lighting candles on Fridays, reciting Hebrew prayers, circumcising baby boys, baking unleavened bread, keeping the Sabbath.

3   Researchers are now finding evidence that some nominally Christian families have handed down Jewish traditions, and have done it amid a fear-inspired secrecy that seems hardly to have lessened over five centuries.

4   In the past two or three years, in remote areas of the Southwest, hundreds of gravestones have been found in old Christian cemeteries with Hebrew inscriptions or Jewish symbols often combined with the cross.

5   Stimulated by the scholarly inquiries, or on their own, young descendants of converso families are searching to find their roots, Jewish and Christian, and comparing their findings.

6   A few of these descendants have returned to Judaism. Others are slowly establishing fragile ties to mainstream Jewish congregations.

7   "I've been here 20 years, and only in the last two or three, after observing me carefully, a handful of these people have made contact with me," said Rabbi Isaac Celnik of Congregation B'nai Israel in Albuquerque.

8   Some come to services, always sitting by themselves, he said. He has been invited five or six times to their homes to lead prayers, often because an elderly relative wants to renew ties to the ancient faith.

9   Still, distrust toward outsiders lingers. "These people lived in fear of persecution for so long, they still look over their shoulders," Rabbi Celnik said. "They are historically conditioned over centuries to be suspicious and alert."

10   **Heritage of Secrecy Is Handed Down**   There are perhaps 1,500 families in New Mexico who have some cognizance of their Jewish heritage, said Frances Hernandez, a professor of comparative literature at the University of Texas at El Paso. "They range from those with only blurred memories of Jewish customs or family legends to others who really are aware of their Judaic background and know what it means," she said. "We're talking of people who survived 200 generations of stress and secrecy, and it's a wonder anything survives."

11   In pursuing the conversos' saga, historians are interviewing families and using data in church records in Mexico City and New Mexico on baptisms, weddings and burials. They have also examined Spanish shipping manifests dating from the 1490's.

12   A few months before Columbus's voyage in 1492, Spain enacted the Edict of Expulsion, compelling Jews to leave or convert to Catholicism under threat of death. Perhaps half of the estimated 200,000 Jews in Spain began an exodus to Portugal, other European countries and North Africa. Others became "New Christians."

13   But even New Christians who prospered found themselves still persecuted, possibly out of envy. And some only pretended to convert. Under continuing pressure from the Inquisition, which began to be felt in Portugal as well, some of the persecuted seized opportunities to come to the New World.

14   When the Inquisition stretched its reach to Mexico, they fled again, crossing deserts and hostile Indian country to the frontier of what is now New Mexico. There they found a measure of safety and obscurity.

15   "We only have started to scrape the surface," said Dr. Stanley Hordes, co-director of a research project on the secret Jews, or "Crypto-Jews," at the University of New Mexico's Latin American Institute.

16   Dr. Hordes, who spoke at the recent third annual meeting of the New Mexico Jewish Historical Society, believes that converso families who fled to remote areas like New Mexico's Mora, Charma and Rio Grande valleys could have settled the first Jewish community in what is now the United States.

17   But other historians and Jewish scholars dispute Dr. Hordes's conclusion, saying Christian families carrying on some Jewish practices or dietary laws do not constitute a Jewish community. Shearith Israel, the Spanish and Portuguese Synagogue established in New Amsterdam in 1654, is considered the first Jewish congregation in North America.

18   Rabbi Marc D. Angel of Shearith Israel said the remnants of Crypto-Jews in New Mexico was a tribute to the human spirit, but he questioned the claim to an early community.

19   "What concerns me is that because of their dramatic story with a movie-like quality, there will be an eagerness to receive them into Judaism and forget there is a formal procedure for reentry after separation that requires instruction, patience and sincerity," he said. "There are no short-cuts."

20   **Getting to Know Distant Relatives**   Dr. Hordes's own inquiry began in 1981 soon after he became New Mexico state historian. His doctoral dissertation at Tulane University was about Crypto-Judaism in Mexico in the 17th century.

21   "People began dropping into my office, leaning across my desk and whispering, 'You know, so-and-so lights candles and does not eat pork.' " Repeated such visits led him to undertake the research project, together with Dr. Tomas C. Atencio, a sociologist at the University of New Mexico.

22   Since 1988, they have interviewed almost 50 converso families, including many who practiced Jewish customs without understanding them, because their families had done so. In the process, the researchers introduced descendants who did not know they were related and who now are comparing their own genealogy searches.

23   Daniel Yocum, a 23-year-old engineering student, suspected he had Jewish roots on his mother's side. He discovered a wedding photograph of his late grandfather wearing a fringed prayer shawl. He has boyhood memories of him baking round, unleavened bread at certain seasons and butchering livestock in the traditional Jewish way.

24   Nora Garcia Herrera, his mother, elaborates on her son's recollections, recalling that her father and mother disagreed about the family's religious practices. "He said it was all right not to kneel to the saints because you don't need an intermediary to talk to God," she recalled. She objected and called him "Judio," Spanish for "Jew," which her children guessed was a bad word. Her father and grandfather were circumcised by an old man in their community. When he died, her father carved a gravemarker with a Star of David.

25   Ramon Salas, 26, a manufacturing analyst at Digital Equipment in Albuquerque, discovered that he was related to Daniel Yocum after tracing his own lineage 17 generations. He computerized his findings and says he has found evidence that Crypto-Jewish families, who often intermarried, used code names so they would recognize each other.

26   Mr. Salas said that, when he asked another cousin if they shared Jewish roots, she shot back, "Use your good Jewish head and you'll come to the realization you have Jewish blood."

27   "I remember I was exhilarated; it knocked my head off," Mr. Salas said. But as one who was raised as a Catholic, and in the eyes of his church will always be a Catholic, he is torn about making a choice. Judaism has an appeal—he lights sabbath candles—but he does not want to lose his attachment to the Catholic community.

28   **Memory and Myth Are Intertwined**   Dennis Duran, a corporate official who lives in Santa Fe, came to the historical society meeting with a copy of his family tree going back 14 generations and showing his kinship to the Salas family. He has collected data suggesting their ancestors were among the Jews who came with Don Juan de Oñate in 1598 to colonize New Mexico. Mr. Duran, who is 36, formally converted to Judaism even before beginning his search for his Jewish heritage.

29   He has recollections of his grandfather secretly praying daily at sundown in a cellar where the family kept fruit and wine, and of playing games as a child with tops, similar to the dreidel of Jewish origin.

30   Paul Marez, a 24-year-old graduate student, is the only one in his family who attends temple services. Family members are practicing Catholics, but he recalls his grandmother preparing for the Sabbath and, after a relative's death, observing a period of mourning and turning mirrors to the wall, as in the Jewish custom.

31   A number of the young adults are counseled about Judaism by Loggie Carrasco, a teacher with a magnetic style. Rabbi Celnik calls her Mama Loggie. "Young people look to her for validation because she is so knowledgeable," he said. "She is their rabbi."

32   Ms. Carrasco said she has traced her family to Seville and Madrid in the early 1600's. She said one ancestor, Manuel Carrasco, was tried in Mexico City by the Inquisition in 1648 for carrying matzo under his hat, which he tried to explain was a remedy for headache. His sugar plantations were confiscated and he disappeared.

33   While protectively withholding the names of conversos, Rabbi Celnik said that for many months he gave religious instruction to an artist from Taos who came weekly, arising at 4 A.M. to travel here. The rabbi also prayed with a dying elderly woman who lived as a Catholic but cherished her Jewish roots.

34   "I went to see her in the hospital," he said. "Her eyes brightened when I came into the room, and she recognized me. It happened to be Passover, and I placed a morsel of matzo on her lip. It meant a lot to her."

35   **Starting to Reconcile Two Disparate Faiths**   Rabbi Celnik said that, among the conversos who go to church, there is a segment that very much wants to return to Judaism. An equally small segment want to be Catholic and Jewish; they are comfortable in both traditions. "But there also is a very small group committed to vengeance against those who return to Judaism, and this is regarded as a genuine threat," the rabbi said. "They are afraid of their own cousins."

36   Rabbi Celnik said this may be the opportune moment for Crypto-Jews to embrace their heritage openly because 1992 marks the 500th anniversary of both Columbus's voyage and the Expulsion Edict.

37   The International Jewish Committee, Sepharad '92, formed to commemorate the anniversary of the expulsion, would welcome the support of the New Mexicans, said Andre Sassoon, the committee vice president.

38   Would they be regarded as genuinely Jewish? "We're a tolerant people," Mr. Sassoon said.

39   "Personally, whether someone is truly a Jew or not, only God can judge, and not mortals."

———————

EXERCISES

Details and Their Meanings

1. What two important historical events occurred in 1492?
2. How many Jews were living in Spain in the fifteenth century? Why did many Jews convert to Catholicism? What happened to those who did not?
3. What is a converso? How many converso families live in New Mexico? What is the relation between conversos and Crypto-Jews?
4. In what ways were some New Mexicans able to uncover their Jewish ancestry?
5. What kinds of rituals have conversos maintained? How has their long exile changed their rituals?
6. Who is Stanley Hordes? Why is he important to conversos?
7. Who is Daniel Yocum? How did he find his cousin?
8. What special significance did the year 1992 have for conversos?

Reading and Critical Thinking

1. Why did Spanish Catholics force Jews to abandon their faith? Why would this be unlikely to happen today? How do you think you would feel if a religious group in power forced you to abandon your faith?
2. What can you infer is one reason that America appealed to Spanish Jews? Was their belief justified?
3. Why does the congregation of Shearith Israel question the claims of Crypto-Jews in New Mexico? Are their questions valid, do you think? Why or why not?
4. What would explain the tendency of converso families to intermarry? How does American society feel about intermarriage? What is your view on this issue?

5. Why are some conversos reluctant to abandon Catholicism? How does their refusal present a problem for their community?
6. What attitude do conversos have toward religion in general? How do you explain their attitude?
7. How can you explain the deterioration of religious tradition among the Crypto-Jews?

The Writer's Strategies

1. What is Kathleen Teltsch's attitude toward her subject? How does she feel about conversos?
2. Who is the original audience for this selection? How can you tell?
3. What is Teltsch's purpose in writing this piece? Is she writing primarily to convey facts or express opinions? How can you decide?
4. What ordering principle does Teltsch use?
5. Why does the writer use subheadings?
6. Where does the writer make use of quotations? Why are quotations important to this essay?
7. What emotion is expressed in the conclusion? Would you call the conclusion powerful, negative, hopeful, or tentative?

Thinking Together

One of the people cited in the selection says that Jews have survived "200 generations of stress and secrecy," which is roughly six thousand years. In small groups, brainstorm to develop a list of reasons you feel that Jews have endured despite centuries of oppression and a list of lessons that contemporary American minorities can learn from the experience of the Jews.

Vocabulary

The following religious or cultural terms are important in the context of the selection. You can determine the meaning of some from their context, but others you will need to look up. Write a definition of each in your own words.

1. conversos (par. 2)
2. unleavened bread (par. 2)
3. exodus (par. 12)

4. Inquisition (par. 13)
5. dreidel (par. 29)
6. Passover (par. 34)

WRITER'S WORKSHOP ━━━━━━━━━━━

Critical Thinking in Writing

1. Suppose you were faced with a dilemma similar to the one faced by fifteenth-century Spanish Jews: you must abandon your identity or else face exile and possibly death. Which alternative would you choose? Write an essay that explains your choice.
2. Some conversos are still afraid of persecution. Do you think this fear is justified? Write a letter to a converso in which you support his or her decision to remain hidden or argue that the time for hiding is at an end.
3. People sometimes choose to hide their religious, racial, or ethnic background in an attempt to assimilate into a dominant culture. Write an essay called "The Crypto-____" (fill in the blank with your own word).

Connecting Ideas

Read Richard T. Schaefer's "Minority, Racial, and Ethnic Groups" (page 179). Do the conversos fit Schaefer's definition of *minority*? Are they truly distinct enough from Jews and Catholics to be considered unique? Make your points with direct references to Kathleen Teltsch's essay.

Roots

Alex Haley

This selection comes from a shortened version of Roots *(1974), Haley's enormously successful novel about his family from the time of his ancestors' capture in Africa until the present day. Haley, who died in 1992, was the ghostwriter of* The Autobiography of Malcolm X *(1964).*

KEY WORDS

saga (par. 4)   an epic story, usually one that covers a great deal of time and has many characters.
lineage (par. 15)   the line of descent from one's ancestors.
profusion (par. 15)   abundant supply.
staccato (par. 20)   composed of abrupt percussive sounds.
din (par. 20)   a great noise.
welled (par. 20)   issued forth like water.

1   MY EARLIEST MEMORY IS of Grandma, Cousin Georgia, Aunt Plus, Aunt Liz and Aunt Till talking on our front porch in Henning, Tenn. At dusk, these wrinkled, graying old ladies would sit in rocking chairs and talk, about slaves and massas and plantations—pieces and patches of family history, passed down across the generations by word of mouth. "Old-timey stuff," Mama would exclaim. She wanted no part of it.

2   The furthest-back person Grandma and the others ever mentioned was "the African." They would tell how he was brought here on a ship to a place called "Naplis" and sold as a slave in Virginia. There he mated with another slave, and had a little girl named Kizzy.

3   When Kizzy became four or five, the old ladies said, her father would point out to her various objects and name them in his native tongue. For example, he would point to a guitar and make a single-syllable sound, *ko*. Pointing to a river that ran near the plantation, he'd say "Kamby Bolongo." And when other slaves addressed him

as Toby—the name given him by his massa—the African would strenuously reject it, insisting that his name was "Kin-tay."

4   Kin-tay often told Kizzy stories about himself. He said that he had been near his village in Africa, chopping wood to make a drum, when he had been set upon by four men, overwhelmed, and kidnaped into slavery. When Kizzy grew up and became a mother, she told her son these stories, and he in turn would tell *his* children. His granddaughter became my grandmother, and she pumped that saga into me as if it were plasma, until I knew by rote the story of the African, and the subsequent generational wending of our family through cotton and tobacco plantations into the Civil War and then freedom.

5   At 17, during World War II, I enlisted in the Coast Guard, and found myself a messboy on a ship in the Southwest Pacific. To fight boredom, I began to teach myself to become a writer. I stayed on in the service after the war, writing every single night, seven nights a week, for eight years before I sold a story to a magazine. My first story in the *Digest* was published in June 1954: "The Harlem Nobody Knows." At age 37, I retired from military service, determined to be a full-time writer. Working with the famous Black Muslim spokesman, I did the actual writing for the book *The Autobiography of Malcolm X.*

6   I remembered still the vivid highlights of my family's story. Could this account possibly be documented for a book? During 1962, between other assignments, I began following the story's trail. In plantation records, wills, census records, I documented bits here, shreds there. By now, Grandma was dead; repeatedly I visited other close sources, most notably our encyclopedic matriarch, "Cousin Georgia" Anderson in Kansas City, Kan. I went as often as I could to the National Archives in Washington, and the Library of Congress, and the Daughters of the American Revolution Library.

7   By 1967, I felt I had the seven generations of the U.S. side documented. But the unknown quotient in the riddle of the past continued to be those strange, sharp, angular sounds spoken by the African himself. Since I lived in New York City, I began going to the United Nations lobby, stopping Africans and asking if they recognized the sounds. Every one of them listened to me, then quickly took off. I can well understand: me with a Tennessee accent, trying to imitate African sounds!

8   Finally, I sought out a linguistics expert who specialized in African languages. To him I repeated the phrases. The sound "Kin-tay," he said, was a Mandinka tribe surname. And "Kamby Bolongo" was probably the Gambia River in Mandinka dialect. Three days later, I was in Africa.

9   In Banjul, the capital of Gambia, I met with a group of Gambians. They told me how for centuries the history of Africa has been preserved. In the other villages of the back country there are old men, called *griots*, who are in effect living archives. Such men know and, on special occasions, tell the cumulative histories of clans, or families, or villages, as those histories have long been told. Since my forefather had said his name was Kin-tay (properly spelled Kinte), and since the Kinte clan was known in Gambia, they would see what they could do to help me.

10   I was back in New York when a registered letter came from Gambia. Word had been passed in the back country, and a *griot* of the Kinte clan had, indeed, been found. His name, the letter said, was Kebba Kanga Fofana. I returned to Gambia and organized a safari to locate him.

11   There is an expression called "the peak experience," a moment which, emotionally, can never again be equaled in your life. I had mine, that first day in the village of Juffure, in the back country in black West Africa.

12   When our 14-man safari arrived within sight of the village, the people came flocking out of their circular mud huts. From a distance I could see a small, old man with a pillbox hat, an off-white robe and an aura of "somebodiness" about him. The people quickly gathered around me in a kind of horseshoe pattern. The old man looked piercingly into my eyes, and he spoke in Mandinka. Translation came from the interpreters I had brought with me.

13   "Yes, we have been told by the forefathers that there are many of us from this place who are in exile in that place called America."

14   Then the old man, who was 73 rains of age—the Gambian way of saying 73 years old, based upon the one rainy season per year—began to tell me the lengthy ancestral history of the Kinte clan. It was clearly a formal occasion for the villagers. They had grown mouse-quiet, and stood rigidly.

15   Out of the *griot's* head came spilling lineage details incredible to hear. He recited who married whom, two or even three centuries back. I was struck not only by the profusion of details, but also by the Biblical pattern of the way he was speaking. It was something like, "—and so-and-so took as a wife so-and-so, and begat so-and-so. . . ."

16   The *griot* had talked for some hours, and had got to about 1750 in our calendar. Now he said, through an interpreter, "About the time the king's soldiers came, the eldest of Omoro's four sons, Kunta, went away from this village to chop wood—and he was never seen again. . . ."

17   Goose pimples came out on me the size of marbles. He just had no way in the world of knowing that what he told me meshed with what I'd heard from the old ladies on the front porch in Henning, Tenn. I got out my notebook, which had in it what Grandma had said about the African. One of the interpreters showed it to the others, and they went to the *griot*, and they all got agitated. Then the *griot* went to the people, and *they* all got agitated.

18   I don't remember anyone giving an order, but those 70-odd people formed a ring around me, moving counterclockwise, chanting, their bodies close together. I can't begin to describe how I felt. A woman broke from the circle, a scowl on her jet-black face, and came charging toward me. She took her baby and almost roughly thrust it out at me. The gesture meant "Take it!" and I did, clasping the baby to me. Whereupon the woman all but snatched the baby away. Another woman did the same with her baby, then another, and another.

19   A year later, a famous professor at Harvard would tell me: "You were participating in one of the oldest ceremonies of humankind, called 'the laying on of hands.' In their way these tribespeople were saying to you, 'Through this flesh, which is us, we are you and you are us.'"

20   Later, as we drove out over the back-country road, I heard the staccato sound of drums. When we approached the next village, people were packed alongside the dusty road, waving, and the din from them welled louder as we came closer. As I stood up in the Land Rover, I finally realized what it was they were all shouting: "Meester Kinte! Meester Kinte!" In their eyes I was the symbol of all black people in the United States whose forefathers had been torn out of Africa while theirs remained.

21   Hands before my face, I began crying—crying as I have never cried in my life. Right at that time, crying was all I could do.

22   I went then to London. I searched and searched, and finally in the British Parliamentary records I found that the "king's soldiers" mentioned by the *griot* referred to a group called "Colonel O'Hare's forces," which had been sent up the Gambia River in 1767 to guard the then British-operated James Fort, a slave fort.

23   I next went to Lloyds of London, where doors were opened for me to research among all kinds of old maritime records. I pored through the records of slave ships that had sailed from Africa. Volumes upon volumes of these records exist. One afternoon about 2:30, during the seventh week of searching, I was going through my 1023rd set of ship records. I picked up a sheet that had on it the reported movements of 30 slave ships, my eyes stopped at No. 18, and

my glance swept across the column entries. This vessel had sailed directly from the Gambia River to America in 1767; her name was the *Lord Ligonier;* and she had arrived at Annapolis (Naplis) the morning of September 29, 1767.

24   Exactly 200 years later, on September 29, 1967, there was nowhere in the world for me to be except standing on a pier at Annapolis, staring seaward across those waters over which my great-great-great-great-grandfather had been brought. And there in Annapolis I inspected the microfilmed records of the *Maryland Gazette.* In the issue of October 1, 1767, on page 3, I found an advertisement informing readers that the *Lord Ligonier* had just arrived from the River Gambia, with "a cargo of choice, healthy SLAVES" to be sold at auction the following Wednesday.

25   In the years since, I have done extensive research in 50 or so libraries, archives and repositories on three continents. I spent a year combing through countless documents to learn about the culture of Gambia's villages in the 18th and 19th centuries. Desiring to sail over the same waters navigated by the *Lord Ligonier,* I flew to Africa and boarded the freighter *African Star.* I forced myself to spend the ten nights of the crossing in the cold, dark cargo hold, stripped to my underwear, lying on my back on a rough, bare plank. But this was sheer luxury compared to the inhuman ordeal suffered by those millions who, chained and shackled, lay in terror and in their own filth in the stinking darkness through voyages averaging 60 to 70 days.

EXERCISES

Details and Their Meanings

1. Where did Alex Haley learn to write? How old was he when he began writing for a living?
2. How old was Haley when he first heard about "the African"? Who told the writer about his heritage?
3. In what year did Haley's search to document his family's story begin? How long did it take him to document the American side of his family? How long did it take him to find "the African"?
4. What documentary resources did Haley use? Which ones could other African Americans also use?
5. Who is Kunta Kinte? How was Kinte captured?

6. Who is Kebba Kanga Fofana? Why is he essential to Haley's family history?
7. How many libraries did Haley consult? How many continents did Haley visit to research his story?
8. What was the *Lord Ligonier*? Where did it come from? How does it figure in Haley's story?

Reading and Critical Thinking

1. Why did Kinte teach his daughter African words? How would this piece be different if he had not done so?
2. Why is it essential to the selection that Haley learned his family story through his grandmother? How would this piece be different if Haley's primary source of information had been his mother? What details of your own family history did you learn from your grandparents? from your parents?
3. What clues enabled Haley to begin his search? Why were these resources unlikely to be available to most African Americans?
4. How did Haley's career enable him to conduct his search relatively easily? Why did Haley go to Gambia? What essential resource was available only there?
5. Why did the Gambian women make Haley touch their babies? How long did it take Haley to figure out the reason? Why did the Gambians call Haley "Meester Kinte"?
6. Why do you think that Haley doesn't mention his father's side of the family?
7. Why did Haley travel to America aboard the *African Star*? What were his accommodations like?

The Writer's Strategies

1. What is the thesis of this selection?
2. What rhetorical strategies does Haley use?
3. Why are names, dates, and other specific details so important? How would the selection be less effective without them?
4. Why is the use of first person essential to this selection? How would the piece be less effective if told in third person?
5. Which paragraphs represent the introduction?
6. What is Haley's opinion of slavery? Where does Haley express it?
7. What paragraph is the conclusion? What new emotion is introduced there?

Thinking Together

In small groups discuss the importance of names in maintaining cultural identity. In an attempt to mask their cultural identities and to assimilate easily into their surrounding culture many people choose, for example, to "Americanize" their given names or surnames. Other people choose to herald their ethnic background by returning to names identified with their particular heritage. How do you account for the differences in approach? Why do we as a society infuse names with as much meaning as we do?

Vocabulary

The following words are part of Alex Haley's African heritage. Some of them are defined in the text. Write a definition of each one.

1. ko (par. 3)
2. Kamby Bolongo (par. 3)
3. Mandinka (par. 8)
4. Gambia (par. 9)
5. griots (par. 9)

WRITER'S WORKSHOP ━━━━━━━━━━━━━━━

Critical Thinking in Writing

1. How much of your family's history do you know? Write an essay entitled "Roots" in which you trace your family's history through as many generations as you can.
2. Imagine that you, like Kunta Kinte, suddenly are stolen from your home and family. Write a detailed essay about what steps you will take to teach your heritage to your children. What do you think it will be important to preserve? How will you make sure that your descendants remember where you were from?
3. Haley writes, "There is an expression called the 'peak experience,' a moment which, emotionally, can never again be equalled in your life." Have you or someone close to you had a "peak experience"? Write an essay to describe and explain it.

Connecting Ideas

Read "Scholars and Descendants," by Kathleen Teltsch (page 418). What major differences can you find between the elders in that piece and Haley's relatives in Henning, Tennessee? How did the manner in which those groups became exiles dictate their relations to past history? What do you think Alex Haley would tell the conversos about the need to discover and embrace their heritage?

Looking Forward, Looking Backward

Robert DeBlois

In this essay, Robert DeBlois, a writer and teacher, offers an unsentimental look at the surprising ways his life changed as the result of an accident.

KEY WORDS

nebulously (par. 1)   in an unformed, shapeless way.
ambivalence (par. 4)   inability to describe, being pulled in
   two directions.
stagnation (par. 15)   failure to progress or develop.
stasis (par. 15)   inactivity, inertness.
hokey (par. 16)   corny, trite.

1   ELEVEN YEARS.

2   When I was in the spinal-cord injury, intensive-care unit of a Boston VA hospital, some union musicians would come in once a month, set up amid the beds of men who would not be walking again, and go through their repertoire. They always started with "The Way We Were" and seemed not to notice the irony of it. I hope they never came to a realization of its significance and stopped playing it out of fear of offending someone. It was an appropriate song. Time looms large at the beginning of the ordeal, and looking back at the past is more pleasant than pondering the future.

3   May 19, 1975, was a warm day in New Hampshire. I was 21 years old and had just finished my junior year at the University of New Hampshire. I went swimming in a nearby river, where I broke my neck when I dove onto a rock. Although not the most intelligent thing I had ever done, it was certainly the most dramatic. A few days later, when the neurosurgeon solemnly told me that, in effect, he wouldn't bet the ranch on my walking again and that my arms would not be of much use either, I took the news right in stride. The

434

doctor was surprised and, I have always suspected, just a little disappointed. I think he was ready for a Hollywood performance in which I would rant and rave and swear through my tears that he was wrong and that, by God, I would walk again and, in fact, would start training for the next Olympics right then and there. "Bring me some barbells, please, Doctor."

4   Shortly after the doctor gave me the news, I was awakened one morning by my new nurse, Lollie Ball. As a symbol of snuffed-out youth, I had been getting the royal treatment by the staff, and Lollie was determined to put some discipline into my life. If the Pillsbury Doughboy had a middle-aged daughter, she would look like Lollie —a powdery white complexion, plump, and jolly behind her no-nonsense manner. "Time to wake up, Robert. Today we are going to brush our teeth."

5   Lollie was one of my first real annoyances after I got hurt, and in this respect she served an important purpose. Annoyances were something I was going to have to get used to. The doctor knew this when he gave me his prognosis. He was solemn because he understood the significance of my injury. Quadriplegic, to me, was just a word.

6   The most immediate annoyance I encountered was hospitals. One of the first thoughts I had after I came to on a grassy slope next to the river was that I would have to endure a couple of weeks in a hospital. It turned out to be six months, and all but the first was spent in a VA hospital, where I was given special permission to occupy an empty bed.

7   Another annoyance I couldn't anticipate when the doctor told me of my future was the lack of privacy I would have. This didn't mean I wouldn't be alone at times (although these times are infrequent). It did mean, though, that I could never really do anything while I was alone. Privacy is being able to do something with your aloneness.

8   The personal-care attendant entered my life. One spends a lot of energy when he has to spend 40 hours a week with someone who is paid to be a companion. Things can get annoying. Like the premed student who didn't know how to make a peanut-butter-and-jelly sandwich. Or the woman who insisted I was discriminating against her when I (my wife, really) wouldn't let her go topless when she worked around the yard, as had been the case with male attendants. Or the woman who had claustrophobia and could not ride elevators, sometimes leaving me to travel through a building at the whim of those who pushed the elevator call buttons.

9   Don't get the feeling it's all fun and games, though. Life became considerably more complex and required more compromise. I began to realize this when I moved to a VA hospital that specialized in spinal-cord injuries. Here the compromised future forced itself upon me in the form of bent-over old men in wheelchairs and men of all ages bedridden with urinary tract infections, made noticeable by the blood-red urine in the bags attached to their beds.

10   If someone were to ask me what I feel I missed out on most, it would not be sex, athletic ability or even the ability to walk. These are things that TV movies concentrate upon because they are easy for physically sound people to understand.

11   What I feel I missed most was the opportunity to experiment with my ideals and ideas as I moved into adulthood, that "real world" which floats nebulously outside the gates of colleges where American adult-children prepare to answer the question "What now?"

12   The question intrigued me. I was anxious to get to the real world, but in an instant the future was transformed into "the long haul." I found myself unable to test my ideals of simplicity, unable to learn that these ideals might have been naive, unable to learn through trial and error that life is, after all, complicated, that it is the rare person who gets to have his life on his own terms and call his own shots. The fact that I have come to these conclusions through another route is no consolation. The pain is in opportunity lost, experience missed.

13   When I was graduated from college, I began teaching, which is what I had planned to do before I got hurt. Before the accident though, teaching was just one of many possibilities. Afterward, it was one of the few realistic choices. And then marriage to the woman who was my girlfriend at the university, whose sense of loyalty is equal to our golden retriever's. Still, the romance was difficult, as was the decision to get married.

14   None of this is to imply that I regret what has happened since the accident. But I cannot keep from wondering. As I understand it, Franklin Roosevelt once mused over whether he became president in spite of his paralysis or because of it. He was referring, I think, not to the public's sympathetic view of him but, rather, to his own ambivalence about his motives to take on challenges and, in effect, to prove himself.

15   For persons who wish to assign qualities of heroism to those of us who have to live with readily discernible disabilities, I would suggest caution. That "normal" people are fascinated by different handicaps is evidenced by the way the media latched onto the disabled a few years ago. For a while there, being crippled almost became chic.

The poorer films depicted characters who heroically salvaged happiness from pathetic despair. The better movies, such as "Coming Home" and "The Other Side of the Mountain," showed that courage does not really enter into the picture. The lack of alternatives takes the heroism out of it. Growth may be painful, but stagnation is more so. Being disabled, like being normal, is a process, not a stasis for which one easy approach or formula can be developed. This is an optimistic idea, not a pessimistic one. It means an anticipation and enthusiasm for the future can still be present. Time will not be denied, but it need not only be faced and endured.

16   This may be a little hokey, but then, being crippled is also a little hokey, a little absurd, a little tragic, a little funny, a little fascinating, plenty weird and plenty frustrating. Eleven years later, this is the way things are. Not exactly the way things were, but at least, looking forward is now about as easy as looking back.

EXERCISES

Details and Their Meanings

1. What is DeBlois's current physical state? What caused his condition? When?
2. How long did DeBlois spend in the hospital? How many hours a week does he now need a personal-care attendant?
3. What are some activities DeBlois says he cannot enjoy? What does he find most regrettable about his situation?
4. What does DeBlois do for a living? How does his current physical state affect this work?
5. Who is Lollie Ball? According to DeBlois, what purpose does she serve?
6. Who is Franklin Roosevelt? What is his connection to the writer?

Reading and Critical Thinking

1. In what year was this piece written? Which paragraphs give you the clues for your answer?
2. What significance does the song title "The Way We Were" have in the context of this selection? How does it provide an ironic comment on DeBlois's life?

3. How did DeBlois react to the news that he would spend his life as a quadriplegic? How do you feel most other people would react? Do you agree that the doctors were probably disappointed at his response? Why or why not? What does DeBlois's reaction tell you about his character?
4. Why did people at the hospital treat DeBlois sympathetically? How would you have reacted if you had met him in the hospital?
5. How has the writer dealt with the limitations of being a quadriplegic? Has he been successful?
6. What conclusions about life has the writer reached as a result of his injury? Is he generally positive or negative? Support your response with details from the text.

The Writer's Strategies

1. What is Robert DeBlois's thesis? Why is first-person narration such an effective strategy for this essay?
2. Comment on the audience for this piece. Is the writer writing for other differently abled people or for those not physically challenged? How can you tell?
3. Where does the writer use examples to advance his narrative? Where are examples specifically omitted?
4. What is the writer's purpose in discussing Franklin Roosevelt? What function does the example of Roosevelt serve?
5. What allusions, or references, to other works are in this selection? How important to appreciating the piece is understanding these references?
6. What is the significance of the title? How does the title relate to the song "The Way We Were"?
7. Comment on the effectiveness of the essay's conclusion.
8. What is the tone—the writer's attitude toward his subject? Is he angry, resigned, sad, hopeful? Support your point with references to the text.

Thinking Together

How does your campus accommodate disabled students, faculty, and staff? In groups, investigate your campus and make a list of places and situations in which a person in a wheelchair would have a difficult time. Some good places to start are stairways, bathrooms, elevators, the cafeteria, and the library, but you can find others. Are the difficulties inevitable, or are they the result of a lack of planning by the building designers? What can be done to increase access for the physically challenged? When your list is complete, you might want to bring it to the attention of your student government or dean.

Vocabulary

Write definitions for the following medical terms from the selection.

1. neurosurgeon (par. 3)
2. prognosis (par. 5)
3. quadriplegic (par. 5)
4. claustrophobia (par. 8)
5. paralysis (par. 14)

WRITER'S WORKSHOP ─────────────

Critical Thinking in Writing

1. The writer's life was changed forever as the result of a single accident. Write a narrative about an accident that happened to you or to someone you know. What was the outcome of this event? Did things work out well or not?
2. The writer says that overcoming an obstacle when you have no choice is not heroic. Many readers would disagree, seeing DeBlois's life as truly heroic because of the way he seems to have overcome an extraordinary obstacle. Would you call DeBlois heroic? Write an essay to answer this question; include your own definition of heroism.
3. Write an entry in your diary or journal from the point of view of DeBlois's personal-care attendant. Write about one day or even one hour in your life. What do you do? How do you feel?

Connecting Ideas

Read Douglas Martin's "Blind Commuter" (page 245). How do you think Robert DeBlois would react to that piece? Does Martin depict the blind commuter, Mr. Torres, as a hero? Do you think disability forces a person to make a virtue out of necessity, or does it require the person to find an inner core of strength?

From Affirmative Action to Affirming Diversity

R. Roosevelt Thomas, Jr.

R. Roosevelt Thomas, Jr., is a professor of business management. In this piece, he suggests that it is time to look at the integration of the work force in a new way.

KEY WORDS

coercion (par. 8) force.
meritocracy (par. 11) a system of advancement according to skills and ability.
repudiate (par. 13) to reject totally.
plateau (par. 22) to remain at the same level.

1 SOONER OR LATER, AFFIRMATIVE action will die a natural death. Its achievements have been stupendous, but the premises that underlie it look increasingly shopworn.

2 Affirmative action was invented on the basis of these five assumptions:

1. Adult white males make up something called the U.S. business mainstream.
2. The U.S. economic edifice is a solid, unchanging institution with more than enough space for everyone.

3. Women, blacks, immigrants and other minorities should be allowed in as a matter of public policy and common decency.
4. Widespread racial, ethnic and sexual prejudice keeps them out.
5. Legal and social coercion are necessary to bring about the change.

3   Today all five of these premises need revising.

4   To begin with, more than half of the U.S. work force now consists of minorities, immigrants and women. In addition, white males will make up only 15 percent of the increase in the work force over the next 10 years. The so-called mainstream is now almost as diverse as the society at large.

5   Second, while the edifice is still big enough for all, it no longer seems stable and invulnerable. In fact, American corporations are scrambling to compete more successfully for markets and labor and to attract all the talent they can find.

6   Third, women and minorities no longer need a boarding pass, but an upgrade. The problem is not getting them in at the entry level; the problem is making better use of their potential at every level, especially in middle-management and leadership positions. This is no longer simply a question of common decency; it is a question of business survival.

7   Fourth, although prejudice is hardly dead, it has suffered some wounds that may eventually prove fatal. American businesses are now filled with progressive people—many of them minorities and women themselves—whose prejudices, where they still exist, are much too deeply suppressed to interfere with recruitment.

8   Fifth, coercion is rarely needed at the recruitment stage. Women and blacks who are seen as having the necessary skills and energy can get *into* the work force relatively easily. It's later on that many of them plateau, lose their drive and quit or get fired. It's later on that their managers' inability to manage diversity hobbles them and the companies they work for.

9   In creating these changes, affirmative action had an essential role to play and played it very well. In many companies and communities, it still plays that role.

10   But affirmative action is an artificial, transitional intervention intended to give managers a chance to correct an imbalance, an injustice, a mistake. Once the numbers mistake has been corrected, I don't think affirmative action alone can cope with the remaining long-term task of creating a work setting geared to the upward mobility of *all* kinds of people, including white males.

11   It is difficult for affirmative action to influence upward mobility even in the short run, primarily because it is perceived to conflict with the meritocracy we favor. For this reason, affirmative action is a red flag to every individual who feels unfairly passed over and a stigma for those who appear to be its beneficiaries.

12   What affirmative action means in practice is an unnatural focus on one group, and what it means too often to too many employees is that someone is playing fast and loose with standards in order to favor that group. Unless we are to compromise our standards, a thing that no competitive company can even contemplate, upward mobility for minorities and women should always be a question of pure competence and character unmuddled by accidents of birth.

13   And that is precisely why we have to learn to manage diversity —to move beyond affirmative action, not to repudiate it.

14   Managing diversity means getting from a heterogeneous work force the same productivity, commitment, quality and profit that we got from the old homogeneous work force.

15   **The correct question today** is not "How are we doing on race relations?" or "Are we promoting enough minority people and women?" but rather "Given the diverse work force I've got, am I getting the productivity, does it work as smoothly, is morale as high, as if every person in the company was the same sex and race and nationality?"

16   When we ask how we're doing on race relations, we inadvertently put our finger on what's wrong with the attitude that underlies affirmative action. So long as racial and gender equality is something we *grant* to minorities and women, there will be no racial and gender equality. What we must do is create an environment where no one is advantaged or disadvantaged, an environment where "we" is everyone.

17   The traditional American image of diversity has been assimilation: the melting pot, where ethnic and racial differences were standardized into a kind of American puree. Now those days are over. The melting pot is the wrong metaphor even in business, for three good reasons.

18   First, if it ever was possible to melt down Scotsmen and Dutchmen and Frenchmen into an indistinguishable broth, you can't do the same with blacks, Asians and women. Their differences don't melt so easily. Second, most people are no longer willing to be melted down, even for eight hours a day—and it's a seller's market

for skills. Third, the thrust of today's non-hierarchical, flexible, collaborative management requires a 10- or 20-fold increase in our tolerance for individuality.

19   So companies are faced with the problem of surviving in a fiercely competitive world with a work force that consists and will continue to consist of unassimilated diversity.

20   **The vision** that company leaders should hold in their imagination and try to communicate to all their managers and employees is an image of fully tapping the human resource potential of every member of the work force. This vision sidesteps the question of equality, plays down the uncomfortable realities of difference, and focuses instead on individual enablement. It doesn't say, "Let *us* give *them* a chance." It assumes a diverse work force that includes us and them. It says, "Let's create an environment where everyone will do their best work."

21   So far, no large company I know of has succeeded in managing diversity to its own satisfaction. But any number have begun to try.

22   Corning Inc. discovered in the early 1980s that talented women and blacks were joining the company—only to plateau or resign. Few reached upper management levels, and no one could say exactly why.

23   In order to break the cycle, the company established two quality improvement teams headed by senior executives, one for black progress and one for women's progress. Mandatory awareness training was introduced for some 7,000 salaried employees— 1½ days for gender awareness, 2½ days for racial awareness.

24   One goal of the training is to identify unconscious company values that work against minorities and women. For example, a number of awareness groups reached the conclusion that working late had so much symbolic value that managers tended to look more at the quantity than at the quality of time spent on the job, with predictably negative effects on employees with dependent-care responsibilities.

25   **Digital Equipment Corp.** helps people get in touch with their stereotypes and false assumptions through what it calls core groups. These voluntary groupings of eight to ten people work with company-trained facilitators whose job is to encourage discussion and self-development and, in the company's words, "to keep people

safe" as they struggle with their prejudices. Digital also runs a voluntary two-day training program called "Understanding the Dynamics of Diversity," which thousands of Digital employees have now taken.

26   Avon Products Inc. has sent racially and ethnically diverse groups of 25 managers at a time to the American Institute for Managing Diversity for the past several years. They spend three weeks confronting their differences and learning to hear and avail themselves of viewpoints they initially disagreed with.

27   Xerox Corp., on the assumption that attitude changes will grow from the daily experience of genuine workplace diversity, has set goals for the number of minorities and women in each division and at every level.

28   One piece of its strategy is a focus on pivotal jobs, a policy Xerox adopted in the 1970s when it first noticed that minorities and women did not have the upward mobility the company wanted to see. By examining the backgrounds of top executives, Xerox was able to identify the key positions that all successful managers had held at lower levels and to set goals for getting minorities and women assigned to such jobs.

29   **A widespread assumption** in many companies, probably absorbed from American culture in general, is that "cream will rise to the top." This unexamined assumption can tend to keep minorities and women from climbing the corporate ladder.

30   In most companies, what passes for cream rising to the top is actually cream being *pushed* to the top by an informal system of mentoring and sponsorship. It is usually difficult to secure a promotion above a certain level without a personal advocate or sponsor. In the context of managing diversity, the question is whether this system works for all employees. Executives who only sponsor people like themselves are not making much of a contribution to the cause of getting the best from every employee.

31   Performance appraisal is another system where unexamined practices and patterns can have pernicious effects. For example, there are companies where official performance appraisals differ substantially from what is said informally, with the result that employees get their most accurate performance feedback through the grapevine. So if the grapevine is closed to minorities and women, they are left at a severe disadvantage.

32   As one white manager observed, "If the blacks around here knew how they were really perceived, there would be a revolt." Maybe so. More important to that business, however, is the fact that without an accurate appraisal of performance, minority and women employees will find it difficult to correct or defend their alleged shortcomings.

33   **There is a simple test** to help managers spot the diversity programs that are going to eat up enormous quantities of time and effort. Surprisingly, perhaps, it is the same test they might use to identify the programs and policies that created their problem in the first place.

34   The test consists of these questions: Does this program, policy or principle give special consideration to one group? Will it contribute to everyone's success, or will it only produce an advantage for blacks or whites or women or men? Is it designed for *them* as opposed to *us?* Whenever the answer is yes, you're not yet on the road to managing diversity.

35   This does not rule out the possibility of addressing issues that relate to a single group. It only underlines the importance of determining that the issue you're addressing does not relate to other groups as well.

36   For example, management in one company noticed that blacks were not moving up in the organization. Before instituting a special program to bring them along, managers conducted interviews to see if they could find the reason for the impasse. What blacks themselves reported was a problem with the quality of supervision. Further interviews showed that other employees too—including white males—were concerned about the quality of supervision and felt that little was being done to foster professional development.

37   Correcting the situation eliminated a problem that affected everyone. In this case, a solution that focused only on blacks would have been out of place.

38   Had the problem consisted of prejudice, on the other hand, a solution based on affirmative action would have been perfectly appropriate.

39   **Let me come full circle.** The ability to manage diversity is the ability to manage your company without unnatural advantage or disadvantage for any member of your diverse work force. The fact remains that you must first have a work force that is diverse at every

level, and if you don't, you're going to need affirmative action to get from here to there.

40   The reason you then want to move beyond affirmative action to managing diversity is because affirmative action fails to deal with the root causes of prejudice and inequality and does little to develop the full potential of every man and woman in the company.

41   In a country seeking competitive advantage in a global economy, we must develop our capacity to accept and empower the diverse human talents of the most diverse nation in the world. Diversity is our reality. We need to make it our strength.

EXERCISES

Details and Their Meanings

1. What are the five assumptions on which affirmative action is based? Why does R. Roosevelt Thomas, Jr. believe these assumptions no longer hold?
2. According to the writer, how effective has affirmative action been in changing conditions? Does the writer believe that affirmative action ought to be continued? Why or why not? What does he see as the most pressing problems now?
3. What is the new question that managers ought to be asking? How does it differ from previous questions? How do the older questions keep alive outdated attitudes?
4. What is the idea of the melting pot? Why is it no longer an appropriate metaphor, according to the writer?
5. What problem did the Corning company discover? What did the company do about the problem? What programs were set up by Digital, Avon, and Xerox corporations? What did these companies see as problems? How did they try to work on those problems?
6. How do mentoring and performance appraisal affect promotion? Have they worked fairly for all people? What problems arise?
7. What, according to the writer, are the compelling reasons to move from affirmative action to managing diversity?

Reading and Critical Thinking

1. Do you agree that affirmative action is based on the five assumptions mentioned by Thomas, or do you see other or more assumptions? What do you think have been the good and bad effects of affirmative action? Do you think the policy is still appropriate?
2. The writer defines the ability to manage diversity as "the ability to manage your company without unnatural advantage or disadvantage for any member of your diverse work force" (paragraph 39). Do you agree with that definition? Why or why not?
3. What distinction does the writer make between cream rising to the top and being pushed to the top? Is the personal-advocate route to promotion fair? Is the writer's picture of this route accurate, do you think? Explain.
4. Do you agree that some groups in the workplace do not get the same chances for advancement as others? which groups, in what circumstances, and why?
5. What are your feelings about programs that are directed toward one particular group? Are they ever useful or warranted? When and why?

The Writer's Strategies

1. What is the thesis of this essay? Where does Thomas state it most directly? What is the point of paragraphs 1 through 12? Why does the writer begin with this subject? How and where does he connect the opening idea with the main idea of the selection?
2. Affirmative action is a sensitive topic about which many people have blunt opinions in favor or in opposition. How does the writer move beyond simply arguing one side or another? How does he show partial support for the policy historically? How does he show current needs? How does he show that the policy has succeeded so well that it has led to a new stage of concerns? What words does he use to emphasize that affirmative action was intended to be only a temporary policy?
3. Where does the writer present questions? To whom are the questions addressed? What purpose would the questions serve for managers? Who is the audience for this selection? How might the questions and the piece as a whole be of interest to other groups?

4. Where are specific corporate situations mentioned? What point do the examples make? How do they fit into the development of the writer's overall argument?
5. What does the writer present in the last three paragraphs? Why?
6. Comment on the title. How does it reflect the themes of the essay?

Thinking Together

In groups compare your experiences with working in multi-ethnic groups. How well did the groups work together? What helped them work well together or hindered them from working well together? What might have been done to improve the way the groups worked together? Compose a list of suggestions for managing diversity to improve cooperation.

Vocabulary

Prefixes, suffixes, and roots contribute to the meanings of the following words from the selection. For each word, first define the meaning of the italicized part and then define the entire word.

1. *in*vulnerable (par. 5)
2. *trans*itional (par. 10)
3. *art*ificial (par. 10)
4. *inter*vention (par. 10)
5. *hetero*geneous (par. 14)
6. *homo*geneous (par. 14)
7. *in*advertently (par. 16)
8. *non-hierarch*ical (par. 18)
9. *en*ablement (par. 20)

WRITER'S WORKSHOP ━━━━━━━━━━

Critical Thinking in Writing

1. Do you think that prejudice is vanishing? State why you agree or disagree with Thomas's observation that "prejudice . . . has suffered some wounds that may eventually prove fatal" (paragraph 7). Use your personal experiences or observations to explain your reasoning.

2. Write a short essay stating and supporting your position about whether affirmative action ought to continue and in what form.

3. In what ways does the writer's concept of managing diversity provide a useful model for thinking about the future? Is *diversity* the best term to describe what you would like to see? Is diversity something to be managed? To what extent does the writer present a corporate point of view that may or may not be applicable to the wider society? Write a short essay to respond to these questions.

Connecting Ideas

R. Roosevelt Thomas, Jr., suggests that the melting-pot idea is out of date. In "The Return of the Melting Pot" (page 450), Alan Wolfe suggests that it is not. In a few paragraphs, compare the positions of these two writers on this issue. How do they present and use the melting-pot idea? Is the melting pot the same thing to both of them? To what extent do they disagree over the appropriateness of the term but not over what is happening in society? To what extent do they disagree more fundamentally about the handling of intergroup relations?

The Return of the Melting Pot

Alan Wolfe

Alan Wolfe is a professor of sociology and political science. In this essay, he compares earlier views of ethnic diversity in the United States with current views.

KEY WORDS

> **nativist** (par. 2)   favoring native-born inhabitants over immigrants.
>
> **entrepreneurial** (par. 5)   taking risks in business ventures.

1   I RECALL FROM MY childhood in Philadelphia that no discussion of ethnicity could begin without two rituals: a quiz and a story.

2   The quiz was designed to convey how truly diverse the American population had become. It generally took the following form: What is the second-largest Irish (or Jewish or Italian or Polish) city in the world? The story, on the other hand, went like this: once upon a time America was an empty land settled, except for Native Americans, mostly by folk from the British Isles. When immigrants began to arrive from the poorer countries of Europe, nativist sentiment and racial prejudice kept them in second-class jobs and ethnic ghettos. But the immigrants were a determined lot—how else to explain the risks they took in coming?—and they worked hard to provide opportunities for their children. The second generation, bilingual and able to keep the old rituals even while adopting new customs, succeeded economically, moving out of ethnic enclaves and up the job ladder. Their children, in turn, assimilated, but at the same time they retained an ethnic identity. America is thus defined, as Lawrence Fuchs puts it, by both the *pluribus* and the *unum*. We are similar because we are different.

3   Since the passage of an immigration reform law in 1965, a new wave of immigration has begun once again to alter the ethnic and

racial composition of the American population. In 1980, 6.2 percent of the American population was foreign born, nowhere near the 13.2 percent of 1930, but far higher than it had been for the previous thirty years. Moreover, the bulk of this new immigration has come not from Europe, but from Third World countries, especially Mexico, the Dominican Republic, India, China, the Philippines, Cuba, and Vietnam.

4   There is, consequently, enough material for a new generation of quizzes. How much higher is the minimum wage in the United States than the average wage in Mexico? (Six times.) Which city receives the most Chinese immigrants: New York, San Francisco, or Los Angeles? (Twice as many come to New York as to San Francisco, two-and-a-half times more to New York than Los Angeles.) What country provides the single largest source of Chicago's new immigrants? (Mexico.) Does Canada or Cambodia send more immigrants to the state of Iowa? (Cambodia.) Where, outside of Samoa, can one find an entire city softball league reserved for Samoans? (San Francisco.) For the following countries, are the educational attainments of the immigrants higher than, similar to, or lower than the American average: Nigeria, Peru, Egypt, England, Canada, the Netherlands, Germany, the Soviet Union, Portugal, and Italy? (The first three are higher, the next four are about the same, and the last three are lower.) From what country came the 12-year-old girl who placed second in a spelling bee in Chattanooga because she could not spell "enchilada"? (Cambodia.) How many new immigrants come each year to live in Oklahoma? (More than a thousand.)

5   Not surprisingly, the new quiz is also accompanied by a follow-up to the story, which in its most recent retellings incorporates these newer groups. It is true, the saga continues, that these immigrants are not primarily Europeans; and because of their race and their foreignness, American nativists are already active, insisting on English as an official language, closing union doors to new workers, and, on extreme occasions, engaging in physical violence. But this will pass, as the earlier nativism passed. For the new immigrants, too, are unusually entrepreneurial, and they, too, are determined for their children to succeed. We should keep our borders open, welcome the new immigrants, allow them to keep their language and culture, and enrich ourselves in the process, since diversity and pluralism will not only generate new sources of economic growth, but they will also contribute to the social mosaic that makes our country distinct.

EXERCISES

Details and Their Meanings

1. What question does the writer recall from his childhood? What point is made by this question?
2. What story was typically told in the writer's childhood? What was the point of the story?
3. In 1965, what happened to change immigration patterns? What was the specific effect of that event? In what ways was immigration after 1965 similar to earlier patterns of immigration? In what ways was it different?
4. What are some of the questions to be asked for a new quiz? What is the point made by these questions? How similar to or different from the earlier quiz questions are they?
5. What is the new story? How is it similar to or different from the old story?
6. How did nativist feeling influence earlier immigrants? How does it influence current immigrants? How permanent was the effect then, and how permanent does the writer think it will be now?
7. What characteristics of the immigrants allowed them to succeed in the past and will allow them to succeed now?
8. What conclusions are drawn from the comparison of earlier and current discussions of ethnicity? What sentence best sums up the main point of this selection?

Reading and Critical Thinking

1. What do the older quiz and story tell you about the way people used to think about diversity in America? How much does re-telling certain facts determine the conclusions that can be drawn? What issues get left out once the quiz and story are granted as starting points?
2. Are the new questions that the writer lists really the first thing you think of when you discuss diversity in the United States now? Why or why not? Where have you seen these questions in evidence? What other questions have you also heard? Where? How do the other questions differ from the ones Wolfe poses?
3. What are the implications of the modern retelling of the assimilation story? What less optimistic stories have you heard?

4. Do you agree that the image of the melting pot is still appropriate? Why or why not?
5. Do you agree that "We should keep our borders open"? Why or why not? Are your reasons similar to or different from the reason Wolfe provides in the last paragraph?
6. In paragraph 2, what does the writer mean when he restates Fuchs's point that "America is thus defined . . . by both the *pluribus* and the *unum*"? Where do these Latin words come from? Do you agree that "We are similar because we are different"? What does that paradoxical statement mean?

The Writer's Strategies

1. Comment on the introductory paragraph. Is it effective? Does it capture and hold your attention? Why or why not?
2. What is the point of starting out by recalling the old quiz and story? How does the theme of quiz and story hold the selection together?
3. How surprising are the facts referred to in the answers to the new quiz? In what ways does Alan Wolfe use both surprise and lack of surprise to make the point about America's diversity?
4. How does the writer compare the period of his childhood to the present? What point is made by the comparison? Why is comparison such a useful rhetorical strategy in this piece?
5. Does the writer ever state his own position on whether the quizzes and stories represent the truth of immigration to this country? What do you think his position is? How does he let the comparisons and assumptions make his point?

Thinking Together

Use the last sentence of this selection as the basis of a discussion in groups. Do you agree that the United States should (1) keep its borders open, (2) welcome new immigrants, (3) and allow new immigrants to keep their language and culture? Report back to the class at large on your group's responses.

Vocabulary

Define the following italicized words, using the essay context.

1. no discussion of *ethnicity* could begin without two *rituals*. (par. 1)
2. moving out of ethnic *enclaves*. (par. 2)

3. America is thus defined . . . by both the *pluribus* and the *unum*. (par. 2)
4. the educational *attainments* of the immigrants. (par. 4)
5. she could not spell *"enchilada"*. (par. 4)
6. *diversity* and *pluralism* will not only generate new sources of economic growth. (par. 5)
7. the social *mosaic* that makes our country *distinct*. (par. 5)

WRITER'S WORKSHOP ━━━━━━━━━━━━━━━

Critical Thinking in Writing

1. Write a list of questions that you think reveal your assumptions about success in America.
2. Write a one-page essay evaluating whether the melting pot is a useful or an appropriate metaphor for thinking about diversity in America.
3. Is America as a society pulling apart into separate groups or moving together, or is something more complicated happening? Write a brief essay expressing your thoughts on the direction in which group relations and national identity are moving in this country.

Connecting Ideas

Reread the last two sentences of Wolfe's essay. Then consider them in light of Sam Moses' "A New Dawn" (page 12), Rosemarie Santini's "An American Dream" (page 24), or Elizabeth Wong's "The Struggle to Be an All-American Girl" (page 32). In what ways do the experiences recorded in those selections support Wolfe's assertions at the end of his essay?

The Fear of Losing a Culture

Richard Rodriguez

*Richard Rodriguez is a respected and widely anthologized writer on
Hispanic affairs. In this essay, he describes the joining of cultures
that he expects will evolve in America.*

KEY WORDS

vacillate (par. 1)   to waver back and forth.
pieties (par. 3)   respectful-sounding phrases.
notoriety (par. 4)   reputation.
litany (par. 5)   a recited series of items.
fledgling (par. 7)   like a young bird just learning to fly.
miscegenation (par. 8)   the mixing of races through marriage.
confluence (par. 9)   a coming together.

1   WHAT IS CULTURE, AFTER all? The immigrant shrugs. Latin Americans
initially come to the U.S. with only the things they need in mind—
not abstractions like culture. They need dollars. They need food.
Maybe they need to get out of the way of bullets. Most of us who
concern ourselves with Hispanic-American culture, as painters,
musicians, writers—or as sons and daughters—are the children of
immigrants. We have grown up on this side of the border, in the
land of Elvis Presley and Thomas Edison. Our lives are prescribed
by the mall, by the 7-Eleven, by the Internal Revenue Service. Our
imaginations vacillate between an Edenic Latin America, which
nevertheless betrayed our parents, and the repellent plate-glass
doors of a real American city, which has been good to us.

2   Hispanic-American culture stands where the past meets the future. The cultural meeting represents not just a Hispanic milestone,
not simply a celebration at the crossroads. America transforms into
pleasure what it cannot avoid. Hispanic-American culture of the
sort that is now in evidence (the teen movie, the rock song) may exist

in an hourglass, may in fact be irrelevant. The U.S. Border Patrol works through the night to arrest the flow of illegal immigrants over the border, even as Americans stand patiently in line for *La Bamba*. While Americans vote to declare, once and for all, that English shall be the official language of the U.S., Madonna starts recording in Spanish.

3   Before a national TV audience, Rita Moreno tells Geraldo Rivera that her dream as an actress is to play a character rather like herself: "I speak English perfectly well . . . I'm not dying from poverty . . . I want to play *that* kind of Hispanic woman, which is to say, an American citizen." This is an actress talking; these are show-biz pieties. But Moreno expresses as well a general Hispanic-American predicament. Hispanics want to belong to America without betraying the past. Yet we fear losing ground in any negotiation with America. Our fear, most of all, is of losing our culture.

4   We come from an expansive, an intimate, culture that has long been judged second-rate by the U.S. Out of pride as much as affection, we are reluctant to give up our past. Our notoriety in the U.S. has been our resistance to assimilation. The guarded symbol of Hispanic-American culture has been the tongue of flame: Spanish. But the remarkable legacy Hispanics carry from Latin America is not language—an inflatable skin—but breath itself, capacity of soul, an inclination to live. The genius of Latin America is the habit of synthesis. We assimilate.

5   What Latin America knows is that people create one another when they meet. In the music of Latin America you will hear the litany of bloodlines: the African drum, the German accordion, the cry from the minaret. The U.S. stands as the opposing New World experiment. In North America the Indian and the European stood separate. Whereas Latin America was formed by a Catholic dream of one world, of meltdown conversion, the U.S. was shaped by Protestant individualism. America has believed its national strength derives from separateness, from diversity. The glamour of the U.S. is the Easter promise: you can be born again in your lifetime. You can separate yourself from your past. You can get a divorce, lose weight, touch up your roots.

6   Immigrants still come for that promise, but the U.S. has wavered in its faith. America is no longer sure that economic strength derives from individualism. And America is no longer sure that there is space enough, sky enough, to sustain the cabin on the prairie. Now, as we near the end of the American Century, two alternative cultures beckon the American imagination: the Asian and the Latin American. Both are highly communal cultures, in contrast to the literalness

of American culture. Americans devour what they might otherwise fear to become. Sushi will make them lean, subtle corporate warriors. Combination Plate No. 3, smothered in mestizo gravy, will burn a hole in their hearts.

7   Latin America offers passion. Latin America has a life—big clouds, unambiguous themes, tragedy, epic—that the U.S., for all its quality of life, yearns to have. Latin America offers an undistressed leisure, a crowded kitchen table, even a full sorrow. Such is the urgency of America's need that it reaches right past a fledgling, homegrown Hispanic-American culture for the darker bottle of Mexican beer, for the denser novel of a Latin American master.

8   For a long time, Hispanics in the U.S. felt hostility. Perhaps because we were preoccupied by nostalgia, we withheld our Latin American gift. We denied the value of assimilation. But as our presence is judged less foreign in America, we will produce a more generous art, less timid, less parochial. Hispanic Americans do not have a pure Latin American art to offer. Expect bastard themes. Expect winking ironies, comic conclusions. For Hispanics live on this side of the border, where Kraft manufactures Mexican-style Velveeta, and where Jack in the Box serves Fajita Pita. Expect marriage. We will change America even as we will be changed. We will disappear with you into a new miscegenation.

9   Along and across the border there remain real conflicts, real fears. But the ancient tear separating Europe from itself—the Catholic Mediterranean from the Protestant north—may yet heal itself in the New World. For generations, Latin America has been the place, the bed, of a confluence of so many races and cultures that Protestant North America shuddered to imagine it.

10   The time has come to imagine it.

EXERCISES

Details and Their Meanings

1. What does Richard Rodriguez suggest are the immediate concerns of Latin American immigrants?
2. What examples does the writer give of the effects of Hispanic culture on mainstream America?

3. Which prominent Hispanic Americans does Rodriguez mention?

4. What does the writer say are the principal strengths of Latin American culture? What is the chief characteristic of North American culture? How is it exactly the opposite of Hispanic culture?

5. According to Rodriguez, which two cultures dominate the American imagination? How are they similar? How do they differ?

6. What does Latin American culture have to offer the United States?

7. How does the experience of living in America modify Latin American art? What is the reason for the change?

Reading and Critical Thinking

1. Why does Rodriguez dismiss culture as a primary concern of immigrants? Do you agree with his point? Why or why not?

2. Why does Rodriguez believe that Latin America "betrayed" immigrants who then came to the United States? Do you think that he is right? Why or why not?

3. What feeling does Rodriguez convey about the relation between Hispanic culture and the Spanish language? Where does he state his position on this issue?

4. In which paragraphs does Rodriguez talk about North American hostility to Hispanic culture? What are the underlying causes of this hostility?

5. What is the irony of the United States's embrace of certain aspects of Latin American culture?

6. What does Rodriguez mean when he says (paragraph 8), "We will change America even as we will be changed"? Do you agree? Why or why not? Will the new culture be Latin American or North American? Explain your response.

The Writer's Strategies

1. What is Rodriguez's thesis? State it in your own words. Which sentences in the essay come closest to stating the main point as you understand it?

2. Why does Rodriguez title this essay, "The Fear of Losing a Culture"? Who is afraid of losing a culture? What does the title have to do with the intended audience? Who is that audience, do you think?

3. What is the primary rhetorical strategy that the writer uses to develop this essay? In which paragraphs does he use specific examples to advance his argument?
4. Is the focus of this essay the United States or Latin America? How do you know? How does the first paragraph relate to the rest of the essay?
5. What is the conclusion of this essay? Is it effective? Explain.
6. In paragraphs 2, 5, and 8, Rodriguez introduces lists, each time using a different technique. Which sentences are lists? How does he highlight them? Why does he use this strategy?

Thinking Together

In class, brainstorm together in groups to produce a list of Hispanic contributions to recent American culture. Your list might include famous individuals, foods, works of art, literature, entertainment, Spanish phrases, and areas of the country where Hispanic culture is prominent. Is Rodriguez correct when he states that the United States is becoming more Latin American?

Vocabulary

This essay contains references and allusions from history and from everyday life. Give a brief explanation of the following terms. If necessary, look them up in a dictionary or some other reference book.

1. Elvis Presley (par. 1)
2. 7-Eleven (par. 1)
3. *La Bamba* (par. 2)
4. Madonna (par. 2)
5. minaret (par. 5)
6. sushi (par. 6)
7. Velveeta (par. 8)
8. Jack in the Box (par. 8)

WRITER'S WORKSHOP ━━━━━━━━━━━━━━

Critical Thinking in Writing

1. Rodriguez correctly points out that the Asian and Hispanic populations are the fastest-growing segments of the U.S. population. By the end of the next century, one of these groups may be the dominant cultural group, just as the descendants of northern

Europeans are now dominant. Imagine that you are still alive one hundred years from now. How will America be different? How will the new Americans, in Rodriguez's words "create one another when they meet" (paragraph 5)? Write a description of the changes you anticipate.

2. Rodriguez believes that America's glamour is that "You can separate yourself from your past" (paragraph 5). Is this a fair comment? In what ways can you see Americans reinventing themselves as a culture or even as individuals? Have you done anything to recreate yourself, like dyeing your hair, dieting, bodybuilding, divorcing, moving to a different part of the country, and so forth? What does reinvention say about you?

3. Write an essay entitled "The Fear of Losing a Culture." In it, deal with your own cultural background or the culture of a friend or relative. What effect has this culture had on mainstream America? Is this culture likely to prevail as time passes?

Connecting Ideas

Read "Kiss of Death," by Armando Rendón (page 91). Prepare a list of the ways in which Rendón says Anglo culture assaults Chicano culture. Imagine a debate between Rendón and Rodriguez. Where do the two writers disagree? Whose position do you feel has more merit? Why?

SIDE BY SIDE

1. Drawing on the ideas and information presented in the selections in this unit, write an essay arguing for the way you think the future of this country ought to be envisioned—as a melting pot, a collection of separate cultures, a diverse mosaic, a shared modern culture, or any other description you would propose.

2. Do you personally identify more with your roots or with some newer version of evolving American culture? Recalling the selections in this unit and the rest of the book, write an essay describing the culture that you feel part of or want to be part of.

3. Imagine that you are given the assignment of filling a time capsule with objects that will not be seen for thousands of years, long after all of the works of modern civilization are gone. What will you include to present a cross section of items that will best describe Americans, in all their diversity, to those people of the future?

Index